Inside the US Navy of 1812–1815

JOHNS HOPKINS BOOKS ON THE WAR OF 1812
Donald R. Hickey, *Series Editor*

INSIDE
THE US NAVY
of 1812–1815

WILLIAM S. DUDLEY

Johns Hopkins University Press
Baltimore

This book was brought to publication with the generous
support of the J. G. Goellner Endowment.

Johns Hopkins University Press
2715 North Charles Street
Baltimore, Maryland 21218-4363
www.press.jhu.edu

Library of Congress Cataloging-in-Publication Data
Names: Dudley, William S., author.
Title: Inside the US Navy of 1812–1815 / William S. Dudley.
Description: Baltimore : Johns Hopkins University Press, 2021. | Series: Johns Hopkins
books on the War of 1812 | Includes bibliographical references and index.
Identifiers: LCCN 2020022453 | ISBN 9781421440514 (hardcover) |
ISBN 9781421440521 (ebook)
Subjects: LCSH: United States. Navy—History—War of 1812. |
United States—History—War of 1812—Naval operations.
Classification: LCC E360 .D833 2021 | DDC 973.5/25—dc23
LC record available at https://lccn.loc.gov/2020022453

A catalog record for this book is available from the British Library.

*Special discounts are available for bulk purchases of this book. For more information,
please contact Special Sales at specialsales@jh.edu.*

Johns Hopkins University Press uses environmentally friendly book materials,
including recycled text paper that is composed of at least 30 percent post-consumer
waste, whenever possible.

To my wife, Donna Tully Dudley, for her love, dedication, and assistance in helping me to produce this work

CONTENTS

Those who have written studies of the War of 1812 usually consider the international context, the strategic interests of the combatants, and the political concerns of the governments who chose to fight rather than negotiate. They also weigh the relative strengths of the opposing forces and soon move on to study the operations of the war. This involves analysis of leadership at the highest levels, the relative orders of battle, the geographic environment, the day-to-day course of battles and campaigns, and the scarcity of funds throughout the war. Administration and logistics, however—matters relating to shipbuilding, supply of ordnance, technical innovations, provisioning, recruitment, transportation, medical care, and discipline—are the bedrock from which operations spring, yet they usually get much less attention.

This book attempts to rebalance the equation, to pay much more attention to how the US Navy provided for its material and logistical needs in a war that pitted one of the world's smallest professional navies against the largest and most successful. My background is that of a historian and documentary editor specializing in selection, annotation, and publication of the early documents of the Navy Department. The present work undertakes to use many of these documents to present a history of the inner workings of the US Navy during the War of 1812–1815. There was neither a navy department nor a secretary of the navy before 1798. The idea of creating a new American navy came about in response to a maritime challenge from several of the Islamic regencies in the Mediterranean during the Confederation period. It was a difficult birth, with economy-minded Democratic-Republicans resisting navalists of the Federalist Party every step of the way. The actual building of the nation's first frigates began under the auspices of Secretary of War Henry Knox and his successor, James McHenry, under the pressure of a burgeoning naval war with Napoleonic France. It was the Adams's administration that realized the new navy would need its own department. President John Adams persuaded Congress to pass legislation to this effect in 1798, and he appointed the Marylander

Benjamin Stoddert as the first secretary of the navy. From 1800 on, though, this was a Federalist navy in a Republican era.

My goal is to explain what it took to build, maintain, man, fit out, provision, and send fighting ships to sea for extended periods of time. First came the issue of navy yards, built on areas of land owned by the government near deep water where ships could be built and launched or hauled out for repairs. The navy yards would also serve as depots where lumber, naval stores, machinery, and ordnance could be stockpiled. Civilian navy agents were responsible for procurement of live oak and white oak timber for ships' hulls, pine and spruce timber for masts and spars, iron for fittings, copper sheets for sheathing hulls, and hemp cordage for standing and running rigging. Shipbuilding required attracting and hiring experienced shipwrights, carpenters, coopers, ironsmiths, and sailmakers to keep ships in operating condition.

The Navy Department had to recruit, train, and retain its officer corps to fulfill seagoing careers, not just for a single cruise or operation. Able and ordinary seamen and even landsmen had to be induced to sign on for work on particular ships with promise of bounties and rewards of other types, especially when privateers were promising more pay and lighter discipline. Navy yards and ships had to continually maintain and replenish their stocks of ordnance and ordnance stores. This meant procurement of well-made ship's guns of various sizes and weights, such as 32-pounder carronades, 24- and 18-pounder long guns for the frigates, and 12- and 6-pounder guns for schooners, sloops, and gunboats. Each gun required an ample stock of round shot of the weight indicated and gunpowder in kegs ready for distribution to gunner's mates when the occasion required. Commanding officers expected all hands to undergo training in the use of cutlasses, muskets, handguns, and small edged weapons, of which each ship kept a supply.

Ship commanders needed to maintain the health of their sailors and marines, keeping them fed, clothed, and healthy in unhealthy environments. In this respect, there was a requirement for naval surgeons and assistant surgeons, medical instruments, and medications for ship sick bays and shore-based naval hospitals. Civilian shore-based navy agents, ships' store keepers, pursers, and paymasters played an important role, operating the navy's peculiar system of supply. I attempt to put a human face on the navy, portraying how Secretaries of the Navy Paul Hamilton and William Jones administered their department and how their commanding officers handled the many issues of command at sea and ashore.

This book considers the problems of high command, the peculiar difficulties of a civilian secretary of the navy running a growing navy without adequate professional staffing. From its very beginning in 1798 the Navy Department's work was handled by a skeleton crew of elderly clerks. During the War of 1812, both

Paul Hamilton and William Jones held this post without sufficient funding, staffing, or professional advice. Hamilton, in particular, was totally ignorant of the ways of the sea, but he was a loyal Madisonian Republican. William Jones, who succeeded Hamilton, was his opposite. Though he too was a Republican, he had served at sea in a privateer during the Revolutionary War, had voyaged around the world as a merchant captain, and was well acquainted with naval officers such as Captains Thomas Truxtun, Hugh Campbell, and William Bainbridge. The navy secretaries had neither a chief of naval operations nor a naval chief of staff on whom they could depend on a day-to-day basis. These civilian executives usually had to depend on senior officers who happened to be close at hand in Washington. I trace how these matters played out politically, in terms of presidential and congressional support, and the operational results for the navy.

In treating all these topics, I draw principally from published and unpublished American and British primary-source documentation as well as from many secondary sources. The letters and reports printed in the four volumes of *The Naval War of 1812: A Documentary History* (1985–2021) and those contained in *American State Papers, Naval Affairs*, volume 1 (1794–1825), are the principal sources of primary documents at the core of this study.

Equally valuable are the landmark secondary studies of Richard V. Barbuto, *Niagara, 1814: America Invades Canada* (2000); Donald R. Hickey, *The War of 1812: A Forgotten Conflict* (Bicentennial Edition, 2012); Harold D. Langley, *A History of Medicine in the Early U.S. Navy* (1995); Kevin D. McCranie, *Utmost Gallantry: The U.S. and Royal Navies at Sea in the War of 1812* (2011); Christopher McKee, *A Gentlemanly and Honorable Profession: The Creation of the U.S. Naval Officer Corps, 1798–1815* (1991); Jerome R. Garitee, *The Republic's Private Navy: The American Privateering Business as Practiced by Baltimore during the War of 1812* (1977); John R. Elting, *Amateurs to Arms! A Military History of the War of 1812* (1991); Donald G. Shomette, *Flotilla: The Patuxent Naval Campaign in the War of 1812* (2009); David Curtis Skaggs, *Thomas Macdonough: Master of Command in the Early U.S. Navy* (2003) and *Oliver Hazard Perry: Honor, Courage, and Patriotism in the Early U.S. Navy* (2006); Skaggs and Gerard T. Altoff, *A Signal Victory: The Lake Erie Campaign, 1812–1813* (1997); and Skaggs and Larry L. Nelson, eds., *The Sixty Years' War for the Great Lakes, 1754–1814* (2001).

I have found useful the following works addressing the British and Canadian perspectives: Brian Arthur, *How Britain Won the War of 1812: The Royal Navy's Blockades of the United States, 1812–1815* (2011); Barry Gough, *Fighting Sail on Lake Huron and Georgian Bay: The War of 1812 and Its Aftermath* (2002); Donald E. Graves's trilogy *Field of Glory: The Battle of Crysler's Farm, 1813* (1999), *And All Their Glory Past: Fort Erie, Plattsburgh, and the Final Battles in the North, 1814*

(2013), and *Where Right and Glory Lead! The Battle of Lundy's Lane, 1814* (2009);
John R. Grodzinski, *Defender of Canada: Sir George Prevost and the War of 1812*
(2013); Faye M. Kert, *Privateering: Patriots and Profits in the War of 1812* (2015);
Andrew Lambert, *The Challenge: America, Britain, and the War of 1812* (2012);
Robert Malcomson, *Lords of the Lake: The Naval War on Lake Ontario, 1812–1814*
(1998); and Roger Morriss, *Cockburn and the British Navy in Transition: Admiral
Sir George Cockburn, 1772–1853* (1997).

I refer to relevant British primary documents and historical accounts for points
of comparison and contrast with the experiences of the US Navy. The challenges
of fighting Great Britain, Europe's dominant naval power, became especially critical as the concurrent war in Europe came to an end. Napoleon's surrender in
1813 meant that British forces could be shifted across the Atlantic to launch a final assault on the United States. The Royal Navy's ships blockaded American
harbors and raided coastal areas of New England, the Chesapeake Bay, southern
Georgia, and the Gulf Coast to pinch off trade and destroy or immobilize US
naval vessels. The blockade wrought economic and financial hardship to many
areas and deprived the US Treasury of its sources of income. This in turn affected
the logistical needs of the navy as well as coastal and land-based commerce in
general. Commanders of naval squadrons on Lakes Ontario, Erie, and Champlain
were under orders to cooperate with their army counterparts when their success
depended on close communications and collaboration with the navy. The same
was true of relations between the British army and the Royal Navy on their side
of the northern lakes. This book considers how the US Navy handled these challenges from 1812 to 1815 and why it managed to survive as well as it did, despite
its losses. Every historian has to make decisions on what events and details to include and exclude. For such decisions in this work and for any errors of fact or
judgment that may be found I alone am responsible.

ACKNOWLEDGMENTS

There are many to whom I am indebted for their assistance as I researched and wrote this book. From my years working at the Naval Historical Center (now the Naval History and Heritage Command), I thank my colleagues Michael J. Crawford, Christine F. Hughes, Charles E. Brodine Jr., Michael A. Palmer, and Tamara M. Smith, who served as editors of *The Naval War of 1812: A Documentary History* (1985–2021). Several other friends and colleagues with whom I worked in various capacities during the years before and including the bicentennial of the War of 1812, namely, Donald G. Shomette, Ralph Eshelman, Scott S. Sheads, Frederick C. Leiner, and Commander Tyrone Martin, USN, former commanding officer of USS *Constitution*, generously shared their special knowledge and historical expertise.

I am especially appreciative of Robert J. Brugger, formerly acquisitions editor at Johns Hopkins University Press, for urging me to get started with writing this book ten years ago. I am most grateful to Professor Donald R. Hickey, series editor, for welcoming this volume as part of the series Johns Hopkins Books on the War of 1812. I am indebted to Charles Raskob Robinson and his colleagues in the American Society of Marine Artists for granting me the use of several high-resolution images of their beautiful artworks. I benefited from the research services of many public and private institutions: US National Archives, Library of Congress, National Archives of the United Kingdom, the Library and Archives of Canada, US Naval History and Heritage Command, Maryland Historical Society, the William L. Clements Library of the University of Michigan, New-York Historical Society, New York Public Library, Mystic Seaport Museum, Peabody-Essex Museum, USS *Constitution* Museum, and the Chesapeake Bay Maritime Museum. I am glad to acknowledge fellow naval historians David C. Skaggs, John B. Hattendorf, and William N. Still Jr. and the naval novelist William H. White, who gave of their valuable time reviewing portions of this book and offered essential suggestions and advice. I am indebted to the professional acquisition and editorial staff of Johns Hopkins University Press, who encouraged and assisted me in the production of this book, including Laura Davulis and Esther Rodriguez. Joanne Allen was a painstaking and vigilant copyeditor.

Finally, I am most grateful to my wife, Donna Tully Dudley, willing reader and commentator on many drafts, for her encouragement and patience during the long years I spent researching and writing this work.

Inside the US Navy of 1812–1815

CHAPTER I

The Resources for Naval War

During the later months of 1811 and early 1812, rumors of impending war spread throughout the Eastern Seaboard from Washington, DC, where Congress had been debating military preparations against Great Britain. After the embarrassing *Chesapeake–Leopard* affair of 1807, many Americans eagerly anticipated an opportunity to avenge the British navy's insult against a US ship of war by firing on it during a time of peace for refusing to hand over British deserters. The reaction to British impressment of American seamen from merchant ships had reached a fever pitch. In the war between France and Britain, warships of both nations had seized American merchant ships sailing as neutral traders that were carrying goods intended for their enemy. In the American Northwest, British outposts stirred up Native American tribes against westward-moving American settlers. The resulting raids stirred a challenge from Indiana's territorial governor, William Henry Harrison, who led an attack against the many tribes at Tippecanoe in 1811. President James Madison asked Congress to authorize a ninety-day embargo on outward-bound shipping, in effect a war warning, to allow American ships then at sea to return before a possible outbreak of hostilities. In early June, after considering the president's presentation of the case for war, Congress voted, with middle Atlantic and southeastern representatives for war and New England's minority against. It is worth pondering the navy's strengths and weaknesses, its material resources, and its readiness for war.

US Navy of the Early Republic

During the waning years of the Revolutionary War the Continental Navy, created by the Second Continental Congress in 1775, gradually faded from sight. It had grown from two small, armed merchantmen to a few small squadrons and cruisers in European waters that achieved some remarkable feats considering its much more numerous and powerful British naval opponent. Ultimately, worn down by combat losses, groundings, and storms, the Continental Navy was left with only a handful of ships at the war's end in 1783. Yet during the war this little navy that had numbered more than fifty ships established its reputation, acquired vessels, created a Marine Corps, trained its officers, recruited sailors, transported munitions from abroad, delivered food for the Continental Army, and distracted the Royal Navy from its primary role in the protection of the British Isles. The Continental Navy played its part, and in company with privateers and the indispensable French navy, helped win the war at sea. Two years later the last Continental Navy frigate, *Alliance*, was sold, and the officers and crew went their separate ways. Yet all was not lost. Memories lingered, and several of these naval officers, such as Captains John Barry, Thomas Truxtun, Silas Talbot, and Richard Dale, survived to serve again, this time in the US Navy.[1]

Soon after President George Washington was inaugurated, Secretary of War Knox urged passage of legislation creating a "naval armament" that would enable the government to come to grips with the challenges posed by Islamic corsairs.[2] The US commissioners in Europe discovered during the 1780s that the only way to protect American merchant ships in the Mediterranean was to pay a high price to the regencies of the Barbary Coast. This was to ensure that American ships would not be captured or, if they were captured, that the United States could ransom the ships and crews from these rapacious seafarers. After considerable debate, Congress passed the Act to Provide a Naval Armament in 1794, which authorized the building of six frigates at six different locations to increase and disperse the nation's shipbuilding capabilities. At the time there were no government shipyards, so these ships were built by private contractors in ports ranging from Gosport (Norfolk), Virginia, to Portsmouth, New Hampshire.

The Navy's Industrial Establishment, 1799–1812

Charles Oscar Paullin, a leading historian of American naval administration, wrote that "in the winter of 1811–1812 on the eve of the war with Great Britain, the Navy Department was unprepared in every essential means, instrument, and material of naval warfare."[3] What the nation lacked was a mature system of military and naval logistics. Such a system requires, first, gathering or manufacturing and deploying the necessary resources—manpower, weapons, and equipment—before the campaign begins. Second, the sources of supply must be continuous, as the campaign and battles will tend to exhaust supplies of men and material. Third, the personnel in charge must show flexibility in adapting their resources as the military situation changes, often in ways unanticipated by planners. And finally, the commanders must consider the effect their operations will have in relation to other theaters of war, and vice versa, where the availability of resources is also in short supply and commanders in both theaters are drawing from the same source.[4]

Logistics Defined

Modern theories of logistics are integrated with military concepts of strategy, operations, and tactics. One definition reads: "Logistics is that branch of administration which embraces the management and provision of supply, evacuation and hospitalization, transportation and service."[5] A naval logistician amplified this idea: "Logistics is the provision of the physical means by which power is exercised by organized forces. In military terms, it is the creation and sustained support of combat forces and weapons. Its objective is maximum sustained combat effectiveness."[6] Another way to think about it is in relation to the levels of warfare that logistics must support:

Strategic level of war: the level of war at which a nation, often as a member of a group of nations, determines national or multinational (alliance or coalition) strategic security objectives and guidance, then develops and uses national resources to achieve those objectives. This comprises a prudent idea or set of ideas for employing the instruments of national power—political, economic, diplomatic, informational, or military—in a synchronized and integrated fashion to achieve theater, national, and/or multinational objectives.

Operational level of war: the level of war at which campaigns and major operations are planned, conducted, and sustained to achieve strategic objectives within theaters or other operational areas.

Tactical level of war: the level of war at which battles and engagements are planned and executed to achieve military objectives assigned to tactical units or task forces.

At the highest level, therefore, logistics start with national resources, capabilities, and purpose. Application of logistics must especially be well integrated at the operational and tactical levels of warfare. These deal with planning and executing the movement and support of forces. They include those aspects of military operations that deal with (1) design and development, acquisition, storage, movement, distribution, maintenance, evacuation, and disposition of materiel; (2) movement, evacuation, and hospitalization of personnel; (3) acquisition or construction, maintenance, operation, and disposition of facilities; and (4) acquisition or furnishing of services. These concepts were worded differently in the early nineteenth century, but the practitioners of the arts of military and naval warfare knew what they needed. However, they were circumscribed by the slow pace of communications, inadequate roads, and the primitive industrial capabilities of their times and had to adapt to the long lead times needed to apply these concepts.[7]

All these factors came into play during the War of 1812 for both the British and American navies with respect to the availability of trained sailors, the supply of gunpowder, ammunition, and guns of various sizes and weights, the existence of protected harbors, the location of navy yards, the availability of timber for shipbuilding, and the presence of skilled civilian artisans to produce war materiel in remote locations. The quality of transport affected the pace of communications between the central government and the battlefront, as well as the availability of accurate intelligence required for shrewd, timely decision making. All these controlled the pace of operations and could make the difference between victory or defeat.

The Navy Yards

During the first year of the war, 1812–13, as the US Navy's ships and men experienced the stress of battle in an operational area of broad scope, it grew ever clearer that the navy would have to depend for its very existence on an established system of logistics to support its distant ships and stations with war material. This system was based on naval shipyards. One of the Navy Department's first acts after its establishment under Secretary Benjamin Stoddert in 1798 was to order surveys and purchases of land from Virginia to New Hampshire where navy yards could be built. Over two years, from 1799 to 1801, lands were selected in Washington, DC, Norfolk (Gosport), Philadelphia, New York (Brooklyn), Boston (Charlestown), and Portsmouth, New Hampshire. In places such as Lakes Erie, Ontario, and Champlain, where navy yards did not exist, they would have to be built, but this did not happen until after the declaration of war in June 1812. If not opposed, the Royal Navy was capable of using these waters to support amphibious expeditions that could deeply penetrate vulnerable sections of the United States, such as Lake Champlain and Lake George and the Hudson River valley. This had happened before, during the French and Indian War and the American Revolutionary War.

Logistics in naval warfare can be defined as a major system of supply directed to maintain and reinforce a nation's operating ships and stations. Its role is to support fighting units with everything they need. To succeed, it must be in place or be built up rapidly when the threat of war becomes apparent. This system includes land-based skilled labor, transportation, ordnance, oak timber for structural repairs, spruce for replacement of spars and masts, recruitment of sailors and marines, uniforms, small clothes, blankets, and medicines to maintain a crew's health. Ships had to possess a medicine chest, pharmacological necessities, basic food provisions, cable, line and rope for running and standing rigging, copper sheets for sheathing the hull, heavy copper rods for hull construction, pig iron for ballast, and iron for repairs to ordnance, belaying pins, gun-elevating screws, gun carriages, and the pintle-and-gudgeon steering system that connected the vessel's rudder to its hull.

The early navy's method of providing these and other supplies was to put in place a number of government navy yards where the thousands of items needed for ship construction and repair could be stockpiled and protected. The more advanced navy yards contained buildings and sheds along a river with access to deep water. Around this area, a wall had to be constructed to prevent pilferage. To enforce security, sentries from a local Marine Corps barracks guarded the gates. They could be called on to maintain discipline among the yard workers, though normally this was a job for the master-at-arms, a senior navy petty officer. The yards also attracted many artisans and mechanics who knew how to forge, shape, create, and repair these items. In ports where there was no government shipyard, the ship's purser would contact the local navy agent, whose job it would be to obtain needed items for the ship from a local private shipyard. It was up to a ship's commanding officer to determine the logistical priorities so that the ship and crew could function properly. He had to understand that this was one of the most important of the elements of command.

Self-Sufficiency in Ships

Often, ships in need of repairs were far distant from a navy yard and had to attend to their own repairs or have the work done in a private shipyard. A national navy needed ships of varying types to operate in shallow rivers or bays and seaworthy vessels capable of withstanding frequent storms at sea as well as the enemy's weapons. Naval legislation called for a set number of commissioned officers, noncommissioned warrant officers, and petty officers in each ship. For example, during 1807, a relatively peaceful year when the pace of naval operations was slow, the largest US Navy ships—USS *President, Constitution,* and *United States,* all 44-gun frigates—were authorized 100 able seamen, and 172 ordinary seamen and boys, and a ship's guard of fifty marines. Smaller frigates and other vessels had fewer officers and enlisted men.

Personnel

The commissioned officers in one of these ships normally included the commanding officer, five lieutenants, one Marine Corps lieutenant, one purser, one surgeon, two surgeon's mates, one sailing master, and sixteen midshipmen. To become a commissioned officer, one had to be recommended by persons of standing to the

US Senate. If selected, the individual received a document signed by the president and the secretary of the navy and approved by the Senate. There was one each of several noncommissioned warrant officers: carpenter, sailmaker, boatswain, gunner, and purser. The social distinction between commissioned and warrant officers was defined by their tasks on board ship—whether tasks of command or physical or manual in nature. The role of purser was vital. He, in effect, was the ship's paymaster and business manager; he had a modicum of college-level education and some experience as a clerk. In 1812 the secretary of the navy elevated pursers to commissioned status. Warrant officers received warrants, similar to commissions, but did not require approval by the Senate.

Finally, there were petty officers, who were essential for the smooth running of the ship: two master's mates, two gunner's mates, two boatswain's mates, one carpenter's mate, one sailmaker's mate, twelve quarter gunners, one quartermaster, one cooper, one armorer, one captain's clerk, a yeoman of the gunroom, and a coxswain (small-boat handler). The ship's captain would name petty officers from among the members of his crew. The 44-gun frigates would, in addition, have a captain's steward, a master-at-arms, and a cook. If a skilled petty officer had many years of experience, the commanding officer could request that the secretary of the navy appoint this individual a warrant officer by providing a document attesting to his appointment, thus placing him in a category between the commissioned officers and the cadre of petty officers.[8] The hard core of the ship's crew was made up of able seamen, those who had been at sea for several years, long enough to "know the ropes," and ordinary seamen, those without long service who needed close supervision both on deck and aloft. A final category was that of landsmen, new recruits right off the farm or village streets who had no seafaring experience. During wartime, a ship's company could increase in the number of supernumeraries, who could provide redundancy to compensate for those killed or wounded in action. On December 14, 1811, an accounting of the navy's enlisted and Marine Corps personnel showed approximately 6,848 plus 272 officers. By the end of the War of 1812 the navy's total manpower had more than doubled, to 15,200 officers and enlisted men by February 8, 1815, due to operations on Lakes Ontario, Huron, Erie, and Champlain, the Atlantic Ocean, and the Gulf Coast. This navy's size had become virtually unsustainable in terms of both costs and the need for skilled personnel.[9]

Pay and Rations

The pay of naval personnel was not calculated to make anyone wealthy. Captains received $100 per month; master commandants, $60; lieutenants, $40;

surgeons, $50; surgeon's mates, $30; and pursers, chaplains, and sailing masters, $40. Warrant officers received $20 per month regardless of specialty, and lowly midshipmen received $11 per month. Each rank also received a small monthly sum for *rations*, which were intended as pocket money for the officers' mess and for the enlisted men, and *necessaries* such as tobacco, sugar, and tea, which were not usually served in a ship. Each ration was worth 20 cents, which seems a pittance by today's standards though each officer received several per day; for example, a captain received six rations; master commandants, five; lieutenants, three; and all warrants and midshipmen, two. All enlisted were paid $9 per month and one ration per day. The navy's cooks (and a steward for the officers) provided each mess with provisions from a ship's food allowances. These rates of pay and rations remained the same throughout the war, except for those serving on the northern lakes, who received a 25 percent increase because of price inflation in those remote areas and the hardships of lake service.[10]

Navy yards employed men with a wide variety of skills and backgrounds, similar to those on board ships. During the first Jefferson administration, Baltimore's Robert Smith was appointed secretary of the navy. In 1804, he proposed legislation confirming Commodore Thomas Tingey as commandant of the Washington Navy Yard. He was allowed a deputy, Master Commandant John Cassin, a staff of thirteen salaried and supervisory employees, and one hundred seamen. Four of the staff were administrative: a clerk to monitor the workforce, a storekeeper to keep track of inventories, a purser to administer the funds at Tingey's disposal, and a surgeon to run the yard's hospital. The workforce included carpenters, plumbers, coopers (barrel makers), block makers, sailmakers, gunners, and boatswains. Over time, as the yard and its responsibilities grew, so did the number of employees. Personnel categories came to include riggers, shipwrights, and blacksmiths. Within less than ten years, the Washington Navy Yard was the most advanced in terms of capability and number of workmen, and it soon became one of the largest industrial activities in Washington, DC.[11] Navy yards in Philadelphia, New York, Boston, Portsmouth, and Gosport (Norfolk) were less advanced, but these ports also had several private shipyards that were accustomed to doing work for the navy.

The Quasi-War with France

With the passage in 1794 of the Act to Provide a Naval Armament, providing for the construction of six frigates, the Federalist naval program got under way.[12] During the second Washington administration, the European war brought French troops, warships, and privateers into the Caribbean. On St. Domingue

(Haiti), Toussaint L'Ouverture had raised a successful rebellion against French rule, and the French navy's ships were there to protect the French Islands from the British, who were making every effort to end French control of the wealthy sugar-producing islands of Martinique and Guadalupe. American merchant ships had been trading with both the French and the British islands, but this had become dangerous.

The Quasi-War with France lasted more than three years, from the inauguration of President John Adams in March 1797 to the ratification of the Treaty of Mortefontaine on December 31, 1801. The primary task of the newly improvised US Navy was to escort American merchant ships to the West Indies and back, defending them from the swarm of French privateers that issued forth from the French islands. In this the United States had the cooperation of the British Royal Navy, as Britain was also at war with the French, the Spanish, and the Dutch. The US Navy did rather well in this short conflict, capturing twenty-six French privateers in 1799 and fifty-eight in 1800 while at the same time having an average of sixteen warships operating in the Caribbean during those two full years of war. Under Commodore Thomas Truxtun, the frigate *Constellation* made its reputation as a fighting ship in engagements with *L'Insurgente*, a capture, and *La Vengeance*, a standoff. The experience gained by the navy's young officers and enlisted men was invaluable in affording opportunities to learn and practice skills they would need later in the Barbary Wars and the War of 1812. Unfortunately, many of the ships accumulated during the Quasi-War were either sold or allowed to deteriorate in the years 1806 to 1812, when the Jeffersonian gunboat experiment was in vogue.[13]

Creation of the Navy Department

With the passage of several acts dealing with the new republic's naval force, President Adams felt an urgent need to find a competent, strong personality to take firm control of naval administration and operations. Secretary of War James McHenry had been out of his depth in planning for and directing the navy's new ships and their commanders. Adams finally selected the Maryland businessman Benjamin Stoddert to fill the post. Stoddert had good military credentials, having fought and been wounded at the battle of Brandywine. He was a friend of many of the leading Federalists and had served as secretary of the Board of War during the Revolution. He had the blessing of former secretary of war Timothy Pickering, who had handled naval matters until his appointment as secretary of state.[14] In Philadelphia, Joshua Humphreys's shipyard had launched the 44-gun frigate *United States* in 1797 and the 36-gun frigate *Philadelphia* in 1799. In

New York, in the following year the shipyard of Peck and Carpenter launched the frigate *New York* and Forman Cheesman's yard launched the 44-gun frigate *President*. Other New York shipwrights, such as the brothers Adam and Noah Brown, Christian Berg, and Henry Eckford, made notable contributions to the US Navy at improvised shipyards on the Great Lakes during the War of 1812. During the years 1808–9, Berg and Eckford joined forces to build the 16-gun brig *Oneida* to enforce the embargo on Lake Ontario.

During the Quasi-War, the Boston area's private shipyards produced several ships for the navy. Edmund Hartt's yard built the 44-gun frigate *Constitution*, launching her in 1797, and then followed with the 36-gun frigate *Boston*. William Hackett's yard in Newburyport built and launched the 20-gun sloop of war *Merrimack* in October 1798, after only seventy-four days on the stocks. The town of Salem contracted with Hackett to build the 36-gun frigate *Essex*. Hackett's men laid her keel in April 1799 and launched her in September. Edward Preble, a veteran of the Revolutionary War at sea who recently had performed well as captain of the revenue cutter *Pickering*, was designated to command *Essex*. In late 1799, at the urging of President John Adams, Secretary of the Navy Benjamin Stoddert assigned Captain Preble, of *Essex*, and Captain James Sever, of the newly launched frigate *Congress*, the task of escorting a small convoy of merchant ships heading for Batavia, in the Dutch East Indies. There they would rendezvous with and escort American merchantmen on their homeward passage. Sever's rigging failed in a storm at sea, and he put back to Norfolk, but Preble continued on with *Essex* into the Indian Ocean and the Sunda Strait, making it the first US Navy ship to reach Pacific waters on an easterly passage.

Meanwhile at Boston, the building of a navy yard was a slow, halting process begun under Secretary of the Navy Stoddert. Working through Higginson and Company, the navy's agent in Boston, he had to acquire the necessary pieces of land from private owners. With the approval of a Federalist-dominated Congress, he had ordered the accumulation of timber to build 74-gun ships of the line, but the signing of a peace treaty with France in 1800 brought an end to the Quasi-War.

The Tripolitan War

At the close of the Quasi-War in 1800, the Jefferson administration ordered Commodore Richard Dale to prepare a squadron of four ships for a Mediterranean cruise to prevent the Barbary powers from "breaking the peace" and to ascertain the state of relations between these powers and the United States. If any or all declared war against the United States, Dale was to blockade their ports and "sink, burn or otherwise destroy their ships and vessels, wherever you find them."[15] When Dale arrived in the Mediterranean, he discovered that the bashaw of Tripoli had already declared war against the United States.

During the course of the first Tripolitan War, American squadrons in the Mediterranean were commanded five successive commodores. Dale was succeeded by Commodore Richard Morris, whose inactivity dissatisfied Washington. Commodore Preble provided bold leadership and applied all the pressure at his disposal against the recalcitrant bashaw. For assistance with diplomacy, Secretary Madison had assigned Tobias Lear, a former consul to Santo Domingo, to work with Preble as consul general to the North African states. After Captain William Bainbridge's frigate *Philadelphia* ran aground in October 1803, it was Preble's decision to burn her while she was in enemy hands. Shortly afterward, Preble received news that the Tunisians were preparing to make war against American shipping because the United States had not paid the tribute it had promised. Preble's response was to call for reinforcements from the United States to continue operations against Tripoli and blockade Tunis at the same time. "These people," he wrote, "must not be humour'd but beaten."[16]

Commodore Preble established valuable bases in the Mediterranean at Sicily and Venice, hired additional seamen, borrowed gunboats and bomb vessels manned by foreign crews, purchased supplies and naval stores, and rebuilt or refitted his ships. All these logistical improvisations were needed for successful naval operations far from the United States. These actions included blockades, shore bombardment, and amphibious operations, enabling American officers to hone valuable fighting skills.

The *Chesapeake–Leopard* Affair

Several of the navy's ships that had been constructed for the Quasi-War were sold during the Barbary Wars; others, such as the frigates *New York*, *Boston*, *Chesapeake*, *Constellation*, and *Congress*, served in the Mediterranean but were laid up in ordinary in the Washington Navy Yard after 1805, the year of the negotiated peace at Tripoli. These ships should have been maintained ready for service, but the Jefferson administration had determined on economy rather than efficiency as its watchword. Further, the president was convinced that the United States would provoke its involvement in a foreign war by maintaining a navy of large ships. His answer for maritime defense was the construction of a flotilla of gunboats, which would cost far less money and employ fewer sailors. Yet, Secretary Robert Smith still had need of the frigates to maintain a presence in the Mediterranean. In 1807, the decision to send Captain James Barron to the Mediterranean as commodore of the squadron protecting American merchant ships required Commodore Tingey to take *Chesapeake* out of ordinary and have it prepared for service.

Finally repaired and fitted out, *Chesapeake* sailed from Washington to Norfolk under the command of Master Commandant Charles Gordon. Encumbered with passengers for Europe and their baggage, the ship was not ready for sea when she arrived in Hampton Roads. Nonetheless, Commodore Barron arrived on board and ordered Gordon to get the ship under way the morning of June 22, 1807. The Royal Navy, when it was learned that *Chesapeake*'s recruiting officers had signed British deserters to fill its complement of sailors, issued orders to retrieve them, by force if necessary. Later that day, the 60-gun HMS *Leopard* signaled a request for *Chesapeake* to halt for dispatches. Barron ordered Gordon to back his sails to receive an officer from *Leopard*. When Barron refused to allow the British officer to inspect his crew for deserters, *Leopard* fired three broadsides, which *Chesapeake* was in no condition to answer. The British reboarded her, mustered the crew, and removed four seamen, claiming that they were British. Barron, by then thoroughly humiliated, had to return to Norfolk, where he reported this disaster to Secretary Smith.[17] The news of this galling event angered President Jefferson, infuriated American naval officers, and aroused the nation. At this point, had Jefferson wanted a war with Great Britain, Congress would have supported him, but he decided that a diplomatic protest was the better option. Yet, this incident remained an open wound and only five years later impelled the United States toward war.

The Weapons of Naval War

It was just as well that Jefferson thought diplomacy the better course. The United States was not prepared for war with Great Britain. The nation's army and militias lacked firm leadership, training, and equipment. After the onset of war, it took more than a year and many humiliating experiences to bring the military up to a standard that could achieve anything near success. The US Navy was better prepared than the army, yet in both ships and personnel it remained much smaller than the Royal Navy. When the war began, the navy had its six original frigates built in the 1790s and a number of smaller vessels, including the frigates *Essex* with 32 guns and *Adams* and *John Adams* with 28; the sloops of war *Hornet* with 20 guns and *Wasp* with 18; the brigs *Syren* and *Argus* with 16 guns and *Vixen* with 14; and the schooners *Enterprise* with 14 guns and *Nautilus* with 12.

This miniature navy of sixteen vessels of varying sizes and rigs faced what at first seemed an overwhelming array of British warships. The United States had no ships of the line, which were three-masted, square-sailed vessels carrying 74 or more guns, while the British had ninety-seven of these ships. The Royal Navy boasted 105 frigates, while the United States had only 9, and the Royal Navy's other 313 vessels, denominated as sloops of war, brigs, schooners, and sloops, vastly outnumbered the US Navy's. It is no wonder that Paul Hamilton, President Madison's first secretary of the navy, questioned whether the nation should risk any of its vessels on the high seas, given such odds. But it was also true that Britain's hundreds of ships were scattered over the seas in remote stations in the North Sea, Jamaica, the Mediterranean Sea, and the Indian Ocean, where they were committed to fighting France and her allies and could not be easily recalled. Seen from this perspective, the US Navy's opportunities improved markedly. Operating on the North American station, based at Halifax, were twenty-three Royal Navy ships and other vessels: five frigates, seventeen brigs, schooners, and sloops, and only one ship of the line.

The US Navy might have possessed ships of the line had the Federalist shipbuilding program of President Adams stood the test of time, but President Jefferson, whose naval policy was far less realistic, was less willing to spend money to build a military and naval establishment. Despite his earlier writings, Jefferson had come to believe in a defensive naval policy dominated by small gunboats for harbor defense. The building of American ships of the line (*Independence, Washington,* and *Franklin*) did not begin until 1813. A third-rate British ship of the line was a very powerful vessel, carrying at least 74 guns on two gun decks. These guns ran from short-range carronades the quarterdeck that could throw a 32-pound shot about 500 yards to long 24-pounders whose range could be as much as a mile and were carried on the upper and lower decks.

A typical "middling size" Royal Navy 74 of the period 1798–1801, such as HMS *Plantagenet*, measured approximately 181 feet in length, 47 feet in beam (width), and 19 feet in depth. For the sake of comparison, the US frigate *Constitution* measured 175 feet between perpendiculars, 44 feet in beam, and 14 feet in depth of hold. Although rated at 44 guns, *Constitution* actually carried 52, compared with *Plantagenet*'s 78. She was equipped with twenty-eight 32-pounders on the lower gun deck, thirty 24-pounders on the upper gun deck, twelve 9-pounders and two 32-pounders on the quarterdeck, and four 18-pounders and two 32 pounders on the forecastle. The number and types of guns varied from class to class, but after 1794, carronades were increasingly used on the quarterdecks and forecastles of the 74s.[18]

Frigates that were characterized as fifth- or sixth-rate ships were not "of the line"; rather, they were used for reconnaissance as the "eyes of the fleet," and being lighter, they were normally more maneuverable than third-rate and heavier ships. Their average armament was 36 or 38 guns on one gun deck for fifth-rate ships and 28 guns for sixth-rate ships. A sloop of war resembled a small sixth-rate frigate with a single deck of guns. The armament carried by most of these ships varied with the period and the personal preference of the commanding officers. Usually the rate of the frigate was lower than the number of guns actually carried; for example, *Constitution* was rated as a 44-gun frigate, but she resembled a 74-gun ship in construction and usually carried 56 guns. The frigates *United States* and *President* were, as *Constitution* was, especially well-built, conceived by Joshua Humphreys as a hybrid or superfrigate, able to defeat any European frigate and swift enough to escape from larger ships of the line. Brigs, which were two-masted vessels with square sails, carried fewer guns than sixth-rates. Schooners were equipped with fore and aft sails on two masts and could hoist one or two square topsails on the foremast, especially when sailing before the wind. They were considered very swift in sailing to windward and could be tacked quickly through the eye of the wind to sail in another direction. Like brigs, schooners usually carried lighter and fewer guns. These vessels were frequently used as dispatch vessels. Schooner-rigged vessels were the favorites of the privateersmen of the War of 1812.

In March 1809, the newly elected president James Madison appointed Paul Hamilton as secretary of the navy. Soon thereafter, many of the navy's gunboats were laid up and *Chesapeake* was ordered to Boston for repairs. In 1810, with the possibility of war, Secretary Hamilton appointed a board made up of Captain John Rodgers, Captain Isaac Chauncey, and Commodore Tingey to evaluate the ships at the Washington Navy Yard. They recommended that *Congress*, *Constellation*, and *Adams* be repaired but averred that *New York* and *Boston* were in such poor condition that they were not worth repairing.

Anglo-American diplomatic tensions had increased as the years passed, and the European war became a war at sea, with both France and Britain seizing neutral American ships alleged to have traded with their enemy. US naval commanders yearned to exact revenge for the *Chesapeake–Leopard* affair. An opportunity arose in May 1811, when a British warship reputed to be HMS *Guerriere* was reported to be halting ships and impressing sailors off the New Jersey coast, Secretary Hamilton ordered Commodore Rodgers to intercept her in *President*, which was then anchored off Annapolis in the Chesapeake Bay.

The *Little Belt* Incident

It was late afternoon on May 16 when Rodgers discovered a ship off the Chesapeake capes that he thought fit the description of *Guerriere*. He overtook the vessel later that night and vainly exchanged questions about the ship's identity with its commander. Finally, one ship fired into the other and several broadsides ensued, with the British ship sustaining more damage and eleven British sailors dead as a result of the battle. When at dawn Rodgers discovered that he had taken on a considerably smaller vessel, the sloop of war HMS *Little Belt*, 22, under fire, he was embarrassed but insisted that his opponent had fired first. Likewise, the Royal Navy captain, Arthur Bingham, claimed that Rodgers's ship had fired first. Rodgers later requested a court of inquiry to find facts, which it did, in his favor.[19] But the Admiralty's finding ridiculed Rodgers's statements and called his actions dishonorable. This incident gave some satisfaction to the US Navy's officers but raised the level of hostility felt by each side. This preceded the convoking of the Twelfth Congress, in November 1811, in which President Madison called for legislation to prepare the nation for war.

Congress authorized repairs for the frigates, but still no new shipbuilding was included. *Constellation* had suffered severe enough decay to warrant a thorough rebuild, which commenced in February 1812 under the watchful eye of Commodore Tingey. The frigate *Adams* required a rebuild and lengthening of its hull at the Washington Navy Yard. Other frigates still in service requiring serious repairs were *Chesapeake* and *John Adams*, both of which had been laid up in Boston. Captain Bainbridge ordered *Chesapeake* to New York for repairs because the Boston Navy Yard lacked sufficient space and timber and a dry dock for hauling ships out of the water. Only six months later, under these conditions, with one-third of the nation's small navy in disrepair or beyond hope of repair, the United States declared war on Great Britain.

The following chapters examine the US Navy's struggle with adversity as the naval war progressed from early victories to near paralysis on the Atlantic Seaboard. Paradoxically, during the same period, bold leadership and innovation on Lakes Ontario, Erie, and Champlain created squadrons where there had been none in 1812. This brought into being the two-front naval war, one on the northern lakes and a second in the Atlantic, the Caribbean, and the Gulf of Mexico, that confronted both navy secretaries Paul Hamilton and William Jones. Finally, though, even the New Orleans naval station, which the financially stricken Navy Department had neglected for years, was able to contribute significantly to the city's defense in 1814–15.

CHAPTER 2

Paul Hamilton's Ordeal

The Onset of War, 1809–1812

In 1809, President James Madison's first secretary of the navy, Paul Hamilton, was not well known in Washington. Madison may have chosen him to provide regional diversity in his cabinet. Previously the owner a of rice plantation in South Carolina, Hamilton arrived at his office without naval or maritime experience of any kind. However, he did share Madison's political views and was not new to governmental administration. He had served one term in the South Carolina House of Representatives (1787–89) and on two occasions in the state's senate (1794, 1798–99) and had been the state's comptroller for five years (1799–1804) before his election to the governorship, a post he held from 1804 to 1806. As a younger man he had served in the state militia during the Revolutionary War, including as a defender at the Siege of Savannah in 1779 and as a participant in the battle of Camden in 1780, and in the capture of Fort Balfour in 1781. Hamilton came to be secretary of the navy with military experience, service in the state legislature, financial expertise, and political experience as governor of an important southern state (fig. 2.1).[1]

How Hamilton came to the notice of President Madison is a matter for conjecture, but as a Revolutionary War veteran and an experienced executive from South Carolina in Democratic-Republican ranks, he likely was noticed by President Thomas Jefferson, who may have recommended him to Madison as a possible candidate for a position in the executive branch at the beginning of Madison's term in 1809. When Hamilton accepted his appointment as navy secretary, the department had been in existence for just ten years and possessed only a small staff, none of whom were or had been naval professionals. Hamilton's predecessors were Benjamin Stoddert, a staunch Maryland Federalist from Georgetown, and Robert Smith, a Maryland Democratic-Republican from Baltimore. They had inhabited offices located in privately owned buildings near the White House. In the execution of their duties they had been served by a small staff, including a chief clerk, who guarded access to the secretary's office, drafted most of the secretary's correspondence, revising as necessary, and also served as the disbursing

Figure 2.1. Secretary of the Navy Paul Hamilton, 1809–1812. Portrait by G. B. Matthews. Courtesy of Navy Art Collection, Washington, DC, US Naval History and Heritage Command, Photograph NH 54747-KN.

officer for the immediate office. Naval officers carefully nurtured their relationship with the chief clerk, who could provide easy access to the secretary.

Secretary Hamilton's Staff

Hamilton's chief clerk, Charles Goldsborough, who had begun his service under Secretary of the Navy Stoddert, supervised two subordinate clerks who functioned as administrative assistants, each with his own area of responsibility. These were educated gentlemen with a generous capacity for paperwork. When Congress called for reports from the secretary, these clerks were the ones who gathered, organized, and formatted the information. In addition to overseeing the other clerks, Goldsborough drafted much of the secretary's routine correspondence and acted in the secretary's place in his rare absences. Another was the departmental registrar, who kept track of the navy's personnel business, assignments, promotions, resignations, and requests for leave; he also prepared commissions and warrants for the signature of the navy secretary or the president. A third clerk disbursed requisitions for money, compared commitments with congressional appropriations, and copied financial statements into the estimate books. Finally, there was a messenger whose job it was to deliver and pick up mail at various offices, summon people for discussions with the secretary, build and keep fires burning, and in general make sure the offices were secure.

Another group under the secretary's supervision was the Navy Department's accountants, located on the first floor of the building. These were the ten professional bookkeepers of considerable seniority who examined the accounts that came into the department from commanding officers, navy agents, and squadrons assigned overseas, paymasters, and pursers. The accountants checked the calculations, compared them with previous statements, and investigated questionable accounts. As the navy's ships and personnel increased in number during the war, it became difficult to keep up with the backlog of accounts, so Congress voted to approve an expansion of the staff to twelve. Thomas Turner, the chief accountant, was a former mayor of Georgetown, a gentleman of great energy and integrity who by 1812 had served for nearly twelve years at his post and enjoyed the trust of two secretaries of the navy. And even though Turner was known to be a Federalist, his skills and devotion to duty were such that he retained his post for sixteen years. It is a matter of interest that although he was under the administrative control of the secretary, his work was subject to audit by the Treasury Department. His appointment, like the secretary's, required confirmation by the Senate, a mark of the importance attached to his post.[2]

The one professional naval officer who worked nearby and could provide immediate technical advice to the secretary was Commodore Thomas Tingey, the commandant of the Washington Navy Yard. Born in London in 1750, Tingey had served at sea in the Royal Navy until 1771 and then emigrated to Philadelphia. He served in merchantmen that traded with the Swedish island of St. Croix. Ultimately, he made friends with Robert Morris and met others, such as Thomas Willing and Thomas Francis, who advanced his career in the world of maritime commerce. When the Quasi-War with France erupted in 1798 and Secretary Benjamin Stoddert was searching for competent commanders for the ships of his expanding navy, Captains Richard Dale and Thomas Truxtun both recommended Tingey. Stoddert offered Tingey command of USS *Ganges*, a converted merchant ship, and he accepted with alacrity. Tingey served with distinction in 1798 and 1799 not only as commander of his own ship but also as commodore of a small squadron. In January 1800, when Stoddert needed to appoint a naval officer to command the newly established Washington Navy Yard, he named Tingey. At the time the title of commandant had not been congressionally authorized, and it would not be until 1804. Remarkably, Tingey then retained the position of commandant until his death in 1829 through many changes of administration and under several secretaries of the navy.[3]

It was Hamilton's good fortune to take up his post as secretary of the navy at a time when Congress's penurious attitude toward the service was beginning to change. During Jefferson's two terms as president, the navy had operated in the Mediterranean against Tripolitan (or Barbary) pirates, but aside from providing for needed ship repairs, Congress had not authorized any significant increases in the strength of the seagoing navy. To protect the nation's trade, Jefferson had favored constructing gunboats for harbor defense and building fortifications near harbor entrances. He and most of his party had wished to avoid adding new ships to the navy because of their expense and because they did not want to provoke the bellicose navies of France and Great Britain. The alarm raised by the *Chesapeake–Leopard* affair in 1807 had only reinforced Jefferson's resolve to keep the European war at a distance.

James Madison's election to the presidency in late 1808 ushered in changes that gave hope to naval officers and congressional navalists. Although at first President Madison himself stood aloof from military and naval affairs, Hamilton came to the navy with few preconceptions and a mind open to the needs of his department. He also had friends in Congress, such as Langdon Cheves, chairman of the House of Representatives Naval Committee, who had been South Carolina's attorney general from 1808 to 1810 and presumably had known Hamilton as governor. He stood for Congress in 1810 and served as the representative of South Carolina's First District until 1816. Known for his eloquence and his advocacy of war with Great Britain, Cheves was one of the War Hawks of the prewar Twelfth Congress, along with John C. Calhoun, William Lowndes, and Henry Clay.

It took Hamilton many months to get settled in Washington, first to find housing and then to bring his family to the capital city. Apparently, his personal finances were in disarray when he left South Carolina. He was deeply in debt, and his creditors were pressing him for payment. He had been compelled to sell his slaves and then his plantation. His family had been living for some months at the estate of his son-in-law, Colonel Morton A. Waring. Hamilton's correspondence with Waring in the autumn of 1810 shows his anxiety about his property and his reputation as well as about the worsening international situation. On October 1 he wrote, "This day and tomorrow are sale days and to me days of anguish to endure. The papers will announce the news from France, but we have no official dispatches yet. If what we have seen may be relied on, our prospect brightens, and Britain must revoke her orders or she will present herself as our single enemy, which would naturally change our situation by relieving us from the embarrassment of having France also to contend with. I have just received a letter from the President who does not appear very sanguine that Britain will act an honorable part towards us."[4] These private and public issues weighed on this conscientious executive as the nation drifted toward war and made it imperative for him to try to strengthen the situation of the navy.

Difficulties with Congress

During the years 1808 to 1810 Congress frequently debated whether the embargo on US trade should be repealed, as it had shown itself to be of little consequence in persuading Britain to alter its wartime policies. Ultimately the majority Jeffersonian Republicans divided over what measures should replace the embargo and whether the navy should be augmented in preparation for possible hostilities. The naval issue was extremely controversial. About half the southern Republicans wished to continue the embargo; the others were undecided whether to repeal or to pursue more vigorous measures. Most of the northern Republicans favored strengthening the navy. Jefferson, Madison, and Albert Gallatin were deeply interested in how their party would emerge from the debate, hoping that it would finally support a consensus position between embargo and war. Yet in this they were to be disappointed.

In March 1809, just before leaving office, Jefferson signed the Non-Intercourse Act, which lifted the embargo, reopening trade with all nations except Great Britain and France; it gave the president the authority to resume trade with either of these two if they ceased violating neutral rights. Confusion followed when Madison was assured by the British minister to the United States that Britain would revoke the orders in council. In response, Madison proclaimed trade with Britain to be legal, only to discover one month later that the prime minister did not agree and had ordered the envoy to return to England. Embarrassment ensued, prompting Madison to issue a new proclamation reviving non-intercourse with Britain in August 1809.

Congress took another tack in 1810, as embodied in Macon's Bill No. 2, authorizing trade with both Britain and France and providing that if either nation ceased its violations of American shipping, the president could terminate American trade with the other. Emperor Napoleon entered the scene and ordered the Duke of Cadore, his foreign minister, to inform the American minister to France that his government would revoke the restrictions on US trade. Cadore, however, told the American minister that the decrees had already been revoked, when in fact they had not. In November 1811, President Madison and Secretary of State James Monroe accepted this statement at face value, opened trade with France, and proclaimed non-intercourse with Great Britain.

The conservative block of southern Republicans, on whom Jefferson had depended, began to weaken as votes were taken (and each time either tabled or defeated) on whether to arm merchant ships, issue letters of marque, or provide naval escorts for US merchant ships. The latter would have required an expansion of the navy, a step many Republicans had traditionally opposed because of the cost of building and maintaining ships and because they questioned the usefulness of a large navy. Federalists too were on the fence regarding how far to go in defending neutral rights and whether a naval expansion would bring on a war they wished to avoid. Republicans from the southeastern coastal states pushed beyond this position as debates continued into 1811. More frequently, they spoke up for their unprotected coastal towns and harbors and for merchants whose ships had been harassed or confiscated on the high seas. While this was happening, however, Republican advocacy for war and naval expansion declined in the New England and middle Atlantic states. In other words, congressional Republicans as a group did not necessarily link going to war with need of a strong navy. They were willing to repair and fit out the navy's frigates and smaller vessels, but they stopped short of building new warships. They were in the anomalous position of being both prowar and anti-navy.[5]

A little more than one year later, with Hamilton on a trip to South Carolina, his office staff again requested that Congress authorize the navy to fit out *United States*, *Essex*, *John Adams*, and *President* as soon as possible and to employ other vessels that might be needed. These vessels were to be stationed at such ports and harbors "as may be expedient" or to cruise on any part of the Atlantic coast. This action evidently pried loose the necessary funds from Congress, as Secretary Hamilton mentioned in his report to Congress in December. The European war in which Great Britain confronted France and her allies had become a North Atlantic war. The United States was struggling to maintain its neutrality and its trade, but the potential for war with either Britain or France was increasingly clear by 1810. Hamilton addressed this issue in a general order sent to Commodore John Rodgers, the senior officer afloat, for distribution to the officers under his command. With reference to the *Chesapeake–Leopard* affair, Hamilton urged, "It is therefore our duty to be prepared and determined at every hazard, to vindicate the injured honor of our Navy, and revive the drooping Spirit of the Nation. Influenced by these considerations, it is expected that while you conduct the force under your command, consistently with the principles of a strict and upright neutrality, you are to maintain and support at every risk and cost, the dignity of our Flag; And, that offering yourself no unjust aggression, you are to submit to none, not even a menace or threat from a force not materially your Superior."[6] The navy's vessels at that time were dispersed along the coast in two minisquadrons.

The ships under Rodgers's immediate command were those of the "northern squadron," based at New York, while those of the "southern squadron," based at Norfolk, sailed under Commodore Stephen Decatur.

In May 1811 Commodore Rodgers's *President* had a brief battle at night with the British sloop of war *Little Belt*, less than half the size and power of *President*. Secretary Hamilton had ordered Rodgers to seek out the frigate *Guerriere*, which had been disrupting shipping off New York. This was a case of mistaken identity, for which Rodgers was maligned in the British press. To clear himself, Rodgers requested a court-martial. It found him innocent of initiating the battle; however, the damage was done, and it heightened the tensions between the US Navy and the Royal Navy.

Preparations for War

As Congress gathered for its annual session in November 1811, many issues awaited resolution. The most pressing of these concerned preparations for a possible war with Great Britain, which had not yet agreed to a settlement of the *Chesapeake–Leopard* affair. His Majesty's government had neither withdrawn the orders in council nor given any thought to revoking impressment involving the United States. Thus, diplomatic efforts to resolve these disputes had failed, giving President Madison little hope of avoiding an armed conflict. Tensions heightened as news of the battle with Native Americans at Tippecanoe on November 7 filtered into Washington. Madison's message to Congress on November 5, 1811, laid out the issues in typically indirect and dispassionate language. He informed the members that France had sent deceptive correspondence claiming to have rescinded legislation against American shipping, when it had not done that, thus provoking the United States into a position favoring trade with France, her colonies, and her allies. This in turn was viewed by the British as a hostile act by the United States. Madison referred to the British as "trampling on rights which no independent nation can relinquish." Congress, he said, "will feel the duty of putting the United States into an armor and an attitude demanded by the crisis." The president asked Congress to fill the ranks of the army and prepare to call up the militia (an auxiliary force) for a limited term, asking also for acceptance of volunteer corps motivated by patriotic ardor. Although the manufacture of small arms and cannons was proceeding, he asked that stock of these weapons be enlarged. As to the navy, he merely urged such provisions "as may be required," without asking specifically for ships to be built or repaired. He referred tangentially to events in "the southern portion of our hemisphere," which he knew would be taken to mean Spanish East Florida, where land-hungry American interlopers were threatening to raise a revolution.[7]

On November 19, Langdon Cheves sent a message to Secretary Hamilton asking seven questions concerning the navy's need of ships and materials, the costs of equipping and manning the ships and smaller vessels, and the current condition and location of the navy's gunboats. Hamilton replied as fully as he could on December 3 with an extensive paper and four annexes. He estimated that the navy could probably protect the nation's trade if, with the continuance of the war in Europe, the navy had half the force that might be sent against it. This meant, he added, that the navy would require twelve ships of the line and twenty well-constructed frigates, including those presently in service. He was confident about obtaining the manning necessary with an increase of pay or bounties.

As to materials, Hamilton was confident of the nation's ability to supply these and recommended an appropriation for a three-year supply of timber, iron, copper, canvas, and hemp. He took care to emphasize the navy's need of a drydock suitable for its largest frigates and certainly if the nation were to build ships of the line. The cost of building twelve ships of the line was $3,998,000; the cost of ten frigates would have been $1,710,000. And these figures did not include the annual maintenance costs. Considering the House's record on naval legislation, it was highly unlikely that Congress would endorse a bill containing this level of expenditure.

After receiving Hamilton's response to his questions and consulting with the Naval Committee, Cheves reported to Congress, commenting on how little the members had previously chosen to do in support of the navy, exhibiting "a spirit so languid, as, while it has preserved the existence of the establishment, has had the impact of loading it with imputations of wasteful expense and comparative inefficiency." He argued that Congress should have acted properly to provide for the enlargement of the navy in proportion to the nation's growth in population, wealth, and commerce, enabling it to expand energetically when faced with a crisis. As the situation stood, however, facing potential conflict with a major naval force, he recommended that all war vessels worthy of repair be immediately repaired, fitted out, and put into active service. He notably failed to include Hamilton's request for twelve ships of the line. He did, however, propose that ten additional 38-gun frigates be built, provided with a sufficient stock of timber, and a (dry) dock suitable for the repair of such vessels to be built in a central and convenient place. Although he knew all this was unlikely to happen, Cheves had spoken his mind and left his committee's bidding on the table in the form of a "bill concerning the naval establishment."[8]

In the following weeks, Hamilton was under pressure as never before to prepare the navy for battle with the Royal Navy. He ordered Captain Hugh Campbell, his commander at St. Marys, Georgia, to withdraw his gunboats from a potential conflict with the Spanish authorities in conformity with President Madison's wishes. General George Matthews, of the Georgia state militia, had joined forces with American settlers in East Florida to overthrow Spanish rule and in fact had seized Amelia Island and the seaport of Fernandina. Madison and Congress had tacitly played along while these actions did not embarrass the government. Yet, with the stirring of sentiments for war against Britain and the need for US naval gunboats in other, more important places, Madison let it be known that Matthews's proceedings in Spanish territory had been unauthorized and that US naval gunboats were to depart from the waters near Fernandina.[9] For the time being the United States was not officially involved; nevertheless, Americans continued their efforts to obtain control of East Florida until the Adams-Onis Treaty of 1819.[10]

The Gunboats

The issue of how to deploy the Navy's gunboats arose as the need for sailors and marines in the larger blue-water ships became more urgent. The gunboats' primary mission was harbor defense, but they could be very useful in protected bays, rivers, or sounds in situations where the lack of wind or the presence of shallows or flats could inhibit the movement of a deeper-draft enemy ship. They were also used to patrol against coastal smugglers, both foreign and domestic, who frequently violated the embargo laws.[11] Built over a number of years (1803–7), these shallow-draft vessels ranged from 45 feet to 70 feet in length and from 16 to 18 feet in beam. They were either schooner- or sloop-rigged and were equipped with oars (or sweeps) for rowing. Their commanders might be lieutenants (rarely), midshipmen (occasionally), or sailing masters (usually), possibly supported by a gunner, steward, and cook, plus fourteen to thirty-three sailors and marines.

Weaponry for gunboats depended on the size of the boat and the number of her crew. Larger gunboats could be equipped with one 24-pounder long gun and an 18-pounder carronade; yet, the larger the gun, the more men were needed to handle and fire it. As a gunboat aged, her timbers weakened, so that after a few years of service she could not stand the shock of the heavier weapons. The guns might be arranged bow and stern, or they might be placed on carriages that could pivot on circle mounts located amidships. The gunboat could also be equipped with low-caliber swivel guns mounted on the railings along its sides. In addition, the crew would be provided with cutlasses, boarding axes, pikes, muskets, and pistols.

For sailors, gunboat duty was generally unpleasant. Messing and sleeping arrangements were cramped, the boats often leaked, and low morale was rampant, as was alcoholism, which often thrived in such an environment. The few officers assigned to gunboats continually begged for orders to larger vessels. Many of the original 200 gunboats built under Jefferson's mandate had been neglected, were no longer fit for service, and lacked sufficient crew members. By December 1811, of a total of 165 gunboats still existing along the Atlantic and Gulf coasts, only 63 were in commission, 95 were laid up, and 7 were under repair. Of those in commission, 20 were stationed at New York, 19 at New Orleans, 11 at St. Marys, 10 at Baltimore, 8 at Norfolk, and 4 at Wilmington, North Carolina, near Cape Fear.[12]

In the spring of 1812, with a growing likelihood of war, Congress passed legislation proclaiming a ninety-day maritime embargo (Madison had requested sixty days) to prevent American ships from sailing into what was likely to be a dangerous war zone and to give fair warning to shipowners and shipmasters overseas to return to their home ports. Possibly, another motive for the declaration was to signal to the British cabinet that war was likely if concessions were not forthcoming. Moderate Senate Republicans amended the embargo bill to increase the number of days from sixty to ninety, hoping the additional time would allow for a British change of heart. For merchants and ship captains, the embargo had the opposite of the intended effect. They readied their ships for sea in haste, loading goods and recruiting crew, to take advantage of what might be the last opportunity to profit in an uncertain international climate.[13]

In the two months remaining before the anticipated outbreak of war, Hamilton did what he could to satisfy the navy's needs. For example, he shifted all available marines from gunboat duty to the frigates that had fewer than the required number of marines and ordered navy yards and stations to test their barrels of gunpowder, many of which they found to contain ineffective powder. He ordered the Marine Corps commandant to ship small arms to the brig *Oneida*, the navy's only vessel on Lake Ontario where she was "near to the probable scene of action," and he attended to a request that the navy strengthen the gunboat crews stationed at Gosport Navy Yard at Norfolk.[14]

The Navy's Medical Concerns

Not least among Hamilton's concerns was caring for the navy's sick and wounded sailors. Before the War of 1812, there were no navy hospitals as such. In 1798 Congress passed An Act for the Relief of Sick and Disabled Seamen. It called for the establishment of a Marine Hospital Fund primarily for the treatment of merchant sailors, but the hospitals also took in the navy's sailors and marines. This medical care was paid for by deducting a small sum (20 cents) in advance from the pay of each officer, sailor, and marine, which the captain of a returning ship would pay to the port customs officer, who in turn would deposit the funds to the credit of the Treasury Department. In that time there were marine (merchant marine) hospitals in Boston and Norfolk but no navy hospitals. The navy agents in certain ports would rent rooms or houses where sailors could convalesce. In 1810 Secretary Hamilton requested that Congress create a special fund for the treatment of naval personnel separate from the fund for the treatment of merchant seamen but financed in the same way. Looking forward to the time when the Navy Department would be able to have its own hospitals, An Act establishing Navy Hospitals, of February 26, 1811, created a board of commissioners of navy hospitals, whose job it was to oversee the expenditures of the Naval Hospital Fund and to procure sites for naval hospitals.[15]

Fortunately, Hamilton was able to depend for advice on several eminent medical officers, such as Edward Cutbush, Lewis Heerman, and Usher Parsons. Cutbush was the senior surgeon of the navy, a graduate of Philadelphia College, and a founding member of the Medical Society of Philadelphia. After the *Chesapeake–Leopard* crisis, Cutbush offered his thoughts in *Observations on the Means of Preserving the Health of Soldiers and Sailors* (1808), the first book published by a US Navy medical officer. He discussed methods of preventing as well as treating sicknesses, stressing the need to keep sick men dry in a well-ventilated space, the need to keep bodies and clothing clean, the need for warmth, rest, avoidance of intoxication, and regular discipline, as well as wholesome provisions and water. These strictures would apply whether the sick men were in sickbay afloat or in a hospital ashore.[16]

In June 1812, as the possibility of war drew ever nearer, Dr. Cutbush advised Hamilton of the availability of a new variety of surgeon's needles for suturing wounds in deep-seated arteries. He had bought some on his own and thought other naval surgeons should be made aware of them. Hamilton soon ordered some for the navy through George Harrison, the navy agent in Philadelphia.[17] Cutbush got back in touch with Hamilton, this time showing his concern for the needs of the four hundred sailors attached to the Delaware River gunboat flotilla. These men were divided into two divisions, each having its own surgeon's mate, but Cutbush asked what was to be done with men who were sick or wounded, as they could not be treated on board the open gunboats, nor was there yet a designated hospital, and the small medical chests on board lacked several essential articles, including tourniquets. Hamilton's response is missing, but it is apparent that there had been little advance preparation for care of sick and wounded sailors.[18] It would not be long before these medical supplies and the naval surgeons were actively employed.

During the three weeks of congressional deliberations, two squadrons of the navy's principal ships, with the exception of USS *Constitution* and *Essex*, assembled under Commodore John Rodgers's orders at a rendezvous inside Sandy

Figure 2.2. Commodore John Rodgers, USN, 1772–1838, commander of the *Atlantic Squadron* and first president of the Board of Navy Commissioners. Oil on wood. Portrait by John Wesley Jarvis, 1814. Photograph courtesy of US Naval Academy Museum, Annapolis, Maryland.

Hook, New Jersey, to await the fateful decision. Both Rodgers and Decatur concurred in this strategy after discussions with Secretary Hamilton. The secretary's main concern was the safety of homecoming merchant ships. Yet, Commodore Rodgers's preference was to sail in force against Great Britain's West India trade.[19] Decatur had to accept this, although he would have preferred to sail in smaller, detached squadrons. At the last minute, after sending Rodgers his cruising orders, the nervous Hamilton sent another dispatch ordering the squadron to stay close to New York so that it could continue to receive his orders. It arrived too late. Rodgers's ships had sailed (fig. 2.2).

War Patrol, June–August 1812

Commodore John Rodgers anchored inside Sandy Hook with his small squadron and remained in suspense about when the orders would arrive. He had the answer to his question by 3:00 p.m. on June 21. Within ten minutes, Rodgers had ordered his ships to weigh anchor and proceed to sea. All the years of British insults and suppressed American anger were now unleashed, and the proud Rodgers was in his element. He sailed in search of a British West India convoy said to be moving with the Gulf Stream toward the British Isles. Under his command was his squadron, comprising his own *President*, 44, Master Commandant James Lawrence's sloop of war *Hornet*, 18, Captain Stephen Decatur Jr.'s frigate *United States*, 44, Captain John Smith's frigate *Congress*, 36, and Master Commandant Arthur Sinclair's brig *Argus*, 16. The other frigates—*Chesapeake*, 38, at Boston awaiting repairs; Captain Isaac Hull's *Constitution*, 44; and Captain David Porter's *Essex*, 32—had received orders to join the squadron when they were ready for sea, but they were unable to comply at that critical time. Porter had applied for permission to enter New York Navy Yard for emergency repairs to his spars and rigging, and Hull was still in the Chesapeake Bay shaking down his ship, swaying on board 24 carronades, and drilling a fresh crew. Hull would have his own rendezvous with the British in a few weeks. Within two days, however, Rodgers's squadron was drawn off his quarry by HMS *Belvidera*, 38, a British frigate on her way to join a British squadron then forming off Halifax under the command of Commodore Philip B. V. Broke.

Rodgers's larger, more heavily armed ship should have been able to overtake and subdue *Belvidera*, but the British captain, Richard Byron, handled his ship more skillfully and made the most of an opportunity to escape.[20] Rodgers, instead of using his ship's greater speed to come up with his enemy, stood off and altered course to fire broadsides at the stern quarters of *Belvidera*. When this had only the effect of slowing his ship, Rodgers returned to a stern chase and commenced firing his bow guns. Suddenly, while he supervised the battery, one of *President*'s guns misfired and exploded, sending shards of iron in all directions. The blast killed one sailor, wounded nine others, and Rodgers suffered a broken leg as he fell to the deck. This was not an auspicious beginning for the cruise that he had hoped might make his reputation and earn him a small fortune.[21]

Captain Hull had been exercising his ship and green crew in the Chesapeake when the war began. His orders were to join Rodgers, but the commodore was in no mood to wait for *Constitution*. Further delayed while waiting to receive his complement of marines, sailors, and spars, Hull did not depart from Annapolis until July 5, though he must have met adverse winds for he did not clear the Virginia Capes until July 12.[22] Five days later, as Hull was sailing northward along the New Jersey coast, his lookouts sighted the sails of four ships nearer the shore. Hull later reported that he had been uncertain whether they were enemy ships or those of Rodgers's squadron. This points up the difficulties of communication at sea at the time; two weeks earlier the squadron had already had its encounter with HMS *Belvidera* and was well over a thousand miles to the east. Hull turned toward these ships to take a closer look. Soon, in the late afternoon, another ship appeared and seemed to be heading toward the squadron. Hull held his course, but when in the evening the unknown ship (HMS *Guerriere*) would not answer his private signal, he correctly assumed that she and the others were enemy ships.

For the next three days, Hull's *Constitution* was the hare and the other five ships were the hounds, relentlessly pursuing her. The solitary American frigate had nearly run into the arms of Commodore Broke's Halifax-based squadron, HMS *Africa*, 64, *Shannon*, 38, *Belvidera*, 36, and *Aeolus*, 32. With the addition of the late-arriving *Guerriere*, 38, Hull had a truly formidable foe intent on his capture. Hull made all sail to escape in a light breeze. In the morning, the wind had dropped to nothing, so Hull ordered his crew into boats to tow ship and ordered two of the deck guns to be brought to the stern cabin windows and two others to be set on the quarterdeck above, facing aft. The wind came up but from the northwest, first favoring the enemy's ships, which approached to within gunshot (two miles).

Lieutenant Charles Morris, Hull's executive officer, recommended that the ship employ kedging (also called warping), using the ship's boats and anchors to haul her forward by bending the anchor cables around the anchor windless and then hauling the ship forward after the anchors had been dropped to the seabed. The British adopted the same technique, but *Constitution*'s crew held their own. This intense labor continued until nearly midnight, when a light breeze sprang up, enabling Hull to hoist his boats and rest his crew. Still, into the next day, *Constitution* gradually increased her lead by wetting the sails to capture every breath of air. The wind gradually increased, and finally a squall enabled Hull to use the poor visibility to his advantage. On the following day, July 20, the British squadron gave up the chase and headed in the direction of New York.[23]

Hull's extraordinary seamanship, his hardworking crew, and favorable winds had made it possible to sail out of harm's way. His orders from Secretary Hamilton required him to put into New York, but he decided that that was unwise, as the enemy squadron would be waiting for him. His next move was to shape a course for Boston in hopes of receiving further orders; he arrived in Massachusetts Bay, off Boston harbor, on July 28. Hull reported that he was short of provisions and had hoped to receive word from Secretary Hamilton about his next assignment. Since he found no instructions waiting, Hull wrote to inform Hamilton that he would head to sea to operate independently if he could not locate Rodgers's squadron. As it turned out, Hull's lack of instructions may have been the best possible circumstance for his own reputation and the morale of the US Navy (map 2.1).[24]

Three weeks later, while Hull was cruising between the Gulf of St. Lawrence and the Grand Banks, he captured some small merchant ships and gained

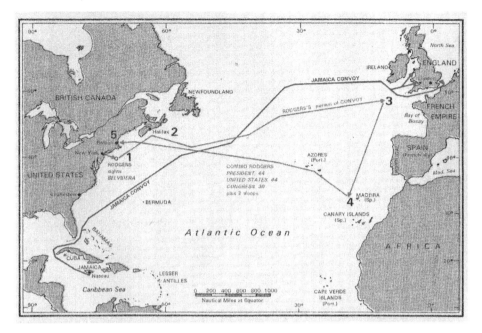

Map 2.1. Cruise of the US fleet, 21 June–31 July 1812. Reprinted by permission from Craig. L. Symonds, *The Naval Institute Historical Atlas of the U.S. Navy*, Cartography by William J. Clipson, © 1995 (Annapolis, MD: Naval Institute Press).

information about a British frigate that had been active in the same area and last seen heading southward. He immediately altered course in that direction. On August 19 he overtook *Guerriere*, 38, at the time commanded by Captain James Richard Dacres. *Guerriere* had been detached from Commodore Broke's squadron to patrol south of Nova Scotia. The ensuing engagement gave the United States one of its most notable victories at sea.

The battle began with Hull's three-hour pursuit of his opponent followed by much maneuvering at close quarters. When the two ships were alongside each other, at no more than a pistol shot's distance, they exchanged broadsides. Within fifteen minutes *Guerriere* was in trouble, having lost her mizzen mast with rigging and sails damaged, and nearly unmanageable. Hull ordered his crew to prepare to board *Guerriere* and take her by hand-to-hand combat, but before the command could be executed, *Guerriere*'s foremast and mainmast fell, leaving the ship a "perfect wreck." Hull then maneuvered *Constitution* several hundred yards away to repair rigging that had been shot away.

As darkness fell, Captain Dacres informed Hull that he had surrendered. Hull's victory was complete. *Guerriere*, he reported, "had not a spar left standing," and her hull was "cut to pieces." Dacres's crew suffered twenty-three killed (including those who died of wounds) and fifty-six wounded, compared with only seven of Hull's crew killed and seven wounded. For this lighter human cost, the US Navy had to thank *Constitution*'s superior strength, heavier guns, and larger, better-trained crew, enabling a more rapid pace of firing and more accurate shooting.

After removing all usable equipment from the shattered *Guerriere* and taking off her surviving crew, Captain Hull ordered the ship burned and set sail for Boston. By coincidence, he had anchored in Nantasket Roads just hours before Rodgers's squadron appeared in the offing. At first, when the early-morning watch reported the approach of these ships, Hull was unsure whether they were friendly or enemy. With no time to hoist anchor, he cut his cable and made all sail to cut off the ships before they could reach Boston harbor and get in ahead of him. One can only imagine his relief when he recognized the Stars and Stripes flying from the mast of *President*. Hull ordered *Guerriere*'s ensign hoisted beneath *Constitution*'s as he led the naval procession into Boston harbor. With his ship securely moored to Long Wharf, Hull welcomed a stream of well-wishers headed by Captains Bainbridge, commandant of the navy yard, Decatur, Lawrence, Sinclair, and others. The celebrations of *Constitution*'s defeat of *Guerriere* went on for two weeks.

With the return of Hull's *Constitution* and then Rodgers's and Decatur's squadrons to Boston at the end of August and Porter's *Essex* to Philadelphia in early September, the logistical burdens of the Navy Department increased in number and weight. A prime example came in the form of a letter from Amos Binney, the navy agent at Boston, who had received multiple requests for supplies and provisions for every warship recently arrived at the port. As he said in his 1822 narrative, "I was but newly appointed, had no experience, no precedents, no forms, no instructions, was obliged to form a whole system from the chaos that surrounded me, [and] was always short or destitute of funds."[25] On August 31, 1812, Binney wrote to Hamilton requesting $4,000 for repairs to the frigates *Constitution* and *President* for damage received in action. In addition, he requested $10,000 for pay, $10,000 for provisions, $2,000 for medicines, and $1,000 for contingencies. Hamilton responded willingly with $6,000 more for repairs than Binney had asked, in all $33,000. In closing, Hamilton added that "we are extremely anxious to get all our public vessels to sea with the least possible delay."[26]

War Patrol, September 1812–April 1813

Secretary of the Navy Hamilton discussed the results of the summer's naval campaign with his commanders in the weeks following the return of Rodgers, Decatur, and Hull. This time, following Decatur's recommendations, he ordered the departure of three small squadrons in the fall; each would start out with two frigates and a brig, which would then separate to cruise in search of enemy convoys.[27] The first squadron was made up of *Constitution* under the command of William Bainbridge, David Porter's *Essex*, and James Lawrence's *Hornet*. A second squadron comprised Stephen Decatur's *United States*, John Smith's *Congress*, and Arthur Sinclair's brig *Argus*. The third squadron, formed under the command of Commodore Rodgers in *President*, included Samuel Evans in *Chesapeake*, 38, and Master Commandant Jacob Jones in the sloop of war *Wasp*, 18. Hull requested leave to take care of family business; Secretary Hamilton later assigned him to command the Boston Navy Yard. At Decatur's suggestion, Rodgers and he combined their squadrons, which sailed from Boston on October 10, 1812, to provide a show of force in case they met any blockaders. *President, United States, Congress*, and *Argus* stayed together for several days before going off on their own. *Chesapeake*'s departure was delayed until December 17 by the need for extensive repairs. Jacob Jones's sloop of war *Wasp*, having returned from a diplomatic voyage to Europe and a short independent patrol off Nova Scotia, was moored at Philadelphia, under orders to rendezvous with Rodgers at sea.[28]

Jones departed from Delaware Bay on October 13, but a violent storm threw him off course and off schedule, damaging his ship in the process. After making repairs, Jones was 250 miles north of Bermuda when, on October 18, he discovered a convoy of British merchant ships, escorted by HM brig *Frolic*, 22, which had also been damaged in a storm. *Frolic* sought to engage *Wasp*, but after a bloody engagement she struck her colors. As *Wasp*'s crew endeavored to repair the damaged *Frolic*, bad luck appeared in the form of HMS *Poictiers*, 74, which rapidly took *Wasp*, recaptured *Frolic*, and took both ships into Bermuda.[29]

Cruising off the Madeira Islands, Decatur's *United States* intercepted HMS *Macedonian*. In a standoff fight Decatur's ship severely punished the ship of Captain Sir John Carden, who eventually struck his colors. Decatur's crew repaired the damaged *Macedonian*, set up a jury rig, and brought her into Newport, Rhode Island, as a prize of war. After further repairs she was recommissioned as a US Navy frigate using the same name, USS *Macedonian*.

Captain William Bainbridge had impatiently awaited his chance for a sea command while in charge of the Boston Navy Yard. Finally, with *Constitution* as his flagship, he cruised first across the Atlantic toward the Azores and then southwest toward Brazil. He paused at the Portuguese island of Fernao de Noronha to leave a message for Porter and then departed for Bahia, Brazil. There he encountered HMS *Java* sailing alone on her way to India with a high-ranking British army officer and his staff on board. In the ensuing three-hour battle, Commodore Bainbridge's *Constitution* dismasted HMS *Java* in a hard-fought engagement in which

Java's commanding officer, Captain Henry Lambert, was fatally wounded. *Java* was too damaged to be sailed as a prize, so Bainbridge destroyed her and returned to Boston, missing his chance to rendezvous with Captain Porter.

Before departing the South Atlantic, Bainbridge advised Captain Lawrence to sail northward to the British entrepôt of Georgetown, Guyana, out of concern that otherwise *Hornet* might be overwhelmed by HMS *Montague*, 74, rumored to be on its way north from Rio de Janeiro. When Lawrence arrived, he discovered first the HM brig *Espeigle* moored close to the mouth of the river, but he dared not approach for fear of uncharted shoals; however, on February 24 fate delivered HM brig *Peacock*, closing from the open sea. *Hornet*'s superior armament, eighteen 32-pounder carronades, gave her the advantage over *Peacock*'s sixteen 24-pounders. After the usual maneuvering for position, Lawrence chose to attack on *Peacock*'s starboard quarter, quickly damaging her rudder and wounding Captain William Peake, who was soon thereafter killed by a double-headed shot. The battle was over in fifteen minutes, though with his enemy in sinking condition, Lawrence was unable to rescue all of her crew and lost three of his own to drowning. *Hornet* returned directly to the United States, slipping through the blockade and anchoring in Holmes Hole (now Vineyard Haven), at the island of Martha's Vineyard, on March 19.[30]

As it turned out, *Chesapeake* and *Essex* were delayed in departure, missed rendezvous, and sailed alone. Cruising from December to April, *Chesapeake*, under the command of Captain Samuel Evans, captured five merchant ships, while David Porter's *Essex*, heading into the South Atlantic, had a meager hunt, but on December 12 he captured HM brig packet *Nocton*, 10 guns, which carried a cargo of specie in the amount of 12,000 pounds sterling.[31] On December 14, Porter arrived at the place agreed upon with Bainbridge for their rendezvous, the Portuguese island of Fernao de Noronha. He departed that same day after picking up the letter that Bainbridge had left for him and sailed for the southern Brazilian province of Santa Catarina.[32] *Essex*'s further adventures took her around Cape Horn into the Pacific, where she operated against the British whaling fleet and Spanish privateers for the next year.

On October 15, sailing off the Grand Banks, Commodore Rodgers's *President* and Captain John Smith's *Congress* captured the royal mail packet *Swallow* en route from Jamaica to Falmouth with a cargo of gold and silver amounting to almost $200,000. Rodgers sent the valuable cargo off in the charge of a civilian American crew whose nearby schooner was near foundering. He ordered the crew to take charge of *Swallow* and sail to an American port for adjudication.[33]

At the end of his first war patrol, Commodore Rodgers had expressed disappointment that his expectations had not been met. He had been unable to bring

HMS *Belvidera* to action and had returned with few prizes. But he did take satisfaction in the fact that the combined squadron of the summer cruise "obliged the enemy to concentrate a considerable portion of his most active force and thereby prevented his capturing an incalculable amount of American property that might otherwise have fallen a sacrifice." Having returned from this second patrol with little to show for his 11,000-mile cruise except the capture of *Swallow*, he regretted the bad luck and bad weather that caused him to miss his quarry and hoped to get back to sea as soon as refitting and a recoppered hull permitted.[34]

By the end of April 1813, American warships had captured or destroyed three British frigates, *Guerriere*, *Macedonian*, and *Java*, the sloop of war *Alert*, and the brigs *Frolic* and *Peacock*, as well as several British merchant ships and fishing vessels. The one American frigate still on patrol after *Hornet*'s return was Captain Samuel Evans's *Chesapeake*, nominally part of Decatur's squadron but very late to arrive on station in the South Atlantic because of delays in fitting out. Secretary Hamilton permitted Evans to follow Commodore Decatur's original orders. He sailed to the eastern Atlantic and gradually made his way southwest into the area off Demerara that Lawrence had just departed. Failing to fall in with merchant convoys, Evans shaped a course for Boston, evaded the blockade and arrived in that port on April 9.

These events boosted national morale and delighted most American citizens, who reelected President James Madison in November 1812, at a time when US military operations on the northern frontier had failed in their objectives and shown weaknesses in leadership and logistical preparations. Faced with a series of unexpected defeats that stunned the British public, the Admiralty reinforced its blockading squadrons and later ruled that in the future British frigates would not undertake single combat with America's large frigates.[35] Within the US Navy, while not all had gone well, a great deal had. The naval events of 1812 showed that American sailors had taken to heart the lessons learned during the Quasi-War with France and the Tripolitan War. Most of the seamen and ships that the Madison administration sent to sea were trained and ready.

These successes should not shade the fact that in addition to *Wasp*, the service lost two other vessels to the British during the first six months of the war. Commodore Broke's squadron discovered and captured Lieutenant William Crane's brig *Nautilus*, 12, outward bound from New York in search of Rodgers's squadron. On July 16, after a six-hour chase, Broke's frigate *Shannon*, 38, overtook *Nautilus*, and Crane, having made every effort to escape, surrendered his command. His was the first US Navy vessel to be captured by the British. Captain Sir James Lucas Yeo's HMS *Southampton*, 38, captured Master Commandant George Reed's brig *Vixen*,14 guns, on November 22 in the Caribbean. Only five days later both vessels ran aground, and their crews had to be rescued in the Bahamas' Crooked Island Passage.[36]

Outbreak of War on the Northern Lakes

When, in July 1812, US armies attacked Canada in three locations, at Detroit, Niagara, and the upper Champlain Valley, the British response came quicker and more forcefully than expected. At the northwestern tip of Lake Huron, a small force of British regulars, augmented by fur traders and a large contingent of Native American allies, attacked Fort Mackinac on July 11, leading to the US garrison commander's capitulation. Major General William Hull's force captured Fort Amherstburg on July 12 but was soon threatened by General Isaac Brock's combined force of regulars, Canadian militia, and First Nation warriors. Hull surrendered at Detroit on August 16. After that, the military balance shifted to the British in the Northwest. On Lake Erie, the Provincial Marine captured the sloop *Cuyahoga*, and with it Hull's baggage containing his papers and correspondence from Washington.

These defeats awakened Americans to the importance of the United States having a naval force on the northern lakes that could assist its armies and contend with the Provincial Marine's small but important flotilla operating on the lower lakes. In effect, these events revealed the extent to which the United States had suffered because it had not reinforced Fort Mackinac before the campaign began and because it had no naval force on Lake Erie to support General Hull. In October, Major General Stephen Van Rensselaer's attack at Niagara (Queenstown) began well but failed because of a lack of reinforcements and good leadership when the New York State militiamen refused orders to leave the state they were under orders to defend. Major General Henry Dearborn's attack on Canada along the Richelieu River was repulsed at the La Colle Mill in November, and no US counterattack was forthcoming. Dearborn sent his troops into winter quarters.[37]

Soon after the declaration of war became known in the Great Lakes region, Lieutenant Melancthon Woolsey, commanding the brig *Oneida*, the navy's only vessel on Lake Ontario, voiced his concern for American shipping on Lake Ontario and the St. Lawrence River. Writing to Secretary Hamilton on June 26, Woolsey reported that he had been in touch with the local militia general Jacob Brown and requested volunteers to act as marines on board *Oneida*. One week later, he wrote again, describing the strength of the British Provincial Marine squadron stationed at Kingston and his concern to protect his base, as well as American trading schooners on the St. Lawrence.[38]

The Provincial Marine, a branch of the Quartermaster General of the British Army based at Kingston, Ontario, had at its disposal the sloops of war *Royal George* and *Earl of Moira* and the schooners *Duke of Gloucester* and *Prince Regent*. With the exception of *Prince Regent*, which was newly built, the other vessels were in dubious condition and in need of repair. Nonetheless, this British squadron outnumbered and outgunned Woolsey's one-ship navy.[39] By mid-July, the threat to American shipping and lake ports was serious enough to prompt Daniel D. Tompkins, the governor of New York, to write to John Bullus, the navy agent at New York, warning of trouble to come if US naval forces were not reinforced on Lake Champlain and Ontario. Bullus forwarded the letter to Secretary Hamilton.[40] Lieutenant Woolsey sent several more dispatches to Hamilton as he sparred with enemy gunboats while trying to save the American merchant schooners that had been trapped down the St. Lawrence after the outbreak of war. Overwhelmed with work related to the navy's operations on the Atlantic and requiring Madison's approval for a new naval initiative on the lakes, it took Hamilton more than a month to launch an operation on the northern lakes.

Logistics at Sackets Harbor

Finally, at the end of August, the secretary ordered Captain Isaac Chauncey to relocate from the New York Navy Yard to Sackets Harbor, taking with him as many of the ship carpenters and other specialists from the New York yard as could be spared. The immediate task was to establish naval bases, shipyards, and a new naval station in order to "obtain command of Lakes Ontario and Erie with the least possible delay." Chauncey was authorized to immediately transport the officers, seamen, marines, ordnance, small arms, and all equipment necessary for these tasks to Sackets Harbor and Buffalo to begin building warships at both locations.[41] This meant a huge increase in responsibility for Chauncey, altering his role from navy yard commandant and base commander to head a major operational command in charge of defending the northern frontier of the United States in cooperation with the army. Luckily, he had in Woolsey a competent second-in-command who did not hesitate to act when necessary. With the assistance of Lieutenant Henry Wells, Woolsey was able to protect and escort several merchant schooners up the St. Lawrence River from Ogdensburg to the safety of Sackets Harbor, where in due time they were purchased for the navy and converted into gunboats for Chauncey's squadron.[42]

The navy storekeeper Samuel Anderson, a confidential clerk who worked for Chauncey, reported to Secretary Hamilton on the difficulties of transporting provisions and ordnance to Sackets Harbor and to Black Rock during October 1812. From New York all the supplies had to travel by steamer 150 miles on the Hudson as far as Albany and then another 200 miles by Durham boats up the Mohawk River, until they reached what had been known during the French and Indian War as the Oneida Carry, a portage of three to four miles to Oneida Creek, which linked the Mohawk to the Oswego River and the lake port of Oswego. In 1792, the Western Inland Lock Navigation Company constructed a canal with locks that linked the Mohawk River to Wood Creek, eliminating the portage to the Oswego River. This improvement markedly eased the transport of people and goods to Lake Oneida and Oswego and was of great military use during the War of 1812. Yet, if there were low water owing to the lack of rainfall, transport would be delayed on the stretch from Utica to Rome. From Oswego, the cargo would be transferred to smaller vessels that would sail eastward along the shore to Sackets Harbor, while their sailors kept a weather eye peeled for the enemy squadron.

If the destination was Lake Erie, the cargo would travel from the Mohawk River to Wood Creek via a canal to Lake Oneida and then down the Onondaga and Seneca Rivers. There, cargo would have to be laboriously offloaded to wagons at Seneca Falls for the remainder of the trip, over 114 miles of rough roads to Black Rock on Lake Erie. In either case, the entire distance was close to 360 miles, and it would take more than a month to complete the trip from Albany to Black Rock. During the winter months, delivery might be easier by sled on snow-covered roads and frozen rivers. These logistical problems required Chauncey to plan well in advance for delivery of shipbuilding materials (except timber), sailcloth, ordnance, and all other goods that could not be obtained locally for use on these remote lakes. There was no better route for New Yorkers to use when it came time to finance and build the Erie Canal, but this would have to wait until 1817, two years after the end of the war.[43]

With so much to do regarding establishment of the navy on Lakes Ontario and Erie, Hamilton also had to concern himself with building another squadron for Lake Champlain. For this post he selected Lieutenant Thomas Macdonough, a battle-tested veteran of the Barbary Wars. At that moment, Macdonough was commanding the US gunboat flotilla at Portland, Maine, but he eagerly took up this new challenge. He would have an autonomous command, responding directly to orders from Washington, not from New York or Sackets Harbor, though he would be dependent on Chauncey for manpower. Hamilton ordered Macdonough to contact General Dearborn, encamped near Albany, for supplies and other assistance. From there, Macdonough traveled north to Plattsburgh, where he contacted Brigadier General Joseph Bloomfield for help equipping the few government vessels still afloat on Lake Champlain. In late October, when he arrived, there were only two decaying sloops under naval control on the lake, both moored at Whitehall, New York, needing officers and seamen. By December 20 Macdonough had three armed sloops, *Growler, President*, and *Eagle*, laid up for the winter at Shelburne, Vermont. In addition, he had acquired two gunboats, each armed with a 12-pounder long gun, and three sloops for use as transports. His main concern was that at Isle aux Noix, the British base on the Richelieu River, the enemy had more vessels, better armed and manned, which Macdonough would have to confront in the spring.[44]

In mid-August the news arrived at Sackets Harbor that William General Hull's army had surrendered after taking Detroit and had fallen into British hands. Secretary of War Eustis had apparently ignored Hull's warning that if the army were to contest the British and Indian control of the upper Great Lakes territory, the navy would first have to establish its supremacy on Lake Erie.[45] This lake was the key to navigation routes for carrying troops, supplies, and First Nations' trade goods from Quebec to Michilimackac. Hull's surrender put the Michigan Territory under threat from allied British and First Nation forces. Settlers in Kentucky and Ohio were sounding the alarm. Hull's defeat made it clear to Madison that a naval force on Lake Erie would be essential for future military operations in the Northwest. Captain Isaac Chauncey, having given orders to build a new base at Sackets Harbor, turned his attention to creating a squadron on Lake Erie. Secretary Hamilton told him that Lake Erie was at least as important as Lake Ontario in terms of national strategy. To supervise the acquisition and building of the Lake Erie warships, Chauncey selected Lieutenant Jesse D. Elliott, whom he had known while serving in the Mediterranean, and ordered him to Buffalo with instructions to contact local military officers and select a convenient situation for a navy yard. In addition, as a first installment of the personnel Elliott would require, Chauncey ordered the officers and men of the small frigate *John Adams* to their new duty station on Lake Erie. Elliott quickly made a name for himself. Not only did he obtain a site for shipbuilding at Black Rock but he also took the initiative to plan and implement a joint cutting-out expedition, capturing two brigs anchored off British-held Fort Erie (fig. 2.3).[46]

Commodore Chauncey's shipwrights had made remarkable progress since their arrival at Sackets Harbor in late September. Henry Eckford and his men from New York had nearly completed the sloop of war *Madison*; however, her armament, twenty-four 32-pounder carronades and two 9-pounder long guns, had not yet arrived. By early November the rest of Chauncey's squadron was ready for sea. He planned to challenge the Provincial Marine squadron that had been

Figure 2.3. Commodore Isaac Chauncey, USN, 1772–1840, commander of US Navy Squadron, Lake Ontario. Portrait by Gilbert Stuart, ca. 1818. Painting in US Naval Academy Museum, Annapolis, Maryland, US Naval History and Heritage Command, Photograph NH 51624.

actively shipping troops and supplies up the lake from Kingston to reinforce Fort George. Having set sail in *Oneida* in company with six schooners on November 8, Chauncey intercepted the *Royal George* on her return and pursued her into Kingston harbor, where they exchanged fire for over an hour, resulting in considerable damage to *Royal George*, later reported to be in a sinking condition when hauled out for repairs. The enemy schooner *Governor Simcoe*, 12 guns, sank in Kingston harbor before she could reach the wharf. On the next day, Chauncey's schooners captured the schooner *Mary Hatt* and the sloop *Elizabeth*, both transports in *Royal George*'s convoy.[47] By the end of November, winter had truly set in at Sackets Harbor, with ice forming on the harbor and around the ships at their moorings. From then until April, the main threat from the enemy might be from British troops attacking across the ice from Kingston. Against this possibility, Chauncey ordered the building of blockhouses and requested army troops and more marines to reinforce the naval base.

Hamilton Resigns

On November 13, 1812, Hamilton submitted a request for the most important leg-islation of his tenure as secretary of the navy. Addressing Burwell Bassett, chair-man of the Naval Committee of the House of Representatives, Hamilton's letter answered a number of questions that had been put to him by the committee con-cerning the enlargement of the navy. He proposed construction of several 76-gun ships of the line and a number of additional 50-gun and 40-gun frigates and 20-gun corvettes. With this request, he enclosed a letter from Captain Charles Stewart warmly and cogently explaining the reasons why this request should be approved.[48] After considerable debate, Congress approved the request. The pres-ident signed on December 23 an act authorizing the building of four 74-gun ships and six 44-gun frigates.

Paradoxically, after six months in which there were several successful naval engagements, the beginning of naval squadrons on the northern lakes, and the passage of the first major naval construction bill in ten years, the newly reelected president James Madison asked Paul Hamilton to resign his post. This news may have come to Hamilton as both a surprise and a relief. He was an honest gentle-man, friendly and approachable, but he was not a first-rate administrator.[49] It was widely rumored in Washington that he had been drinking heavily, but it was also true that he had been under immense strain since the beginning of the war and had personal financial difficulties. Having heard complaints from Congress about Hamilton's mismanagement, the president had lost confidence in his navy secre-tary's abilities. Empowered by reelection, he knew this was the time to find a suc-cessor. Madison met with Hamilton on December 28 and asked for his resigna-tion. Hamilton, though taken aback, duly complied. In his letter of resignation he asked Madison to write something complimentary in reply, which would "be a valuable legacy to my children." In his letter of acceptance, the president com-mended Hamilton's "patriotic merits and private virtues," as well as his "faithful zeal, uniform exertions, and unimpeachable integrity."[50]

CHAPTER 3

William Jones's Challenge
A Two-Front Naval War

The frigid winter of 1812–13 gave the United States and Great Britain a pause to adjust to the radical changes that war brought. During the summer and fall, prospects for an early peace had been tested and found wanting. Reconciliation between the warring Anglo-American cousins would not be forthcoming until military and naval actions and political pressure brought forth meaningful negotiations. For Britain, this meant strengthening its thinly stretched naval blockade on the Atlantic, reinforcing military and naval forces in Upper Canada, and planning a strategy for raiding vulnerable areas of the American coast. For the United States, the new year brought a realization that conquest of Canada would not be easily accomplished, that far more men were needed for its armies in the north, and that squadrons would have to be built on the Great Lakes and Lake Champlain.

The end of the first year of the war coincided with the results of the US presidential election of 1812, and the important decisions President Madison made after his reelection. He needed to strengthen the leadership of the Navy and War Departments. Responding to Madison's request, Secretary of the Navy Paul Hamilton resigned at the end of December. As shown in the previous chapter, Hamilton's administrative skills were not adequate to meet the pressures of war. Madison asked Secretary of War William Eustis to step down as well. The painful humiliation of the US Army in the wake of its failed invasions of Canada was the result of several factors, including congressional neglect of the army's condition, the failure to approve the administration's request to finance the war, the professional military's aging leadership, and the military's lack of attention to recent innovations in warfare. The blame for this was commonly laid at the feet of Secretary of War Eustis, but as a physician he was a poor choice for this important administrative office in the first place.

President Madison had selected Eustis not for his expertise in military matters but because he was an Anti-Federalist from Massachusetts, where Madison had few supporters. Eustis had served as a camp surgeon in the Continental Army and had been present at Lexington as a militiaman and at Bunker Hill, where he was attached to an artillery unit. He continued to serve in the army until the end of the Revolutionary War. He had run twice as a Republican for a seat in the House of Representatives and defeated Josiah Quincy each time. Madison therefore selected him mainly based on his Republican zeal, his congressional credentials, and his patriotism. His term as secretary of war was marked by quarrels with Major General Wilkinson about his unhealthy army encampment in Louisiana. Wilkinson's own misbehaviors, which were many, should have been cause for his removal from command of the army. Eustis tried to improve the army's logistical system by reestablishing the positions of quartermaster general, commissary general of purchases, and commissary general of ordnance, but a recalcitrant Congress refused to approve these essential posts. The defeats suffered by the army during the summer and fall of 1812 undermined what was left of Eustis's congressional support, and he offered Madison his resignation.

The president chose as Eustis's successor John Armstrong, who had served for six years (1804–10) as US ambassador to France. He was a Continental Army veteran and had served briefly as a US senator from New York, but he was a man of entirely different character from Eustis. A staunch pro-Madison Republican, Armstrong was based in New York State, where many other Republicans of an independent stripe supported Governor George Clinton. Madison's trusted colleague Treasury Secretary Albert Gallatin recommended Armstrong over others such as Governor Daniel Tompkins of New York, who might have been more manageable. Armstrong would prove to be a difficult personality at the head of the War Department because although intelligent, he was also stubborn, irascible, and indolent.[1]

The Selection of William Jones

These cabinet choices may have been imperfect and difficult, but the president's selection of the man who would be the next secretary of the navy was well considered and brilliant: William Jones, of Philadelphia, would serve as the navy's key civilian administrator for nearly the duration of the war, accepting the position in January 1813 and resigning in November 1814. Born in Philadelphia in 1760, Jones went into mercantile business at an early age. During the Revolutionary War he joined a company of volunteer infantry at age 16 and fought in the battles of Trenton and Princeton, New Jersey. He later served with distinction under Thomas Truxtun on the Pennsylvania state privateer *St. James*. During this service, Jones was wounded twice and captured by the British. After the war, he became associated with the Philadelphia merchant Samuel Clarke, with whom he established the merchant house of Jones and Clarke, with offices in Charleston and Philadelphia.[2] Jones himself commanded ships on far-flung trading voyages and became expert in matters of trade, navigation, and maritime insurance. He declined an invitation to serve as President Jefferson's secretary of the navy in 1801 but instead ran for election to the House of Representatives for Philadelphia's First District. He served in Congress for one term, as a Democratic-Republican, from 1801 to 1803 (fig. 3.1).

Jones began his duties in the Navy Department in early January 1813 with a sense of patriotic purpose and a desire to reform what he saw as a department that was understaffed and run by a few clerks of long tenure and corrupt practices that had been tolerated or overlooked by his predecessor Paul Hamilton. One of his first steps was to ask for the resignation of Chief Clerk Charles Goldsborough, who he claimed was responsible for the disorganized state of the department, which he had supervised for the past twelve years. Goldsborough was embarrassed, naturally enough, and asked to be given time to arrange his departure as well as another position in the department, suggesting the position of storekeeper at Portsmouth, New Hampshire, which he knew was vacant. Jones assented to this arrangement but quickly went about selecting a successor. Working through Secretary of State Monroe, Jones inquired about Benjamin Homans, an acquaintance of Vice President Eldbridge Gerry's. Gerry recommended Homans as a

Figure 3.1. Secretary of the Navy William Jones, 1813–1814. Portrait by Gilbert Stuart. Courtesy of Navy Art Collection, Washington, DC, US Naval History and Heritage Command, Photograph NH 54764-KN.

dedicated and honest man who had organized the office of the secretary of Massachusetts, a good Republican, and a former ship captain. Homans accepted and held the job for a decade, apparently working well for the three navy secretaries who administered the department from 1813 to 1823.[3]

In March 1813, Homans arrived in Washington to begin his next job but was dismayed to find that the clerks he had to work with were inhospitable because he had supplanted their accustomed boss Charles Goldsborough and were reluctant to share the information Homans needed to get on with his work. Homans had to ask Jones to expedite the collaboration of Thomas Turner, the department's well-seasoned and all-important accountant who was also the fourth auditor of the Treasury Department. Next, Homans found fault with the Navy Department's storekeepers, whose returns were irregular and overwhelmed with trivia. He found disorder in record keeping and needed new filing cases to reorganize the office in a systematic way. He assured Jones, at the end of a lengthy memo, that given time, he would put things in good order.[4]

While regularizing his office staff, Jones also had to deal with congressional requests for information about the best method of reforming the management of the navy. This had begun even before Jones assumed the office. Lieutenant Charles Morris, Hull's first lieutenant during the fight with *Guerriere*, was apparently between assignments during the interim between Hamilton's departure and Jones's arrival in Washington. Congressman Langdon Cheves, chairman of the House Naval Committee, had sent a letter to Morris asking for his opinion on reforms needed in the Navy Department. Morris had not held back; he had sent a lengthy enumeration of practices he thought reflected inefficiencies and abuses. Aware that the new secretary would soon be in position, he had sent a copy of his remarks to William Jones.

Reforms for the Navy Department

Morris first brought up the matter of navy agents, who did the purchasing of items for the navy's ships. They were permitted to reward themselves for these services by charging a commission on every purchase. This system could be exploited, Morris thought, by purchasing from vendors charging the highest prices. It would be cheaper for the government to put the agents on a fixed salary and require them to purchase on the best terms for the government. They should also be required to swear an oath at the time of their quarterly settlements that they had complied with these regulations.

That Morris was also concerned about the government's method of contracting shows that this troublesome concern of modern times is nothing new. He felt that contracting practices were "too loose" and that inadequate security was required for performance of contracts. At times, agents would make an unauthorized advance without being able to ascertain the vendor's compliance. To remedy this, Morris prescribed sealed bids for vendors hoping to obtain a naval contract and recommended that no advances should be made except when the government could obtain sufficient security or bond from the vendor.

In a third area, Morris complained that there was a lack of system for classes of vessel and their accoutrements, or furniture and equipment. Commanding officers were allowed to exercise discretion on how to equip their ships, and often commanders disagreed about what a ship needed. This resulted in occasional extravagances based on the whim of the ship's commander, for which the service should not pay. The department should issue regulations forbidding alterations in a ship's configuration unless specifically authorized by the secretary of the navy or a squadron commodore.

There were often delays in a ship's readiness for departure from a port or navy yard because of lack of appropriate, oft-needed equipment in the yard's supply depot. A lack of planning or foresight on the part of navy agents or yard commandants could (and did) lead to ships being unavailable when they were most needed for service. US navy yards, Morris opined, should each have a drydock to accommodate a ship needing hull inspections or rudder repairs and cleaning below the waterline. The lack of such a facility meant that a ship had to be emptied of stores and equipment and heaved down at great effort and risk of damage to the ship, not to mention the delay imposed by all the preparations for this operation.

Further, Morris condemned the usefulness of the Jeffersonian-era gunboats. He maintained that their use was only feasible for harbor defense or when operating in shoal water. Their lack of significant force meant that no officer would be put in charge of them, and they would not provide a midshipman an adequate field of experience for naval warfare. Far better, he proposed, to place gunboats under military command at a fort or harbor defense battery or under the supervision of sea officers who had no part in the regular navy establishment.

Morris encouraged Congressman Cheves to consider establishing a board of senior naval officers to advise the head of the Navy Department and to ensure that all regulations of the service be carried out, to supervise the awarding of contracts, examine accounts of officers in charge of stores (supplies), and test and evaluate midshipmen up for promotion. He advised that this board have under its direction a surgeon general and a contractor general. These last suggestions were prescient, foreshadowing the establishment of the Board of Navy Commissioners in 1815 and, further into the future, Navy Department bureaus in charge of supply, navigation, ordnance, and construction.[5]

Three weeks later Secretary Jones followed suit with his own recommendations for "better organization of the Navy Department" addressed to Congressman Burwell Bassett, the new chairman of the Naval Committee. Jones, like Morris, wanted a more centralized supply system. He suggested that there should be a naval purveyor's department under a purveyor general with as many deputies as necessary to manage an efficient contracting system, with the secretary of the department having oversight and general direction. He also requested an increased appropriation for more clerks for his office and more billets for captains to serve as commanding officers of the new 74-gun ships and to provide replacements for any who might be wounded or killed in combat. The most significant requests were for appropriation of funds for six small frigates or corvettes for escorting the coastal trade and attacking the enemy's shipping and a further reduction in the number of gunboats in service.[6] Jones's highest priorities included providing more seamen for the frigates and reducing the expenses of the Navy Department. Captain Morris had argued for more gunboats for harbor defense, but this was not an urgent necessity for Jones. Before leaving office, Hamilton had requested the building of four ships of the line and six additional heavy (44-gun) frigates. These were authorized on January 2, 1813, but none of them got to sea before the end of the war. Jones thus added more intermediate-class frigates to the navy's wish list. One of these one was *Argus*, built at the Washington Navy Yard, while the other five were built under private contract, *Erie* and *Ontario* at Baltimore, *Wasp* at Newburyport, *Peacock* at New York, and *Frolic* at Boston. The last three named were launched and commissioned and performed well during 1814–15. Although completed, launched, and commissioned, *Erie* and *Ontario* were unable to depart Chesapeake Bay until after the war because of the British blockade.

When Jones lifted his eyes from matters of naval reform and ship construction to the great challenges ahead, he grew philosophical. In a letter to his wife, he admitted that the task he had accepted would prove Herculean, but he observed that as he got deeper into the job, "the terrors appear to diminish with the serious contemplation I have given to the subject." He knew that though he was well acquainted with maritime matters and political concerns, there would be difficult moments ahead. Yet he felt that if he were reasonably competent and virtuous, he would survive, and he asked her to understand and "not to mind it" when these things occurred.[7]

William Jones and the Second Front

What made the new navy secretary's job so daunting was its two operational theaters, which would demand all his ingenuity and strength of character. It is a byword of military theory that it is unwise for a nation to try to fight two wars simultaneously, and yet this was a conundrum the Madisonian strategy had created. There was the developing naval war in the Atlantic, in which the diminutive US Navy faced the much larger, globally deployed British Royal Navy, but on the US-Canadian borderlands and lakes there was a different kind of war to be fought. This involved the building of ships and naval stations on the shores of the lakes, transporting experienced officers, crews, and equipment from the Atlantic to the lakes, and recruiting and training military forces in the Michigan Territory that had already tasted defeat at the hands of the British and their First Nation allies in the 1812 campaign. The major issues for the secretary would be those of logistics. He would have to deploy the tools of naval warfare to commanders who needed them when they required them and where they were located. In case of shortages, the secretary would be called upon to make difficult choices, depending on the nature of the threat faced and how quickly the resources could be made available.

Judging from the arrival of reports in Jones's office, it was the building of the navy's bases on the Great Lakes that first claimed his attention. One of the first items to cross his desk was Captain Isaac Chauncey's letter addressed to Paul Hamilton. Chauncey, unaware of Hamilton's departure, was on a tour of naval facilities on Lake Erie. He wrote from Presque Isle, at Erie, Pennsylvania, commenting on Sailing Master Daniel Dobbins's progress in constructing gunboats for the Lake Erie squadron. Dobbins was a master mariner with many years' experience on merchant schooners on Lakes Erie and Huron. After the surrender of William Hull's army at Detroit, at the urging of Major General David Mead (Sixteenth Division, Pennsylvania Militia), Dobbins visited Washington in September to inform President Madison of the strength of the Canadian Provincial Marine on the lakes.[8] He urged that Erie, Pennsylvania, would provide an ideal place to build and base a naval flotilla. It was well protected from the immense lake, though too shallow for large warships. It was probably inevitable that Dobbins and Lieutenant Jesse Elliott clashed on this subject. Elliott was selected by Chauncey as his second-in-command on Lake Erie, but Elliott was not as well informed about Presque Isle as Dobbins. Dobbins had not been a part of the Regular Navy and had no status until Secretary Hamilton gave him the rank of sailing master and ordered him back to Erie. It is probable that Elliott's animosity over Dobbin's preferment arose because of this and the fact that Elliott was Commodore Chauncey's chosen officer in charge on Lake Erie matters.

Dobbins, Chauncey wrote, had commenced building four gunboats, but they were too small for lake-cruising; however, he could alter and lengthen the two that were least advanced in construction. Chauncey was right to object. Gunboats of the Jeffersonian variety were totally inappropriate for lake warfare, however adequate they might be for defending harbors and shallow water sounds. But it was Secretary Hamilton who ordered Dobbins to build "gunboats," about which he knew as little as he did about Lake Erie. Chauncey had ordered three ship carpenters to travel to Erie to hasten the process. He admired the harbor at Presque Isle for its breadth and the ease with which it could be defended, yet he regretted its shallow depth. The navy depot at Black Rock was within cannon shot of Canada's Fort Erie; for that reason it was a riskier location for a navy yard than Presque Isle. The area had fine timber resources, although cordage and iron would have to be procured from Pittsburgh.[9] Carrying these items from Pittsburgh to Presque Isle would be done more quickly and with less effort and expense than carrying them from New York via Albany. They would transit by barge on the Alleghany River and French Creek. Iron might be obtained in some quantity from Buffalo, but there were no adequate ropewalks in the Buffalo area at that time.[10]

From Erie, Chauncey traveled east to inspect Black Rock, the American naval base on the right bank of the Niagara River about two miles north of Buffalo. The problem with using Black Rock as a base was its position in sight of and within range of Fort Erie on the opposite bank. Chauncey realized that he could not afford to run this risk during the winter. He had ordered all vessels then at Black Rock—the captured brig *Caledonia* and four purchased lake schooners, *Contractor* (later renamed *Trippe*), *Amelia*, *Catherine*, and *Ohio*—to be moved into a creek behind Squaw Island, where they would be safe from ice floes and from the British guns across the river. He ordered the building of a blockhouse for the protection of the vessels and to provide shelter for the men and their equipment, as well as the rigging, sails, spars, and anchors, all of which had been stored in remote places around Buffalo, now to be brought together in one location and placed in the charge of Lieutenant John Pettigrew, USN, the new commander at Black Rock.[11] Naval operations on the lakes would cease until the breaking up of ice and the re-rigging of the schooners in the spring. Upon his return to Sackets Harbor in mid-January, Chauncey reported to Secretary Jones that several deserters from *Royal George* had informed him that the enemy's military strength at Kingston, Ontario, was about 1,000 men and that new warships were under construction there and at York, following the arrival of 150 ship carpenters and 50 sailors. Chauncey thought the British would make a desperate effort to regain control of the lake in the ensuing summer and that it was essential to expedite construction of another ship to be ready to meet the British challenge. He also thought he should meet with General Dearborn in Albany and visit New York City to make logistical arrangements for the 1813 campaign season.[12]

British Reinforcements in Canada

North and east of Lake Ontario, the British were likewise intensifying their preparations. They had taken the first steps in this direction in late 1807 after they realized the strength of the American response to the *Chesapeake–Leopard* incident. At this time, Major General Sir George Prevost, born into a military family in colonial New Jersey, was a veteran of more than thirty years' service in the British army, much of it fighting the French in the Caribbean. He had served recently as lieutenant governor of Portsmouth, England, and was on the verge of being posted to the Continent with a joint expeditionary force headed for Denmark. In late 1807 the secretary of state for war and the colonies countermanded these plans and ordered Prevost to sail with an infantry brigade to Halifax, where he assumed the local rank of lieutenant general to become the governor and commander general of the Maritime Provinces. Essentially, Prevost was there to prepare Canada for war, but during a tour of inspection he found that he had troop shortages owing to the demand for regulars in Portugal. Dire news arrived from Portugal, where French forces had invaded from Spain and were threatening British army defensive positions on the outskirts of Lisbon. For the same reason, the Royal Navy had reduced its allotment of ships to the North American Station in order to reinforce its Channel and North Sea squadrons. The Anglo-French battles for Portugal and Spain had become the main British concern.[13]

Thus, within a year British alarm over *Chesapeake–Leopard* had faded as Jefferson left the White House and the more flexible James Madison relaxed the strict US trade laws. Prevost proceeded to prepare the Maritime Provinces however he could. He would have to compensate for the lack of sufficient numbers of regular troops by raising the militia's pay, improving training, and strengthening discipline and then redeploy them when and where needed. He was also ordered to gather intelligence about US military forces deploying to the borderlands, spread discord in the northern states, and encourage trade with Americans who inclined to disobey their government's laws prohibiting commerce outside the United States. In addition, Prevost was strategically placed to succeed the ailing General Sir James Henry Craig as captain general and governor in chief should it become necessary. In the midst of all this, the Crown was uneasy about French military activity in the Caribbean, where it controlled the islands of Guadeloupe and Martinique.

In August 1808, Prevost received orders to leave Halifax temporarily and take command of troops for an invasion of Martinique in cooperation with Lieutenant General Sir George Beckwith, who then commanded in the Windward Islands. Their campaign was remarkably short and successful, begun and completed within the month of February 1809, with the French commander yielding in an unconditional surrender. Soon, Prevost was back in Halifax enjoying the celebrations of his household and the community at large, but this pleasant interlude would not last long. Anglo-American relations took another turn for the worse in 1810.

The Madison administration was anxious to resume its neutral trading with both Britain and France, but neither nation would allow the United States to trade with the other without suffering consequences. Under Macon's Bill No. 2, the United States would suspend its non-intercourse policy and open trade with the nation that first agreed to suspend its punitive acts against American shipping and then refuse trade with the other unless it would agree to the neutral trade. This measure was exploited by Napoleon's government, which deceitfully promised to drop its retaliatory measures against the United States but allowed them to remain in place and continued to sequester American ships and imprison their crews. The US government, preferring Britain to be its trading partner, ignored this fraudulent practice, hoping to force Britain to drop its constraints on American trade. Yet the British government recognized this and under the orders in council refused to stop the seizing of American merchant ships suspected of trading with France.

The next sign that a new Anglo-American crisis was brewing came in May 1811 with the furor caused by the *President–Little Belt* incident. This incident outraged Royal Navy officers as much as the *Chesapeake–Leopard* incident had offended US Navy officers three years earlier. With hostile feelings at a near boiling point, the British hastened to place Major General Prevost where they wanted him. Governor General James Craig had sent his letter requesting permission to resign his position in June 1811. This opened the way for Prevost, who quickly stepped down as governor general of Nova Scotia to become governor general of Canada, arriving in Quebec in September after a three-week voyage on board HMS *Melampus*.

At this point, Prevost was empowered to prepare Canada for war with the neighboring United States, and much was to be done, although there were limitations on his scope of authority. He did not have the Crown's permission to declare war, nor could he take the offensive. His role was to be a defensive one of preventing and repelling the attacks that might come from the United States. Britain's strategic priorities placed greater importance on warfare on the European continent; thereafter, trained men and needed supplies were not to be wasted elsewhere. Thus, Prevost had to walk a narrow path when it came to actual operations and not overextend his forces to the point of being in an embarrassing predicament.[14] Other observers, including some of his subordinates, did not realize the limitations that had been placed on Prevost and criticized him as being overly cautious and lacking in aggressive spirit.

It is important to recognize that when Prevost took the reins in Quebec, he did not have a subordinate Royal Navy officer on his staff assigned to preparing for naval operations on the Great Lakes. Rather, he had to depend on the officers of the Provincial Marine, a branch of the British army's quartermaster general's department. Soon after his arrival Prevost requested a report from the quartermaster general on the condition of the Provincial Marine with a view to probable operations on the lakes. The deputy quartermaster general, Lieutenant Colonel A. H. Pye, responded to the effect that virtually nothing was left of the vessels formerly on Lake Champlain. On Lakes Erie and Ontario, there were several vessels under the supervision of Provincial Marine officers. At Amherstburg, at the western end of Lake Erie, were the ship *Camden*, which was rotten and unfit for duty, the sloop of war *Queen Charlotte*, 16, which was much newer and could be made ready for service, and the brig *General Hunter*, 14, deemed serviceable but beginning to decay.

On Lake Ontario, at Kingston, were *Duke of Kent*, a vessel beyond hope of repair but being used as a barracks ship, the sloops of war *Earl of Moira*,14, and *Royal George*, 22, and the schooners *Governor Simcoe*, 14, and *Duke of Gloucester*, 12, the latter described as the most useful vessel on the lake. Pye's report warned that Amherstburg might not be a safe haven for ships considering its proximity to Detroit, the probable scene of action, and even Kingston was thought to be too open to attack, being so close to "the enemy's country," meaning the US Navy's base at Sackets Harbor, some forty miles distant. The report closes with guarded remarks suggesting that the ships' commanding officers might need to be replaced with younger, more efficient men.[15]

As he considered the preparations for the summer with the likelihood of war, Prevost had to contend with immense logistical problems owing to the length of his supply lines, which stretched 700 miles from Quebec to Amherstburg and 400 miles from Quebec to Kingston. The roads were primitive and difficult during inclement weather. The most difficult stretch was the part of the route along the St. Lawrence River, as bateaux had to negotiate 180 miles of rapids between Montreal and Kingston, although this was easier in winter, when sleighs could be used. Once men and supplies reached Kingston, the use of sailing vessels made travel much easier and quicker if the winds cooperated. Prevost's transportation problems were akin to those of the American commodore Chauncey, who had to send his men and supplies from New York City to Albany and thence via the Mohawk River, the Oswego River, and Lake Ontario to Sackets Harbor or Buffalo and Erie, Pennsylvania. Prevost also had to consider the security of his transport up the St. Lawrence River, as it closed on the US border for the last 100 miles to Kingston. There, with only the river itself defining the borders of the two hostile neighbors, boat attacks and raids across the frozen river could easily be made against British convoys, sleighs, and wagons.

The Provincial Marine still dominated Lake Ontario, opposed only by the American navy brig *Oneida*. This was to change with the onset of hostilities after June 18, 1812. Lieutenant Melancthon Woolsey, the American officer commanding *Oneida*, quickly realized that he had to gather and protect the American trading schooners on the lakes and rivers or they would be seized by the British. But the immediate threat came from Provincial Marine vessels stationed at Kingston. He had another vessel in mind, the schooner *Julia*, based at Oswego, but she was privately owned. He approached the owner with an offer to purchase for the navy, but the owner refused, whereupon Woolsey immediately seized the vessel and armed her with an available 32-pounder long gun.

On July 19 the Provincial Marine vessels appeared off Sackets Harbor endeavoring to capture *Oneida*, but Woolsey cleverly anchored his brig beneath a shore battery and transferred his spare guns to the battery. He was able to beat off the enemy squadron with no damage to his own ship. This brief lake action showed how serious the war had quickly become in the US–Canadian borderlands.[16] Ten days later, Woolsey sent *Julia* down the St. Lawrence to Ogdensburg, where a number of American trading schooners were gathered awaiting an escort. Unexpectedly, Prevost and the American general Henry Dearborn agreed upon a truce while the British waited to see if the news of the withdrawal of orders in council would have any effect in Washington; it did not, but the truce from August 8 to September 4 gave *Julia* enough time to bring the schooners back to the lake and into the safety of Sackets Harbor. Woolsey reported that "we can now muster eight or nine fine schooners—two of them can carry 32 pounders, one—two twenty fours, and the rest will average eight light guns each, say nines and sixes."[17]

Commodore Chauncey at Sackets Harbor

These vessels became the nucleus of the Lake Ontario squadron after Commodore Chauncey arrived at Sackets Harbor in September. Chauncey armed the schooners and reinforced the fort at Sackets Harbor for their protection. Then he ordered Henry Eckford, the New York shipwright, to commence the construction of a sloop of war that would be USS *Madison*, the 24-gun flagship of the Lake Ontario squadron.[18] With *Oneida* and the schooners *Conquest, Hamilton, Governor Tompkins, Pert, Julia,* and *Growler,* he conducted a sweep of the lake in November and caught up with the Provincial Marine's *Royal George* and other vessels at Kingston harbor. He did not capture his opponent but damaged her and sank the schooner *Simcoe*; with this flourish, the lake came under American control and remained so for the rest of the campaign season.

By December 1, Chauncey had decided that the time had come to "lay up," or deactivate, his vessels and bring their sailors ashore, except for a skeleton crew available for emergencies. No sooner had he given this order than he began worrying about the security of the squadron, as the freezing of the lake might enable the British to effect a raid without need of boats. Intelligence gained from a flag-of-truce mission to Kingston had given rise to a rumor of British troop reinforcements arriving there from Montreal. Given this possibility, the commodore sent a letter to General Dearborn at Albany asking for regular troops to guard the base, in addition to the militia and marines already at his disposal. Dearborn had served his country well in the Revolutionary War and as Jefferson's secretary of war. For the sake of his reputation, he probably should have stepped out of military life in 1809, but he remained in the militia. So in 1812, at 61 years of age, he was recalled to active service as the senior major general officer in the army. Secretary Armstrong placed Dearborn in charge of the right division of the American army, stationed at Greenbush, near Albany and at Plattsburgh (the left division would be sent to the Buffalo/Niagara sector).

The news of Chauncey's attack on *Royal George* at Kingston apparently convinced Prevost of the urgent need for naval reinforcements. In December he wrote to Earl Bathurst, secretary for war, at Whitehall Palace and Admiral John Borlase Warren, commander of the North Atlantic Station, recommending that the Royal Navy take command of the lakes squadrons and that a detachment of officers and men be sent to replace the Provincial Marine. With Bathurst concurring, Warren eventually sent three commanders, six lieutenants, and two gunners to oversee the conversion process. Warren followed up by recommending an additional 550 sailors (including officers) and that an experienced master and commander be sent as commodore to command on the lakes under the dual oversight of Prevost and Warren. He selected Commander Sir James Lucas Yeo for this important role, one that he conceivably deserved because of the energy and bravery he had exhibited in his earlier commands during service against the French in the Mediterranean and the Caribbean.[19] By virtue of the broad scope of his new responsibilities, commanding Royal Navy squadrons forming on Lakes Ontario, Erie, and Champlain, Sir James was promoted to post captain and assumed the traditional title of commodore.

Royal Navy on the Lakes

Commodore Yeo's orders from the Admiralty committed him to cooperate with Prevost. He was directed not to undertake any operations without Prevost's full concurrence and approval and to obey the orders that he might receive from the governor general from time to time. He was also to operate under the supervision of Admiral Warren and to respond to direction from the Admiralty. All of this meant that Yeo had to respond to several masters and to comply with the general tenor of his instructions, which were to wage a defensive campaign against the American naval forces confronting him. Given the situation, Yeo had to tread carefully to avoid annoying his seniors yet take advantage of any openings that fortune would allow. In time, the question of command authority became a major issue in the relationship between the Royal Navy and the British army in Canada during the war. In the event, Yeo and his contingent were unable to arrive at Quebec until May 1813, several weeks after the breakup of ice on Lake Ontario, which signaled the beginning of the 1813 naval and military campaign season.

The junior officers whom Admiral Warren ordered to North America included several lieutenants who, as acting commanders, served with distinction in important posts on the northern lakes: Robert Heriot Barclay, later commodore of the Lake Erie squadron; Robert Finnis, who died commanding *Queen Charlotte* in the Lake Erie battle; and Daniel Pring, who commanded the brig *Linnet* during the Battle of Lake Champlain. These officers arrived at Kingston in early April, more than a month before Yeo. For their first few weeks, they served as officers in the Lake Ontario squadron. Lieutenant Barclay was ordered to take charge of HMS *Wolfe*, a 23-gun corvette (sloop of war), and being senior, he also had overall command of the Point Frederick naval shipyard at Kingston. Lieutenant Pring was selected as the new commander of the 22-gun corvette *Royal George*; and Finnis was given command of the older brig *Earl of Moira*, with 16 guns. These arrangements held until the arrival of Captain Yeo, who, as commodore, altered these assignments and ordered Barclay with a few officers and enlisted to Amherstburg, where he would assume command of the Provincial Marine vessels on Lake Erie, thenceforth to be called the Royal Navy Lake Erie Squadron.[20] All these changes occurred in the midst of urgent operations during the last week of May 1813. Commodore Chauncey's squadron was then engaged in the landings at Fort George, while Governor General Prevost and Commodore Yeo took advantage of Chauncey's absence to attack his base at Sackets Harbor.

Building the US Naval Squadron on Lake Erie

As William Jones took stock of his new office and began reading through the accumulating correspondence from his commanders, he was quick to encourage Chauncey's energetic undertakings at Sackets Harbor. Likewise, the commodore

Figure 3.2. Commodore Oliver Hazard Perry, USN, 1785–1819, commander of US Navy Squadron, Lake Erie. Portrait by Edward L. Mooney after John Wesley Jarvis (1839). Painting in US Naval Academy Museum, transferred from the US Naval Lyceum, 1892. Official US Navy photograph, US Naval History and Heritage Command, KN-2783.

kept Jones informed with frequent letters. One topic uppermost in Chauncey's mind was his need for a capable subordinate officer to command the Lake Erie squadron while he superintended operations from his remote station at Sackets Harbor. He had been highly satisfied with the work of Master Commandant Jesse D. Elliott as his second-in-command on Lake Ontario, but Elliott could not cover both posts.

Of the many officers yearning for service at sea, most would have opted for a blue-water command on the Atlantic; fewer would have chosen to serve on the Great Lakes freshwater seas. Yet one experienced officer then assigned to command gunboats based at Newport, Rhode Island, entreated both Secretary Hamilton and Secretary Jones for a warfighting assignment rather than one limited to harbor defense. Master Commandant Oliver Hazard Perry had served in the Mediterranean under Commodore John Rodgers, who thought well of him, and Perry was likely known to Commodore Chauncey as one of the young lieutenants who had served on the Barbary Coast during the years 1801–7, when

Chauncey commanded *Chesapeake, John Adams,* and *Hornet.* In November 1812 Perry wrote to Hamilton asking for an assignment to "the Lakes," saying that he could bring fifty or sixty of the men then assigned to the gunboats who were willing to serve under him.[21] Perry also wrote directly to Chauncey on January 1, 1813, offering his services, to which Chauncey replied, "You are the very person I want for a particular service where you may gain honor for yourself and reputation for your country" (fig. 3.2).[22]

Joint US Amphibious Operations at York and Niagara

Chauncey tended to believe whatever intelligence there was showing the growing strength of the British garrison at Kingston. This put him on edge because the plan he had previously concerted with General Dearborn calculated a direct amphibious attack on Kingston "with 1,000 picked men" in order to destroy the Provincial Marine and cut British communications with York, Fort George, and Burlington at the western end of the lake. At least that was their plan at the end of January.[23] Then the estimates of the enemy's numbers began to increase. The strategy for the 1813 campaign had been discussed in the president's cabinet. Secretary of War Armstrong had recommended a joint amphibious attack at Kingston, which, if successful, could be followed by attacks at York and Fort George at the mouth of the Niagara River. At the time, probably in early January 1813, he first estimated the enemy's strength at 2,100 troops between Fort Erie and Kingston. Against them he proposed to send General Dearborn's troops from their encampment at Greenbush (near Albany) and others stationed at Lake Champlain to Sackets Harbor, all told perhaps 4,000 men, even though it meant stripping the defenses of eastern New York State.

After Dearborn traveled to Sackets Harbor, he learned from Chauncey that the latest intelligence revealed 6,000 to 8,000 enemy troops ready to cross the ice and attack Sackets Harbor. This was an absolute fabrication. According to a Canadian military historian, there were no more than 413 regulars and 450 militia at Kingston at the time.[24] What had happened to cause the increase in the estimate? It was probably the result of a clever bit of disinformation spread by deserters from Canada. That it may have seemed credible to the American commodore was a coincidence. Governor General Prevost had made a rapid tour of inspection, leaving Quebec on February 17 and reaching Prescott four days later. On February 7 a group of 200 American riflemen led by Benjamin Forsyth staged a raid across the St. Lawrence from Ogdensburg to Brockville (Elizabethtown), seizing supplies, freeing American prisoners, and capturing several British. After Prevost's party passed Brockville heading for Niagara on February 21, the British responded in kind with a force of about 500 men, forcing Forsyth's band to retreat from Ogdensburg.[25] The result of all this activity and the setback for American skirmishers added to the rumors that generally flowed about Sackets Harbor that winter.

Chauncey, like Dearborn, was an anxious, worrying type and perhaps gullible of rumors reaching him from Canada. It is likely that the British raid was viewed as being made possible by reinforcements accompanying Prevost, which it was not. Chauncey and Dearborn agreed to propose an alternative to the Kingston attack; they would instead attack York and posts at the western end of the lake. In this, their superior numbers would overwhelm the British. If all went well, they could then turn back and attack Kingston. Secretary of War Armstrong, ever ready to shift so that negative results could be blamed on someone else, agreed to the change in plans even while warning that it would leave Sackets Harbor without a defensive force. As it turned out, the British force at Kingston was only about 2,000 troops, though that was temporary. When warmer weather and British troops and naval reinforcements arrived, the American opportunity at Kingston vanished.

When Jones received Chauncey's news that Armstrong had approved a change in strategy, he told Chauncey that while the president had agreed, their main concern at the time was that the naval and military "harmonize" the movements of their combined forces. An amphibious attack at York and Fort George would be simultaneous with the US Army's thrust across the Niagara at Fort Erie and Chippewa. If this succeeded, it would free the navy's vessels from their difficult position under the enemy's Fort Erie guns at Black Rock, enabling them to sail west to join with Perry at Presque Isle, an all-important move that would be vital to bringing Lake Erie under American control.[26]

Building the Lake Erie Squadron

Master Commandant Perry arrived at Erie on March 27 and set to work in a whirlwind of activity to carry out his orders to confront the enemy with a battle squadron in the shortest possible time. For this to happen, Perry had to order the basic supplies and men required to build ships in a wilderness. Ship's timbers would be cut from the surrounding forests. The ship carpenters Noah and Adam Brown, whom Chauncey had requested from New York City, arrived in late March and had laid the keels for two brigs of 360 tons each and four armed schooners by the end of April. Iron fastenings, anchors, and cordage were manufactured and shipped from Pittsburgh, while sailcloth would come from Philadelphia. Chauncey had told Perry he would send him James Sacket, a sailmaker from New York City, to shape and sew the sails as required. The guns required for these vessels included thirty-seven 32-pounder carronades and two long 9-pounders for the brigs and one 32-pounder long gun for each of the gunboats. These would come either from the naval depot at Black Rock or from Pittsburgh.[27]

While Perry was engaged in building his ships, his military counterpart, Major General William Henry Harrison, established his headquarters at Fort Stephenson, on the lower Sandusky River. In late May, with his men hard at work completing the brigs at Presque Isle, Perry had a unique opportunity to join Commodore Chauncey's squadron at Niagara, where Chauncey and Dearborn were about to launch an amphibious landing to capture Fort George. At Chauncey's invitation, Perry sailed to Black Rock and traveled to Fort Niagara, where he joined the military and naval officers of the expedition. Perry volunteered to organize the naval aspects of the troop landings and in this capacity worked out the details with Colonels Winfield Scott and Alexander Macomb. This involved loading several hundred boats with troops, horses, artillery, and ammunition and orchestrating the boats' movements so that the navy's squadron could provide gunfire support, which suppressed the enemy's efforts to thwart the invasion before it could gain a foothold on the Canadian shore. The Americans landed despite opposition and pressed on toward Fort George, which the British abandoned as they retreated westward toward Burlington, Ontario.

The American attack on Fort George created ripples of concern all the way from Fort Erie to Amherstburg and Fort Malden. The British garrison abandoned Fort Erie and withdrew toward Burlington on May 25. This meant that British naval command, control, and communications on Lake Erie had to be based on the waters between Long Point, on the north shore of the lake, and the naval base at Amherstburg. Few supplies could be obtained except those that could be hauled overland from Burlington, on Lake Ontario, to Long Point Bay, on Lake Erie, or on the rough lakeside roads some two hundred miles to Amherstburg. If Perry were able to move his fleet from its protected anchorage inside Presque Isle Bay to the lake, this would imperil British communications with Kingston, Montreal, and Quebec. One should keep in mind that Commander Barclay, the newly appointed Royal Navy commodore on Lake Erie, had only just arrived, on June 5, to assume his new duties.

Still far from ready for battle, Perry needed more sailors for his squadron. Commodore Chauncey, as commander in chief on the Great Lakes, was obliged to provide or arrange for them to be sent to Perry. In June, Perry notified Secretary Jones of his return from Buffalo in company with five vessels, one small brig, *Caledonia*, the schooners *Ohio*, *Amelia*, and *Somers* and the sloop *Trippe*. Each was manned by 50 seamen provided by Chauncey and aided by soldiers provided by General Dearborn. Against the Niagara's swift current and rapids, these men and sailors hauled the ships from Black Rock to Buffalo. From that port, Perry sailed his ships along the south shore of Lake Erie, all the while keeping a sharp lookout for Commodore Barclay's squadron.[28]

After returning to Presque Isle on June 18, Perry took stock of his situation. Both brigs had been brought over the shallow water bar. They were rigged, the sails readied, and the guns mounted. Perry had not yet received from Pittsburgh an adequate quantity of shot and the anchors for the brigs. He informed Secretary Jones that his eleven vessels now needed their full complement of officers, seamen, and marines. The squadron required 260 men for the brigs (130 each), 112 men for the four larger schooners (28 each), 50 men for the small brig *Caledonia*, and 35 men for the three schooners and one sloop he had brought from Buffalo. Available to him were only 159 men; he still lacked 403 hands.[29]

Barclay, on the far side of the lake, was having similar problems. For the six vessels he planned to use in the anticipated battle, he required 440 seamen, but despite his pleas Commodore Yeo sent very few, preferring to keep the most experienced hands for his own squadron. In the end, Barclay prevailed on General Henry Procter to provide enough men from his own troops, the Forty-first Regiment of Foot and the Royal Newfoundland Regiment to fulfill Barclay's needs, although most were landsmen.[30]

It was during this period, from early June to mid-July, that Commodore Barclay had a fleeting opportunity to destroy Perry's burgeoning naval establishment. Barclay had discussed such a raid with General Procter, asking whether the general would be willing to collaborate by providing some of his regular troops to land near Erie and attack Perry's base while the warships stood off and provided shore bombardment. Procter indicated that he was willing if he could obtain sufficient reinforcements to protect Fort Malden from an attack by General Harrison during their absence at Erie. To get permission and the reinforcements, Barclay and Procter wrote to their immediate commanders, Commodore Yeo and Governor General Prevost, respectively. Prevost responded, encouraging his naval and military commanders to cooperate and said that he personally would send 200 men of the Forty-first Regiment to Amherstburg. Upon receipt of this encouraging news, Procter and Barclay proceeded with preparations for a combined attack on Erie. Yet Yeo and Prevost were simultaneously concerned about the American offensive on the Niagara Peninsula and its threat to Burlington. They concluded that as long as the situation on the peninsula was in doubt, their Lake Erie commanders had to be left to their own devices. Prevost's newly appointed commander of the center division, Major General Sir Francis de Rottenburg, provided the final stroke to Procter when he wrote that he needed the troops for a raid on Black Rock and could give no assistance for the projected attack on Erie. Thus passed what was probably Barclay's best opportunity to crush Perry's squadron before it was actually launched on Lake Erie.

As the season wore on, Perry became worried as the sailors were only trickling in from Sackets Harbor and Black Rock. By July the situation was desperate. Perry came to believe that Chauncey was providing fewer hands than he had promised, keeping the most skilled, experienced men for his own Lake Ontario squadron. Near the end of July, Perry wrote to his superior suggesting that Chauncey had sent him the dregs of his supply of sailors: "The men that came by Mr. Champlin are a motley set, blacks, soldiers and boys, I cannot think you saw them after they were selected—I am however pleased to see anything in the shape of a man."[31]

Chauncey lost no time in replying from his location off Burlington Bay, at the western end of Lake Ontario. He was furious at being directly questioned about his intentions to support Perry fully in his manpower needs. He made this statement, remarkable for his time: "I have yet to learn that the color of the skin or cut and trimmings of the coat can affect a man's qualifications or his usefulness—I have nearly 50 Blacks on board of this Ship [*General Pike*] and many are amongst my best men and those people you call Soldiers have been to Sea from 2 to 17 years, and I presume you will find them as good and useful as any men on board your vessel."[32] In the same letter, Chauncey also criticized Perry for intimating that it would be better to have a command independent of Chauncey's because of the slow communications between Sackets Harbor and Presque Isle. Yet, Perry's statement accorded with the facts. Weather, terrain, and local command problems may well have distracted Chauncey during his operations on Lake Ontario. Secretary Jones agreed with Perry about the need for direct communications and often wrote him directly instead of working through Chauncey when he thought it urgent.

The secretary acted to calm Perry's irascible nature when he received a letter in which Perry requested a change of command because of the poor relationship that had festered between himself and Chauncey. Jones pointed out that the bad feelings that had arisen would only undermine the progress that had been made and would redound by ruining Perry's reputation. He reminded Perry that "it is the duty of an officer . . . to sacrifice all personal motives and feelings when in collision with the public good." After receiving this thoughtful reprimand, Perry avoided further conflict with Chauncey, who, for his part, continued to support Perry's fleet with what men and supplies he could spare from his own squadron.[33]

By early August, all vessels of the American squadron at Erie had been brought over the sand bar that separated the bay at Presque Isle from the vastness of Lake Erie. Lifting heavy vessels over the bar was no mean feat, especially with regard to the brigs *Lawrence* and *Niagara*. The direction of wind and tide could also affect the depth of water over the bar from day to day. In late summer, at mean low water, the bar gave clearance of only about 4 feet, while the brigs drew approximately 9 feet. Thus, the brigs had to be lifted at least 5 feet to clear the bar. In order for this to occur, Noah Brown's ship carpenters had to build and rig two enormous boxlike structures called camels, to which valves and pumps were fastened. The two camels were then pumped full of water and connected by ropes and beams that extended through the gunports on either side of *Lawrence* and over the camels. The men pumped out both camels, so that they lifted by their buoyancy both themselves and the brig they supported. After *Lawrence* cleared the bar, she was quickly reequipped with all her spars, sails, guns, munitions, water casks, and other supplies on board and made ready for sea. *Lawrence* and two schooners could defend *Niagara* and the other vessels as they too were brought over the bar. It is surprising that this feat of nautical engineering was not interrupted by the enemy's vessels, which could have wreaked havoc had they appeared at an opportune time. This was when Perry's fleet was at its most vulnerable. Barclay was well aware of the progress being made by Perry in preparing his squadron as he had established a distant blockade covering the approach to Presque Isle Bay (fig. 3.3).

Figure 3.3. Cameling the brigs: lifting USS *Niagara* and USS *Lawrence* over the bar at Presque Isle. Pencil sketch by Peter Rindlisbacher. Used courtesy of the artist.

Logistical Problems for Commodore Barclay

On three occasions the blockaders were present, once for ten days, July 19 to 29, but then they disappeared for a crucial period of five days, just before Perry completed preparations to brings his flotilla into the lake. Americans at Erie thought it curious that the British blockaders from Amherstburg had not attempted to interfere. Commodore Barclay, however, had ordered his vessels to Long Point, on the north shore of the lake, for resupply. While undoubtedly important, this purpose could hardly substitute for the opportunity to destroy Perry's squadron as it undertook this delicate and essential operation. Still, Barclay had other factors to consider. His flagship, *Detroit*, had an inadequate supply of men and guns for a fight at that time. He was also concerned about the defenses of the Presque Isle peninsula and Perry's guard boats, and he preferred to delay the day of battle until his squadron was as ready as it could be.[34] Barclay was under constant pressure from his army counterpart, General Procter, who had problems of his own, not least of which was the supply of food for the 14,000 First Nation warriors and their families who had arrived at Fort Malden and for his regular and militia troops as well. These shortages were partly due to the warriors' vandalism of the farms in the vicinity. Cattle had been needlessly slaughtered for their horns and tails, with no meat taken from the carcasses. There was little government cash to pay farmers for their supplies, and in Upper Canada wheat and corn were in short supply. Procter had also run short of ammunition and the articles of trade prized by his Northwest First Nation allies. Without these commodities, he feared losing their loyalty to the British cause.[35]

Thus, desperate because of logistical difficulties and shortages, the British commanders on Lake Erie faced an opponent on the south side of the lake who had faced similar difficulties in preparing for a battle. The difference was that although Governor General Prevost had promised support, his principal commanders, General Rottenberg and Commodore Yeo, had pressing needs of their own at Niagara and on Lake Ontario. As he realized he could not make good on his promises, Prevost had sent word to Procter and Barclay that "you must endeavor to obtain your ordnance and naval stores from the enemy."[36] Perry, on the other hand, with Secretary Jones's full support in Washington and Commodore Chauncey's somewhat grudging cooperation, had been able to surmount those logistical problems with ingenuity and persistence. Fortunately, as it turned out, his military counterpart, Major General William Henry Harrison, was willing and able to provide men from his army to make up for Perry's deficit of sailors. The final weeks before battle during the month of August and the first week of September brought these elements into high relief.

CHAPTER 4

From Lake Erie to Lake Huron

Commodore Perry and Major General Harrison continued to correspond and plan for their eventual expedition. Now at sea, Perry put his squadron through tactical maneuvers and also exercised his gun crews, a good many of whom were volunteers from Harrison's army. There was no time to lose, for he did not know when Barclay would dare to bring out his ships. In mid-August Perry's squadron sailed to Sandusky Bay and signaled by gunfire to Harrison's units ashore that Perry was ready to meet Harrison to coordinate plans.

Harrison, accompanied by his staff and a delegation of allied Native Americans from the Delaware, Shawnee, and Wyandotte tribes, came on board for a lengthy conference. The results of the meeting were that Perry agreed to reconnoiter Barclay's squadron where it was anchored off Fort Malden for the purpose of taunting him into action out on the lake. Still lacking sufficient seamen, Perry asked Harrison to provide him with volunteers from the army, which the general agreed to do. He provided 130 soldiers from the Army of the Northwest to Perry's squadron.[1] Finally, they agreed to an amphibious assault on the British base if Barclay had not chosen to engage the American squadron by mid-September. Their concern was that autumn storms might hinder the movement of troops and the navy's ability to protect and supply the army as it made its move toward the Canadian shore. For their part, the Native Americans left the conference much impressed by the great guns of Perry's fleet and the confidence they witnessed among the American officers. This helped spread trust among Harrison's other Native American allies and engendered discouragement among the native warriors allied to the British.[2]

Sickness in Perry's Squadron

During most of August and early September, Perry based his squadron at Put-in-Bay on South Bass Island, near the western end of Lake Erie. As Put-in-Bay was within one day's sailing of both Harrison's base at the mouth of the Sandusky River and the enemy base at Amherstburg, this seems a strategically sound decision. However, there were other factors to consider. For one thing, the harbor at

Put-in-Bay was not a healthy place to be with several ships in company. Ill health was generally an issue on the lakes—caused by poor hygiene, bad food, and tainted water. Unless commanding officers made it a point to demand strict standards of hygiene and nourishment for their men, an entire encampment or community could become subject to sickness and low morale. One of the maladies that prevailed on military as well as naval bases was then called "remittent bilious fever," which perhaps was a form of malaria, accompanied by dysentery, nausea, and fever.[3] This must have been a cause for concern to Perry, and his medical men had to deal with the consequences. Put-in-Bay on South Bass Island was quite sheltered, with deep water close to shore, so it was considered a safe harbor in every breeze but a southwesterly. Yet, there was not an ever-freshening current flowing along the shore, so the water grew stagnant as the effluence of hundreds of men and their trash went overboard. What made it worse, the water used for drinking and cooking likely came from the bay, which was being used as a sewer. Some in the crews of these vessels were unhealthy when they departed Erie. On July 6, Perry's squadron doctor, Surgeon's Mate Usher Parsons, recorded 70 men sick; on July 17, the number had risen to 81; and on September 9, the day before the Battle of Lake Erie, 87. The commodore himself was laid low from time to time, as were two other naval surgeons attached to the squadron, as well as Parsons, who was stationed on board the brig *Lawrence*.[4]

Preparing for Battle

Meanwhile, Commodore Barclay was anxiously awaiting the completion of his new ship *Detroit* at Amherstburg. She had been ready to launch as of July 20 but still lacked enough ordnance, ammunition, and seamen to be sure of success. The sixteen 24-pounders and two long 12-pounders he had expected had been captured by the Americans during their April attack on York. Like Perry across the lake, Barclay needed to complete his crews from the ranks of the army In early August, in need of 250 to 300 men, he asked General Procter to provide him with guns from Fort Malden as well as 150 men from the Forty-first Regiment and 60 from the Royal Newfoundland Regiment to complete his complement of landsmen to serve as marines and deckhands to work the ship.[5] *Detroit* ended up with a diverse assortment of ordnance: long guns—eight 9-pounders, six 12-pounders, one 18-pounder (centerline pivot), and two 24-pounders—supplemented with carronades, one 24-pounder and one 18-pounder. This mixture of weights and calibers portended trouble on the gundeck, where balls and powder bags of different sizes would have to be distributed to each gun crew, to be handled rapidly in the heat and din of battle. The other vessels, *Queen Charlotte*, *Lady Prevost*,

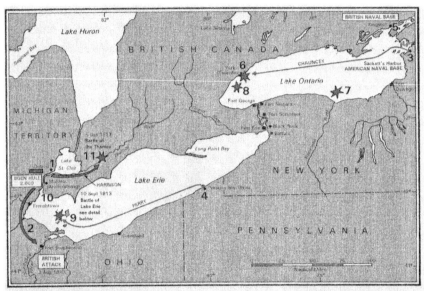

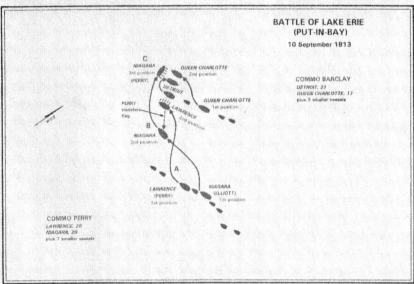

Map 4.1. Great Lakes, Battle of Lake Erie, 10 September 1813. Reprinted by permission from Craig. L. Symonds, *The Naval Institute Historical Atlas of the U.S. Navy,* Cartography by William J. Clipson, © 1995 (Annapolis, MD: Naval Institute Press).

General Hunter, Little Belt, and *Chippawa,* likewise had a variety of somewhat lighter guns (long 12-, 9-, and 6-pounders) but fewer carronades, making the vessels more dangerous for the Americans at long ranges than at short ranges.[6]

Perry's order of battle included nine vessels, the two brigs *Lawrence* and *Niagara,* each mounting eighteen 32-pounder carronades and two 12-pounder long guns; *Caledonia,* a smaller brig with two 24-pounder long guns and one 32-pounder carronade; *Ariel,* a large schooner mounting four 12-pounder long guns; *Somers,* one long 24-pounder and one 32-pounder carronade; *Scorpion,* one long 32-pounder and one 24-pounder carronade; *Porcupine,* one long 32-pounder; *Tigress,* equipped with one long 32-pounder; and *Trippe,* a sloop, armed with one long 24-pounder. Two American vessels would miss the battle: the schooner *Ohio* had been sent to Erie to pick up supplies, and the schooner *Amelia,* deemed unfit for battle, remained at Erie. For Barclay's smaller, more lightly armed vessels, Perry's squadron posed a powerful and dangerous threat, especially at close ranges, where the heavy carronades could wreak havoc amid the enemy's rigging and crew (map 4.1).

The Battle of Lake Erie

When the day of battle finally came, it was Commodore Barclay who brought it on. He had waited with ships prepared for Perry to attack while the British ships were at anchor under the guns of Fort Malden, but Perry chose to have battle in open water, where there was room to maneuver. Barclay, who had repeatedly requested more men and material, only to have them denied, had no other honorable choice but to fight it out on the lake, where Perry was waiting for him. On September 10 Perry's lookouts sighted the enemy squadron at a distance of perhaps twenty miles to the west of Put-in-Bay with a light breeze from the southwest. The American squadron made haste to sortie and form up, but the wind prevented a direct attack on the British. Perry had to tack to find sea room west of the islands, and even then, he did not have the weather gauge. Barclay at first had the advantage of the windward position, meaning that he could determine the time and point of attack, but the wind did not hold and soon dropped to nothing. When the breeze sprang up again, it came in light from the southeast, favoring Perry's squadron, and he took advantage of it. The commodore had rehearsed the scenario with his captains, arranged his ships according to their strength and capabilities each time, but the final formation did not represent those he had recommended earlier. His first orders had demanded that all ships stay in strict line formation, with each vessel contending with its enemy opposite number. In the final meeting, Perry instructed each commander to target a specific enemy ship. Thus, *Lawrence* would take on Barclay's *Detroit*, while Elliott's *Niagara* would attack the brig *Queen Charlotte*, and the smaller vessels had their targets as well. Yet, as the battle developed, Elliott held *Niagara* back, which had the effect of stalling the schooners in his train.[7]

When the two flotillas met, the heavier schooners *Scorpion* and *Ariel* led the American line, with Commodore Perry's flagship, *Lawrence*, close astern. The other powerful brig, *Niagara*, under the command of Master Commandant Jesse Elliott, followed at a distance, leading several schooners equipped with long guns. Commodore Barclay deployed his squadron in line, headed by *Chippawa*, with *Detroit*, the commodore's flagship, and supporting ships, *General Hunter*, *Queen Charlotte*, *Lady Prevost*, and *Little Belt*, following close behind. Although Perry had the weather gauge, most of his vessels were not grouped closely enough for mutual support. As a result, his brig *Lawrence* took major punishment from the long guns of *Detroit* and *Queen Charlotte* as he closed with them. When finally within carronade range, *Lawrence* too scored many hits on the enemy between wind and water, but the carnage among Perry's crew and damage to the ship put his flagship out of action. As the naval surgeon Parsons described it, "The wounded began to come down before the *Lawrence* opened her battery and I for one felt impatient at the delay. In proper time, however, as it proved, the dogs of war were let loose from leash, and it seemed as though heaven and earth were at logger-heads. For more than two hours little could be heard but the deafening thunders of our own broadsides, the crash of balls dashing through our timbers, and the shrieks of our wounded. These were brought down faster than I could attend to them, farther than to stay the bleeding or support the shattered limbs with splints and pass them forward to the berth deck."[8]

Perry Shifts His Flag

During this time, both *Detroit* and *Queen Charlotte* suffered grievous personnel casualties. Commodore Barclay was severely wounded by a wooden splinter in the leg, while Captain Finnis, commander of *Queen Charlotte*, was killed as she received severe blows from *Caledonia*'s long 32-pounder, and the first lieutenant was fatally wounded. The leading petty officers on board were killed or wounded, as well. The battle raged for more than two hours. At this critical point, Perry, who had miraculously escaped being wounded, called for a boat crew to row him several hundred yards across the water to *Niagara*, which he boarded, taking command. He then ordered Elliott to take his cutter and bring up the schooners which had lagged astern, unable to take part in the battle. Perry ordered the undamaged

Niagara to make sail to direct her carronades on *Detroit*, raking her from bow to stern. Having broken through the British line, Perry directed *Niagara*'s port battery against *Chippawa* and *Lady Prevost*, which soon were in no condition to continue the fight. The senior surviving officers of the British vessels, most so damaged as to be unmanageable, hauled down their ensigns. The human toll was staggering. In the British squadron, 3 officers were killed and 9 wounded, including all the commanding officers; of the enlisted, there were 85 killed and 38 wounded. The Americans suffered 8 officers killed and 3 wounded, 24 enlisted killed and 88 wounded. This brought the total casualties for the day to 135 British and 123 American.[9]

Commodore Perry's famous victory message to Harrison resonated in its brevity: "Dear General: We have met the enemy and they are ours: Two ships, two brigs, one schooner and one sloop. Yours with great respect and esteem, O.H. Perry." Even though the numbers of casualties on the two sides were similar, the British naval control of Lake Erie was eliminated, enabling Harrison's army to advance across the lake, the withdrawal of British troops toward Lake Ontario, their abandonment of Fort Malden, and the burning of Amherstburg. Perry and Harrison saw this as their great opportunity to follow up the naval battle with a pursuit of the enemy and its Native American allies, whom they solidly defeated at the battle of the Thames. This brought relief to the Americans, who had settled in the Northwest, and dismay to British subjects living in Upper Canada, who knew that hard times lay ahead if they did not have control over Lake Erie. For the First Nations of the Northwest, the death of Tecumseh at the battle of the Thames was a devastating setback. They understood that they would be on their own in defending the land they considered their ancestral hunting grounds and hard pressed by increasing waves of American immigrants attempting to settle in their territory.

The Battle of the Thames

Soon to follow the complete American victory at the Battle of Lake Erie was Harrison and Perry's amphibious invasion of Canada. This required Perry first to provide transportation to army units for the reoccupation of Detroit, which had been evacuated by the British in the days following the battle. Harrison planned a two-pronged approach to invade Canada. The Kentucky volunteer cavalry regiment under the command of Colonel Richard M. Johnson marched overland to liberate Detroit and then moved eastward to cross the Detroit River, which it did not accomplish until October 1. Harrison's much larger army of forty-five hundred moved in phases by water, using eighty bateaux (oar- and sail-propelled Durham boats) that had been built in Cleveland for that purpose.[10] Perry carried the troops from the Portage River and the Marblehead Peninsula near Sandusky Bay to South Bass Island and from there to tiny Middle Sister Island, just short of the Canadian shore. On September 25 and 26, Perry's vessels towed the bateaux toward the shore, prepared to cover the landings with gunfire in case of British opposition. Such was not the case, as General Procter had ordered a retreat as soon as landing operations began. Arriving at Amherstburg on September 27, the American troops found that the British had destroyed Fort Malden and burned the town. Then began the pursuit of Procter, who had chosen to retreat instead of making a stand as urged by Tecumseh and his chiefs. Procter's goal was to reach Burlington and join up with General John Vincent's army on the Niagara Peninsula. This was a false hope. Proctor's force made slow progress due to bad roads, considerable baggage, the number of civilians accompanying, the exhausted troops, and the lack of a shrewd plan of retreat.

Wanting not to miss the action and to provide support to the army, Perry and Elliott participated in the chase after Procter. Perry borrowed a horse from the cavalry and rode with Harrison as an aide-de-camp, while Elliott took charge of the gunboats *Scorpion*, *Tigress*, and *Porcupine* on the Thames River, enabling the troops' river crossings while providing gunfire support and transportation of supplies. Within a few days, the American troops caught up, and Procter was forced into an improvised battle near Moraviantown, a small settlement on the Thames River. The result was a complete defeat of Procter's army and his First Nation allies, compounded by the death of Tecumseh, the redoubtable Shawnee chieftain.[11] The entire operation from the Battle of Lake Erie to the battle of the Thames was made possible by the extraordinary degree of cooperation between Perry and Harrison, a great example of unity of effort in a military campaign, virtually unheard of in the War of 1812.

Commodore Perry, having received many compliments and a promotion to captain as a result of the battle, was anxious to be relieved and requested leave at his family's home in Newport before any new assignments.[12] Chauncey, his immediate superior, though pleased with the victory on Lake Erie (he was due a significant portion of the prize money), was dismayed that Perry was communicating directly with Secretary Jones instead of with him. He felt that Perry, though successful in battle, had not really finished the job. The Lake Erie squadron and its British prizes needed after-action repairs and would require protection from British reprisals during the late fall and winter months.[13] Nonetheless, Jones granted Perry's request to be reassigned after a period of leave.

Captain Jesse Elliott in Command at Erie

The secretary followed by stating that Captain Jesse Elliott, whom he had promoted after the battle, would succeed to command of Lake Erie, under Chauncey's orders, but Elliott would still be required to communicate directly to the Navy Department anything of importance that was deemed urgent. For the time being, until the end of October, Elliott's sailors were primarily concerned with rebuilding the fleet, preparing for winter, and strengthening the shore defenses at Erie. A new worry arose near the end of October when Elliott learned that four of the squadron's vessels that had been sent to Black Rock with General Harrison after the Erie battle had been driven ashore by a vicious storm. These were the schooners *Ariel*, *Chippawa*, and *Little Belt* and the sloop *Trippe*. Intervening events on the Niagara Peninsula and at Fort Niagara would have a fatal effect on these vessels. The departure from Niagara of the greater part of the US Army for an expedition against Montreal left only a weak force under Brigadier General George McClure to protect Fort George, Fort Erie, and Fort Niagara. On December 10, a spoiling raid by Americans troops and a rogue force of Canadian Volunteers burned the towns of Newark, Queenston, and other communities on the Canadian side of the Niagara. This precipitated a response in kind led by the British general Phineas Riall, who on December 18 took possession of Fort Niagara and with equal savagery burned all the communities on the American (eastern) bank of the Niagara all the way to and including Black Rock and Buffalo by the end of the month. The raiding force also destroyed American vessels that had been driven ashore, thereby eliminating some of Elliott's Lake Erie squadron. The question might well be raised in retrospect as to why the recovery of these vessels could not have been accomplished in the month or more that had passed since their grounding. Apparently, no one with sufficient authority and fortitude had been left in charge of the naval station at Black Rock, and it was not near the top of Elliott's worry list. Elliott warned Secretary Jones that an escaped American prisoner of war had provided information indicating that the British were planning an attack on Erie and the US squadron's ships across the lake ice. He recommended calling out two thousand Pennsylvania) militia until the end of March to protect his base.[14]

December was not yet half over when Commodore Yeo suggested to Governor General Prevost that it would be highly desirable to attack Elliott's base at Erie for the purpose of destroying the brigs *Lawrence* and *Niagara* and seizing the smaller ones. The next step would be to use these smaller vessels to attack the small shipkeeping force left at Put-in-Bay with the idea of recapturing *Detroit* and *Queen Charlotte* before they could be destroyed. He suggested building the frames of a flotilla of fourteen smaller vessels in great secrecy and then transporting them to Long Point, where they could be assembled and provided with tight-fitting hides instead of planks in just a few hours. From Long Point the flotilla could be launched as soon as the lake was free of ice and sent to attack Erie. Yeo's argument about attacking Erie first and then Put-in-Bay had some merit, but his means of accomplishing this seems far-fetched, since it was unknown whether skin-covered flotillas could make the voyage safely and whether the preparations could be accomplished in secrecy. The plan was not put into effect, but it does show the lengths to which the British naval commander was willing to go to regain command of Lake Erie.[15]

A second British plan to attack during the winter was not an idle rumor. This was a season when many of the preparations for a summer campaign would be made. The trails and roads were usually frozen, and snow made it easier and quicker to transport heavy loads and personnel by sleighs rather than in wagons. Lieutenant General Gordon Drummond, Procter's replacement as commander of the right division (or flank) of the British army in North America, urged such an expedition to Prevost as early as January 21, 1814. His plan involved moving a force of more than seventeen hundred men, including seamen and marines, and all necessary provisions by sleighs first from Burlington Heights to Amherstburg via the Thames River and then from Amherstburg to Put-in-Bay by a direct over-the-ice march of forty miles in order to destroy the two American prizes, *Detroit* and *Queen Charlotte*, laid up there. He also expressed concern that if the enemy became aware of the impending attack, it might take steps to reinforce the troops at Detroit.[16] Prevost expressed reservations about the practicality of the plan of attack, and two weeks later Drummond expressed his own doubts given the "peculiarly uncommon mildness of the season." His informants had explained to him that the lake was insufficiently frozen and unsafe, and he reluctantly gave up the idea.[17]

But Prevost had larger objectives in mind for the 1814 summer campaign. The strategy he laid out was to protect the commanding post of Fort Mackinac (pronounced Mackinaw) in upper Lake Huron, which the British had seized from a small US Army garrison in July 1812. He was quite certain that the US Navy would make a major effort to recover the fort during the summer. British control of this place was critical to control of communications with British outposts in the upper Mississippi River valley. Likewise, Prevost felt it was absolutely necessary to make a show of strength to retain the loyalty of their First Nation allies. As he eloquently wrote, "I consider it [the preservation of Michilimacinack] as of vital importance as respects our Indian alliance, it being the rallying point, the last link by which their Warriors still faithfully cling to our interest. Severed from that, they will find themselves an abandoned people deserted by us in their utmost need and reduced by despair to seek mercy from their bitterest foe—then the charm of British influence would be dissolved & hopeless becomes the prospect of ever gaining their confidence."[18]

Planning the 1814 Campaign

To Prevost and those commanders who were concerned about British control of the upper lakes, 1814 would be a critical year. Since they no longer were dominant on Lake Erie, their supply lines to and from Fort Mackinac had to be shifted to an overland and river trail, leading from York across the Upper Canada peninsula to Lake Simcoe and from there to Penetanguishene on Nottawasaga Bay. From there, supplies and personnel could be conveyed by boat to Mackinac Island or its neighbor St. Joseph's Island in the straits separating Lake Huron from Lake Superior. The less practical alternative was the traditional canoe route used by the fur traders via the Ottawa River flowing northwest from York to Lake Nipissing and from there to the French River, many miles north of Nottawasaga Bay.

Prevost planned to reinforce the fort in the spring, sending three hundred men and provisions for twelve months. He informed General Drummond that he would require two companies of marines, a number of seamen, and a naval lieutenant to man the armed trading schooner *Nancy* and a flotilla of gunboats yet to be built at Penetanguishene.[19] The absence of passable roads in that northern wilderness would cause delay, as would the lack of competent boat builders, who would have to be drafted from those at work in Kingston on the ships that Commodore Yeo had ordered for this Lake Ontario squadron. Thus, the lack of sufficient logistical support for the forthcoming operations had already begun to impact the coming campaign season for British forces in Upper Canada.[20]

For the administration of James Madison, planning for a renewed campaign in the US-Canadian borderlands was problematic. The launching of its failed St. Lawrence campaign against Montreal in the fall of 1813 had denuded Niagara of any significant American land forces and leaders. The British raids on Fort Niagara and Buffalo in December showed the weakness of the American defenses in that region. The one bright moment for American arms on Lake Erie and at the battle of the Thames was not followed up, as it might have been, by sending American troops to Burlington Heights and the Niagara Peninsula from the west. The British would no doubt attempt to strengthen their positions on Niagara at an early opportunity in the spring and might reassert themselves in an attempt to recover control of western Ontario and even Detroit. Madison's military leadership needed to implement a purge of disgraced senior generals such as James

Wilkinson, Wade Hampton, Morgan Lewis, and Henry Dearborn. Secretary of War Armstrong showed his willingness to do that by appointing a group of younger, more energetic officers, including Winfield Scott, Edmund Gaines, Jacob Brown, Alexander Macomb, and George Izard to positions of key responsibility. Unfortunately, Armstrong's personal dislike of William Henry Harrison led ultimately to Harrison's resignation. In his place, Armstrong appointed Tennessee militia general Andrew Jackson to the rank of major general in charge of the militias of Tennessee and Kentucky in their ongoing war with the Creek Indians in western Georgia, Alabama, and the Mississippi Territory.

Madison's cabinet decided on an attempt to retake the Niagara Peninsula, strengthen the American position at Sackets Harbor, prepare for an expedition below Kingston on the St. Lawrence River, and launch a renewed attack on Montreal. Much of this depended on the navy doing its part. The US naval squadron under Commodore Chauncey was to reassert control of Lake Ontario in order to assist the army at Niagara. Commodore Arthur Sinclair would lead a naval squadron into Lake Huron to eliminate British control of the upper lakes, and Commodore Macdonough was to defeat British naval forces building on Lake Champlain to block its use as a possible invasion route into the United States.

By April, American naval plans had already been made to launch an expedition into Lake Huron to recapture Fort Mackinac. Commodore Chauncey, still the superior of Captain Jesse Elliott, who was in charge of the Erie squadron, sent orders to Elliott to be ready for departure "as soon as the Ice will permit for the purpose of reducing the posts of the Enemy on that Lake." He instructed Elliott to take *Niagara* and *Lawrence* with other vessels as needed "to accomplish this object (taking care to select those drawing the least water)." He was then to sail to Put-in-Bay and get *Detroit* and *Queen Charlotte* under way for Detroit, where he would moor them in the charge of shipkeepers under the guard of troops provided by the commanding general in charge of that garrison.

As soon as that could be accomplished, Elliott should proceed into Lake Huron via Lake St. Clair, having taken on board troops provided for the expedition, capture Fort Mackinac, and leave troops there as a garrison to protect the fort. Presuming this was done successfully, Elliott should sail for St. Joseph Island to reduce the British outpost there and then proceed to Matchedoc, in Georgian Bay, to destroy the shipyard. Chauncey laid out these orders in a rather breezy way without considering the great difficulties that Elliott might encounter along the way in terms of weather, navigation, geography, and whatever obstacles the enemy might choose to throw in his path. As an example, he casually mentioned that if by any chance the opportunity presented itself, Elliott might also send one of his vessels into Lake Michigan "if it could accomplish anything beneficial."[21]

Commodore Arthur Sinclair Relieves Captain Elliott

While these orders were being sent from Sackets Harbor, President Madison and his cabinet were making further alterations to plans for the 1814 summer campaign plan in the American-Canadian borderlands. As the large scope of the effort to send a squadron to the upper lakes became apparent, Secretary Jones decided that it would be necessary to create a separate and independent command under Captain Arthur Sinclair, an experienced officer senior to Captain Elliott, who had been far less effective than hoped during his time in charge of the Lake Erie station.[22] Elliott's tenure after Perry's departure had been a time of discontent, disorganization, and consequently low morale. Much of this had been brought about by Elliott's feelings of persecution and his churlish attitude toward those of Perry's supporters who still remained at Erie. Jones may have received word of this from others but certainly gained a sense that all was not well from Captain Arthur Sinclair's earliest reports from Erie.[23] Sinclair in earlier days had served as a young lieutenant in the Mediterranean and most recently had commanded the brig *Argus* in Captain Decatur's Atlantic squadron. Jones mentioned to Sinclair that Elliott had expressed a wish for more active duty under Chauncey on Lake Ontario, so there he was sent, later to take command of the brig *Sylph*, 16 guns.

On April 1, 1814, Secretary Jones informed Sinclair that "the enemy it is understood is making effort to create a force on Lake Huron; and the moment is at hand when our Squadron on Lake Erie must be actively employed, not only in keeping secure possession of that Lake, but a part of the Squadron must immediately proceed into Lake Huron in order to rout the enemy, retake Michilimackinac, take St. Joseph's, and thus secure the entire command of the Upper Lakes."[24] While Jones's orders to Sinclair were very similar to the orders Chauncey sent to Elliott, the fact that both letters were sent on the same day indicate a disconnect between Jones and Chauncey. Although he did not say it in so many words, Jones had lost confidence in Elliott, but he had not yet communicated this to Chauncey, who still believed himself to be in charge of the Lake Erie station.

The Lake Huron Expedition

Be that as it may, Sinclair found that he had much work to do to prepare for an expedition. The purser Samuel Hambleton had been severely wounded in the Battle of Lake Erie while helping to work the guns on board *Lawrence*. He stayed in his assigned position while Dr. Usher Parsons tended his wounds but departed for his next duty station in March 1814.[25] There was no immediate replacement.

As Sinclair stated in early May, "There has been no responsible person whose duty it is to keep copies of requisitions, receipts, returns of expenditures, etc., I am using every possible exertion in my power to give you a correct and circumstantial account of what has been done, what requires doing, what is on hand, and what is required to complete the outfits of the intended expedition."[26] From this state of confusion, it is clear that the squadron at Erie was definitely not "ready for departure as soon as the ice has cleared," to use Chauncey's expression. It would seem that not only Elliott but the commodore himself would be at least partially to blame for having neglected the affairs of the Erie naval station while Elliott was in charge. A visit of inspection by Chauncey would have revealed this state of affairs in a matter of days; however, he had departed Sackets Harbor in late December for a two-month period of official travel and personal leave to visit the Navy Department in Washington and his family in New York. For a squadron commander, this was an extraordinarily lengthy absence; while it might have been permissible in peacetime, in the midst of a war, when preparations for the upcoming campaign were of utmost importance, it was an extravagant waste of time. As a result, the US Navy's lake squadrons at both Sackets Harbor and Erie were late in starting their operations, a circumstance of which the British took full advantage.

Although previously agreed upon, the US Lake Huron expedition design was not easily decided in Washington. Secretary of War Armstrong had at first gone along with plans to organize a joint expedition. Learning of a British buildup of naval and military forces on Lake Ontario, he changed his mind, dismissing the Lake Huron expedition as unnecessary. He intended the American army to endeavor to recapture Fort Erie and Queenston and possibly attack Burlington Heights. This would require, he believed, the navy's services on both Lakes Erie and Ontario. Secretary Jones still felt that taking British outposts on Lake Huron would require strong army and naval components. This strategic thrust was needed to eliminate British influence in the Lake Superior–Lake Michigan–Upper Mississippi region and provide safety for settlers on the northwest frontier.[27] President Madison, acting to smooth over the matter, proposed a compromise whereby Jones would order the navy to divide its forces, sending some vessels to Huron and keeping the stronger portion on Lake Erie to assist the army. Jones complied, yet this was not the end of the matter. Commodore Sinclair was distressed to learn of his change of orders, for in late May he had received new intelligence that indicated the British had been quietly sending troops, ordnance, and civilian artisans north from York by way of Lake Simcoe to strengthen their fortifications and build a lake force to protect their communications from the Americans.[28] Sinclair's letter gave Jones the information he needed to refute Armstrong's arguments and to quiet Madison's doubts. On June 1, Jones revoked his change of orders, informing Sinclair that he should now proceed to execute the original plan without delay.[29]

And yet, there was delay. Sinclair could not resist the impulse to participate in a raid on Port Dover, in western Ontario near Long Point. His military counterpart was Colonel John B. Campbell of the US Army Eleventh Regiment. He was eager to prove himself by reducing the enemy's logistical ability to sustain armies in the field. Sinclair's cooperation was essential, and he did not demur, despite his orders to get under way for Lake Huron. On May 13, Sinclair reported that there were a half dozen flour mills near Long Point, on the opposite side of Lake Erie. These mills were providing flour for the bread being supplied to British troops and their First Nation allies. The mills were not well guarded and were within easy reach of the shore. The two men gathered and embarked some eight hundred infantry (including units of pro-American Canadians belonging to Joseph Willcock's Canadian Volunteers) and transported them to the Canadian shore near Dover, Ontario, landing them on May 14 with orders to burn Ryerse's and Finch's mills and others as far as Turkey Point.[30] In the absence of concerted opposition, these troops apparently felt free to destroy private homes of those they conceived were "old Tories" who had fled the United States during and after the Revolutionary War.[31] For those innocents targeted on the receiving end of this violence, it was a frightening and inhumane experience. British authorities declared the destruction of private property to be outrageous, equating these deeds with the American troops who burned Newark and other communities on the Niagara Peninsula in December 1813.[32] It is worth noting that in the aftermath of this event Commodore Sinclair, informed Secretary Jones: "I am sorry to learn that several private houses were also destroyed which was so contrary to my wish and to the idea I have of our true policy to those people that I had used every argument against it before his [Colonel Campbell's] departure and was under the impression that he accorded with me most fully." Sinclair's report did not state that he had accompanied the raid but had placed Lieutenant John Packett, recently transferred from USS *Constitution*, in direct command of the naval vessels that transported the seven hundred troops. Also accompanying the raid was Lieutenant Benjamin Hyde, USMC, in charge of a detachment of twenty-five marines. Although Canadian sources state that six schooners delivered the expedition, but US naval records do not name the vessels or their commanders. Campbell later stated to Armstrong that "this expedition was undertaken by me without orders and upon my own responsibility. I have done the enemy some injury and returned without the loss of a man." Armstrong disavowed responsibility for Campbell's actions and ordered a court of inquiry. This was held under the auspices of Major General Jacob Brown, who, after hearing the evidence, decided that Campbell may have made errors in judgment in burning homes but that there was not sufficient reason to convene a trial by court-martial.

One of the unanticipated results of this successful raid was the determination of the British to retaliate on the United States when the opportunity arose, as it did in the Chesapeake campaign in later 1814. As reprehensible it may have seemed, this kind of warfare was fully consistent with what both sides were doing in 1814, waging war on their enemy's civilian and military logistics in order to preempt or derail plans in execution by destroying the material strengths of their opponent. It was, in effect, a form of economic and psychological warfare.

Sinclair did not set sail for Lake Huron from Erie until June 18, using the brig *Niagara* as his flagship, in company with the brigs *Lawrence* (Lt. Daniel Dexter), *Caledonia* (Lt. Thomas Holdup Stevens), and *Hunter*, the schooners *Tigress* (Sailing Master Stephen Champlin), *Scorpion* (Lt. Daniel Turner), and *Ohio* (Lt. Samuel Woodhouse), and two unnamed supply vessels. He intended to put in at Detroit to pick up an army contingent and then proceed north through Lake St. Clair to its source on Lake Huron.[33] On June 23, Lieutenant Colonel George Croghan and some one thousand soldiers embarked on the squadron's vessels, which then left for the waters of Lake St. Clair, which proved bothersome, being shallow and swept by a contrary current coming south from Lake Huron. After sending out boats to mark the channel, anchoring several times, off-loading the soldiers to lighten his vessels, and clearing the rapids, Sinclair finally sailed out of Lake St. Clair in a six-knot breeze and entered Huron on July 13.[34] It had taken almost three weeks from the time the squadron left Detroit to accomplish this feat, made all the more difficult by the lack of adequate charts and a pilot's knowledge of local waters.[35]

Sinclair could now refocus his thoughts on his mission, which was threefold: to destroy the British shipyard at Matchedoc in Severn Sound off Georgian Bay; to reduce the fur-trading establishment at St. Joseph Island; and to recapture the fort on Mackinac Island, thus gaining command of Lake Huron. After pausing to reembark the troops from Fort Gratiot, the squadron set sail on a northeasterly course for Matchedoc. Beset with fog and unfamiliar with the geography of the rock-strewn eastern part of Lake Huron, he was unable to locate the entrance to Georgian Bay. He prudently decided to wait for better weather and visibility. Tacking to the northwest, the squadron arrived off Thunder Island and within a few hours had St. Joseph Island and the Michigan Straits in sight. During the next days, Sinclair's men plundered and destroyed the abandoned fort and trading post on St. Joseph, taking only what they could use. Meanwhile, on July 21 the squadron discovered and captured the schooner *Mink*, a small trading vessel laden with 230 barrels of flour. Sinclair sent the *Scorpion* and other boats to reconnoiter the St. Marys River, which provides access to Lake Superior through the Sault Sainte Marie rapids. Here they found an extensive Hudson Bay Company trading post with outbuildings, livestock, and a sawmill. Again, the troops destroyed everything that could not be taken away. The point of this attack was to damage the British fur trade and the enemy's links to the First Nation tribes. This attack accomplished one of the expedition's objectives, but the more important task was to capture Fort Mackinac.

The British at Prairie du Chien

The officer in charge of the British post on Mackinac Island was Lieutenant Colonel Robert McDouall, who had been sent there in February to build up the fort's defenses and supplies. This was the westernmost military post in British North America. As the commander, McDouall had responsibility for protecting British fur-trading interests in this vast region that included the former French trading post located at Prairie du Chien, where the Wisconsin River joins the upper Mississippi River. He allied himself with the tribes of the Upper Peninsula of Michigan and modern Wisconsin. He was obligated to coordinate British-Indian military actions throughout the region from his headquarters at Fort Michilimackinac. The fur traders were an important link because of their long association with the First Nations they depended on for the trade. Although the Madison administration had shown little interest in that settlement until then, Governor William Clark, of the Missouri Territory, had awakened to the possibility of the British using Prairie du Chien as a springboard for military operations against St. Louis. In June 1814 he moved up the Mississippi River and landed a small military force there to build a fort named for the Kentucky governor Isaac Shelby.

News of this encroachment soon arrived at McDouall's headquarters, whereupon he quickly sent a small expedition of regulars, fur traders, and First Nation allies to oust the enemy intruders. A small mixed force of Michigan Fencibles, Mississippi Volunteers, and First Nation warriors under the command of Captain William McKay took the trade route through the lakes to Green Bay via the Fox River and portaged to the Wisconsin River. Arriving at Prairie du Chien, they lost no time in attacking Fort Shelby and placed it under siege for three days, July 17–20. By this time, bands of First Nation warriors had joined McKay's force, bringing it to about 650, outnumbering the 150 Americans who manned the fort and a small gunboat left behind by Governor Clark. The Americans' position was untenable. They soon surrendered and were allowed to return to St. Louis.

Captain McKay determined to retain control of the post and renamed it Fort McKay. His successors successfully defended the fort against two attempts to recapture it, in July and August, but were ordered to withdraw from Prairie du Chien in 1815 according to the terms of the Treaty of Ghent.

The Assault on Fort Mackinac

At virtually the same time, McKay reported to Lieutenant General Drummond that his First Nation informants had told him of Sinclair's ships being on the St. Clair River in June with the intention of making an attack on Fort Mackinac in August. McDouall speculated that this expedition might have been conceived after the Americans heard of the recent British expedition sent from Mackinac to capture the American outpost at Prairie du Chien. As this force would necessarily have depleted the strength of the troops available to defend Fort Mackinac, he reasoned that this intelligence had stimulated American commanders to strike while the British were in a weakened position.[36]

Perched high on the rocky bluffs of Mackinac Island, the fort was nearly impregnable if manned by a few capable defenders. Commodore Sinclair declared it "by nature a perfect Gibraltar, being a high inaccessible Rock on three sides except on the west . . . surrounded by an impenetrable forest intersected by deep ravines, apparently caused by volcanic eruption, on the fourth he [the enemy] has two strong forts—the lowest of which is between one and two hundred feet above the water."[37] After an extended period of reconnaissance and exploration of about two weeks, Sinclair landed Colonel Croghan and his army on the rather narrow beach, where they were fired on by British troops, militia, and First Nation warriors, well concealed in the thick woods, boulders, and shrubbery. While Sinclair's ships' guns covered the landing with gunfire support, they could not elevate to reach the position of the enemy's forts, a sure disadvantage when Croghan's attacking forces climbed above the range of the ships' guns. The farther they advanced, the more the elements became separated. The higher they climbed, the more exposed they were to the enemy's breastworks and artillery fire. The early wounding and killing of his principal officers led to confusion and ultimately retreat after about three hours of combat. The Americans suffered only 12 killed, 39 wounded, and 3 missing, a small proportion of some 700 troops that had landed with Croghan, leading to the conclusion that the expedition leaders had allowed too much time to pass between first appearing offshore and the amphibious landing, allowing the British to prepare their defenses. Whatever the reason, whether fear, uncertainty, or lack of organization, this failure to launch the amphibious attack immediately encouraged the British and enabled them to continue to fortify their position. With this repulse the United States lost its last opportunity to capture the strategic Mackinac Island stronghold that was key to access to the Mississippi headwaters for the duration of the war.[38]

The final acts of the Lake Huron drama feature two distant events, Sinclair's penetration of the mysteries of Georgian Bay and the US Navy's loss of two small yet significant armed schooners. Departing from Michilimackinac, Commodore Sinclair was bent on returning to the scene of his first failure, that of finding access to Georgian Bay and the British depot at Nottawasaga, one of the key ports on the lake from which most trading goods and other supplies were sent to Michilimackinac, Green Bay, and other far-flung trading posts. Sinclair's sailors had captured an unidentified individual in the schooner *Mink* who was willing to guide Sinclair's ships to Nottawasaga Bay for a price. As Sinclair wrote, "The navigation is dangerous and difficult and so obscured by rocks and bushes that no stranger could ever find it. I have however availed myself of the means of discovering it. I have agreed on a reward for this man, under the promise of secrecy, and the penalty of death in the case of failure, who is one of very few who have ever been there and who is to conduct me to the river and portage."[39]

In Search of the Schooner *Nancy*

Meanwhile, Lieutenant Miller Worsley, RN, the new captain of the schooner *Nancy*, prepared for her next voyage to Fort Mackinac. He had already departed Penetanguishene when a bateau pilot intercepted him with a message from Colonel McDouall warning him that Mackinac expected an attack and that Sinclair's squadron would soon be on its way to seek out and destroy *Nancy*. The best advice he could give Worsley was to return to Penetanguishene, warp his schooner as high up the river as possible, and build a blockhouse for her defense. Worsley immediately reversed course and followed these recommendations to the letter, even though it put him directly in harm's way. Within days of his completing this task, the Americans showed up, brought their brig and schooners into the river, and bombarded *Nancy* and the blockhouse. Owing to the stout defense offered by Worsley and his sailors, Sinclair's attack took the better part of a day and finally accomplished its purpose, destroying *Nancy*, her valuable cargo, and the blockhouse. Though long after the fact, one wonders whether McDouall might better have suggested any one of a number of hidden harbors on Huron's northern shore that might have provided better protection. Sinclair was bound to discover Penetanguishene sooner than later, and *Nancy*'s absence would have only frustrated and lengthened his search into the stormy season, which the commodore was anxious to avoid. As it was, Worsley and most of his crew escaped into the wilderness and lived to fight another day.[40]

The Capture of the US Schooners *Tigress* and *Scorpion*

Mindful that his vessels were much needed on Lake Erie for the support of US troops fighting on the Niagara Peninsula, Sinclair departed Nottawasaga in haste for Detroit, leaving behind only the two schooners *Tigress* and *Scorpion* to disrupt, if they could, the enemy's commerce and communications on the lake. They were to blockade the Nottawasaga Bay and to patrol and survey the islands, especially in the northern part of the lake, until about October 1, when blinding snow and ice storms would make sailing the lake too dangerous. The commanders of *Scorpion* and *Tigress* soon quit their Nottawasaga station owing to severe storms and poor anchorages and sailed to the area between St. Joseph's Island and the French River, intending to cut off the enemy's boats and canoes transiting from and to Lake Huron. During this time, they unwisely became separated from each other, thereby allowing an opportunity for the enemy to attack one while the other was absent.

In actuality, the two schooners were too weak a force to attempt to control such a wide and uncharted body of water, and the British naturally took advantage of that situation. Lieutenant Worsley quickly recovered from his loss of *Nancy* and was determined to gain revenge. He gathered his small crew and set sail for Fort Mackinac in a canoe, returning to Mackinac Island, where he conferred with Colonel McDouall about his plan to attack the two American schooners and regaining control of the lake. McDouall enthusiastically provided boats under the command of Lieutenant Andrew Bulger, of the Royal Newfoundland Regiment, manned by both soldiers and First Nation allies. In the evening of September 3 they stealthily attacked the schooner *Tigress*, which had anchored for the night. Caught by surprise, Sailing Master Champlain and his crew put up a fight but were quickly overcome. Lieutenants Worsley and Bulger quickly manned *Tigress* with their own men, sent the prisoners ashore at Mackinac Island, and prepared an ambush for the *Scorpion*, which approached them two days later and anchored about two miles away. At dawn on September 6, *Tigress* approached *Scorpion* under partial sail with US colors hoisted. On board *Scorpion*, Lieutenant Daniel Turner's men caught sight of *Tigress* at the last minute and sounded the alarm, but it was too late. The British swarmed aboard and captured the ship within five minutes. For the Americans, this was a doubly embarrassing turn of events. Commodore Sinclair had explicitly warned them about this possibility,[41] but being overconfident, they had let down their guard and been taken prisoners. The two schooners had suddenly become the Royal Navy's prizes and a means of commanding the lake in their own way. The work of the US Navy's summer campaign on Lake Huron was undone, and with the exception of the destruction of the Hudson Bay Company post, *Nancy*, and her cargo, there was little to show for it.[42]

Missed Opportunities

Even before returning to Lake Erie, Commodore Sinclair found his services called for at the eastern end of the lake, where on July 3 the US Army had launched an attack on British positions on the Niagara Peninsula. During Sinclair's return voyage, Major General Jacob Brown had requested the navy's assistance in covering his rear guard at Fort Erie.[43] However, Lieutenant Edmund Kennedy, whom Sinclair had left in charge at Presque Isle, had received orders from Secretary Jones to decline cooperation because he had another mission, the delivery of British prisoners of war from Sandusky, Ohio, to a point in British territory.[44] Apparently, Jones had not been officially informed about Brown's need for assistance from the Lake Erie squadron during ongoing operations. Otherwise, it would seem highly irregular for delivery of prisoners of war to take precedence over the army's need for navy protection. When Jones finally did receive official notification of Brown's request, he countermanded his orders to Kennedy and ordered him to place the four schooners *Ohio*, *Porcupine*, *Somers*, and *Lady Prevost* at Brown's disposal.[45] By this time, of course, the general had much less need of the navy's assistance. The battles of Chippawa and Lundy's Lane had been fought, with the struggle on the peninsula stalemated. Brown was most disappointed that the navy had been unable to come to his assistance on either Lake Erie or Lake Ontario during his hours of need.[46] This illustrates the need for army and navy commanding officers to be able to reach an understanding on the scene and not have to write to Washington for instructions. This situation cried out for unity of effort between navy and army. A perfect but rare example was the interservice cooperation between Perry and Harrison in 1813. The appointment of a single flag officer with joint authority, a commander whose responsibility was to attain the overall objective rather than service-specific ones, was not even a remote possibility in the early nineteenth century. By the onset of World War II, with large armies and navies and much improved communications, this idea's time had come.

Whether the presence of Kennedy's schooners made much of a contribution to General Brown's position is questionable. Under the command of Lieutenant Augustus Conkling, they were the targets of a British cutting-out expedition on the evening of August 12, while anchored off Fort Erie. Commander Alexander Dobbs, RN, had gathered a team of sailors and soldiers, cut a trail across the woods between Lakes Ontario and Erie, and launched a gig and five bateaux near the schooners' anchorage. Both *Ohio* and *Somers* were taken by surprise in a short fight. *Porcupine* might have been captured as well, but during the action the British cut the cables of *Ohio* and *Somers*, so that they drifted away toward the rapids. The *Porcupine* crew had stayed to perform their shore-bombardment mission, firing on the British besiegers of Fort Erie. On the following night, they might have been taken as well; however, their anchor dragged, so they cut their remaining cable and by skilled sailing escaped the rapids and returned to Presque Isle.[47]

Before the end of October one more calamity overtook Sinclair's troubled squadron. The brig *Caledonia*, which had survived all else, was driven ashore by a storm at Presque Isle after her cable parted. Then one of her crew members accidentally or intentionally set her on fire. Only by heroic efforts was she saved from the threat of exploding. Her commander, Thomas Holdup Stevens, had to swim from shore to get on board and heave the powder overboard. Even so, the brig was much scorched, especially toward her stern, rendering *Caledonia* unusable until she was eventually rebuilt. Finally, too, Sinclair was able to deliver the 550 prisoners of war the United States had held for nearly a year to the British at Long Point. From Jones, Sinclair humbly requested leave to visit his family; he said that having served so long on the lakes, he would prefer a transfer to the command of "a frigate where glory may be won."[48] Sinclair was only too conscious that during his time at Erie much of what had been won by Perry in 1813 had been lost. The failure to take Fort Mackinac had undermined the prospects of US influence over the northwestern territories and the First Nation warriors. And with the capture of *Scorpion*, *Tigress*, *Ohio*, and *Somers* as well as the wreck of *Caledonia*, the Lake Erie squadron had lost much of its flexibility as a fighting unit. It was not all his fault, but he knew that as the commander he would ultimately be held responsible.

CHAPTER 5

Sailors, Privateers, and Munitions

One year into the war, the United States found itself facing challenges only a few had anticipated. The war had begun with Americans believing that somehow it was a war they could win despite a lack of preparations, slim fiscal resources, a poorly trained army, and only a small navy facing the much larger professional armed forces of Great Britain, a nation that had been at war in Europe for nearly twenty years. Along with these realities, there had been in general a naive lack of respect for the capability of the enemy. This attitude had apparently reinforced in others a belief that militant emotion, patriotic zeal, and love of nation could substitute for a carefully considered national strategy, competent leadership, and well-organized lines of supply.[1]

By midsummer 1813 the distant military defeats and the naval victories of 1812 had become a spur to renewed action, but conditions had changed. The Madison administration knew it was in an existential struggle. The Royal Navy had begun to reinforce its North Atlantic station with clusters of frigates and ships of the line off key American ports. The first British sailors had arrived in Canada to take control of the vessels of the Provincial Marine at Kingston and Amherstburg and to build squadrons to oppose those the Americans were building on Lakes Ontario, Erie, and Champlain.

Recruiting

With the naval operations having begun on the Great Lakes, the US Navy had to reorient its distribution of personnel and shipbuilding capacity; the more ships that were built at Sackets Harbor and Erie, the more shipwrights and sailors were required at those northern ports. These experienced artisans and sailors needed on the lakes had to come from Atlantic seaports such as New York, Newport, New London, and Boston. When the frigates *United States* and *Macedonian* were prevented from escaping through Block Island Sound and New York harbor, some of their crews were drafted to man the Lake Ontario and Lake Erie squadrons. On February 18 Captain Stephen Decatur Jr. wrote to Secretary Jones with concern:

The men ordered from the *Argus*, for the Lakes, have been selected, and are now at the disposal of Lt. Woolcott Chauncey [Capt. Isaac Chauncey's brother]. As it is probable that there will be time to hear again from the department before the men leave this [place], I have taken the liberty to address you on this subject, begging that my zeal for the good of the service may plead my excuse for doing so— The *Argus* is nearly ready for sea—she may in the course of two weeks meet the enemy, and with her old crew, which were well disciplin'd, I should not fear the result of a contest with an equal force—she will not be near as efficient with a new crew until time shall be afforded to discipline them—fifty volunteers might have been obtained from the *Adams*, the *Alert* [formerly HMS *Alert*] and the Gun Boats. Those men are not liable to be drafted for service other than the defense of the harbor of New York. These men are equally good with the men of the *Argus* and will not require more reorganization than those of the *Argus* would when turn'd over to other vessels—If Sir this view of the subject shou'd induce you to alter your determination, there may yet be time to countermand your first order.[2]

Unfortunately for Decatur and *Argus*'s commander, Lieutenant William Henry Allen, Secretary Jones did not relent.[3] One month later, Captain Isaac Chauncey reported from Sackets Harbor that the crews of *John Adams*, then refitting in New York, and *Alert* were anxious to join him on the lakes. He needed five hundred men by June 1. As he had not heard from Jones, he had taken the liberty of asking Captain Hull to open a rendezvous in Boston "to recruit as many men as he can" until he heard again from the Navy Department.[4] Commodore William Bainbridge informed Jones in late April that he had "transferred fifty more of the frigate *Constitution*'s crew and forwarded them to Sackets Harbor to serve under the command of Captain Isaac Chauncey which makes one hundred and fifty of the crew of the *Constitution* sent to the Lakes."[5] It was readily apparent to these officers that the sending of experienced seamen to the lakes' commands would drain talent from the ships preparing to sail from the Atlantic ports. The men sent to the lakes would have to be replaced in the Atlantic seaports by those recruited at gatherings known by the traditional nautical term *rendezvous*. These were staged outside pubs, where a drummer and fifer would start playing to attract attention and a ship's officer would loudly announce the offered terms of engagement and a bounty for signing up for the duration of the cruise.

A good example of this recruiting practice occurred when Lieutenant Isaac Hull served in *Constitution* under Captain Silas Talbot in 1799 thirteen years earlier. The ship had returned from the Caribbean to Boston and the previous captain had gone ashore, leaving Hull in charge with instructions to refit the ship and recruit new crew members. He "established his headquarters at Priscilla

Broader's Federal Eagle Tavern, with William Hammond, fifer and William Higgins, drummer, to play a siren song to wandering sailors and 'to indulge and humor the Johns in a farewell frolic,' along with a boat's crew to take the enlistees off to the ship. Bartholomew Broader served up punch to the recruits. Business was brisk; by the middle of the month, Hull had enrolled 113 men. There was always a risk that these men would take their advance pay and abscond; Hull implored Talbot that they might be kept on board as much as possible."[6] If the men deserted while ashore to fetch stores or provisions and fill water casks, it was the recruiting officer's task to send out a search party to capture them. It was only when the ship was out of reach of the shore that the recruiter's job was truly complete.

Privateers and the Navy

The shortage of sailors available to the navy was made worse by competition from privateers that had been fitting out since the beginning of the war. Since colonial times private sea captains had been encouraged by the government to equip their ships with guns and small arms to wage war on the enemy's commerce. Indeed, during the congressional debates over the building of the first frigates, there had been many who, like Albert Gallatin (R-PA) in 1797, believed that encouraging privateers would prove a better defense of commerce than building a navy, because "we ought not to borrow institutions from other nations for which we are not fit."[7] When Gallatin became President Jefferson's secretary of the treasury in 1801, he administered the nation's and the navy's finances on the basis of strict economy. But after the Quasi-War with France, the Tripolitan War, and the *Chesapeake–Leopard* affair, even he agreed that it was necessary to have a navy, though on a limited basis. During the years 1809–11, while serving in the Madison administration, Gallatin held the line on naval expenditures, limiting the Navy Department to an average $1.6 million per year. This allowed for maintenance and operations of the navy's small establishment but no new shipbuilding; however, Gallatin's system of economy could not withstand the pressures brought by the outbreak of hostilities.

In 1812, within a month of the outbreak of the war, Congress approved privateering in An Act Concerning Letters of Marque, Prizes, and Prize Goods on July 26. In several seaports there was a rush to send out privateers during the first months of the war because the British had not yet established a blockade. This practice provided both a material and a strategic benefit to the administration as well as an opportunity for enrichment on the part of the shipowners and crews. Madison's government was under no illusion about the task ahead for the navy and was eager to encourage privateering. Privateers acted, in effect, as an independent naval force operating against British commerce. They multiplied the Royal Navy's work to protect merchant convoys, diverting its convoy escorts and frustrating the ships engaged in blockade duty (fig. 5.1).

Authorities vary in their estimates of the number of American privateers commissioned during the war. Faye Kert's recent study of both US and British/provincial privateers posits that the US government issued at least 600 letters of marque (commissions) for American privateers during the war. Of these, 246 succeeded in capturing 1,941 prizes, although 762, nearly 40 percent of those taken, were recaptured by the British. The vessel types included ships, brigs, schooners, xebecs, and even boats as small as seven tons. All told, they carried approximately 21,509 seamen and were armed with 2,428 guns.[8] It is also true that many privateersmen (an estimated 6,500) who bravely set out to make their fortunes either did not return or ended their careers as prisoners, held either at Melville Island near Halifax or in England's famous Dartmoor Prison, and were not released until 1815.[9]

Figure 5.1. Catch Me If You Can, Baltimore privateer in the War of 1812. Oil on canvas. Painting by Patrick O'Brien. Used courtesy of the artist.

Still, there was a certain cachet attached to sailing out for patriotism and profit, especially in swift-sailing, armed pilot schooners, which were often able to escape from and return to American ports despite the blockade. Overall, these privateers made a significant dent in British merchants' trade, raising insurance rates and prompting the Royal Navy to establish a convoy system for the protection of their ships and cargoes. As expressed in the title of Jerome Garitee's classic study of maritime Baltimore during the War of 1812, American privateers were "the republic's private navy."[10]

Although sailors in the US Navy and those on privateers at all times experienced similar risks in battle and the physical hazards of sea duty, many preferred privateering. For one thing, the rewards were greater if the privateering vessel had a lucky and skillful commander. For every prize that was sent into a friendly port and was determined to be a fair capture, the ship and her cargo were auctioned off in an admiralty proceeding. The magistrate determined court costs and distributed 2 percent of the proceeds of the sale to the customs office for the benefit of a seamen's fund. Of the remainder, 50 percent went to the US government, and the other 50 percent was divided among the ship's owner, captain, and crew. Although the owners received the lion's share, the commanders did well enough, and the crew split the rest according to articles of agreement signed at the beginning of a voyage. The privateer crews generally received better pay than the navy's sailors, who had endured longer voyages and stricter discipline.

On the other hand, privateers were subject to certain regulations. According to section 15 of the act authorizing the issuance of letters of marque and reprisal (privateer commissions), "All offences committed by any officer or seaman on board any such vessel [letter of marque or privateer] during the present hostilities against Great Britain, shall be tried and punished, when committed, as the like offences by any person belonging to the public ships of war of the United States."[11] Several instances demonstrate how commanding officers of private armed ships took advantage of this act. Joshua Barney, when commanding the privateer *Rossie* in September 1812, put two sailors under arrest and sent them to Master Commandant Oliver Hazard Perry, who was then commanding gunboats at Newport, Rhode Island, requesting that they be tried by court-martial. One of them, Thomas Holden, had been the chief mate on board the British merchantman *Jeanie* when that ship was captured by *Rossie*. Barney had discovered that not only was Holden an American citizen but he had served as acting gunner in the American frigate *General Greene* in November 1802. Barney considered him a deserter from the US Navy and a hostile as well since he was serving on a British ship after the declaration of war. The second man, John Nerbon, had served in *Rossie* under Barney's command and was accused of cowardice in that he had abandoned his post during combat. Although Barney had transferred the men to Perry's command to be put on trial, Perry wrote to Secretary Jones pointing out that Barney should have directed his request to Jones but had not since he was in a hurry to put to sea. It is not known whether these two men were finally court-martialed for their misdeeds.[12]

An unusual example of US Navy interaction with an American privateer took place at Provincetown, Massachusetts, in early January 1813. Since the beginning of the war the sleek, dark-hulled schooner *Liverpool Packet*, operating out of Halifax, had enjoyed a highly successful season off the New England coast. Under the command of Joseph Barss Jr., she had captured twenty-one American vessels by the end of the year.[13] Boston merchants were furious that this relatively small privateer had taken such a toll of their coastal traders. Commodore John Rodgers's frigate *President* was in Boston, refitting in Charlestown Navy Yard. A group of merchants determined to purchase and fit out a 100-ton schooner named *Commodore Hull* to protect their shipping and appealed to Rodgers for assistance. As *President* was not then available, they asked Rodgers if he would consent to manning *Commodore Hull* with available members of his crew. They requested that this vessel escort merchant vessels from Martha's Vineyard to Boston as protection against *Liverpool Packet*. After informing Secretary Jones of this proposal, Rodgers offered Lieutenant Henry S. Newcomb four midshipmen and forty-five seamen to crew this vessel. *Commodore Hull*, armed with four 6-pounder carriage guns, was larger than *Liverpool Packet*, though the Halifax privateer was more heavily armed, mounted five guns—two 4-pounders, one 6-pounder, and two 12-pounder carronades—manned by a crew of forty seamen.

Commodore Hull was at anchor in Provincetown's Cape Cod harbor on her way to Martha's Vineyard when she was hailed by the master of another schooner, the privateer *Anaconda*, asking permission to send an officer, Lieutenant Miller, to speak with Newcomb. Miller's purpose was to ask the identity of the schooner, as *Commodore Hull* was not showing her colors. *Anaconda*'s crew suspected her of being British because her sails appeared to be made of English duck and members of the crew were wearing fur caps like those worn by Canadian sailors. When Newcomb refused to identify his ship and nationality, Miller withdrew and returned to *Anaconda*. As *Commodore Hull* hoisted anchor and got under way, *Anaconda*'s acting captain, Lieutenant George Burbank, ordered a gun to be fired across her bow. To the consternation of all, the gun was loaded and wounded Lieutenant Newcomb and two of his two seamen. As Burbank later explained, he believed *Commodore Hull* to be *Liverpool Packet* because of Newcomb's failure to communicate clearly his own and his ship's identity. The ensuing uproar resulted in Commodore Rodgers ordering a court-martial of Burbank. This embarrassing case, involving an American privateer schooner firing on another American schooner, temporarily under navy command, was not resolved until March 11, 1813. Burbank was held prisoner at the Marine Barracks at Charlestown for approximately six weeks. In his own defense, Burbank stated that he had given Newcomb ample opportunity to reveal his and the schooner's identity during Lieutenant Miller's visit to *Commodore Hull*. When Newcomb had gotten his vessel under way, Burbank had determined to prevent its departure and ordered a bow gun to fire a warning shot across his bow, but he had fired not just once but three times, resulting in the unintended injury. He insisted that he had not intended to insult the flag of the United States, saying that he had not believed the schooner was an American vessel.[14] The court-martial ended with Burbank's acquittal; Commodore Rodgers gave his approval of the verdict and ordered the prisoner's release. This episode dramatized the high feelings running at that time regarding the depredations committed by *Liverpool Packet* and how the US Navy could sometimes be at cross-purposes with American privateers, bringing them to heel under naval regulations.

Gunpowder: The Mid-Atlantic Powder Mills

During the years after the Revolutionary War, gunpowder manufacture was in the hands of small-scale proprietors and importers, though it is unlikely that either Britain or France was the source of these imports. After 1789, France was convulsed in its own revolution. The resulting conflicts and later French governments were furious about the Americans' negotiation of Jay's Treaty with Great Britain in 1794. One fortunate result of the French Revolution was the arrival in the United States of affluent French émigrés anxious to escape the violent aftermath and social upheaval of the 1790s. Among these was Eleuthere Irenee Du Pont, who had received training in the chemical laboratory of the French scientist Antoine Lavoisier, the director of the Royal Gunpowder Administration from 1775 to 1792. Having observed that American gunpowder was of poor quality, Du Pont determined that this created an opportunity for him to apply his skills. He purchased land in the Brandywine Valley, near Wilmington, Delaware, in 1800. There, endowed with his specialized training and family backing, he built a small powder mill and furnished it with machinery imported from France.

While Du Pont's powder plant flourished in the years leading up to the War of 1812, others were entering the gunpowder business as well. The Bellona Powder Mill began operations in Belleville, New Jersey, at a site near the Passaic River, in 1810 or 1811.[15] The owners were John P. Decatur, a brother of Captain Stephen Decatur Jr., USN,[16] Dr. John Bullus, a naval surgeon, and John Rucker, of the

New York firm Bullus, Decatur & Rucker. Dr. Bullus, a former naval surgeon, was a relatively affluent gentleman who from 1810 was employed as the navy agent for New York. This firm had hired several immigrants originally brought from Ireland to work at the DuPont mill. The Bellona firm apparently did well for three years but suffered a disastrous explosion on April 20, 1814, killing eleven workers and badly wounding three more as reported in the *Newark Centinel* of April 26, 1814. Decatur and Rucker were on their way to the mill when the explosion occurred but survived because they were not in the immediate vicinity.[17] Other powder mills were being built throughout the United States at that time owing to the war's great demand for explosives. Another one worthy of note was Israel Whelen's Nitre Powder Mill on Cobbs Creek, near Haverford, Pennsylvania, which reportedly produced eight hundred thousand barrels of gunpowder during that conflict.[18]

In Maryland, within twenty years of the end of the Revolutionary War, entrepreneurs were opening powder works. One, within three miles of Baltimore at Gwynne's Falls and operated by William Lorman, obtained orders from the US government and operated from 1791 to 1812, when an explosion occurred that terminated the business. Another, under the ownership of navy agent James Beatty, was the more successful Bellona Mills, located at Jones Falls, which went into operation in 1801 and became a leading competitor of the DuPont Nemours powder works at Hagley.[19] The Bellona manufactory in 1810 was capable of making thirty-two quarter casks per day. Beatty later incorporated the company by an act of the General Assembly on April 16, 1815.[20] The company's agent, Aaron R. Levering (1784–1852), served during the war as captain of the Baltimore Independent Blues, the Sixth Maryland Regiment, which was held in reserve during the battle of North Point, on September 12, 1814. By 1816 the company was able to enter into contracts for one hundred thousand pounds of different powders.[21]

The Levering Powder Mill, located seven miles from Baltimore, was in business from 1808 until 1817, when it was destroyed in an explosion. It is evident that as soon as the federal government was established under the US Constitution, it enabled the newly created War Department to issue contracts for munitions from powder works for the army and the soon-to-be-created navy. This made conditions favorable for private suppliers of arms, armaments, and gunpowder to go into the business of fulfilling government contracts. Those in Maryland, close to the seat of the new government, were quick to take advantage of this opportunity. According to Treasury Secretary Albert Gallatin's report in 1810, the Maryland powder mills were producing twice as much as DuPont and led the nation in the production of gunpowder.[22] Until recent years DuPont was commonly held to be the major supplier of the navy's gunpowder.[23] The army provided a major market for DuPont's powder in the years leading up to the War of 1812, so it should not be surprising that most of the navy's gunpowder orders during the war were filled primarily by the Maryland and New Jersey gunpowder mills. This fact is admitted in Du Pont's own letters on the subject.[24]

Another source of gunpowder for the navy was the powder mills of Dr. Thomas Ewell, a chemist and naval surgeon attached to the Washington Navy Yard.[25] In 1811 he sought to augment his medical practice by providing gunpowder for the navy. Although Ewell had been appointed a naval surgeon and cultivated relations with Commodore Tingey at the navy yard, he seems to have been an importunate and quarrelsome individual, finding fault where he could not find favor. As the son-in-law of Benjamin Stoddert, Ewell had connections in Washington. Stoddert and a group of friends bought property near Bladensburg, where Ewell set up his first powder mill. Ewell appealed to Secretary of the Navy Hamilton for contracts to provide gunpowder for the navy. Hamilton allowed him to compete for a contract, but Ewell had trouble gaining the navy's approval of his powder's quality. As he did not get a contract, he wrote a series of remarkable letters to President James Madison requesting a reversal.[26] In the process he accused several of the navy's officers of conspiring against him. These included Secretary Jones, Captain Charles Morris, former chief clerk of the navy Charles Goldsborough, Commandant Thomas Tingey of the Washington Navy Yard, and Salvador Catalano, sailing master and acting gunner at the Washington Navy Yard.[27] With all these figures arrayed against him, it is a wonder that he was ever able to get a contract. However, perhaps because of his persistence in writing to President Madison and a pressing wartime need for powder, the navy granted Ewell an opportunity to have further tests. Ewell's product eventually met navy standards, and he was offered contracts until the end of the war.[28]

In the trans-Appalachian West, small independent powder works were prevalent during this period in several counties of south-central Kentucky. In 1810 there were sixty-three gunpowder mills producing about 115,716 pounds of powder annually. The abundance of caves that could be exploited for saltpeter may explain this phenomenon. These businesses flourished during the War of 1812, in which many Kentuckians took part, though the powder-mill industry declined rapidly in the depression that followed the war. Kentucky was a probable source of the powder that supplied the navy's New Orleans station. One powder works located in Hart County was that of John Court, on Lynn Camp Creek, near a wagon road. The powder he manufactured is said to have been shipped down the Green River by flatboat and to have arrived in New Orleans in time to be used by General Andrew Jackson's troops at the Battle of New Orleans.[29]

On the Verge of War

As the probability of war became apparent in the early months of 1812, Secretary Hamilton took the step of asking all commands to check the condition of their ordnance supplies and report back to him. On May 8, Captain Samuel Evans, commandant of the navy yard at Gosport (Norfolk), replied that with respect to gunpowder, he had tested nearly one hundred barrels of gunpowder in the yard's magazine comparable to the gunpowder that had been approved for use on board the frigate *United States*. In test-firing a three-pound ball from a 3-inch howitzer, the results were far from encouraging. The frigate's powder threw the shot 452 feet, but the powder from the barrels tested yielded on average only one third of that distance. This showed the gunner's lack of attention to the powder in storage, which tended to lose strength over time unless the powder kegs were kept airtight and dry and regularly "turned" to keep the powder fresh.[30] Captain John Dent reported the following items needed for the gunboats on the Charleston and Wilmington stations, which may be taken as typical for commands of that size. The list, abbreviated here to include only those items pertaining to ordnance and edged weapons, shows that Dent's command was greatly impoverished in terms of the weapons needed for war.[31]

- 400 barrels powder
- 50 barrels priming powder
- 300 white match rope
- 200 muskets with cartouch (cartridge) boxes
- 150 pairs of pistols with cartouch boxes
- 200 sabres
- 200 boarding axes
- 24 sponges and rammers for 32 pounders
- 24 sponges and rammers for 24 pounders
- 24 sponges and rammers for 18 pounders
- 24 sponges and rammers for 12 pounder carronades
- 50 dressed sheep skins for sponges
- 12 gunlocks for 32 pounders
- 4 gun-scrapers for 32 pounders
- 4 gun-scrapers for 24 pounders
- 4 gun-scrapers for 18 pounders
- 4 gun-scrapers for 12 pounders
- 4 gun-scrapers for 9 pounders

At the Washington Navy Yard, Captain Tingey was also in need of munitions. He wrote Secretary Hamilton in early July that "we can at this time supply only the match rope. Of 18-pounder round shot we have not one, over the indent for the frigate *Constellation*—of 24-pounder round shot we have not one in the yard since the departure of *Constellation*. Of the 100 barrels gun powder lately by your order shipped to Charleston, I could only ship 50 and have not 10 left in the magazine, nor have we more port-fire than necessary for the *Constellation* and other immediate wants." Three days later he wrote, "The indents for the frigate *Constellation* state the want of one hundred muskets and bayonets, fifty pair of pistols, and one hundred cutlasses. Of the former we have none fit for use. Of the latter, only sufficient for the gunboats."[32]

From Boston's Charlestown Navy Yard, Commandant William Bainbridge wrote that he had tested all the gunpowder belonging to the navy at the Boston magazine and had condemned 146 casks of powder (14,600 lb.) including 31 casks (2,085 lb.) belonging to the sloop of war *John Adams* and 23 casks (2,229 lb.) belonging to the frigate *Chesapeake*. Thus, approximately one third of each ship's powder had been declared ineffective. A total of 19,814 pounds of gunpowder had deteriorated, leading Bainbridge to ask Secretary Hamilton whether he should sell the bad powder or pay to have it "remanufactured." This is an appalling indication of the navy's unpreparedness, at least at the Boston naval station.[33]

At New Orleans the situation was similar, though the station was smaller and given less importance. Captain John Shaw, the officer in charge, responded to Hamilton that although he had plenty of shot on hand, he needed muskets and pistols better fit for service, as well as gunpowder. The secretary sent a requisition to General William Helms, navy agent at Newport, Tennessee,[34] to provide Shaw with 100 tons of assorted shot, 200 barrels of gunpowder, 40,000 pounds of assorted cordage, and 15,000 gallons of whiskey, adding that a tenth of the powder had to be fine for priming the guns. The normal transit time for letters from Washington to New Orleans was about a month, and delivery of supplies took much longer. Shaw wrote in late October that he was in desperate need of powder, having barely enough to supply the ship *Louisiana*, much less the gunboats on that station.[35]

Thus, although the manufacture of gunpowder at the outset of the war seemed adequate, it was the poor distribution and care of the powder already in storage that was cause for alarm among commanders of naval stations. Secretary Jones's appointment of Benjamin Homans as chief clerk brought changes. Homans's predecessor, Charles Goldsborough, had served as chief clerk since 1800. Although energetic, he seems to have lacked a sense of system, which navy secretaries

Robert Smith and Paul Hamilton had either failed to notice or neglected to chastise. Jones, with a merchant's sense of efficiency, took note immediately and dismissed Goldsborough. Homans took steps to improve the department's record-keeping in order to provide oversight of logistical matters such as supply, manpower, and timely communication, as can be seen in his comments to the secretary regarding matters at the Navy Department: "The storekeepers' returns are irregular, many deficient, and some of them greatly overcharged with details of small articles not worth enumerating;—if a regular form of Returns were adopted, it would aid them and simplify the entry under Classification of the most important Supplies. There are no Returns (that I have seen) of Gunpowder for the Navy Magazine nor do I know of any rule for supplying each ship."[36] Once the powder was brought on board ship in 100-pound barrels, they were lowered into a copper-lined magazine located on the lowest (orlop) deck, below the waterline. In that space, the gunner packed fifty cylinders' worth of broadsides on open shelves in case of an immediate need. The powder containers were turned every six months to prevent the saltpeter from settling. While working in the magazine, gunner's mates would wear felt slippers to avoid making sparks, which could cause a disastrous explosion. Special precautions had to be taken to prevent dampness from entering the magazine, for that too could reduce the effectiveness of the powder. This damp powder has been attributed as the reason why the US frigate *Chesapeake*'s shot was unable to penetrate the hull of HMS *Shannon* during their battle on June 1, 1813.[37]

Arming the Fleet

The navy's small 1812 fleet was equipped with a variety of guns used as main armaments. Naval ships were classified according to the number of guns they carried. Consider first the largest American frigates, or "44s," as they were often called. The descriptive number has nothing to do with the ships' measurements other than the number of guns these vessels were authorized and designed to carry. The US Navy's classification system was based on the Royal Navy's ordering of the ships that would sail in a "line of battle." Naval ships, while perhaps appearing similar to a layman's eyes, varied according to the dimensions of the hull, the ship's displacement, the number and size of their sails, and their seaworthiness under all conditions, especially in combat. There were design limitations and compromises in the amount of weight a ship's hull could accommodate in making the best speed, according to the velocity of the wind encountered. Above all, the naval architects and shipwrights had to consider the likely enemies their ships would encounter and the necessity of defeating or outrunning them.

By the late eighteenth and early nineteenth centuries, the Admiralty classified the largest ships in a line of battle, labeling as "first-rates" those armed with 100 or more guns arranged on three decks. These powerful floating fortresses were often used as flagships of the fleet, though they were not the swiftest and had to accommodate an enormous number of men. "Second-rates" were those equipped with from 80 to 98 guns, and the "third-rates," which made up most of the battle line, were called "74s" and "three-deckers." In descending order next were the "two-deckers," the "fourth-rates," the "fifth-rates," and the "sixth-rates." The fourth-rates were denominated as frigates never intended to sail in the battle line. These ships, often called the "eyes of the fleet," were designed for speed and maneuverability to act as screening vessels or blockaders; the largest fourth-rates carried from 44 to 60 guns, and the third-rates, 38 or 40 guns. The fifth-rate ships, often called *corvettes*, were armed with from 28 to 32 guns, all on a single deck, while the sixth-rate ships, or sloops of war, carried no more than 18 to 20 guns. These lighter vessels often served as convoy escorts or did patrol to interrupt an enemy's coastal trade. There were, of course, smaller vessels such as brigs, cutters, and the more specialized bomb vessels, fireships, and gunboats, which carried guns of lesser weight and range. It should be noted that regardless of a ship's rate, the commanding officer often added a few guns to the battery if the added weight did not interfere with the ship's handling and speed.[38]

The US Navy's ship-rating system also depended on the number of guns its ships and other vessels carried. The 74s were still in the building stage at Boston, Portsmouth, Philadelphia, and Washington and saw no action during the war. The usual battery of guns on board a frigate included both long-range guns, which could reach effectively over one mile, and shorter-range carronades (fondly called "smashers"), which could not be fired accurately at more than a half mile. The carronades were killers in more ways than one. They often were fired with less powder than the long guns, traveled more slowly, and when hitting a ship's side or bulwark tended to splinter the wood rather than to produce a hole, the result being many wounded by the shards or splinters generated by the impact. The wounds tended to be deep, and the wood difficult to extract, causing serious and often fatal infections. By June 1812 the American 44s, or "superfrigates," as they are sometimes called, carried from fifty-four to fifty-six guns—thirty long 24-pounders on the spar deck and twenty to twenty-four 32-pounder short-range carronades (*Constitution*) or 42-pounder carronades (*United States* and *President*) on the gun deck—and two long 24-pounder bow chasers. The number and size of guns carried during the war would vary slightly, depending on their availability and the whims of the ships' commanding officers. The smaller 38-gun frigates, *Constellation* and *Congress*, carried ten 24-pounder carronades and twenty-eight

18-pounder long guns. The frigate *Chesapeake* was armed with twenty long 18-pounders, twenty 32-pounder carronades, and one long shifting 18-pounder.

The armament of the 32-gun frigate *Essex* was originally twenty-six long 12-pounder guns on the spar deck and sixteen 24-pounder carronades on the gun deck. This mix of gun sizes was well chosen when she was launched in 1799. After service in the Mediterranean, *Essex* returned to the Washington Navy Yard for decommissioning. After recommissioning, she went back on embargo duty under the command of Captain John Smith, who, while at the Norfolk Navy Yard in 1810, requested Secretary Hamilton's permission to have *Essex*'s main battery modified, substituting 32-pounder carronades for most of her long guns.[39] Hamilton, who had been in office only one year, approved this unwise request to carry sixteen 32-pounder carronades and two long 18-pounders on the spar deck and twenty-four 32-pounders and four long 18s on her gun deck.[40] This made *Essex* vulnerable to being caught by an enemy ship with a battery of long guns and unable to respond effectively. But this still does not explain why Porter finally sailed from the Delaware River on October 28, 1812, without reducing his ship's excessive dependence on carronades after Hamilton had finally relented in their last exchange of letters in 1811.[41] One can only conclude that either the long guns Porter wanted were unavailable or he was so impatient to depart that he could wait no longer for the delivery of these guns. The British frigates *Phoebe* and *Cherub* took advantage of this disparity in 1814, during a battle off Valparaiso, when they were able to stand off with their long guns to batter the storm-damaged *Essex* because she was unable to reach them with her carronades.

Master Commandant Charles Ludlow, commander of the light frigate *John Adams*, in July 1812 was impressed with neither her seaworthiness nor her armament. After sailing her from Boston to New York, he remarked to Secretary Hamilton that "she cannot pass for more than a tolerable sailing merchant ship, and so crank [unstable] that a ship of 20 guns ought to take her in what would generally be call'd a topgallant breese for Ships of War." Later, as acting commandant of the New York Navy Yard, he wrote that "she has at present [only] 30 men attached to her without having a Gun nor grain of powder on board. These are men I have no control over, owing to her being commanded by a Senior Officer to myself, if it could be so arranged, they would be of infinite service to the Yard & [Gun]Boats at present."[42] Commodore Isaac Chauncey, whom Ludlow had succeeded, had taken most of the ship's crew and armament with him to the naval base at Sackets Harbor.[43] The sad story of the *John Adams* is that even though she was fitted for thirty guns, twenty-four 12-pounders and six 24-pounders, required a crew of 220 men, and had an excellent record of service during the Barbary Wars, she was not called upon to fight in the War of 1812 after service with Commodore Rodgers's squadron. She returned to Boston and remained there until ordered to New York under Ludlow's command. There she remained, denuded of armament and sailors, until 1814. Whether this neglect was due to her relatively poor sailing qualities or simply the need for her sailors and arms elsewhere is not clear. The only service she would provide at the New York Navy Yard was as the potential support ship for the gunboats assigned to protect New York. According to a report requested of Secretary Hamilton by Senator Samuel Smith, of the officers required to man an enlarged navy in December 1812, *John Adams* would rate one master commandant, one lieutenant, one surgeon, one surgeon's mate, and eight midshipmen.

The 28-gun frigate *Adams* had her own share of bad luck after serving in the Mediterranean. She returned to the Washington Navy Yard to be placed in ordinary along with the old frigates *New York*, *Boston*, and *Essex*. *Adams* was used as a receiving ship from 1811 to 1812. This meant the sailors assigned to a ship that had not arrived could lodge in *Adams* temporarily until their next ship was available. In this condition, however, *Adams* lacked maintenance and gradually deteriorated. In 1812 Commodore Tingey debated whether she was worth repairing but finally approved extensive repairs. The shipwrights at the navy yard cut out the decay and rebuilt her, adding a fifteen-foot extension, making her lines the same as those of *John Adams*, at about 128 feet in length overall.[44] Her main armament in 1814 contained twenty-six long 18-pounders and one 12-pounder on the quarterdeck. The commander's distribution of this armament was probably twelve long guns to a side and two to be used as stern chasers. She was ready to sail in 1813 under the command of Captain Charles Morris, but because of the presence of a powerful British squadron he was unable to make use of Chesapeake Bay, much less to penetrate the blockade off the Virginia Capes until early 1814.[45]

The US Navy's next smaller frigates were properly called sloops of war. They were still known as ships, having three masts and rigged for square sails, but they were lighter and shorter and carried fewer guns than the frigates. *Hornet*, built as a brig (square-rigged with two masts) in Baltimore in 1805, had been converted to a ship in 1811 and was armed with eighteen 32-pounder carronades and two long 12-pounder long guns. She measured about 107 feet in length and 30 feet in beam. The Washington-built *Wasp* was a ship similar in dimensions to *Hornet*, measuring 105 feet in length with 30 feet in beam. She carried sixteen 32-pounder carronades and two long 12-pounder long guns.

The navy's six brigs come next, though they were not all of the same size and weaponry. Completed in 1803, the Boston-built *Argus* and the Philadelphia-built *Syren* both carried eighteen guns, sixteen 24-pounder carronades and two long 12-pounders as chase guns. They measured about 95 feet in length and 27 feet in beam. *Nautilus* and *Vixen* were both built as 12-gun schooners in 1803 and later re-rigged as brigs. They were officially rated as 14-gun brigs, but each carried sixteen 18-pounder carronades. *Nautilus* was slightly larger at 87 feet in length and 23 feet in beam. *Vixen* measured about 84 feet in length with a beam of 22 feet. *Nautilus*, commanded by Lieutenant William Crane, was unlucky in being captured by a British squadron off Long island in July 1812, the first US Navy vessel to be captured. *Vixen* suffered a similar fate, being captured by HMS *Southampton* in November 1812; both victor and vanquished wrecked on a reef near the British West Indies soon thereafter. Two other vessels, *Enterprise* and *Viper*, made up the remainder of the navy's flotilla (with the exception of gunboats) at the onset of the war.

Built in 1799 on Maryland's Eastern Shore as a 12-gun schooner, *Enterprise* endured several years of Barbary Wars service in the Mediterranean and was thoroughly repaired and strengthened at the Venice arsenal.[46] She had been serving under Commodore Edward Preble's overall command during 1803–4. He ordered her rearmed with fourteen 18-pounder carronades and two long 9-pounders. Back on the American coast in 1805, she operated on embargo patrol, in 1811 earning another overhaul at the Washington Navy Yard, where the shipwrights re-rigged her as a brig before she was recommissioned in early 1812. The brig *Viper* was originally the 12-gun *Ferret*, built at Norfolk Navy Yard in 1809 as a cutter, then altered to a brig in 1810. Measuring 73 feet in length and nearly 24 feet in beam, she carried twelve 18-pounder carronades and two long 9-pounders.

The Foundries

A logical question to raise is where the navy's guns came from. Were the sources of supply in the United States or overseas? Of the several iron foundries that had produced cannons during the Revolutionary War, most were located in New England. With the end of that war, some of these foundries went out of business, but after the creation of the War Department and the building of the first frigates, the foundries that provided the navy's guns, long 24-pounders, were the Hope Furnace, of Rhode Island, operated by Brown, Francis, and Company, and the Cecil Furnace, in Cecil County, Maryland, operated by Samuel Hughes. Hughes provided twenty-eight guns for the arming of the frigate *Constellation*. David Waterman's Salisbury Furnace, in Salisbury, Connecticut, provided guns for the frigates *Congress* and *Chesapeake* in 1799 and 1800.

In March 1797, Secretary of War James McHenry ordered Captain Samuel Nicholson, of *Constitution*, to visit the Hope Furnace and receive the 24-pounders they had manufactured. He was further ordered to arrange for transport of the guns to Boston and provide instructions for construction of the guns' carriages.[47] Secretary of the Navy Benjamin Stoddert announced in 1798 that the Navy Department had need of 396 guns for its ships, and he entered into a contract with William Lane of Philadelphia and William Salter of New Jersey to produce one-third of those guns for the price of twenty-three thousand dollars.[48]

At about the same time, Henry Foxall, an experienced ironworker from Ireland, became superintendent of the Eagle Foundry, on the Schuylkill River at Philadelphia. Foxall had a superior knowledge of the iron-making business learned from his father and from employment as a furnace man at Funtley's Forge under Henry Cort, a major supplier of iron for the Plymouth Dockyard. Cort developed and patented a rolling mill and the "puddling process," which dramatically improved the strength of iron bar being produced. After Cort's financial failure in the mid-1780s, Foxall took his family to Ireland, where he worked at County Antrim's Arigna Iron Works. Because of religious and political upheaval in Ireland, he decided to emigrate, stealthily, to the United States in 1795. Britain at that time had laws against subjects with such technical knowledge leaving the country. Arriving at Philadelphia, he was fortunate to meet Robert Morris Jr., son of the financier, with whom he set up the Eagle Foundry.[49] Foxall filled orders from the War Department for iron shot and small guns for the ship *Crescent*, being built for the dey of Algiers. He soon built a boring machine for his mill and began to produce carronades for the navy. Secretary of War Pickering was pleased with the quality of Foxall's work. As he wrote to Secretary Stoddert, "Mr. Foxall is the only founder on whom we can depend for further improvements, and particularly for casting that very useful gun called the *carronade*. . . . The U. States are really indebted to him for the improvements he has introduced among us."[50] The high quality of Foxall's work would determine much of his success as an iron founder. Other firms, such as Salisbury Furnace, had problems with their cannons' failure to "stand proof," a test firing to evaluate their ability to withstand the pressures of continual firing in battle. The Navy Department turned to Foxall's Eagle Foundry and Hughes's Cecil Foundry to provide guns needed for *Adams* and the other frigates and sloops of war when the Salisbury Furnace failed to produce ordnance of sufficiently high quality.

The decision taken by Congress in 1789 to move the federal capital from New York to Washington caused a major shift of public attention to the resources of the Potomac region and its hinterlands. By 1798, work had begun on the site, but little progress had been made. An observant visitor could see that the White House was still under construction, some muddy roads had been laid out according to Major L'Enfant's plan, several hotels and rooming houses existed for travelers and congressmen, and workers' cottages abounded. There many farmhouses, animal sheds, and barns for hay, and fields for corn and other crops surrounded the small village that had sprung up. People who, like Henry Foxall, sought to remain in close contact with the government's contracting authority, began to move their homes and works to locations near Washington. In 1800, Foxall established his Columbia Foundry on the Georgetown bank of the Potomac River, where he had access to the early skirting canals around the falls and rapids. This location was ideal, for he was able to negotiate use of a federally owned source of iron ore from Friend's Orebank, a rich vein of limestone and iron ore on the Virginia side of the Potomac above Harper's Ferry, as well as Keep Tryst, an iron forge several miles downriver near Antietam Creek. He was thus able to obtain a reliable supply of pig iron for casting guns and ammunition that he could provide to the armed forces.[51]

During 1807–8, Foxall's Columbia Foundry cast more than one hundred guns for the navy, including twenty 32-pounders for *Constitution*. He continued as part owner of the Eagle Foundry and also had a hand in the establishment of the Virginia Manufactory of Arms, a state-owned foundry near Richmond. Virginia had considered establishing the foundry earlier, but Foxall's high cost estimate had deterred the project until the 1807 *Chesapeake–Leopard* incident off the Virginia Capes raised the prospect of a war with Great Britain. Then, one year later, Superintendent John Clarke agreed to Foxall's price of five thousand dollars. In return, Foxall promised to build and provide the equipment for casting, boring, and finishing cannons. He further agreed to send his own men to assemble the plant and, presumably, to instruct Clarke's workmen in the production methods. The Columbia workers would remain until the foundry had produced and proved a 6-pounder, at which point the Virginians would be on their own.[52] The project was completed in 1809, and Foxall's reputation spread, to his benefit, in Washington and beyond. The Columbia Foundry cast guns for the War Department as well as for the navy before and during the War of 1812, including the famous Columbiad, a chambered gun preferred by the army.

Between 1798 and 1812 there was, according to the armament historian Spencer Tucker, a time when the US Navy borrowed guns from other services or purchased imported guns, mostly from British sources. To fight the French and then the Barbary corsairs, the navy was building and purchasing ships at such a rate that domestic foundries could not keep up with the demand for guns of varying sizes and weight. The War Department supplied some 24-pounders for the frigate *United States*, and the governor of Massachusetts provided some 18-pounders for *Constitution* from the fort on Castle Island when the navy's order for 12-pounders failed to arrive. Likewise, the navy requested guns from the War Department in 1800 for the frigate *Philadelphia*. During the Quasi-War with

France, when the United States and Britain were fighting their common enemy, the navy obtained some 24-pounder French guns from the British dating back to the Revolutionary War. Private contractors acting on behalf of the United States purchased guns ranging from 4- to 24-pounders from sources in London. George Harrison, later the navy's agent in Philadelphia, offered to sell to the secretary of the navy 163 guns cast and proved in the Carron Foundry in Scotland.[53]

One of the most important munitions orders Foxall received, from the Navy Department in February 1813, was for fifty 32-pounder carronades to be sent to Erie, Pennsylvania, via Pittsburgh for Commodore Perry's brigs *Lawrence* and *Niagara*. Commodore Tingey's ordnance workers proved the guns and then sent them overland to Oliver Ormsby, the Pittsburgh navy agent. He had them transferred to barges to be hauled up the Alleghany River and French Creek to the naval station at Erie. The entire transit took forty days, the shipment arriving in mid-April, well before the completion of the brigs. These were the guns that helped Perry defeat the British squadron on Lake Erie on September 10, 1813.

The Columbia Foundry provided much of the navy's armaments during the war but by no means all. The Principio Foundry, in Cecil County, Maryland, was actively involved until a British raiding party from Rear Admiral Cochrane's Chesapeake Bay squadron attacked targets in the Havre de Grace area in the spring of 1813.[54] Cockburn reported "taking from the battery at Havre, six guns, 12 and 6-pounders; disabled ready for sending from foundry five 24-pounders, taking away 28 32-pounders, disabled in the boring house and foundry eight guns and four carronades of different calibres—total 51 guns and 130 stand of arms." This raid effectively ruined the foundry for the duration of the war and removed one of Foxall's foremost competitors in the production of guns for the government.[55] But, there were others, also located in Maryland. One was the Aetna (or Etna) furnace, at Curtis Creek in Anne Arundel County, about eight miles south of Baltimore. This furnace, owned by John E. Dorsey, forged ammunition and gun carriages, as described in one contract calling for "300 tons of heavy shot, 18 and 24 pounders deliverable at Baltimore, @ 72$, 10 tons of grape shot, @ 120$, 60 gun carriages (travelling) @ with timbers complete 40 for 6-pounders @215$ apiece, [and] 20 for 24 pounders @ 245$ apiece." Dorsey's firm also supplied "light 18-pounders" for eight of Commodore Joshua Barney's gunboats being built at St. Michaels.[56] There is no doubt, however, that Henry Foxall's Columbia Foundry and the Eagle Foundry, of which he was a part owner, supplied most of the guns and shot produced for the navy during the War of 1812. The reasons for this were not only his virtual monopoly but also the fine qualities of his weapons, which led both the War Department and the Navy Department to insist that other foundries produce weapons to the exact specifications and proof that Foxall demanded of his foundries.[57] There were, of course, many other needs for iron on board the navy's ships: pig iron was required for ballast; anchors; hoops for barrels; the camboose, or cooking stove; pots for cooking; crowbars; hinges for storage lockers; fittings for masts and spars; and the belaying pins used to secure the ship's lines and ropes on each mast. A ship armorer's main job was to use his iron forge to keep the ship in good repair. In short, there was no substitute for the iron that Henry Foxall and others provided for the early American navy.

For the navy, the situation was becoming more difficult by mid-1813. The two-front war had become a necessity, making it essential for the Navy Department to begin building squadrons on three of the northern lakes. The Secretary had sent commanders to each of these frontier naval bases: Commodore (Captain) Isaac Chauncey to Sackets Harbor, New York, on Lake Ontario; Commodore (Master Commandant) Oliver Hazard Perry to Erie, Pennsylvania, on Lake Erie; and Commodore (Master Commandant) Thomas Macdonough to Vergennes, Vermont, on Lake Champlain. Their enemy counterparts were engaged in similar squadron building on the northern shores of the lakes. Each of these commanders had to build his flotilla from the keel up or purchase and arm trading local schooners in the shortest possible time. The lakes commodores were short of sailors, shipwrights, supplies, and ordnance, all of which had to be drawn from naval stations and navy yards on the Atlantic coast. The stations most affected were those at Boston and New York. Commodore Chauncey, who had overall command on both Lake Ontario and Lake Erie, depleted the New York (Brooklyn) Navy Yard with drafts of men and guns from the frigate *John Adams*. Commodore Bainbridge acceded to Chauncey's request for sailors by sending a draft of sailors from USS *Constitution*, which was at the Charlestown (Boston) Navy Yard undergoing repairs and fitting out for its next war patrol.

Privateers

To bolster the US Navy's efforts, the Madison administration, despite falling short in other areas, had foreseen the size disparity between the US Navy and the Royal Navy and acted to send out privateers a month after declaring war. Their goal was the capture of British merchantmen as they plied the trade routes between the British Isles and the West Indies. The prospect of fighting for profits and patriotism was exciting. The response from northern seaports was immediate. Merchants at New England's ports, such as Newburyport, Marblehead, and Newport, had anticipated the privateering act, An Act Concerning Letters of Marque, Prizes, and Prize Goods, and had begun to convert some of their fastest sailing vessels, mostly schooners, for use in wartime. Shipowners in New York, Philadelphia, and Baltimore followed suit. This rush to privateers had its negative effects as well. Sailors waiting for a ship knew that privateers, if successful, paid better than the navy, and most privateer masters were more relaxed in discipline that were navy captains. The navy's recruiters had to open rendezvous and beat the drums loudly to attract out-of-work sailors. They also had to offer bounties for signing on to a voyage in competition with the privateers. Once at sea, naval commanders had to contend with privateer masters, who were prone to using flags of foreign nations as a ruse, leaving other ships in the dark as to their nationality until they were lured alongside. But even sailors in privateers were subject to naval discipline and court-martial if they overstepped their bounds, showed contempt for their commanders, or fired on US Navy ships by mistake or as the result of poor judgment, as occurred in the case of the navy's *Commodore Hull* and the privateer *Anaconda*. The strengthening of the British blockade also had its impact on privateers. The happy hunting grounds of 1812 had disappeared by the summer of 1813. More American privateers were being snapped up by British cruisers, especially off the New England coast, where the proximity of the Royal Navy's base at Halifax was a threat to Yankee cruisers on the prowl.

The US Navy faced critical shortages of war material at the outset of the War of 1812 thanks to years of congressional opposition to enlarging and supplying the navy with what it would need in time of war. Letters to the secretary of the navy from station commanders along the coast showed their need of men, guns, ammunition, gunpowder, small arms, and edged weapons, as mentioned. The barrels of gunpowder in storage for the frigates required close attention to prevent spoilage because of moisture and deteriorating mixture if they were not regularly turned. This was particularly the case at Boston when Commodore Bainbridge's June 1812 inspection found that one-third of the powder of the frigates *John Adams* and *Chesapeake* had spoiled. Fortunately, the nation's ability to manufacture gunpowder domestically had improved since the Du Pont family established its powder mill in Delaware and since several other private firms had taken root in Pennsylvania, New Jersey, and Maryland.

Equally important for the army and the emerging navy, the growth of the iron industry had proceeded apace since the mid-1790s, coincidentally with the eruption of the naval wars with France in the Caribbean and the Barbary Coast regencies in the Mediterranean. There was a symbiotic relationship between the military's need for forged iron guns and round shot and the response of entrepreneurs of the iron industry. Iron was required not only for weapons of all types but also for building and rigging ships. It was essential for maintaining the strength of a ship's complex structure of interdependent masts, spars, and cordage under tension. The navy became highly dependent on Samuel Hughes's Principio Foundry and Henry Foxall's Columbia Foundry during the War of 1812. After the British attack on Havre de Grace and the destruction of the Principio Foundry in 1813, the continued output of Foxall's foundry became indispensable for the navy.

CHAPTER 6

The British Blockade of 1813–1814

One of the time-honored techniques of maritime warfare is the establishment of a blockade off an enemy's coast. It should be fairly clear that the nation that attempts a blockade must have sea control, at least in the immediate area of the conflict. If that were not the case, the blockaded nation would be justified in protesting that the warships were engaged in only a "paper blockade," a blockade in name only, which was considered illegal under international law. The goals of naval blockade are to destroy or render useless an enemy's warships and to interfere with and preferably ruin that nation's seaborne commerce. The strategy of a sea blockade is twofold. First, it assumes that the blockading nation has sufficient naval vessels at hand to effectively guard the coast and its sea approaches. It does no good for a nation to declare a blockade that it cannot or does not intend to enforce thoroughly. Second, in application, it is designed to prevent or discourage an enemy's warships and merchant vessels from departing from or returning to a port. If rigorously applied, this strategy can throttle a nation's navy and trade and damage its economy, thereby diminishing its resources and undermining the morale of the enemy population. Depending on the number of ships available, the blockading nation may choose to establish a close, loose, or distant blockade, or a combination of all these, if it has a sufficient number of ships.

A Legacy of Blockading

Long before the War of 1812, in keeping with Britain's sense of being an island kingdom, the Crown nurtured its navy and for centuries protected its colonies, escorted convoys, conducted blockades, and harried the ports of its European enemies, especially when invasion threatened. During the Seven Years' War the Royal Navy was adept at preventing French warships from the unfettered use of Brest, Rochefort, and other Atlantic and Channel bases when sending fleets to the West Indies and Canada.[1] During its war against the rebellious United States, Great Britain again resorted to naval blockade to discourage privateering, coastal trade, and shipping to and from the West Indies and France. Royal Navy ships also escorted convoys and participated in amphibious operations and so lacked enough vessels to cover the lengthy, indented American coastline from Massachusetts to Georgia. For that reason the Admiralty had barely enough ships in the Channel fleet to prevent an invasion supported by the French and Spanish navies.[2] British blockades were again in use in European waters during the wars of the French Revolution and the Napoleonic Wars.[3] By the outbreak of the War of 1812 many generations of the Royal Navy's admirals, captains, and commanders, having been trained in the tradition of fighting at sea against the French and others for nearly sixty years, had few problems in executing blockade and raiding strategies against the United States if the required ships were available.[4]

The British blockade of the American coast during the War of 1812 was relatively thin at the outset but increased in effectiveness in 1813. Although the French fleet was considerably weaker after the Battle of Trafalgar in 1805, the British were again obliged to keep watch on enemy bases on the coasts of Normandy and Brittany and to protect the British West Indies. This prolonged conflict coincided with the onset of war between the United States and Britain. Given the great distance from Europe and the few regular troops Britain had in Canada, a naval blockade was essential for demonstrating to the United States that its government would pay a serious price for its declaration of war. By September 27, 1812, when Admiral Warren succeeded Vice Admiral Herbert Sawyer as commander in chief, the Admiralty had unified and thereby expanded the North American Station, at Halifax, to include all stations and commands from Nova Scotia and Newfoundland to Jamaica and the Leeward Islands, an area of vast extent. The neutral trade, as well as Britain's need for American grain and other goods to supply its armies fighting the French in Portugal and Spain, was a complicating factor. For this reason, the British consul in Boston was authorized to issue licenses to merchant ship captains that allowed them to pass through the blockade. Until 1814 the Royal Navy also allowed neutral vessels to enter Boston and New York in the hope of weaning the northeastern states away from the federal government at Washington. The Admiralty steadily drew down its assets at its Halifax, Jamaica, and Leeward Islands bases from 1810 to 1812. At Halifax, the number of ships dropped from 33 to 23. In July 1812 the Admiralty's ships at Halifax included one ship of the line, 5 frigates, and 17 smaller vessels (brigs, schooners, and sloops). Its ability to increase the number of vessels on this station in case of an emergency was very limited.[5] Thus, after the Madison administration declared war and the possibility of negotiating a halt to hostilities ended, it was about four months before the first blockading ships showed up off US ports.

The increasing effectiveness of the blockade along the Atlantic coast pinched off maritime transport of ship's timber as well as the heavy armament needed for ships and fortifications. This strategy forced the US Navy of 1812 to take up innovative tactics that today are considered part of asymmetrical warfare, the techniques favored by smaller, weaker powers in conflict with larger, wealthier, more capable enemies. The US declaration of war dealt the Board of Admiralty a strategic surprise. Most of the Royal Navy's ships of the line were committed to guarding the English Channel and keeping a close blockade of the rugged Breton and Biscay coast against a breakout of the French navy. They had sent Admiral Warren to Halifax to replace Admiral Sawyer, who the more senior admirals thought had failed to give timely notification of the outbreak of war and the sailing of the American squadron. The few warships at Warren's disposal at Halifax were barely more numerous than the combined American squadron under Commodore Rodgers. The other assets of Warren's unified command were based far to the south, primarily at Jamaica but also eastward at Barbados and the Windward Islands, where they were beyond the reach of rapid communications and timely response. Under these circumstances, British commanders were compelled to attend to their first priority, defending British trade, rather than attacking American merchantmen. In the waters near coastal Maine and Nova Scotia, Royal Navy cruisers scooped up several American small privateers and the revenue cutter *Commodore Barry* during July and August 1812.[6] But farther afield, the American navy reaped the advantage of its technologically advanced heavier frigates and the element of surprise.

To the British, their early losses were embarrassing, especially as they fell to American ships and sailors, whom they had underestimated in terms of both seamanship and gunnery. Admiral Warren was made to feel the brunt of the Admiralty's dissatisfaction. His response was that he had to cover a vast coastline with relatively few ships and required reinforcements to stem the flow of American warships and privateers. At the same time, he pointed out the superior size of the American frigates, their increased number of heavy guns compared with British frigates, and their superior sailing qualities. He recommended that the Admiralty consider preparing some modified (razeed) 74-gun ships to counter these larger enemy frigates.[7] Although Warren had not yet received the news, the British high command on December 26, 1812, had approved the establishment of "a complete and vigorous Blockade of the Ports and Harbors of the Bay of the Chesapeake and of the River Delaware."[8]

The major problem confronting William Jones, the new secretary of the navy, as he entered office in January 1813 was the arrival of more British blockading vessels off the American coast. He became fully aware of the blockade when Captain Charles Stewart, commander of *Constellation*, 36, attempted to leave Chesapeake Bay. His ship had undergone a lengthy and extensive rebuild at the Washington Navy Yard. Although this had been scheduled years earlier, it had been postponed. The lack of timber, equipment, and ordnance had delayed completion of the yard's work until her recommissioning on October 11, 1812. During the weeks that followed, boats brought anchors, guns, and provisions for *Constellation*, which apparently was still in need of filling its complement, as evidenced by the opening of a recruiting rendezvous in Alexandria. Secretary Hamilton had asked Stewart for help persuading Congress to authorize a new round of shipbuilding. He had complied with a letter of November 12 arguing for the construction of heavy frigates and ships of the line. This communication had a positive effect: on December 23, 1812, Congress authorized the building of three 74-gun ships of the line, *Franklin*, *Washington*, and *Independence*, and six 44-gun frigates. The first three frigates would be named *Columbia*, *Guerriere*, and *Java*, but because of the blockade none was ready for sea before the war ended.

By then, Captain Stewart had become concerned that the formation of ice on the Potomac might soon prevent his departure. In early December, Stewart got under way, though his frigate was still not completely ready for sea. He put in at Annapolis to continue preparations in accord with instructions from Secretary Jones. Although not satisfied with the tests of his gunpowder and lacking spare sails and other equipment, Stewart sailed for Hampton Roads, anxious to escape Chesapeake Bay before British blockaders took position off the Virginia Capes. To his chagrin, Stewart discovered on February 2, the day he sailed his ship into Hampton Roads, that seven Royal Navy war vessels (two ships of the line, three frigates, a brig, and a schooner) had arrived off Cape Henry, making their way into the bay, where they anchored in Lynnhaven Roads, off present-day Little Creek. He had little choice other than to lighten ship and haul her up the Elizabeth River to above Craney Island, where she could be protected by the guns of Fort Norfolk and the Navy gunboat flotilla. And that is where *Constellation* stayed for the remainder of the war, testimony to the difficulty of a frigate escaping through a close blockade. While privateers from Baltimore often did slip out through the capes, the Royal Navy had targeted *Constellation* because she could have done great damage to British trading vessels if she had escaped.

Admiral Warren had informed the Admiralty of his dire need of blockading vessels. In late March 1813, the First Lord of the Admiralty informed Warren in a private letter that he had determined to lengthen the blockade by well over a thousand miles, including all the principal ports south of Rhode Island, including New Orleans, reminding Warren that this was not to be "a mere paper blockade." He added that "the providing of sufficient convoys between Quebec and Halifax & the West Indies will not escape your attention, nor the husbanding and refitting your force by having a certain number only engaged in cruising, so that the whole may be kept as effective as possible, & your blockading vessels be occasionally relieved."[9] All this was probably unnecessary advice for Warren, though it makes clear how many tasks his ships were simultaneously to perform. Paradoxically, the problem for the Admiralty was that at that moment it could not provide Warren with more ships, the only means of truly enforcing the blockade and making clear that it was not a paper blockade.

Protecting the Seaports

Upon assuming his position as secretary, Jones added to the navy's shopping list. And he discovered that he had inherited from Paul Hamilton several other burdens. One was the posture of the Navy Department with regard to citizens' concerns for the safety of their ports and shipping in view of the increasing British naval threats. One of Jones's earliest acts was to order a reduction in the number of gunboats in service. He believed this would save funds on maintenance and put the available seamen to better use. Only 50 out of approximately 150 gunboats were sufficiently serviceable to remain active; the rest were to be laid up but remained available in case of emergency. Of those gunboats in service, Jones assigned 15 to New York, 5 to the Delaware River, 6 to the Georgia coast, and 10 to New Orleans; 14 remained active on Chesapeake Bay (mostly assigned to Norfolk).[10] But in several cities this did not go over well. In fact, Jones began to receive suggestions from citizens about what the navy might do to help protect the nation's seaports.

New York City

One of the first suggestions was from Jacob Lewis, formerly captain of the privateer *Bunker Hill*, who had been appointed a master commandant recently, in November 1812. He had been given command of the New York gunboat flotilla but wanted to be assured that the navy would fully support the gunboats as Secretary Hamilton had promised. He stated that it was obvious that the navy's preference was to man frigates ahead of gunboats but warned that this would place in jeopardy the defense of harbors such as New York's. He reminded Jones that Secretary Hamilton had intended to place the entire defense of the harbor under his (Lewis's) command and said he hoped the new secretary would make it so.[11] It seems that Lewis had a rather exaggerated idea of his own authority, but he did not realize that until it was severely checked by Jones.

When British blockaders first appeared off New York in April 1813, Lewis summoned the gunboats into service and then was embarrassed to find that he did not have enough sailors to man the gunboats and had incurred expenses he was not authorized to make. Jones reprimanded him for acting prematurely and without sufficient cause, as there was no real emergency. Jones told him that in the future he would not approve Lewis's actions unless there was the threat of an immediate attack in which case he would have to man the gunboats with volunteers, but not without explicit approval from Jones himself. Jones was clearly concerned with matters of both expense and authority. He did not want his subordinate commanders acting without orders in a way he considered extravagant.[12] Lewis's unhappy rejoinder referred to a previous arrangement between the New York City government and the Navy Department regarding pay and rations whereby the city would advance the pay for gunboat officers and sailors, while the federal government would provide the rations. Apparently, the New York attorney Nicholas Fish, a member of the city's common council, had pressured Lewis to activate the flotilla when the council heard that the enemy was at the gates. Lewis tried to assure Jones that no gunboats had actually moved from their moorings at Sandy Hook and that he had spent no additional funds. Later on, Jones wrote to Fish explaining his gunboat policy and his desire to economize on the use of gunboats whenever it could be done without undermining public safety.[13] Fish, a Revolutionary War veteran and politically active attorney, was an important political figure in New York. He had run for the lieutenant governorship of the state only to be defeated by the former mayor Dewitt Clinton in 1811. Though Fish was a Federalist, Jones clearly felt that he was owed a letter of explanation regarding the navy's position with respect to protecting the port of New York.

Savannah, Georgia, and St. Marys, Florida

What was true of New York applied also to other middle Atlantic and southeastern seaports. The navy did not have enough seamen to man the gunboats available to protect the ports. Secretary Jones's letter of early February to Captain Hugh Campbell, at the St. Marys station, enumerated the restraints. No more than six gunboats were to be retained in commission, with thirty men allotted to each, including a commander (probably a sailing master), two midshipmen, two master's mates, an acting gunner, a steward, a cook, eight able seamen, and sixteen ordinary seamen and boys. He allowed the brig *Troup* (formerly *Princess Amelia*, a British packet), named for congressman George Troup, to be retained for the protection of Savannah. She was to be commanded by a lieutenant and a small crew of eighty-seven officers and men. The names of all other men retained for service would be reported to the Navy Department. The brig *Enterprise*, 16, under the command of Johnston Blakeley, was then at Savannah, having recently arrived from New Orleans. Jones instructed Campbell to make sure that any excess officers and seamen would be made available to *Enterprise* or any other cruising vessel.[14] Two months later, in April 1813, Blakeley anxiously wrote to Jones pleading for orders to go on war patrol, fearing that he was losing an opportunity to gain in reputation and promotion while sitting idly in port or being engaged in minor coastal transport duties for Commodore Campbell.[15] This communication bore fruit. Within three weeks Campbell received orders from Jones to immediately release *Enterprise* and order Blakeley to report to Captain Isaac Hull, commandant at the Portsmouth Naval Shipyard. Although at sea at the time this order arrived at Savannah, *Enterprise* finally arrived in Portsmouth in late June.

Charleston, South Carolina

At Charleston, Captain John Dent had his hands full protecting that station's extensive coastal waterways. He hastened to respond to Jones's gunboat-reduction order, but he tactfully reminded the secretary that he actually had the schooners *Ferret*, 9, *Alligator*, 4, and *Nonsuch*, 14, as well as several barges, not gunboats, under his command. There were two active gunboats, *No. 7* and *No. 167*, at the Wilmington station under the command of Sailing Master Thomas N. Gautier. After receiving a letter from North Carolina representative William Rufus King concerning the extensive though lightly defended North Carolina coast, Jones made haste to respond and then informed Gautier that he would have to bring into service four additional gunboats, making a total of six, of which three were to be stationed at Wilmington, two at Ocracoke, and one at Beaufort. He would be able to add the services of a Dr. Morrison, who would serve as a surgeon's mate for his command, and the navy agent Joshua Potts would be ordered to act as his purser. Finally, Sailing Master Gautier would no longer be under the command of Captain Dent at Charleston but would report directly to Jones at the Navy Department.[16]

Wilmington, Delaware, and Philadelphia, Pennsylvania

On the Delaware River, Wilmington and Philadelphia community leaders had formed committees for the defense of their ports and had sent letters to Secretary Jones asking for reinforcements of the navy gunboat flotilla assigned to the Delaware. Jones's Philadelphia friend Manuel Eyre wrote at length advising him that a committee was raising funds to build a number of row galleys and barges to augment the gunboats. He suggested that perhaps the Navy Department would man these vessels or that if not, they would seek out volunteers. The committee, he wrote, was also desirous that a vessel be fitted out to act as a store ship for the flotilla and could furnish a swift schooner to be a tender for the augmented flotilla. The committee was preparing to send a deputation to Washington to call on government departments. Eyre knew that Jones would not wish to deal with this group and was hoping that Jones would respond in such a way as to make this unnecessary. Though his letter was friendly in tone, Eyre must have seemed presumptuous in asking for a reply "by return of post" in which he hoped Jones would agree "immediately" to these requests "at the expense of the government." In an equally long response, Jones pushed back on Eyre's request. Giving an example of British raiding mobility in the Chesapeake, Jones pointed out that it was wiser for the government, whose responsibility was to provide for the safety of the nation, to husband its strength for when and where it was most needed than to respond to the many communities whose concern was a general though not imminent threat. In his opinion, the force already allotted to defense of the Delaware, ten gunboats and two block sloops equipped with two long 18-pounders and two 24-pounder carronades, with fifty men in each vessel, would be adequate if well managed. He ridiculed the idea of open launches and barges as an invitation to slaughter and added that manning them might "unman" the gunboats and sloops, which would not be a promotion of the public good. In closing, he assured Eyre that his natural predilections would not allow him to neglect his native city.[17] Ultimately, the good citizens of Philadelphia contributed to their own defense by building several barges under the auspices of the Philadelphia Corporation Flotilla Committee and then offered them to the navy. In his response, Secretary Jones relented and offered to buy three barges, one large gunboat, *Northern Liberties*, and the schooner *Helen*, to be used as a supply and hospital ship for the flotilla, later named the Delaware Flotilla.[18]

At nearly the same time that Jones was in correspondence with the citizens of Philadelphia, he was dealing with similar requests from Baltimore's merchants. The presence of British ships in the lower Chesapeake meant that merchantmen from Baltimore were encountering difficulty leaving the bay. Beginning in early April and into May, the British staged destructive raids on waterfront communities in the upper reaches of the Chesapeake Bay, on the Sassafras and Elk Rivers, and at Havre de Grace, at the mouth of the Susquehanna, and probed the Patapsco River, the gateway to Baltimore. At the battle of Craney Island, in June 1813, British troops met with a costly reverse owing to the cooperation among *Constellation*'s crew, the Virginia militia, and a squadron of US Navy gunboats. Likewise at St. Michaels, boat attacks on the town on two occasions in August 1813 met with stout opposition from Maryland militia units. The resistance of US gunboats off Norfolk and Craney Island saved *Constellation* and gave hope to bayside communities that something could be done.

These raids struck fear into the hearts of bayside residents and raised doubts about the safety of Baltimore and the state capital at Annapolis. A committee of underwriters representing Baltimore's insurance industry wrote to the secretary of the navy proposing to finance the arming of some fast sailing schooners (idle privateers) that would screen or escort Baltimore's merchant ships to protect them from the enemy's boats. There were many coves where flotillas of armed cutters and longboats from the larger warships in the bay could conceal themselves until a hapless Baltimore trader sailed by and then row after them in hot pursuit. This could be an especially effective tactic during the Chesapeake's frequent calms, when larger merchantmen would be less able to escape the British squadron's nimble oared boats. The committee asked only that the US government reimburse the insurers for their efforts and return the schooners in operational condition. Jones responded that the navy's slender resources comprised only a few gunboats at Washington and Norfolk, in addition to the cutter *Scorpion*, 4, and the schooner *Asp*, 3. All he could do was station a small flotilla of gunboats at the mouth of the Potomac to render assistance when possible. He could not spare any vessels to escort the Baltimore traders and therefore appreciated whatever cooperation the Baltimore committee could produce for their defense.[19]

Baltimore, Maryland

Maryland's senator Samuel Smith, chairman of the Senate Naval Committee and veteran of the Revolutionary War, likewise entered into correspondence with Jones concerning the defense of Baltimore. As a member of the city's Committee of Public Safety, he organized a Corps of Seamen, which recommended building a flotilla of eight armed barges sixty to seventy feet in length to be propelled by both sails and oars. This recommendation was coordinated with legislation in the Maryland Assembly to obtain state funding for these and other efforts to protect Baltimore. In the meantime, Smith had apparently been in contact with Captain Charles Gordon, commander of the navy's gunboats at Baltimore, regarding his thoughts on hiring privateer schooners and their crews to provide some protection for Baltimore's mariners in the absence of help from Washington. Gordon had written to Jones making this suggestion without mentioning Smith, but the secretary picked up the idea and adopted it as his own.[20]

Gordon was ready when Jones ordered him on April 15 to take command of the small force of privateers that the city of Baltimore promised to loan to the navy to act, in effect, as a squadron of observation.[21] Those privateers were the schooners *Revenge*, 17; *Comet*, 14; *Patapsco*, 14; and the diminutive *Wasp*, 3; as well as US gunboat *No. 138*.[22] Their mission was to reconnoiter the enemy and protect merchantmen sailing from Baltimore as they attempted to run the gauntlet of light British cruisers and armed boats that lay in wait down the bay. It took Gordon several weeks to man and arm the schooners and then train them to navy standards. Finally, they sailed and spent the month of June cruising in the lower bay. He reported seeing two enemy 74s, four frigates, and one brig lying close to the flagship. Gordon reported that "the positioning of their fleet prevents any offensive action on our part," implying that he was overly cautious in committing his schooners to his mission and that perhaps no Baltimore merchant ships were able to escape the blockade during that month. He returned earlier than expected because of the flotilla's short supplies of provisions and water. This was the end of an innovative plan for public-private naval cooperation, and the best that might be said was that no ships or lives were lost in the attempt.[23] However, this led to the creation of a more adventurous plan that was to play out over the next year thanks to the efforts of Joshua Barney, a famed Revolutionary War sailor and War of 1812 privateersman who could not abide inaction while the Royal Navy flaunted its domination of Chesapeake Bay.

Senator Smith had been well acquainted with Captain Barney since revolutionary times, as they had both joined the struggle for independence, Barney in the Continental Navy and privateers and Smith as an officer in the Maryland Line of the Continental Army. In the postrevolutionary years, Smith and Barney frequently disagreed on politics, with Barney supporting the Federalist cause and Smith, along with his brother Robert, aligned with the Democratic-Republican Party. Barney, though born to a farming family, was a thorough seafaring man who in peacetime sailed as a merchant captain. During the 1790s Barney was offered the command of one of the navy's first frigates but displayed a fulsome sense of honor and pride when he refused the offer because he would have been outranked as captain by Silas Talbot, whom he did not respect. During the Quasi-War with France, he accepted a commission from the French revolutionary government so that he could again fight against the British he so detested. At the outbreak of the War of 1812, as one of the first captains to receive a privateering commission, he made many captures and a small fortune during two cruises in the schooner *Rossie*. When, in the spring and summer of 1813, he was without a ship to command, Barney could not resist being drawn into the excitement about the British navy's exploits in the Chesapeake and what this might portend for Baltimore and its trade. No doubt privy to Senator Smith's efforts to prepare the city's defenses and to protect its shipping, he wrote a now historic letter to Secretary Jones concerning the urgency of establishing a barge flotilla to offset the British navy's dominance in the bay. In his letter, Barney took over where Senator Smith and Captain Gordon had left the matter. He noted the presence of eleven Royal Navy ships of the line and thirty-three frigates, as well as smaller enemy vessels and their Royal Marine complements. In his estimate, the British could possibly count as many as eight thousand combatants who could be thrown against the weakly defended Chesapeake shores. In essence, he wrote, "the question is how to meet this force with a probability of success."[24]

In a well-framed argument, Barney confidently proposed a force of about twenty shoal draft barges, or row galleys, each carrying at least one heavy gun and both oars and sails, that could be used in flying-squadron formations to watch and harass the enemy. These craft could operate from shoals, where the enemy could not reach but from which the barges could sally forth and damage whatever the British chose to use against them. Twenty American flotilla barges would each be manned by 50 officers, sailors, and soldiers, totaling 1,000 officers and men. Each barge could be equipped with one 24-pounder long gun and small arms. Barney suggested that to make the force even more effective, three or four light fast-sailing vessels could be added for use as fireships if the British attempted to anchor. Barney further recommended that old ship hulks be sunk in the channels of the Potomac and Patapsco Rivers to obstruct passage of deep-draft enemy warships, which might attempt to attack the cities of Washington and Baltimore. Armed schooners and floating batteries (block sloops) could be emplaced to reinforce shore batteries protecting the approaches to these ports.

Finally, regarding the issue of expense, which he knew Jones would bring up, Barney estimated that the cost of building fifty barges would be no more than half the cost of building one frigate. In any event, he concluded, "we have no other mode of defense left us." Secretary Jones, though not a partisan of barge warfare, concluded that it was his only option for providing naval defense of Chesapeake Bay and yielded to Barney's arguments. Jones conferred on Barney the rank of acting master commandant of a barge flotilla for operations in the upper Chesapeake. He confided to Barney that this was to be an independent command, reporting directly to Jones and no one else. The officers under his command would be given rank as sailing masters in the navy and would be in charge of the petty officers and enlisted men, all subject to the rules and regulations of the navy as well as receiving the usual pay and rations. They were to be assigned to twelve months of service with the flotilla, and they would not be subject to the draft of any other service. To recruit the needed seamen, Jones ordered Barney to open a rendezvous to sign up "as many men as will man the whole of the new and old barges."[25]

Building the 74s

While the navy's frigates dodged British blockaders and hunted their prey on the high seas, Secretary Jones had major logistical problems to solve in building the long-delayed ships of the line. In late 1798, during the US Navy's Quasi-War with

France, Secretary Benjamin Stoddert proposed building twelve 74-gun ships, the same number of frigates, and twenty or thirty smaller vessels. He believed that these would be sufficient to protect the coast, provide security from invasion, safeguard commerce, and guarantee future peace. Without such a force, the United States would be unable to resist insults and to punish aggression and might indeed be unable to sustain the union of all the states.[26] Stoddert received enough encouragement to request that Joshua Humphreys draw initial plans for the 74s. These ships of the line were to measure 178 feet from stem to stern, 48 feet, 6 inches in breadth, and 19 feet, 6 inches in depth of hold. As discussion of these plans progressed, the secretary decided that the ships should carry 32-pounder guns as standard armament on all decks instead of the mixture of 32s (gun deck), 28s (spar deck), and 9s (quarterdeck and forecastle), even though this required increased displacement and a lengthening of the ship by 5 feet in the midship section, to 183 feet between perpendiculars.

In the closing days of the Adams administration, Congress did not authorize construction of these large warships, but Stoddert and Humphreys had planted the idea, and the plans survived to be used thirteen years later during the War of 1812. Stoddert had also sent orders for contractors to begin cutting the timbers required for six of the 74s, which, when they arrived, were put into storage ponds at the federal navy yards for eventual use when needed. A dozen years later, however, Captain William Bainbridge, at the Charlestown Navy Yard, discovered that many of the timbers that had been set aside were by then "quite decayed" or had been removed by agents of the War Department.[27]

In his November 1812 message to Burwell Bassett, chairman of the House Naval Committee, Secretary Paul Hamilton revived the project of building 74s but referred to them as 76-gun ships, intending them to be of more impressive construction and strength than their British counterpart of 74 guns. Another reason for the increase in the number of guns was a nod of patriotism to the year of American independence, 1776.[28] The House Naval Committee debated the issue for nearly a month, finally concluding its labors on December 23 in a bill that authorized the building and fitting out of four 74-gun ships and six 44-gun frigates. President Madison signed this bill, entitled "An Act to Increase the Navy of the United States," on January 2, 1813. It was the first major naval construction bill in more than a decade.

William Jones anticipated a tightening of the blockade as the months passed. Taking advantage of the favorable turn of naval events in 1812, he pressed Congress for more and smaller ships, such as sloops of war, or corvettes. These vessels were three-masted and ship-rigged though smaller than frigates in profile, having only one gun deck. Yet they were to be powerful, equipped with eighteen

32-pounder carronades and four long 12-pounders. As he explained to Senator Samuel Smith, "Their force is inferior only to a frigate—their cost and expenditure only about one third in actual service, and in pursuit of the commerce and light cruisers of the enemy, three sloops of the class proposed may reasonably be expected to produce a much greater effect than a single frigate. . . . Moreover, they may be more useful in our own waters and the protection of our coasting trade against the depredations of the enemy's light cruisers."[29]

The renewed effort to build 74-gun ships signaled a desire for a more significant, respectable navy and was a nod to the aspirations of the service's senior officers. The 74-gun ship had emerged in the eighteenth century from an innovative French design to become the primary element in the lengthy battle lines of both the British and French fleets. But, in 1813, the US Navy was very far from having enough ships for what could be described as a battle line. Instead of a handful of ships of the line, the Americans required a much larger number of nimble, well-armed cruisers that could serve as commerce destroyers. Secretary Jones understood that and would soon demonstrate a more realistic course in asking Congress to authorize building a class of powerful sloops of war that would be less costly and more quickly built. In a circular to his senior commanders then in port, namely, Rodgers, Bainbridge, Decatur, Stewart, and Morris, he outlined the strategy that would guide them in the months to come:

> It . . . is intended to dispatch all our public ships, now in port, as soon as possible in such positions as may be best adapted to destroy the commerce of the enemy, from the Cape of Good Hope to Cape Clear [off the coast of County Cork, Ireland], and to continue out as long as possible, as long as the means of subsistence be procured in any quarter. If anything can draw the attention of the enemy from the annoyance of our coast for the protection of his own rich and exposed commercial fleets, it will be a course of this nature, and if this effect can be produced, the twofold objective of increasing the pressure on the enemy and relieving ourselves will be obtained.[30]

Nevertheless, Jones must have recognized an eventual need for the 74s, because he proceeded to order construction to begin on three of the four ships of the line authorized by Congress. As early as February 8, 1813, he wrote William Doughty, the new naval constructor at the Washington Navy Yard, to request that he inform Captain Tingey and take charge of the mold loft, with all of its drafts, plans, books, and instruments. Jones wanted to have a report on all the timber on hand for construction of a new frigate in the yard, and he wished to inspect the drafts for construction of a 74-gun ship, as well as the plans for the frigate *Congress*.[31] On the very next day, he wrote to Amos Binney, the navy agent at Boston, to order the immediate procurement of the materials to build a 74-gun ship at Boston. If timber were not on hand, he was to have the trees cut during the winter season to avoid another year's delay.[32] With a sense of urgency, Jones moved on to communicate with George Harrison, the navy's agent in Philadelphia. He reported that he desired the shipwrights Samuel Humphreys and Charles Penrose to collaborate in the building of a 74-gun ship at the Philadelphia Navy Yard while James and Franklin Grice started to superintend and direct work in their private shipyard on a new 44-gun frigate to be completed "to a cleat." He ordered Harrison to oversee their purchase and collection of all the timber necessary for the project (fig. 6.1).[33]

In April, Captain Isaac Hull, then in charge of the Boston Navy Yard, received orders to command the Portsmouth Navy Yard in New Hampshire. There he was to commence construction of the 74-gun ship *Washington* with timbers that had been sent in the late 1790s by Secretary Stoddert. Hull soon discovered that much of the supply of live oak had either rotted in the holding areas (docks) or been used

Figure 6.1. USS *Washington*, 74, built at Portsmouth, New Hampshire, 1814. Watercolor by Francois Roux, 1829. US Naval History and Heritage Command, Photograph NH 63582.

for other purposes. Bainbridge, replacing Hull at Boston, had the same experience, although judging from their subsequent correspondence, Bainbridge had an ampler supply.[34] The live oak could only be obtained from the southern coastal areas, as had been the case in the 1790s; after cutting, shaping, and shipping, it would have to be seasoned to have maximum strength. Live oak was reputed to have five times the durability of the white oak traditionally used in New England for structural members in shipbuilding.[35] Its disadvantage was its density, its great weight, and the difficulty of cutting and transporting. The navy had bought the timber from landowners on Ossabaw, Blackbeard, St. Simon, and Hawkins Islands in Georgia in the 1790s, but as these became extensively logged between 1800 and 1815, new sources were sought in Florida and Louisiana.[36] Plaguing both Bainbridge and Hull at the time were the British blockaders, who were interdicting coastal shipping, hence the difficulty of obtaining more live oak.[37] Because of the terrible condition of roads at the time and the great distance from the source to the shipyards in the middle Atlantic and New England seaports, if they were not shipped by water, these massive, weighty timbers simply would not be available. Bainbridge had a larger supply of live oak than did Hull, and Jones strongly opposed substituting white oak in lieu of live oak. Bainbridge needed white oak for hull planking, so the two commandants arranged a swap of these essential materials.[38]

By August 1813, Hull still lacked sufficient live oak. He was eventually able to persuade Jones that the white oak was perfectly seasoned and that substituting it for live oak would not negatively affect the ship's longevity.[39] Jones had his way in altering the original design for the 74. He wished to enlarge the hull, lengthening it by 5 feet to 190 feet overall and widening it by 10 inches to 54 feet. This made the American 74s somewhat larger than those of Britain and France. Apparently, he had consulted Joshua Humphreys about the wisdom of doing this, and the latter, then well into his retirement, had agreed. But whether Humphreys also agreed to altering the sheer from concave to practically horizontal, or "straight," is not known. Jones, who fancied himself a naval architect, insisted on this change to both Hull and Bainbridge. This had an unfortunate effect on the ships' seaworthiness, resulting in a loss of buoyancy that reduced the ships' freeboard and tended to submerge their lower gunports in heavy winds and seas.[40] Writing to Jones later in the year, Hull said he still had doubts about altering the sheer of the 74s: "It is clearly my opinion that they are to [too] straight and that they will be hogged in six months after they are launched, if they are not in the launching itself. . . . You did not ask my opinion on this subject, consequently, it is an intrusion, but I hope you will pardon it when I assure you that I have been led to it from no other views than that of being devoted to the service."[41]

Jones, who had already given his judgment on this issue and agreed with Bainbridge, did not respond. To protect his precious ship, Hull made further requests. He proposed to build a housing to cover the ship's frame completely during the harsh New Hampshire winter and storehouses for the preservation of supplies, as well as an ammunition magazine. To discourage British raiding parties, Hull requisitioned guns. He managed to gather thirty of varying caliber, which he distributed to four fortifications covering the approaches to Portsmouth harbor. It was more difficult to find soldiers and militia to man the batteries owing to the lack of enthusiasm of New Hampshire's Federalist governor, John Taylor Gilman, toward even defensive military activities until an actual threat appeared. Ultimately, Secretary Jones provided a guard of US Marines for the navy yard and ordered two brigs, *Enterprise* and *Siren*, to provide protection for shipping along the Massachusetts–New Hampshire coast.[42] *Siren*, commanded by Captain Bainbridge's brother Joseph, did not arrive, having put in at Boston for extensive repairs, but *Enterprise*, commanded by Master Commandant William Burrows, did her duty in a decisive defeat of the HM brig *Boxer* off Monhegan Island, about thirty miles to the east of Portland, Maine, on September 5, 1813.[43] Samuel Blyth, *Boxer*'s commander, had long been harassing New England's coastal trade and privateers while being complicit in protecting ongoing smuggling operations. Both Burrows and Blyth were killed in the close action that took many more British sailors' lives than it did American lives because of *Enterprise*'s heavier guns and more accurate firing. The two commanding officers were buried side by side in an elaborate funeral ceremony in Portland on September 8.

The Blockade Strengthens

By midsummer 1813 the Royal Navy's presence off the US coast was triple what it had been when the United States declared war in June 1812. Admiral Warren had stationed ships of the line, each paired with one or two frigates, strategically along the most likely commercial routes. *La Hogue*, 74, and *Tenedos*, 44, were on the northern edge of the Grand Banks. *Poictiers*, 74, and *Maidstone*, 36, patrolled off Sable Island, Nova Scotia. *Ramillies*, 74, and *Loire*, 40, were on distant blockade off Boston, while *Majestic*, 58, *Junon*, 38, and *Wasp*, 18, held inshore stations guarding the entrance to Massachusetts Bay. On Rhode Island Sound *Orpheus*, 36, and *Loup Cervier*, 18, controlled access to Newport, while four ships, *Valiant*, 74, *Acasta*, 44, *Atalante*, 18, and *Borer*, 14, patrolled from New London to Block Island and eastern Long Island. Farther south, *Plantagenet*, 74, was stationed off Sandy Hook and had access to New York; the entrance to Delaware Bay was guarded by *Statira*, 38, *Belvidera*, 36, and *Morgiana*, 18; and *Dragon*, 74, *Lacedemonian*, 38, *Armide*, 38,

Doterel, 18, and *Mohawk*, 12, dominated Chesapeake Bay. These vessels were in constant motion, reinforcing each other as necessary and occasionally changing station due to bad weather or the need for repairs, in which case the nearest base was Halifax. The wisdom of these arrangements became apparent on June 1, 1813, when *Shannon*, then stationed off Boston, defeated and captured the frigate *Chesapeake*. On that same day, Commodore Robert Oliver's *Valiant*, in company with *Acasta* and *Orpheus*, blocked the escape of Commodore Decatur's frigates *United States* and *Macedonian* at Block Island, forcing the American ships to turn back to New London, where they remained for the duration of the war.[44]

Smuggling and the Licensed Trade

While this news was truly discouraging, Secretary William Jones kept to his task. The Navy Department did not grind to a halt, but events became more difficult for him to manage. For one thing, with more blockading ships on station, there was an increase in the smuggling trade, which in part had become his responsibility to discourage, especially on the northern coast of New England. With a good number of New Englanders disenchanted with the war and, if they were fisherman or merchant sailors, deprived of their usual ways of earning a living, many had turned to smuggling with their contacts in the Maritime Provinces.

The British policy of encouraging the "licensed trade" caused additional frustration for Secretary Jones. With the British army then fighting against the French army in Spain, there was an enormous need for flour and other foodstuffs for British troops in Spain, timber for English dockyards, and cattle and flour for the British West Indies. Consequently, British consulates were authorized by the Crown to issue licenses to American merchantmen allowing them to pass through the blockade after they had been halted and inspected. Surprisingly, the United States had not prohibited the licensed trade with the enemy even though war had been declared and was being actively fought on the high seas. That the Madison administration had not acted to make the trade illegal by late December 1812 aroused Commodore Stephen Decatur's indignation. He forwarded to Secretary Hamilton several licenses seized from the American ship *Mandarin*, stating, "I thought it might be of some service to have the government apprised of the extent to which this trade seemed enlarging itself under the protection of the Enemy and of the individuals involved in it."[45] For their part, British consuls encouraged these licensed American traders to sail under a foreign flag and included language in the documents permitting vessels to sail to a neutral port such as St. Bartholomew to avoid seizure of the licenses by US naval commanders, as Decatur had done.[46]

Early in 1813, President Madison finally decided to act on the question of the licensed trade. He sent a special message to Congress asking for legislation to outlaw the use of foreign trading licenses and to ban ships from trading under a foreign flag. The House of Representatives cooperated, but the Senate refused because the Federalists from New England did not want their merchant constituents to be denied the use of these licenses. This congressional policy remained in effect another six months despite its unpatriotic acceptance of trading with the enemy.

It was not until a ruling by the Supreme Court associate justice Joseph Story on a case involving the frigate *Chesapeake* that the government position changed.[47] In December 1812, *Chesapeake*, then commanded by Captain Samuel Evans, was cruising off the Atlantic coast when Evans hailed and halted the ship *Julia*, an American merchantman returning from Lisbon to Boston. On inspection, she was found to possess on board several documents of British origin, including one of the infamous "Sidmouths," a license permitting *Julia* to pass through the blockade unmolested by British blockaders.[48] This was reason enough to claim her as a prize of war. Evans placed a navy prize master on board and sent her to her intended destination. At that point the master, who was a part owner, objected to the condemnation proceedings, claiming ignorance of the documents found on board. This defense was refuted on testimony of the prize master and others of the crew. The Massachusetts circuit court ruled for the government's claim of fair capture in July 1813. *Julia*'s owners appealed, and the case ended up in the US Supreme Court where Justice Story wrote a scathing opinion upholding the lower court's opinion, stating that "it is sufficient to declare as the result . . . that we hold that the sailing on a voyage under the license and passport of protection of the enemy in furtherance of his views or interests constitutes such an act of illegality as subjects the ship and cargo to confiscation as a prize of war, and that the facts of the present case afford irrefragable evidence of such illegality."[49]

In late July 1813, Jones issued a general order to his senior officers informing them that certain "profligate citizens" had been observed proceeding toward the enemy's ships with the apparent intention of supplying them with produce, water, and intelligence on the whereabouts of US naval and military forces. He urged his officers to be vigilant in the execution of measures to prevent passing assistance and intelligence to the enemy, but they were to take care not to injure those (presumably fisherman) who were "pursuing their lawful occupations."[50]

The Cruise of *Essex*, 1812–1814

The frigate *Essex*, 36, was one of the subscription ships that had been built and transferred to the navy by the citizens of Salem, Massachusetts, at the outset of the

Quasi-War with France. She had been an active ship for most of her career and had been commanded by Captain Edward Preble on a voyage to Sumatra in 1801, making her the first US Navy warship to sail into the Indian and Pacific Oceans. At the outbreak of the War of 1812, Captain David Porter informed the Navy Department that his ship was not yet ready for sea, needing repairs to her bottom copper and her masts. When Porter sailed on July 3, *Essex* was in fighting trim; however, he later complained to Secretary Hamilton about his main armament being a battery of 32-pounder carronades (powerful but short-range), when he would have preferred long guns or at least a combination of the two types. This would have given him the option of fighting at long or shorter distances when conditions favored. This shortcoming had a disastrous effect later in Porter's cruise (map 6.1).

Captain Porter's *Essex* had been assigned to operate with Commodore Bainbridge's squadron in the South Atlantic.[51] He sailed from the Delaware River in late October. En route, Porter overtook and captured the brig *Nocton*, a British packet carrying $55,000 in specie. He failed to find Bainbridge at the island of Fernao de Noronha but picked up a message from him held by the Brazilian authorities. Porter steered for Cabo Frio but again could find no trace. Heading southward, Porter sailed for Santa Catarina, in southern Brazil, the most remote of rendezvous points mentioned by Bainbridge. He arrived there short of provisions on January 20, 1813, and found no sign of Bainbridge.

By then so far south and without definite instructions, Porter had a difficult choice: he could either head for the shipping lanes off St. Helena, far to the east, or interpret his discretionary orders so liberally as to depart for the Pacific Ocean. Earlier in his career he had asked for but been denied permission to conduct a voyage of exploration in the Pacific, so perhaps this explains his next move. He rounded Cape Horn and shaped a course for Valparaiso. Then he cruised off the west coast of South America for the next fifteen months, until March 1814, when his luck ran out.[52]

The political situation in Chile was turbulent when Porter arrived. Since the French invasion of Spain in 1807, the Viceroyalty of Peru had been divided between royalists, who favored the king of Spain, and those who favored a republican style of government. In Chile, a junta led by President Jose Miguel Carrera pronounced itself in opposition to the viceroy and in favor of self-rule for Chile. Thus, when Porter's *Essex* arrived in Valparaiso, he and other anti-royalists saw his ship as a possible ally in their uprising. Joel Poinsett, the American consul general, served as intermediary between Porter and the junta, assisting in resupply of Porter's ship. When Porter found that American merchant shipping had been harassed by royalist privateers, he proceeded to retake the American vessels and pursue the privateers.

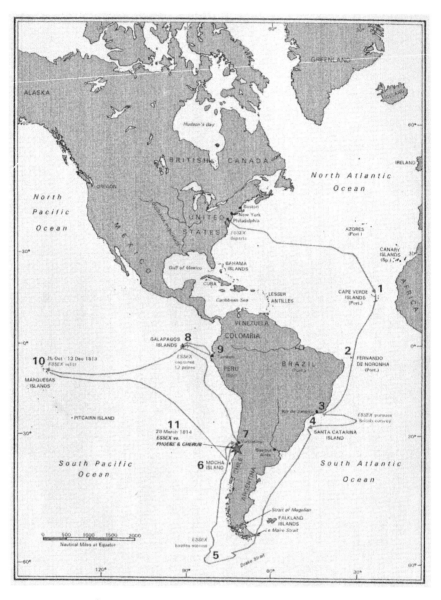

Map 6.1. Cruise of USS *Essex*, December 1812–March 1814. Reprinted by permission from Craig. L. Symonds, *The Naval Institute Historical Atlas of the U.S. Navy*, Cartography by William J. Clipson, © 1995 (Annapolis, MD: Naval Institute Press).

For several months, from April until early October 1813, Porter made his base of operations the Galapagos Islands, off Ecuador. During this time, *Essex* captured twelve British whaling vessels, while provisioning the crew from the islands and the captured ships. But after nearly a year at sea, Porter realized that *Essex* needed extensive repairs, and the crew was delighted to learn he had chosen the Marquesas Islands for their new base. There Porter and his officers had to contend with local feuds among tribes anxious to have the Americans and their weapons as allies. By this time, Porter had learned that the Admiralty had been informed of *Essex*'s rampage in the Pacific and sent HMS *Phoebe*, 36, *Cherub*, 18, and *Raccoon*, 18, to search for and destroy her. In December, with his repairs complete, Porter believed his next mission was to confront Captain James Hillyar's *Phoebe*, then awaiting *Essex*'s return to Valparaiso.[53]

Porter reached Valparaiso in January, but when Hillyar arrived a month later with the sloop of war *Cherub* in company, the odds shifted against Porter. Although *Raccoon* had been sent on to Astoria to assist the Canadian Northwest Company's outpost, *Phoebe* and *Cherub*, combined, surpassed *Essex* in the number and, most importantly, the type of guns they carried, which included long guns as well as carronades. They blockaded the port to prevent *Essex*'s escape. Porter tried to challenge Hillyar to a one-on-one engagement, but Hillyar refused.

After six weeks of waiting, Porter knew he had a chance to break into the open sea when a storm swept into Valparaiso Bay. Riding a fierce gale, Porter conned *Essex* out of the harbor, followed by his British opponents. Suddenly, a gust snapped *Essex*'s main topmast, crippling her speed and maneuverability. Porter sailed for the eastern side of the bay and anchored within Chile's territorial limits, where he thought the Royal Navy's respect for international law would protect him from attack. Sadly for Porter and his crew, Hillyar now saw his main chance and attacked with long guns, carefully standing clear of Porter's carronades. *Phoebe* and *Cherub* pounded *Essex* until she was unable to fight any further. His crew having suffered severe casualties, fifty-eight dead and sixty-five wounded, Porter surrendered. Captain Hillyar gave Porter and his men their paroles and allowed them to sail back to the United States in *Essex Junior*, one of the prizes he had taken. Near the end of Porter's long voyage in *Essex Junior*, he encountered HMS *Saturn*, commanded by Captain James Nash, off Sandy Hook. Porter produced the safe conduct provided to him by Captain Hillyar. As all seemed in order, Nash allowed Porter to proceed, but two hours later, without explanation, *Saturn* again detained Porter's ship. That night, Porter escaped in his ship's whaleboat and made landfall at Babylon, Long Island, thanks to a timely fog bank.[54] Porter arrived safely back in New York in July 1814, just in time to travel south to Washington and assist Commodore Rodgers in the defense of Alexandria. One of Porter's surviving officers was his adopted son, David Glasgow Farragut, later an admiral in the Civil War. At the age of twelve, Midshipman Farragut commanded one of Porter's prizes in the eastern Pacific.[55]

The increasing effectiveness of the British blockade along the Atlantic coast pinched off maritime transport of ship's timber, such as live oak, as well as heavy armament needed for ships and fortifications. This strategy forced the US Navy to take up innovative tactics that today are considered part of asymmetrical warfare, the techniques favored by smaller, weaker powers in conflict with larger, wealthier, more capable enemies. These tactics include barge warfare on estuaries and internal waterways, the shift of naval assets from the seacoast to lake warfare, encouragement of privateering, mine warfare, and technical innovation in ship propulsion, namely, application of steam technology in naval shipbuilding. Future chapters demonstrate how these logistical techniques came into play as Americans sought to continue the war against their more powerful British enemy.

CHAPTER 7

Managing the Navy Department

During his first weeks in office, Secretary William Jones found himself overwhelmed by the details of supplying the Navy Department. He proposed to remedy this by creating a purveyor's (supply) department with attendant deputies to whom he could delegate the contracting for the provisions needed by the navy's ships and stations. This department's deputies would reside in seaport towns, where the state of the market for various necessities could be ascertained. The navy secretary would retain central and general direction of all important contracts to be entered into by the purveyor. This was an eminently reasonable proposal, yet two days after sending it to Congress, Jones withdrew it, stating that on second thought he would prefer to test the idea before making a formal request and that in view of other pressing financial needs he would be content for the time being with adding two clerks to his office staff.[1] With that decision, William Jones had to shoulder the responsibility of acting as his own purveyor general.

Supplies and Provisions

The secretary's day-to-day concerns ranged from the mundane to the hugely important. On the very day that he presented this concern about contracting, he also informed the House Naval Committee of his intention to commence construction of six sloops of war, a major addition to the plans for constructing ships of the line and frigates that Hamilton had proposed in November 1812. The procurement, distribution, and recordation of transactions for myriad items and jobs needed for ships and shipyards were a major part of the Navy Department's workload.

Beginning in 1794, it became immediately apparent that hundreds of contracted individuals would be involved in the creation of a navy. Secretary of War Henry Knox sent out the following notice to all concerned in this business:

To the Agents:
  Sirs: You having accepted of the agency of the ship of war to be built at
  _____, are to consider the rules herein specified as the general principles
  whereby to govern yourselves in the execution of your agency.

1st. You are to provide all the artificers and laborers of all descriptions, except the contractor or master builder, necessary to build a ship of _____ guns, the number to be such, from time to time, as will be able to operate with greatest effect; these workmen to be provided upon the best terms, by the day, week, or month, as you shall judge conducive to the public interests.

2^{d}. You are also to purchase such materials for the construction and equipment of the said ship as shall not otherwise be provided by special contracts, under the orders of the Secretary of the Treasury, and to pay all other incidental or contingent expenses.

3^{d}. All workmen and materials for building the said ship, are to be obtained by you upon the estimate or requisition in writing by the constructor, countersigned by the captain or superintendent. Other articles or labor, necessary for the rigging or equipment of the ship, are to be obtained by you upon the estimate of the principal artificer in each branch, and also countersigned by the captain.[2]

These rules governing the relations of the agents and officials responsible to the government for the construction, repair, and supply of these and future warships remained relatively unchanged except that with the creation of the Department of the Navy in 1798 Secretary of the Navy Stoddert replaced Secretary of War McHenry. Following this essential act, the department laid down rules for the internal administration of its ships in the *Marine Rules and Regulations* of 1798 and in *Naval Regulations of 1802*. In the latter document the specific duties of ships' officers were elaborated by department.[3]

The Navy Agents

Acting under the aegis of the secretary, the navy agents were civilians, perhaps merchants, often in business for themselves, whose duties were to purchase naval supplies such as timber, rope, canvas, and other equipment for building and fitting out ships, cannons, gunpowder, muskets, provisions (food and beverages), clothing, tobacco, and other items considered necessary for crews' comfort. Some agents lived far from the sea, such as Oliver Ormsby, at Pittsburgh, who supplied the naval station at Erie, Pennsylvania, and General William Helms, at Newport, Tennessee, who supplied the New Orleans naval station. Others previously had resided abroad at the Mediterranean ports of Palermo, Messina, and Syracuse in Sicily, from which the navy's operating squadrons were supplied during the Barbary Wars.[4] The letter of appointment of John Broadbent, an American merchant in Messina, shows what was expected of a navy agent in a foreign port:

Sir, I do hereby appoint you agent for the squadron of the United States under my command in the Mediterranean. Authorizing you to purchase supplies as may be wanted for the use of said squadron, to issue the same and to transact all business as is generally transacted by Agents. You will at all times supply the ships & vessels of the squadron with such articles as they want, on the requisition of their respective commanders, taking duplicate receipts for the same. From the representation I have made to the navy department, I have no doubt that the President of the U.S. will confirm you as Navy Agent for this place.[5]

Those navy agents who were most active during the War of 1812 were John Bullus, New York; George Harrison, Philadelphia; Oliver Ormsby, Pittsburgh; Josiah Randall, Annapolis; Amos Binney, Boston; Samuel Storer, Portland; John Langdon, Portsmouth; James Beatty, Baltimore; John Robertson, Charleston; William Joyner, Beaufort, South Carolina; John K. Smith, New Orleans; and General William Helms, Newport, Tennessee. At the beginning of the war most navy agents were understocked and overwhelmed by the demands from the fleet. Boston's agent, Amos Binney, recalled in 1822 what it had been like when Commodore Rodgers's squadron returned to Boston:

In August. or September [1812], the whole squadron came into port. Every ship required complete supplies of provisions and every kind of stores. I was but newly appointed, had no experience, no precedents, no forms, no instructions; was obliged to form a whole system from the chaos that surrounded me, was always short or destitute of funds. I resorted to the bank and to my friends for money on loans and on interest, was soon overwhelmed with requisitions from the public ships in every department—pursers, boatswains, carpenters, gunners, armorers, and frequently had half a dozen midshipmen, with as many boats' crews calling for stores, etc. I could not be with or serve everyone at once, and hence was obliged to confide much of the business in detail to persons I believed honest and faithful.[6]

Pursers

The Navy Department required each command to have a purser or acting purser, who would act as the ship's supply officer and paymaster. Pursers were warrant officers, not in the line of command, and thus could not be promoted. To qualify for a purser's warrant, they had to establish a record of work in a counting house or other business establishment or a familiarity with ship's business, having previously served as a captain's clerk or chaplain. There was no prescribed course of training for the position, which may explain why a number of pursers were unable to settle their accounts at the end of their careers and remained indebted to the government for the rest of their lives.

When a ship or station needed supplies, it was the purser's responsibility to send or deliver requisitions for these supplies to the navy agents. If no agent was available, the purser would have to pay for the supplies on the local economy and keep exact records of government monies expended and copies of receipts given. The purser was directly responsible to the commanding officer for attending to the provisioning of the ship, but as the ship's "money man," he also reported to the navy accountant (fourth auditor) in the Treasury Department for all the funds placed at his disposal. The purser paid the salaries of the ship's officers and the wages of the enlisted men, as well as the bills for ship's provisions, stores, and consumables. The purser had an assigned steward to whom he could delegate the distribution of what in today's navy would be called "small stores," articles of clothing, and items of comfort sailors craved that were not part of the ship's rations, such as coffee, tea, sugar, and tobacco. The purser was allowed to charge a commission of 10–12 percent on these items, which augmented his small salary and rations allowance; however, some unethical pursers exploited sailors by charging excessive rates on the goods he sold them. This provided grounds for congressional investigations and explained the poor reputation of pursers in general among the navy's enlisted men.[7]

An example from before the War of 1812 of the provisions needed for a ship with a crew of four hundred sailors on a six-month (longer than usual) cruise would be those for *Constitution* under the command of Captain Edward Preble. According to the Boston merchant Samuel Brown's accounts, when Preble was preparing to depart for the Mediterranean in 1803 his purser, James Deblois, needed the following: 20,000 lb. bread, 1,300 lb. rice, 36,000 lb. butter, 31,200 lb. pork, 650 gal. molasses, 10,400 lb. flour, 650 gal. vinegar, 5,200 lb. suet, 500 lb. wax candles, 1,300 lb. peas/beans, and 500 lb. molded tallow candles.[8] On inspection, one finds that this allowed only a quarter pound of bread, a quarter pound of pork, barely a handful of rice, and small quantities of the other provisions per man per day. This made for many meager meals for the crew during half a year unless other sources of resupply were found.

Commodore Preble's internal standing orders for the purser's duties, elaborating on the *Naval Regulations of 1802*, provide a revealing insight into a purser's routine on board any taut navy ship.[9] There were eight orders, paraphrased below:

1. On arrival in port, the purser is to take early measures to supply the ship with fuel and necessities of every sort to last at least until the ship is sched-

uled to be resupplied. In case of any difficulties, he is to state such in writing to the commanding officer before the ship is ready for sea.

2. He is required to see that the purser's steward and attendant keep the stewards' room, the bread room, and the passageway clean and neatly arranged.

3. The key to the stewards' room is to be kept by the first lieutenant or the commanding officer, who will deliver it to the purser from 7 until 10 in the morning and from 4 until 7 in the afternoon and at such other times as may be necessary.

4. Upon receiving slops (clothing), the purser is to examine them carefully for size and quality and report to the captain any that prove to be different in size and quality.

5. The purser is to pay great attention to the instructions directing which of the oldest provisions are to be served first in order to prevent having to do vast surveys because of keeping provisions, especially cheese, overly long.

6. No change or alteration whatever is to be made in the ship's company provisions without the captain's particular direction.

7. The purser is to visit every Saturday the stewards' room, the bread room, and the slops room with the master and carpenter to point out any leaks, damp, or injuries his stores may be suffering from those or any other causes. On no account should a selection of choice pieces of beef be taken for the officers when it is being cut up for the ship's company, and no choice pieces of salt meat are to be set aside for the officers when they are intended for the whole ship's company. Officers do not select for their own use the best wine or spirits when they are intended for the Ship's Company.

8. The purser is to make immediate notice to the captain on the discovery of any provisions that may be found unwholesome or unfit for men to eat and to report without delay any instance of any part of the crew that refuses the provisions, or murmurs at, or complain of the quality of these provisions.[10]

While Commodore Preble's detailed orders were based on the naval regulations of that time, it is fair to presume that later ship commanders generally followed suit and may have made slight modifications, depending on the personalities and preferences of those commanders. It is notable that Preble took care that no favoritism was to be shown to officers when it came to distributing portions of meat, wine, and spirits.

A captain's main responsibility to the navy and his crew was to maintain operational readiness in all respects and upon return from a war patrol to have his ship repaired and refitted. As Commodore Rodgers wrote to Secretary Hamilton in January 1813, "Just returned back from an 11,000-mile cruise in company with *Congress* (Captain John Smith), experienced much weather, both ships will require considerable outfit in spars, sails, and rigging. *President's* copper defective in several places. Will be necessary to heave her out. *President* has a sprung mainmast— needs a new one." While this work went on at the Boston Navy Yard, Rodgers had to order the recruiting of new crew members to replace those whose enlistments had expired; at the same time, it was essential to requisition provisions for those exhausted during the cruise. Since the ship would have to be careened, or as he said, "heaved out," that is, pulled over first onto one side and then onto the other, in order to inspect and replace the copper sheathing on its hull, everything of significant weight, including ballast and guns, would have to be removed to avoid unnecessary stress on the hull. Only after the completion of this work on both sides of the hull could the ship be re-rigged, reballasted, and reprovisioned. Rodgers concluded, "I am anxious to get to Sea again, and no time shall be lost in refitting both Ships."[11]

Provisioning for Operations

For those commanders preparing their ships to return to sea in early 1813, refitting and reprovisioning for long-term operations was critical. The key was to avoid having to return to their home ports during the relatively mild weather of late spring and summer, when they would have to contend with the layered distant and coastal blockade of British 74s and frigates. As Captain Decatur expressed it to Secretary Jones, "From the information I have of the preparation of the enemy there is no doubt that our whole coast will be lined with his men of war during the summer months. This presents but little difficulty to our going out but will render our return during the mild season extremely hazardous. I would prefer to remain out as long as possible and by all means until the approach of the autumnal equinox when the attention of the enemy will be occupied in providing for his own safety." Decatur intended to take on board as much provisioning as possible and recommended that the government send a "confidential agent" in a neutral ship to Cape Verde to wait with supplies for his arrival.[12]

Whether Secretary Jones implemented this suggestion is not documented; the likely conclusion is that he did not. Nonetheless, the idea bore fruit in 1815, when a cruise carried out by the brig *Hornet* (James Biddle) and the sloop of war *Peacock* (Lewis Warrington) made rendezvous with the storeship schooner *Tom Bowline* (B. V. Hoffman) at the islands of Tristan da Cunha in the South Atlantic.[13] Soon thereafter, on March 23, *Hornet* engaged HMS *Penguin* in a fierce battle from which Biddle survived wounded though victorious. *Tom Bowline* provided a valuable service by taking on board the British prisoners and delivering them to Rio de Janeiro. The damaged *Hornet* and her consorts remained at Tristan for two weeks, repairing and provisioning, before *Hornet* returned to New York and *Peacock* extended her cruise into the Indian Ocean.

Coping with the Blockade

In late March 1813, Secretary Jones took stock of his situation. He had reduced the number of gunboats in commission in order to provide seamen and officers for seagoing ships and the lakes flotillas. At the same time, he was seeking to tamp down the many requests from citizens concerned about the safety of their seaports. Many people understood that soon British warships would bring the war to American waters, and they wondered who would provide protection for their waterfront homes and businesses. Jones had to work to placate those concerned while taking the long view of the navy he was intent on building. He was undertaking to move forward his favorite projects, such as the building of the 74s and the development of a new class of sloops of war, the ship-sloops. His orders had gone out to navy agents to procure the timbers necessary for the shipbuilding. He had sent orders for the building of several more 44-gun frigates and was urging his commanders on the northern lakes to push ahead in the building of their squadrons, which were sure to be challenged by their British counterparts in the months ahead. One of the last ship-to-ship battles of the 1812–13 campaign season had ended well. Captain James Lawrence, of the sloop of war *Hornet*, had returned to Holmes Hole (now Vineyard Haven), Martha's Vineyard, with news of his complete victory over the HM brig *Peacock* (William Peake).[14] As a reward, Lawrence was due for rotation ashore, and Jones obliged with orders to take command of the New York Navy Yard, succeeding Master Commandant William Crane.

Unfortunately for Lawrence, this assignment was not long-lived. Captain Samuel Evans, commander of the frigate *Chesapeake*, returned in early April from a three-month cruise that had taken him as far south as the Demerara (British Guiana) coast of South America. His meager capture of five vessels did not impress Secretary Jones, whose main concern was that he refit as soon as possible and get out to sea. As Jones wrote, "Time . . . is precious, for the effect of our limited force depends on its constant activity and enter prize." But Evans was exhausted, and his eyesight suffered from an old wound. He first asked to be given a shore command in order to recuperate but then requested a leave of absence. Faced with this, Jones again had to shuffle his commandants at the New York Navy Yard, reassigning James Lawrence first to the New York Navy Yard to replace Evans, then to *Constitution*, and finally to *Chesapeake* when Captain Charles Stewart, senior to Lawrence, requested the command of *Constitution*.[15] Thus, despite his longings for home and hearth, Lawrence ended up on a ship he did not want to command, at least at that time. Why? Secretary Jones had run out of options. *Chesapeake* was available, he lacked other officers with the requisite qualifications, and Lawrence had these qualities plus a sterling reputation in the eyes of the public.

In the midst of getting the navy's ships ready for sea in the second season of the war, Jones was approached by the wealthy fur trader John Jacob Astor, who made a remarkable request. Astor's American Fur Company had founded a sub-sidiary, the Pacific Fur Company, which had established a fur-trading post in 1811 near the mouth of the Columbia River in the "Oregon Country," in the Pacific Northwest, overlapping with British-claimed territory. Astor was concerned, with reason, that the outbreak of war would result in a British attack on his trading post, and he urged the secretary to send a well-supplied navy ship to Astoria to assert dominance in the region and protect American (and his) claims. It had be-come known that the Montreal-based Northwest Company had designs on As-tor's trading post. Jones, with President Madison's assent, ordered Master Com-mandant William Crane to prepare the frigate *John Adams* for this special, secret mission. Crane visited Jones at his Washington office and received oral instruc-tions. Jones followed up with specific orders in writing, based on his own experi-ence in long-distance merchant voyages:

> The nature of the service requires very great attention to the equipment, Stores and provisions, with a view to the utmost possible extension of time, and of such na-ture and quality as will occupy the least space, be least liable to decay, and com-prehend the most vegetable and anti-scorbutic substances. Your hospital Stores must be laid in with great judgment, and your provisions should comprehend a large proportion of Rice, kiln-dried Indian Meal, Molasses, Sourcrout, essence of spruce, Cremtatar, Slops, vinegar, beans and flour packed in tight barrels with the inside of the staves and heads charred to a coal, pickled cucumbers, &, &, and a great abundance of dried herbs, pressed into boxes, for culinary and medicinal purposes. . . . Your Military Stores must be of the best description and put up with care. You will require a skilled Armorer and a good Smith, with tools and conve-niences for erecting a forge, with a supply of bar, bolt, and hoop iron.[16]

Jones was careful to instruct this young officer who would be involved in a highly sensitive mission at a great distance from home waters. The secretary showed his tendency toward a detailed management style when it suited his purposes, in this case for logistical preparations. For the next two months, Crane labored to make alterations to his ship and recruit a crew and officers to his liking. He was nearly ready to depart when Jones suddenly canceled his orders. Much to Astor's consternation, the demands of the war on Lake Ontario had superseded his project. One can only imagine the disappointment of Commander Crane, as well, when he received orders sending him and his crew to join Commodore Chauncey's squadron at Sackets Harbor.

"The Inglorious First of June"

On the Atlantic coast, the navy's frigates were having increasing difficulties in executing their planned operations. Having taken command of *Chesapeake*, Captain James Lawrence had to deal with a crew that had not received their reward of prize money from their previous cruise, under Captain Evans. There was a dispute between Captain Evans and Commodore Decatur as to whether Decatur deserved a commodore's share since he had been absent and ashore, preparing a new squadron for operations.[17] In his situation, Lawrence had no say in the delivery of the prize money, but he felt under pressure to take his ship to sea regardless of whether the crew had been properly paid. The crew, however, felt differently and voiced their discontent to Lawrence the day before they sailed. For their complaints, Lawrence reportedly called them a "set of rascals" and directed them to prepare to get the ship under way. At the same time, Lawrence was having a similar dispute with Commodore Bainbridge over the prize money gained from Lawrence's defeat of HMS *Peacock* in March 2013. Bainbridge was claiming the commodore's share, though he had been hundreds of miles away from the scene of the action. Lawrence and Bainbridge met the evening before *Chesapeake*'s last sortie to resolve the issue.

On the morning of June 1, 1813, Lawrence's mood must have been unsettled as he unmoored his ship and prepared to give battle to HMS *Shannon*, commanded by Captain Philip Broke, waiting a few miles off Cape Ann. The battle was a disaster for the US Navy. Through an excess of zeal, Lawrence threw caution to the wind and aligned his ship for a yardarm-to-yardarm brawl, when he could have maneuvered more adroitly or waited to avoid battle altogether. Some three months earlier, Secretary Jones had ordered that his captains' primary objective was the British merchant fleet, not their warships.[18] Lawrence, however, was a proud man. He probably saw *Shannon*'s bold lack of maneuver as a personal challenge and chose to disregard the wishes of the secretary. The battle was a short one, lasting only twenty minutes. *Shannon* gained the upper hand through superior gunnery and grappled *Chesapeake* close as they battered each other. Lawrence fell fatally wounded and was taken below as Captain Broke and *Shannon*'s crew boarded and gained the victory. When last seen in American waters,

Chesapeake was under Royal Navy command escorted by *Shannon* as they headed for Halifax.[19]

Chesapeake's defeat and capture delivered a blow to the navy's morale since it was completely unexpected after the frigate victories of the previous year, but that was not the only impact. In the confusion of battle, neither Lawrence nor his officers had thought to dispose of the ship's signal books; thus a valuable set of the navy's secret signals had fallen into Captain Broke's hands. The Admiralty realized that this coup meant that British ships equipped with the American signals could lure their enemy into close quarters and proceeded to have copies made for British cruisers. Likewise, Secretary Jones was quick to act. As he wrote Bainbridge, "It is indeed a source of regret that our signals should have fallen into the hands of the enemy; and it is certainly of utmost importance that they should be so constructed, as that private Signals would be unintelligible to him." He ordered Bainbridge to confer with Captains Hull and Decatur to prepare new signals and to take every opportunity to inform the other commanders that the enemy was in possession of the American signals. Bainbridge did so and advised Jones that commanders, having read the private signals, should destroy them and only communicate them to the first lieutenant on the probability of getting into action and then only "with the strictest injunction of secrecy." Jones replied that he had accepted Bainbridge's signal system with some modifications. He confided that Bainbridge's former first lieutenant, Master Commandant George Parker, would deliver the packet of new signals and requested Bainbridge to provide copies to all the commanders on his station.[20]

On the same day that James Lawrence and *Chesapeake* suffered defeat, Commodore Stephen Decatur Jr. in *United States*, Captain Jacob Jones in *Macedonian*, and Master Commandant James Biddle in *Hornet*, 20, attempted a long-delayed sortie from the confining waters of Long Island Sound. The British had established a blockade off Sandy Hook with the ship of the line *Valiant*, 74, and the frigate *Acasta*, 44 and had stationed the ships of the line *Ramilies*, 74, and *Orpheus*, 36, off Montauk Point. Decatur and Jones had attempted a breakout via New York harbor in late May but had been frustrated by a reverse in the weather. The impatient Decatur, sensing that he might have better luck forcing his way out through the eastern end of the Sound, waited for the best wind and tide and sailed toward Newport and Block Island on June 1. But, as he reported it, he discovered more British warships than expected guarding the Block Island Channel, with more powerful ships off Montauk. Before they could make contact, Decatur turned back his ships and sought safety up the Thames River at Groton, where Fort Trumbull offered protection. Unfortunately for Decatur, this provided an ideal opportunity for the Royal Navy's ships to bottle up these two fine frigates for the next eighteen months. There is, however, another side to this story.

In his circular letter to all captains in port refitting, Secretary Jones transmitted his recommended cruising policy for the ensuing campaign season thusly: "Cruising singly, will . . . afford to our gallant commanders a fair opportunity of displaying distinctly their judgement, skill, & enterprize, and of reaping the laurel of Fame and its solid appendages [money], which so extended a field of Capture, without impairing the means of continuing the pursuit, cannot fail to produce."[21] Decatur was then in New York refitting his frigate *United States* and looking forward to a cruise in company with the sloop of war *Argus*, commanded by Lieutenant William Henry Allen, who had been his first lieutenant in *United States* at the time of the *Macedonian* engagement. After that battle, Decatur selected Allen to take command of the prize. In response to Jones's request for a plan, Decatur stated that he would shape a course east of Bermuda to avoid the British cruisers "to the northward," then head toward the eastward edge of the Grand Bank, veering toward Ushant and sweeping southward along the coast of Portugal, crossing the track of British merchantmen returning from the Cape of Good Hope, Brazil, and the West Indies. He proposed to stay with *Argus* as long as he could to seek out HMS *Aeolus*, which had been blockading off Charleston. After dealing with this threat, he would continue alone, as Jones had suggested, but he wanted *Argus* to remain in the same general area. This plan apparently met with Jones's approval, but in mid-May it happened that the secretary had an urgent use for *Argus* on another mission, that of delivering Georgia congressman William H. Crawford as the new US minister to France.

Jones had to select another officer and ship to replace *Argus*. His choice was Master Commandant James Biddle, commander of the sloop of war *Hornet*. When Decatur, with *Macedonian*, now commanded by Jacob Jones, and Biddle's *Hornet*, decided to sortie via Long Island Sound instead of Sandy Hook, he did not know that HMS *Valiant*'s commander, Captain Robert Oliver, had decided to exchange stations with Captain Thomas Hardy, in HMS *Ramillies*, who had been waiting off Montauk Point. Both of these Royal Navy captains wanted the opportunity to defeat Decatur, but Oliver had seniority. He ordered Hardy to sail immediately for New York, while he, Oliver, sailed in company with the frigate *Acasta* to be at Montauk in time to confront Decatur and his small squadron. This shift of blockaders actually left both Montauk and New York uncovered in the time it took for the British commanders to change stations, about thirty-six hours. Had Decatur feinted and turned back to New York after disappearing into the Sound, he might have had a window of a few hours to escape without cost or delay. What actually happened was that when Decatur, Jones, and Biddle made their move on the morning of June 1, they were outward bound, well past Montauk Point, when the lookouts sighted *Valiant* and *Acasta* under their lee near Block Island, but they also saw three other vessels in the distance that might have been British warships. They were not, yet because their identity was uncertain, Decatur reversed course and sailed back to New London, almost overtaken by *Acasta*. Though Biddle's *Hornet* later escaped, *United States* and *Macedonian* were bottled up in the Thames River for the remainder of the war, and most of their crew were distributed to the lakes squadrons. The loss of three US Navy frigates in one day made June 1, 1813, in the words of the late American historian William Dunne, "the Inglorious First of June," a play on the phrase "The Glorious First of June," used to describe the British admiral Lord Richard Howe's victory over the French fleet on June 1, 1794.[22]

USS *Argus* in British Waters

Although Master Commandant Allen missed out on the disappointing result of the Decatur sortie, he departed in *Argus* soon afterward on a solitary cruise that would have its successful moments and a devastating conclusion. Secretary Jones's orders to Allen, dated June 5, required him to carry the new minister to France, William H. Crawford, landing him at Brest, Lorient, or another port he could safely enter. He cautioned Allen against any diversion until he had completed his primary mission. That done, Allen was to "make the enemy feel the effect of our hostility" by attacking British commerce, fisheries, and coastal trade. This, he assured Allen, would produce an astounding sensation. The secretary even proposed that the cruising ground extend from the English Channel, along the coast of Ireland, across to the northwest coast of England, and then through the Faroe Island passage so as to be in the way of the fleets traveling to and from Archangel. Departing on June 18, *Argus* made a swift passage of a little over three weeks, entering Lorient, on the coast of Brittany.[23]

After a quick reprovisioning, *Argus* sailed on July 20 and headed for Ireland. During the next three weeks, Allen captured and burned vessels in the English Channel and on the southern and western coasts of Ireland, including River Shannon. As Jones had predicted, *Argus*'s captures and ship burnings gained much attention in the seaports on both sides of the St. George's Channel and the Irish Sea. Before long, this news reached the Admiralty, where the reaction was swift. Vice Admiral Edward Thornbrough, commander in chief of the Irish station, based at Cork, had heard reports of enemy-vessel activity but assumed that it was an American privateer. Only after receiving an eyewitness action report from a lieutenant manning the signal station on Kerry Head, on the south side of the River Shannon, did he realize that she was a more heavily armed American brig. On August 11, the captains of some of the ships that Allen destroyed gave their accounts directly to the admiral. From that moment, Thornbrough advised the only warships then available—*Leonidas*, 38, *Jalouse*, 26, and the brig *Pelican*, 18—of *Argus*'s last known position and likely cruising grounds.[24] It was *Pelican*, under Lieutenant John Maples's command, that found the quarry in the early-morning light of August 14 off St. David's Head, Wales. In the forthcoming battle, *Pelican*'s battery of sixteen 32-pounder carronades and two long 6-pounder guns had the advantage over *Argus*'s sixteen 24-pounder carronades and two long 12-pounders.

In the few minutes available while *Pelican* bore down on him, Lieutenant Allen may have thought briefly about avoiding combat altogether. *Argus* was remarkably fast, as had been shown in his transatlantic passage. He might well have escaped by turning downwind and spreading all sail. He had an exhausted crew already made short-handed by sending off prize crews, yet Allen had an acute sense of personal honor, similar to that of the late Captain James Lawrence. He must have found it impossible to turn down what he probably saw as a fair fight between similar ships. Secretary Jones had admonished Allen to seek out mainly the enemy's commerce, but he had provided an additional clause in his orders that permitted Allen to capture and destroy the "light cruizers of the enemy."[25] The two ships were only 200 yards distant as firing commenced. *Pelican*'s gunners were more accurate as her 32-pounders shredded *Argus*'s hull and fatally wounded Captain Allen and many crew members within the first few minutes. The first lieutenant took over, but he was knocked unconscious by grapeshot, whereupon Lieutenant Howard Allen replaced him. *Argus*'s gunfire was high and inaccurate, taking only a small toll of *Pelican*'s crew and rigging. Although lack of much previous gunnery action and crew exhaustion might explain this, later comments by surviving crew suggested that some sailors might have been intoxicated or hung over from taking liberties with a prize vessel's stores of rum or wine the night before. For the Americans, the battle's casualties amounted to ten dead, including Lieutenant William Allen, who had been mortally wounded, with thirteen others having wounds ranging from severe to slight. Captain Maples's well-handled *Pelican* suffered only two dead and five wounded. Whatever the reasons, Allen had suffered a tragic defeat after a great run of luck. *Argus* had taken nineteen prizes, more than any other single US Navy vessel during the course of the war.[26] The taking of prizes was not, however, the only objective; the other was to create alarm in Britain and embarrass the Admiralty with an American warship attacking shipping in coastal waters in the manner of John Paul Jones's raids off Whitehaven and Flamborough Head in 1778 and 1779. Such moves distracted the enemy, requiring him to shift resources suddenly from tasks such as escort of convoys and blockade of the continental European coastline. In this, at least, Allen had successfully carried out Secretary Jones's strategy.

Medical Needs at Sea

Argus's relatively high number of casualties provides an opportunity to discuss medical arrangements on this and other US Navy ships and how sick and wounded sailors were treated. In the years leading up to the navy's establishment, Congress created several laws providing for the building, arming, manning, and equipping of its ships. Concerns for sailors' health is evident in the texts of these acts, depending on the size of the ships. For example, the large 44-gun frigates would carry a complement of one surgeon and two surgeon's mates to care for an estimated 400 sailors; a 36-gun frigate of 340 men would be limited to one surgeon and one surgeon's mate; the same with a 32-gun frigate of 260 men, a 22-gun ship of 180 men, and a 20-gun ship of 160 men. Smaller ships and schooners or cutters would have only a surgeon's mate. Gunboats might have either one surgeon or surgeon's mate assigned to an entire flotilla.

Following approval by the Senate and the House of Representatives, and signed by President John Adams, a new law was promulgated on April 23, 1800, An Act for the Better Government of the Navy of the United States. Article 29 stated, in part, that "the duties of a commanding officer included that he shall cause a convenient place to be set apart for sick or disabled men, to which he shall have them removed with their hammocks and bedding, when the surgeon shall so advise, and shall direct that some of the crew attend them and keep the place clean; and if necessary, that cradles and buckets with covers be made for their use." This space came to be called the "sick bay." Sailors with maladies needing treatment were instructed to report to the sick bay, located at the forward part of the berth deck, at the time of "sick call," normally early in the day. During this time, an officer or petty officer would take an accounting of those present and absent from the division. Any sailors missing and not accounted for on the sick list would provoke a search throughout the ship. The surgeon or surgeon's mate would report the numbers of sick and hurt sailors to the commanding officer twice each day. At the beginning of the War of 1812, the navy employed forty-six surgeons and surgeon's mates attached to its ships and stations. By the end of the war, that number had tripled, as had the number of ships and their multiple needs for medical professionals. As in civilian life, sickness, disease, and accidents were a part of everyday life for sailors, and occasionally combat at sea could make things much more perilous. In emergencies, a ship's captain would need every available hand, so keeping men healthy and active was an important part of his duties as commander.

Work on deck or in the rigging of a rolling, plunging ship could be dangerous. Any number of incidents could occur that would bruise, lacerate, or burn a sailor or crush his limbs. Sailors working aloft in a storm at night were especially prone to losing their balance or losing their grip on a rope, sail, or part of the standing rigging of the ship. A loose cannon that had broken free from its gun port lashings could crush or maim a man. Falls from aloft were not infrequent and could be fatal. A sailor could become ill and unable to work as a result of insect-borne diseases such as yellow fever and malaria or from venereal diseases, tuberculosis, and a host of other diseases. Another disease that could demobilize a ship's crew was scurvy, caused by a lack of vitamin C in the diet. The cure was application of citric acid, and by the early nineteenth century this was widely known, but ships could quickly run out of their supply of lemons, limes, and oranges, broccoli, onions, tomatoes, and a few other anti-scorbutics, leaving the sailors at risk on a long voyage.

Other duties required of a surgeon were listed in the *Navy Regulations of 1802.* He was to inspect the necessaries on board for the use of sick men; visit the sailors under his care twice a day or more often if required; and see that the surgeon's mates were doing their duty so that none suffered for want of due attendance and relief. He was to inform the captain daily of the state of his patients; those sent to hospitals must take with them an account of the time and manner of their getting ill and how they had been treated. The surgeon was to be ready with mates and attendants in an engagement (battle), having at hand all things necessary for stopping blood and dressing wounds. He must keep a daybook of their practice containing the names of patients, their hurts, their distempers, when they were taken ill, when they recovered, their death, their prescriptions, and their method of treatment when under care. From the daybook, the surgeon must maintain two journals, one containing his physical, the other his surgical, practice. These were to be sent to the secretary of the navy at the end of every cruise. Stores for the medical department were to be furnished upon his requisition, and he would be held responsible for their expenditure. The surgeon would be held responsible for his receipts and expenditures of such stores and must transfer an account thereof to the accountant of the navy at the end of every cruise.[27]

During battle in a frigate, the surgeon and his assistants would operate in a space on the lowest (orlop) deck, below the waterline, just above the bilge, where round shot from the enemy's guns would be unlikely to do damage. If the ship were smaller or a brig, as in the case of *Argus*, the operating area would be located in the berth deck's sick bay. There, the surgeon would assemble his instruments, medicine chest, and operating table and prepare to assist wounded sailors who were brought down from the main (spar) or gun deck, where they worked the guns and were exposed to enemy fire and the deadly splinters that came from round shot hitting bulwarks and ship's timbers. Surgeons were prepared to deal with broken limbs and puncture wounds but lacked modern antiseptics and anesthesia. The closest they could come to anesthesia was a tincture of opium called laudanum, which would induce a coma-like sleep and dull the pain. Absent that, whiskey or rum would provide the patient some distraction while the surgeon amputated and cauterized an arm or leg to prevent gangrene.

In the aftermath of *Argus*'s battle with *Pelican*, the American surgeon James Inderwick's journal included, in part, the following remarks concerning dead and wounded:

> Mr. William W. Edwards—Midshipman—Killed by shot in the head; Mr. Richard Delphy, Do. [Ditto], Had both legs nearly shot off at the knees—he survived the action about 3 hours; Joshua Jones—Seaman—Killed; Geo. Gardner—Seaman—His thigh taken off by a round shot close to his body, he lived about ½ an hour; Jno. Finlay—Seaman—his head was shot off at the close of the action. William Moulton—Seaman—Killed. The following were wounded. William H. Allen—Commander—His left knee was shattered by a cannon shot. Amputation of that thigh was performed about 2 hours after the action—an Anodyne was previously administered—an Anodyne at night. Lieut. Watson—1st Part of Scalp on the upper part of the head torn off by a grape shot—the bone denuded. It was lightly dressed, and he returned and took command of the deck. [He is] now on board the *Pelican*. Mr. Colin McCloud—Boatswain—received a severe lacerated wound on the upper part of the thigh, a slight one on the face and a contusion on the right shoulder. Dressed simply with lint and roller Bandage. . . . Joseph Jordan—Boatswain's Mate—Has a wound through the left thigh the bone fractured and splintered—the back part of the right thigh carried off—and nearly the whole of the fleshy nates carried away—Dressed with lint imbued with Ol Olivar [olive oil?]—gave a large Anodyne—repeated it at night—case hopeless.[28]

In Washington, when Secretary Jones brought the disheartening news of *Argus*'s defeat to President Madison, he asked the secretary a pointed question, "Would it be amiss to instruct such crews positively never to fight where they can avoid it and employ themselves entirely in destroying the commerce of the enemy?"[29] This brought the lesson clearly home to the navy's secretary. Jones reacted affirmatively and positively in his instructions to Master Commandant Lewis Warrington, commander of the new USS *Peacock*, before he set sail on his next cruise. Yet the British also took a lesson from *Argus*'s romp in their coastal waters. The Admiralty increased the number of warships assigned to the Cork squadron and did not reduce its watchfulness in coastal waters during the remainder of the war.

Faced with setbacks such as these, Secretary Jones was open to suggestions from ingenious members of the public to wage a kind of guerrilla warfare against the Royal Navy's blockaders. He and others persuaded Congress to pass legislation offering rewards to anyone who successfully destroyed an enemy warship. When British warships operated close to shore in the Chesapeake Bay or Long Island Sound, they provided a temptation to those brave enough to approach with explosives of various types. Some of these inventive persons and their attempts at what some have called asymmetrical warfare are discussed in chapter 8.

CHAPTER 8

Naval Innovation and Inventions

The realization that the nation was at war in June 1812 produced many and varied reactions among the American public. From a surge of voices came cries of patriotic ardor as well as expressions of doubt and fear in the newspapers of the day and public prints reflecting the people's thoughts. Those given to pragmatic actions contemplated what they as individuals could do, whether it was to make money from war mobilization or to participate in the conflict in some meaningful way, such as joining a militia or volunteering for the army that was being enlarged. Expressions of doubt and fear came from tales of Native American brutality, captivity, and rape spreading from the frontier, as it was obvious that the British foe would be allied to Native Americans, whose methods of war were well known from colonial, revolutionary, and later times.[1] The news of the Fort Dearborn massacre by Potawatomi of citizens evacuating Chicago on August 15, 1812, horrified many Americans. The Potawatomi ambushed and killed many of the men, women, and children and took the rest into captivity. Likewise, General William Hull's surrender at Detroit that same month was inspired by his fears that Native Americans allied with the British would massacre his army and the citizens of Detroit should his army of untested troops be defeated by the British. The collapse of the American offensive in the west led to an outbreak of Native American warfare in the Michigan territory and beyond. It would take more than a year of campaigning for the army under Major General William Henry Harrison, combined with Commodore Oliver Hazard Perry's victory on Lake Erie, to stabilize that frontier.

On the Atlantic, aggressive British ships patrolled the indented New England coast and sailed into Long Island Sound, isolating Block Island, Martha's Vineyard, and Nantucket Island. Not satisfied with blockading the Virginia Capes, a strong enemy squadron invaded the waters of the Chesapeake Bay, attempting to halt American trade, capture Baltimore privateers, and suppress armed resistance by creating a reign of terror among the largely agricultural populace, who were unsupported by any force but untrained militia. Such provocations, however, inspired innovative countermoves. The navy secretary's support of local efforts to defend seaports by strengthening naval defenses at Philadelphia, Baltimore, New

York, and other ports was discussed in chapter 6. The proximity of the enemy's ships also inspired individuals to offer their services to the government in the invention, construction, and use of weapons that would catch the more powerful, unprepared enemy by surprise.

Robert Fulton and Undersea Warfare

The foremost of these inventors was Robert Fulton, commonly thought of as a steamboat designer, and so he was, but the multitalented Fulton also became an innovator in undersea-weapons technology. First, attempting to start a career as an artist, he traveled from the United States to England in the 1780s and began his studies with the Anglo-American artist Benjamin West, then president of the Royal Academy, and soon earned a modest income painting portraits and landscapes. Soon, however, he found that his artistic talents were not receiving enough patronage, and he became fascinated with the merging of steam engineering with water transportation at a time when canal building was gaining public attention. He teamed up with a partner and built a crude paddle-driven steam tugboat. He began experimenting with submarines intended to blow up warships. The French and British navies were fighting in the early phases of the wars of the French Revolution. Seeking the patronage of the French government, Fulton spent the years 1797 to 1801 in France. There, with financial support from his friend Joel Barlow, US minister to France, he built *Nautilus*, a submersible that some have called the first practical submarine.[2] Napoleon lacked confidence in Fulton's invention and refused to engage his services. In 1804, the British, under the threat of French invasion, shrewdly invited Fulton to England, where he demonstrated his submarine and explosive devices he called "torpedoes" (mines). He gained a contract from the government to carry out further experiments but learned after the Battle of Trafalgar in 1805 that the British were no longer interested, since they considered the French no longer capable of mounting an invasion.

In late 1806, following these failed attempts to gain French or British support for his inventions, Fulton returned to the United States. Within a month, he wrote to President Jefferson asking for an opportunity to demonstrate his torpedo devices to the administration and members of Congress. Residing in Washington at Joel Barlow's home, Kalorama, near Rock Creek, Fulton invited Secretary of State James Madison and Secretary of the Navy Robert Smith for dinner and a personal briefing and discussion on his weapons experiments.[3] Six months later, on June 22, 1807, the nation was brought to the brink of war over the *Chesapeake–Leopard* incident. On July 20, Fulton took full advantage of the war scare by staging a demonstration of his torpedo blowing up a ship in New York harbor in front of Secretary of War Henry Dearborn and many others. Fulton reported the event to Jefferson in detail and explained that he had endeavored to locate the torpedo under the hull of the target.[4] Jefferson responded that although he understood the usefulness of the weapon, he had yet to be convinced of its practicality. The visionary president also mentioned his interest in how a submarine could be used to fire a torpedo. In fact, he wished "to see a corps of young men trained to this service and a corps of naval engineers to practice and use them."[5] The war scare over the *Chesapeake–Leopard* incident slowly faded, but the nation and the navy had taken note of Britain's hostility and its continuing refusal to change its impressment policy.

As the administration's interest in torpedoes waned, the ever-active Fulton soon began work designing a commercial steamboat in partnership with the wealthy Robert R. Livingston, whom Fulton had encountered in Paris as the minister to France. Livingston had previously obtained a license to develop steamboats in New York, with exclusive rights to navigate on the Hudson River. With their combined talents and resources, Fulton's steamboat *Clermont* became a reality in 1807 and was soon making regular passages of the 140-mile trip from New York to Albany in thirty hours, as opposed to three days by sailing vessel (fig. 8.1).

Figure 8.1. Robert Fulton, 1765–1815, self-portrait. Engraving by Robert Fulton. Courtesy of Commander Charles Bittinger from an original (1941) in the William R. Nelson Gallery, Kansas City, Missouri, US Naval History and Heritage Command, Photograph NH 49451.

Fulton's Torpedo (Mine) Warfare

By 1810, with the failure of the Jefferson and Madison administrations' economic sanctions, the dramatic aftermath of the *Chesapeake–Leopard* incident, and the continuing pressure of impressment, talk of war against Britain become more frequent. Fulton approached Navy Secretary Paul Hamilton with a request for assistance to demonstrate his undersea weapons for possible use by the navy department. In January, Fulton sent a copy of his pamphlet *Torpedo War, and Submarine Explosions* to every member of Congress. He then met with President Madison, former president Jefferson, and several congressmen at Joel Barlow's residence to acquaint them with his experiments on the use of torpedoes to attack ships in defense of American harbors.

On February 17, 1810, Fulton gave a speech at Long's Hotel, in Washington, DC, to an audience of some two hundred people on the subject of submarine warfare and freedom of the seas. Fulton had developed a unique theory based on his premise that the main threats to freedom of the seas came from national navies. To eliminate this threat, he had designed underwater weapons that would, he thought, discourage countries from building navies. As he explained it, floating torpedoes, underwater guns, and the submarine, when fully developed and successfully tested, would be so devasting that conventional warships would become useless. At the time, Fulton's ideas seemed revolutionary. It was in Fulton's nature to be open and enthusiastic about these possibilities. He did not spend his time thinking about whether the navies themselves would adopt his ideas and make them part of their maritime arsenals to create their own version of "freedom of the seas."

On February 21, 1810, Senator Stephen R. Bradley, of Vermont, reported his committee's opinion that if practical experiments could demonstrate that Fulton's ideas could be used in actual operations, they would no doubt be widely adopted by governments that did not "expect to exercise an undue influence on the seas." Bradley wrote that it was the unanimous view of his committee that "a sum ought to be appropriated by the government and experiments made," under the direction of the secretary of the navy, to determine to what extent it would be expedient for Congress to employ the torpedo or submarine explosions for the protection of American seaports. A bill authorizing the expenditure of five thousand dollars for this purpose was approved on March 2, 1810.[6]

Fulton provided Congress with a remarkably complete report on how he had experimented in the past, along with engravings of anchored torpedoes, spar torpedoes, guns that fired underwater, and floating torpedoes. Regarding those who had criticized his proposed methods of warfare, Fulton told an anecdote (possibly apocryphal) about the British admiral John Jervis, 1st Earl of St. Vincent. When told about the experiment and the destruction of the brig *Dorothea*, the admiral had reflected and then said, "Pitt [the prime minister who had commissioned Fulton] was the greatest fool who ever existed, to encourage a mode of war which they who commanded the seas did not want, and which if successful, would deprive them of it." Fulton went on to criticize those who considered undersea warfare dishonorable and inhumane. Fulton added that if the British were warned of the existence of mines in American harbors and nevertheless chose to send ships into those harbors, then the blame shifted to the attacker, not to the American defenders. However much sophistry there may be in this argument, Fulton's apparent message was that all modes of warfare could be considered inhumane but that the perpetrators had to decide what was the greater or lesser evil. He also boasted that his weapons would make navies irrelevant and spread freedom of the seas. In his eagerness to convey his ideas and sell his inventions, Fulton tended strongly toward exaggeration, which may have been counterproductive, bringing forth skepticism in his audience.

Following the demonstrations in Washington and New York during 1810, the distinguished committee of congressmen and military and naval officers who had witnessed them provided individual comments to Secretary Hamilton about the efficacy of Fulton's underwater weapons. The committee summarized the comments by stating, "[These papers] show that Mr. Fulton has not, in the opinion of the majority of the committee, proved that the government ought to rely on his system as a means of national defense. Mr. Fulton states, however, that he has made important improvements since the experiments were made; and as he appears very confident of success, it is contemplated to authorize further experiments in order to ascertain the effect of such improvements." Commodore John Rodgers, one of the naval officers who witnessed the demonstrations, was more than unimpressed: he thought Fulton's claims about the marine torpedo were "exorbitant, misleading, and threatened the nation's security in that it distracted attention from what Congress ought to be doing for the navy."[7]

The only member to fully approve of Fulton's efforts was Livingston, Fulton's partner in the building of the *Clermont*.[8] Livingston praised Fulton's weapons, saying,

> I view this new application of powder as one of the most important military discoveries which some centuries have produced. It appears to me capable of effecting the absolute security of your ports against naval aggressions; provided that, in conjunction with it, the usual means necessary to occupy an enemy's attention are not neglected. . . . I would therefore earnestly recommend the further prosecution

of the experiments already commenced and upon a larger scale, nor do I think that trifling miscarriages, arising from want of practice and nautical skill, should stifle in its birth a discovery that may lead to consequences, the extent and importance of which it is impossible at this moment to foresee.[9]

Fulton's Experiments

Soon after the US declaration of war against Britain, Fulton again wrote to Secretary Hamilton. This time he asked him to approve use of the remaining half of the original five-thousand-dollar appropriation "to construct 10 or 12 Torpedoes with all their apparatus and of such a size to do execution." He suggested that the navy establish a corps of torpedomen by offering a premium of two thousand dollars per gun of an enemy vessel destroyed by using torpedoes. The bonus would encourage anyone who might wish to join "a kind of sea fencibles [naval militia] who would exercise themselves and watch for every opportunity to attack or annoy the enemy."[10] Although no answer to Fulton's request has been found, he managed to build the torpedoes and to obtain firelocks for them from the Harper's Ferry arsenal.[11] With the arrival of British warships in Delaware Bay, the Chesapeake Bay, and Long Island Sound, it seemed that Fulton's moment had come at last. The timing coincided with Congress's enactment of a bill on March 3, 1813, urging "any person or persons, in any manner whatsoever whilst such armed [British] vessel shall so remain within the jurisdiction of the United States, to burn, sink or destroy every such armed vessel; and for that purpose, to use torpedoes, submarine instruments, any other destructive machine whatever." As a reward, anyone who successfully destroyed such a vessel would receive a bounty of one-half its value and one-half the value of its guns, tackle, and apparel, to be paid out of the US Treasury.[12]

Fulton proposed a torpedo attack on a British warship in Delaware Bay in a letter to Navy Secretary Jones seeking the cooperation of the Navy Department. The architect Benjamin Latrobe had introduced Fulton to Samuel Swartwout, a soldier of fortune once in the service of Aaron Burr. Fulton wrote to Jones in the hope that he would "aid Mr. Swartwout in carrying my submarine engines into effect. The depredations of the enemy and the times demand every exertion of mind and nerve. Mr. Swartwout is a gentleman of great energy and resource. And I hope any impression which may have existed against him will not interfere in this case to impede or injure a good cause or an experiment on the enemy which, if successful will be of incalculable importance."[13]

Fulton contracted with Swartwout to hire and train men to deploy his torpedoes to sink HMS *Poictiers*, 74, then stationed in Delaware Bay. The contract, dated March 26, 1813, stated that he would supply Swartwout with six torpedoes and two whaleboats to be commissioned as privateers. Fulton's instructions specified that the boats should be painted a faint gray and that the men should wear white waistcoats and white hats to blend in with the gray paint at night. Swartwout launched his crew into the Delaware River. The crew was about to attack *Poictiers* when Delaware's governor, Joseph Haslet, ordered Swartwout to desist because there were American prisoners on board the ship. It is unknown how Governor Haslet found out about the plan.[14]

Fulton's experiments inspired others to carry out attacks on British warships in the Chesapeake Bay. President Madison received a letter from Elijah Mix, a US Navy sailing master from Baltimore who was serving under Captain Charles Gordon, officer in charge of the gunboats at Baltimore. That a warrant officer on active duty would be so bold as to write directly to the president is astounding in itself, yet he wrote as if he were a civilian, not supplying his rank, unit, or commanding officer. Mix had volunteered to lead a crew in attacking British warships then dominating the bay.[15] As Mix mentioned to Madison, the ship he had in mind was anchored off New Point Comfort, Virginia. Although he made several attempts, none damaged HMS *Plantagenet*, a 74-gun ship, although a near miss on July 24, 1813, got the Royal Navy's attention. Madison apparently thought well of the project and forwarded the letter to Secretary Jones, who gave his blessing to this arrangement. He wrote to Gordon that "a Mr. Elijah Mix will call upon you by my order to furnish him with such aid in carrying into effect his plans for the destruction of the enemy's ships now off the Patapsco, as I have encouraged him to expect; viz: you will furnish him with 500 lbs. of powder, a boat or boats and six men, provided he can prevail upon that number of men, fit for the enterprise, to volunteer their services. His plan is that of Fulton's Torpedo. He is an intrepid, zealous man and means to perform this service in person."[16] As early as mid-June, Rear Admiral Cockburn notified his superior, Admiral James Warren, that HMS *Victorious* had picked up "one of the Powder Machines commonly known made to explode underwater and thereby cause immediate destruction to whatever it may come into contact with."[17]

Commodore Decatur vs. Commodore Hardy

At about the same time that Elijah Mix and his crew were attempting to sink *Plantagenet* in the Chesapeake Bay, other efforts were being made to destroy HMS *Ramilies*, 74, the flagship of Rear Admiral Sir Thomas Masterman Hardy, located off New London in Long Island Sound. In this scheme, Master Commandant Jacob Lewis, commander of the New York gunboat flotilla, employed one John

Scudder and other volunteers to load the merchant schooner *Eagle* with provisions in hogsheads and to hide a similar hogshead filled with gunpowder attached to a cord fastened to a gunlock that, when moved, would ignite a train of gunpowder leading to the explosive. They sailed *Eagle* as if to make for New London, knowing that when she was sighted, the British would send barges to capture and bring her to the flagship. The crew abandoned *Eagle* near the Connecticut shore and then fired desultory shots as if to deter the boarding party.[18] The plan nearly succeeded; the British seized *Eagle* and towed her to HMS *Ramilies*, tying her off next to a vessel astern. As a crew from the flagship began to unload *Eagle*, they triggered the explosion, killing the ten-man boarding party and destroying the barges alongside. As Admiral Hardy reported, "Under the circumstances, it is most providential that the schooner was not taken alongside this ship, as it appears to me quite evident that the naval stores and provisions were placed in her as an inducement to do so." Admiral Warren added his endorsement, calling the attack a "diabolical and cowardly contrivance of the enemy; indeed, the daily attempts practiced by Commodore Decatur and the Americans against that valuable officer Sir Thomas Hardy and the ships under his orders . . . by means of torpedoes, fire vessels, and other infernal machines are beyond conception."[19] Admiral Warren told his flag captain, Henry Hotham, to prepare a general order to contend with this kind of attack by instructing ship commanders not to permit any prize or boat to be brought alongside their ships, and he stated that "any American vessel or boat with whom it is necessary to communicate shall be kept at a proper distance or anchored before an examination shall take place."[20]

Fulton and Swartwout continued their conversations and agreed to another contract. This time Swartwout agreed to attempt an attack on a British warship in Long Island Sound using one of Fulton's devices. If he succeeded in destroying the ship, Swartwout would receive three-fourths, and Fulton, one-fourth, of the congressional reward to be paid by the government, according to the act of March 3, 1813.[21] Swartwout, James Weldon, and others tried to ensnare *Ramillies* and *Orpheus* with Fulton's floating torpedo, but their efforts were unsuccessful, in part because Hardy frequently shifted anchorages to avoid these attacks. Meanwhile, the contriving inventor was already deep in thought, conceiving his revolutionary steam frigate.[22]

Commodore Decatur was far from idle during these summer months. Although his ships were bottled up in the Thames River, he had his reputation to repair. He had been embarrassed by his inability to break out of the Long Island Sound in early June. In this situation, he encouraged Robert Fulton and others to attack Admiral Hardy's flagship, *Ramillies*, and the frigate *Orpheus*, commanded by Captain Robert Pigot. He planned boat attacks on the British ships' crews on their occasional visits to Gardiner's Island and others, when they were vulnerable; and he accepted volunteers to guide his men to their targets. New London citizens, aware of Decatur's predicament and his attempts to attack the blockaders, worried about possible retribution the enemy might carry out, such as raiding or bombarding the town. Most Connecticut people shared the New England Federalists' position regarding the war—that it was unwise, unnecessary, and harmful for their economy and safety. Many merchants had already been put out of business by the government's embargoes on the import-export trade. It was therefore with a jaundiced eye that New Londoners witnessed the commodore's efforts to strike back at the British warships in the Sound. As James De Kay has written, a "majority of New London's citizens still held him [Decatur] personally responsible for the blockade and were not prepared to forgive him for it."[23]

The Gardiner's Island Incident

Joshua Penny, an Easthampton, Long Island, seaman who volunteered to help Decatur, was an American-born merchant seamen who had served in several British warships after being impressed. After several years, Penny escaped and returned home; he was engaged in the coasting trade when the war broke out. He sold his schooner and determined to do what he could to gain revenge. Penny was well acquainted with the waters around Gardiner's Island, in the bight between Orient and Montauk Points.[24] Decatur sent selected members of his crew and volunteers to wage a kind of guerrilla warfare against Hardy's ships. It was only natural that the commodore would want to make use of Penny's knowledge of his home waters.

On the night of July 26, Penny acted as pilot for a landing party of four launches manned with sailors from *United States* and *Macedonian* and guided them to Gardiner's Island, where *Ramillies* and *Orpheus* were anchored. According to Penny's memoir, written soon after the war, the raid was meant to capture the commanding officers of the British ships, who frequently went ashore to dine with John Lyon Gardiner, the "Lord of the Manor" and owner of the island. In the event, however, Admiral Hardy and Captain Pigot did not go ashore, but a small group of ship's officers and enlisted men from *Orpheus* did, in order to pick up supplies, a regular practice that Gardiner tolerated, under duress.

Penny's landing party captured seven men—two lieutenants, a sailing master, and four others. The Americans gave them a choice between parole and being taken back to the US squadron as prisoners. The senior British lieutenant chose parole, and they were let go, free to return to their ship after agreeing not to participate further in the war without being properly exchanged. How Hardy and Pigot reacted to this news is not known but can easily be imagined, as the Royal

Navy would lose the services of two valuable lieutenants, a sailing master, and the other men, if Hardy chose to respect their capture and paroles as legitimate.

When Penny and his crew returned to New London, Decatur commended his leadership and told him he would command a boat on the next expedition. Penny returned to his Easthampton farm at Three Mile Harbor, although friends warned him that the British now knew his name and his location and wanted to capture him. Some days later, *Ramillies* returned to Gardiner's Bay. Hardy sent a team of sailors ashore, dragged Penny from his bed, and brought him to the flagship. From interrogations, Hardy learned that Penny, in addition to capturing his sailors, had been an impressed sailor who deserted from His Majesty's ships. Hardy ordered him put in irons and sent him for imprisonment to Halifax, where he remained until the end of the war.[25]

This episode had greater ramifications. When President Madison learned that Penny, a civilian, had been imprisoned, he made a formal protest to the British. He then retaliated and sent an order to John Mason,[26] the American commissary general of prisoners and superintendent of alien enemies to the effect that a British civilian of similar status should be seized and given the same treatment in the United States until Penny was released. This was also to show that if the British persisted, further steps would be taken.[27]

Fulton and Decatur

Following the Gardiner's Island incident, Decatur turned to Robert Fulton, with whom he had opened a correspondence. Fulton expressed interest in demonstrating the submerged gun device that he had already tried out with the cooperation of Master Commandant Jacob Lewis at New York. As Lewis described it to Jones, "A hundred pounder [Columbiad] cannon was placed in a box with the muzzle through its side, the water prevented from entering. Into the box, the gun charged with Ten pounds of powder and a ball—the box sunk in five feet of water—a target placed at 25 feet distance under water and the Peace [*sic*] discharged, without injury—the ball entered a very Considerable distance into the Target, which was of three feet thickness." Eight days later the experiment was repeated with even better results, confirming that a 100-pounder Columbiad would perform this act more effectively through three feet of oak than a long 24-pounder.[28] It remained to be seen how such a weapon could be brought stealthily alongside a British warship to deliver the devastating blow. So far as is known, Fulton never had a chance to put his underwater cannon to the supreme test.

Immediately after these experiments, Fulton wrote a remarkably detailed letter to Thomas Jefferson, at Monticello, containing diagrams of the seven experiments he had conducted, each with a different amount of powder. He then explained an entirely new concept: how the waterproof underwater cannon could be fitted into the side of an attacking *steam-driven* vessel "to bring her up to the enemy in a calm or light breezes . . . the steam engine would give a Vessel of this description the means of playing round the Enemy to take choice of position on her Bow or quarter and with little or no risk sink everything which came into our waters." He continued, confidently, that for six hundred thousand dollars, the cost of building one 74, he could build seven steamers and that in an attack in American waters surely one of them could get as close as 8 or 10 feet to fire the underwater gun with devastating effect.[29] Soon after receiving this letter, Jefferson wrote to Madison, then at his Montpelier estate recovering from illness. Jefferson's words showed his immediate respect for the inventor's genius and that he understood the need for what a later generation would call asymmetrical warfare:

> Mr. Fulton's ingenuity is inexhaustible, and his disinterested devotion of it to his country very laudable. if his present device depended on me, I should try it, on the judgment of an officer so well skilled as Decatur. it is one of those experiments which neither the personal interest nor the faculties of a private individual can ever bring into use, while it is highly interesting to the nation. intersected as we are by many and deep waters, and unable to meet the enemy on them with an equal force, our only hope is in the discovery of the means which ingenuity may devise whereby the weak may defend themselves against the strong. this is done at land by fortifications, and, not being against any law of nature, we may hope that something equivalent may be discovered for the water.[30]

Fulton's exuberance overflowed as he wrote to Commodore Decatur a month later to describe the steam warship he had in mind. Fulton assured Decatur that although his steam warship would have masts, sails, and rigging, it would be designed so that masts could be lowered before an engagement to avoid entanglement with the enemy's rigging and would approach the target using steam power only. This seemed to excite Decatur, who quickly replied that the only other danger was the enemy's boarding from boats. To combat the risk of boarders, the commodore recommended designing a steeply sloping deck with sharp steel spikes pointing upward that could be covered by boards until going alongside the enemy. He also recommended having 13-inch shells loaded with powder and musket balls ready to fire at the boats.[31] Following this exchange, Decatur spent eighteen months, while awaiting a chance to break out of New London harbor, scheming how to bring Hardy's *Ramillies* to action. One of these opportunities arose during a stretch of bad weather in December 1813. He prepared his ships for the precise moment, with cold and stormy weather approaching from the northwest.

Yet, just when he was ready to depart, his lookouts reported what they believed were a pair of blue light signals on shore alerting the British to Decatur's planned sortie. Once again, the commodore canceled the operation. He placed the blame on suspected Federalist traitors or British spies in New London. He reported this in a letter to Secretary Jones, copies of which appeared in the press. The good citizens of New London, and New England Federalists generally, took umbrage at this allegation, which Decatur was never able to prove. It was from this event that the phrase "Blue Light Federalist" entered the American political lexicon, referring to any Federalist whose patriotism was suspect.[32]

Demologos

During the autumn of 1813, Fulton attended to his many civilian steamboat interests while developing the plans for a steam-driven warship, suggested in his correspondence with Thomas Jefferson and Commodore Decatur. Fulton named the vessel *Demologos*, a made-up Greek phrase interpreted loosely as "spirit of the people," but the US Navy never adopted this name. Newspapers often referred to her as "the steam battery." The navy officially preferred to refer to her as *Fulton the First*. The plans and a model of the steamer were ready for display and discussion by mid-December. Fulton assembled a group of friends and notables who would be helpful in advancing his ideas. These gentlemen met at Fulton's New York home on Christmas Eve to organize themselves as the Coast and Harbor Defense Company, of which General Henry Dearborn was elected president; Fulton, engineer; and Thomas Morris, secretary. The purpose of the committee was "to obtain the patronage of the general [Dearborn], the state government, and the corporation of this city and to endeavor to raise by subscription or otherwise the necessary funds to build a vessel on the plan proposed by Mr. Fulton."[33] Among these committeemen, Adam Brown stands out. Brown was a principal New York shipbuilder who, with his brother Noah, had supervised construction of warships on Lakes Erie, Ontario, and Champlain. Decatur and Lewis were the unofficial Navy Department representatives, and Cadwallader Colden was Fulton's lawyer. Colonel Isaac Bronson, of Connecticut, had been a surgeon in the Continental army and was by this time a successful banker and insurance man in New York. John Bogert was the captain of a Hudson River trading sloop. Nathan Sandford was one of Fulton's political connections, an attorney then serving as a senator in the New York State legislature in Albany. Samuel L. Mitchill, MD, a Columbia University professor and attorney, was one of New York State's representatives in Congress. Henry Rutgers, an attorney, former colonel in the Continental army, and New York State legislator, had been a navy agent during

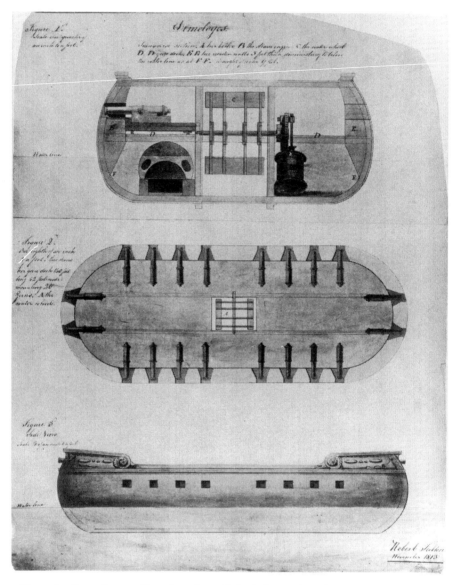

Figure 8.2. Steam battery *Demologos* (later *Fulton's Steam Frigate*). Drawing by Robert Fulton, November 1813, showing the ship's general arrangement. US Naval History and Heritage Command, Photograph NH 61883.

the Tripolitan War and was a civic leader in New York City who headed a committee for the defense of New York City in June 1812. Oliver Wolcott Jr., an attorney, former US circuit court judge, and businessman, was later governor of Connecticut. John R. Livingston was the younger brother of Fulton's deceased partner, Robert R. Livingston, chancellor of New York State and former minister to France. This group of powerful, skilled, and largely wealthy individuals were a socially significant team who could not only raise funds but also apply political influence when necessary.

The committee met formally for the first time on December 27, 1813. They voted to issue a stock offering for a company to be called the Coast and Harbor Defense Company. The company would sell fifteen hundred shares at one hundred dollars per share to build a double-hulled steam-driven vessel 130 feet in length, 50 feet in width, and capable of moving at a rate of five knots. The steam engine would turn a paddle wheel between the two catamaran hulls. For armament, this steam battery would carry twenty-four long 24- or 32-pounders and would contain a furnace for red-hot shot. To help sell this project, the committee obtained a letter of endorsement from seven well-known naval officers: Captains Decatur, Jacob Jones, Samuel Evans, and Oliver Hazard Perry and Master Commandants James Biddle, Lewis Warrington, and Jacob Lewis. Fulton circulated his plans and the officers' endorsement to Secretary Jones and members of Congress. Jones expressed his deep interest and "recommended its adoption without hesitation" to the chairmen of the House Naval Committee and the Senate Naval Committee in February 1814. Congress approved a bill to provide five hundred thousand dollars to construct a floating battery "to attack and destroy any of the ships of the enemy which may approach the shores or enter the waters of the United States" (fig. 8.2).[34]

Building *Demologos*

Even though Congress swiftly appropriated more than adequate funds for Fulton's steam warship, those funds were slow to arrive when they were needed. The inventor wrote to President Madison in March to try to shake these funds loose from the Navy Department, protesting that "I have not yet heard from the secretary of the Navy giving me orders to proceed or where to find funds." Jones was slow to act and later claimed that he had had "to give the matter mature consideration and to determine whether it would be compatible with a multiplicity of other pressing war needs."[35] Jones also asked a number of basic questions about the design, which must have infuriated Fulton, who thought there was no time to spare. Ultimately, the secretary gave in, accepting Fulton's plans and writing that he would make every effort to find the necessary resources. To give the secretary his due, his primary concerns at this time were preparations for the summer campaigns on Lake Ontario and Lake Champlain, where shipbuilding projects were the key to defending the northern borders and supporting military operations at Niagara and Plattsburgh. Other projects he was pushing forward were the building of three 74s at Portsmouth, Boston, and Philadelphia and completion of the sloops of war he had proposed in 1813, *Erie*, *Ontario*, *Wasp*, *Peacock*, and *Frolic*, and the frigates *Columbia*, *Guerriere*, and *Java*.

For the time being, Fulton and his committee had to provide the funds needed by dipping into their personal accounts. The Brown brothers' shipyard on the East River laid *Demologos*'s keel on 20 June, but remaining construction proceeded by fits and starts owing to a shortage of skilled labor and the slow delivery of needed supplies of timber, copper, lead, and coal. The blockade frequently interrupted the coastal shipping trade, making transportation more costly and time-consuming. While the Browns' yard constructed the vessel, Fulton's metalworkers were building the steam engine, the paddle wheel, and their associated parts. Once the ship was launched, the mechanics at Fulton's yard would have the time-consuming job of placing the engine and its connecting pipes within the hulls. *Demologos*'s engine machinery involved two boilers, 22 feet in length and 12 feet in diameter, located in one hull, connected to the vertical 48-inch cylinder containing a piston with a five-foot stroke in the other hull. Fired by wood, steam from the boilers drove the piston, which was linked by crosshead, connecting rods, cranks, and flywheel to the 16-foot-diameter paddle wheel placed in the race, a large, 15-foot gap between the parallel hulls. The excess gases were expelled upward through flues to two stacks placed in line, fore and aft, on the spar deck. This engine was capable of 120 horsepower and would be able to drive the vessel at five to six knots. At launching, *Demologos* had an overall length of 152 feet; beam, 57 feet; and depth, 20 feet. Her sides were 4 feet, 10 inches thick, and she drew 11 feet when fully loaded.[36] The extreme ends of her superstructure were rounded and double-ended, with linked twin rudders at each end so that she could move forward or backward and still be under control. The heavy framing connecting the hulls and the massive side planking protected the engine machinery from enemy fire. Immediately above the engine was the gun deck, equipped with enough gunports for thirty 32-pounder long guns, fifteen on each side. While some authorities have suggested that the ship was equipped with thirty guns, others indicate that the correct number was twenty-four. Fulton's early sketches show gunports for only twenty guns, eight on each side and two each at the bow and stern.[37] Apparently, as Fulton elaborated on his plans, his estimate of the number of guns that could be carried increased. The open spar deck, immediately above the gun deck, originally had no bulwarks or gunports. Secretary Jones selected Captain David Porter, commander of the late US frigate *Essex*, to command *Demologos*.[38] It was he who recommended to Fulton that the ship be equipped with two masts, lateen-rigged sails, jibs, and a bulwarks on the spar deck for sailors' protection. The spar deck was also to carry launches nested for the captain's use.[39]

Horse teams hauled the two dozen 24-pounder long guns over the muddy New Jersey roads from Philadelphia, and the Browns' yard built carriages to accommodate the heavy guns. At times, work halted for lack of funds to pay the men. When this happened, the commissioners had to pledge some of their own funds to bring the men back on the job. Nonetheless, four months later all was in readiness. The launch took place on Saturday, October 29, before an excited, curious crowd huddled near the launching site in Brooklyn.[40] *Demologos* launched smoothly into the East River, carrying her new commander and several hundred notables, to the cheers of some fifteen thousand onlookers. Captain Jacob Lewis's navy gunboat flotilla and the steamboats *Paragon* and *Fulton* saluted her with guns and whistles as she slid down the ways and into her element.[41] According to his biographer, Captain Porter was initially "somewhat distrustful of such an intrusion into his world of wood and canvas," but he changed his mind that day. As Porter wrote to Jones, "She promises to meet our most sanguine expectations, proving to be buoyant, shallow-drafted, and easily maneuverable."[42]

It took several more months for *Demologos*'s engine to be completed, installed, tested, and ready for sea trials. On her first steam-powered cruise, on June 1, 1815, she stemmed both wind and tide and proceeded down the New York harbor, took the salutes of Forts Wadsworth and Hamilton at the Narrows, and returned to her berth near Paulus Hook, New Jersey. On July 4, *Demologos* steamed as far as Sandy Hook, a distance of 53 miles, in eight hours and twenty minutes, averaging 2.5 miles per hour against a current of 3 miles per hour, indicating capability to steam at slightly over 5 miles per hour under ideal conditions. In September, she made another voyage to the sea carrying a full load of armament, equaling her earlier speed and trouble-free trials, thus supporting Fulton's predictions in fulfillment of his promises to Secretary of the Navy Jones. In all, it had been a remarkable performance, lending a breath of reality to Fulton's dream that "this invention, practiced to its utmost powers, must produce a total revolution in maritime war and political relations of the United States with Europe."[43]

For all the years of effort, expense, and persuasion that Fulton and his supporters put into his steam-frigate project, they were unable to produce the completed warship in time for the supreme test, a battle between *Demologos* and a Royal Navy ship of the line. Sadly, Robert Fulton did not live to see her sea trials. He died on February 24, 1815, from pneumonia as the result of exposure in walking across the ice of the Hudson River and helping a friend out of the frigid waters after he had fallen though the ice. The Coast and Harbor Defense Committee and the navy nevertheless continued to support the project to completion, despite Fulton's death and the news that the War of 1812 had ended with the ratification of the Treaty of Ghent on February 13.

The engineers continued to tinker with the engine. According to Samuel Mitchill's report to Secretary of the Navy Benjamin Crowninshield, the boilers required greater or better-focused drafts of air to raise the steam pressure needed for sustained cruising speed and the waterwheel needed to be elevated to decrease "wallow." These improvements made, Mitchill declared the problems solved and recommended that "further experiments should be made to determine the effect of the entire weight of cannons and stores upon her draft, to find out the quantity and quality of fuel she consumes, the size of crew she requires and what practice and discipline they may require different from other vessels."[44]

Commodore Thomas Macdonough replaced Commodore Porter as commanding officer of *Demologos* in late 1814 and held that post until July 1815, when he was assigned to the command of the Portsmouth Navy Yard. Secretary Jones transferred *Demologos* to the care of the commandant of the Brooklyn Navy Yard, Captain Samuel Evans, who delegated command of the ship to Captain Joseph Bainbridge. This experimental steamship went on one last cruise on June 18, 1817. With President James Monroe on board, she steamed to Staten Island, allowing him a view of the forts at the Narrows and a visit to the home of Vice President Daniel Tompkins. After her return to the Brooklyn Navy Yard, Captain Evans ordered yard workers to construct a roof over *Demologos*'s spar deck and converted her to a receiving ship, where sailors lodged awaiting their next cruise. There she ended her days, moored 200 yards offshore until June 6, 1829, when a powder-magazine explosion blew her apart, killing twenty-nine sailors and wounding twenty-three more.

Robert Fulton is better known for his commercial steamboat enterprises than for his experimentation with naval mines, primitive submarines, and underwater guns and *Demologos*. These were his contributions to the defense of the United States during the War of 1812. All these projects taken together, combined with his invention of the first steam-driven warship, complete with catamaran hull and protected paddle-wheel propulsion, showed him to be a visionary naval architect almost a half century ahead of his time. Even though paddle-wheel technology was ill-suited for oceangoing warships, Fulton's combining of steam technology with an understanding of the principles of ship design pointed the way. He pioneered in applying the technology of the Industrial Revolution to seafaring and naval warfare and was well aware that others would have to carry forward and perfect his inventions.

Naval Machine Guns and Other Weapons

Secretary Jones was open to unusual proposals from the public on how to distress the enemy. As in the case of Robert Fulton, he encouraged inventors of new weapons in an effort to make up for years of unpreparedness and to gain an advantage over the enemy. Several years before the War of 1812, Joseph G. Chambers, a Revolutionary War army veteran, developed several versions of repeating arms: pistols, muskets, and a large swivel-mounted, seven-barreled gun that could discharge more than one hundred rounds with one trigger pull. Through the navy agent George Harrison, in Philadelphia, Jones ordered ten swivel guns for the use of the Delaware gunboat flotilla, but these apparently never arrived. The disgruntled Jones would soon lose patience with the gunsmith, who made many excuses for his failure to deliver.[45]

Despite this setback, Commodore Isaac Chauncey was eager to obtain them after seeing a demonstration. He wrote to Jones asking for twenty swivels and one hundred of the repeating muskets for his Lake Ontario squadron. Likewise, Commodore Bainbridge ordered eight swivels, fifty repeating muskets, and one hundred pistols of similar capability for the use of USS *Independence*, then under construction in the Charlestown Navy Yard. Jones witnessed a demonstration of the swivels at the Washington Navy Yard and wrote enthusiastically to Chauncey, "They are a truly astonishing and potent weapon. I recommend them to your attention. Two of those in each Top, to be fired in succession upon the deck of your adversary would not fail to clear it entirely in five minutes. It is utterly impossible for any body of men to withstand such a shower of balls in quick succession, sweeping the deck from stem to stern."[46] Upon the arrival of the first shipment, Chauncey distributed the twelve swivels to his squadron, four each to *Superior*, *Mohawk*, and *General Pike*. Interestingly, intelligence about Chauncey's acquisition of these unusual weapons reached the British by means of an "informant" who traveled from Sackets Harbor to deliver the news to Commander Charles Owen, RN, at Fort Wellington, Prescott, Ontario. Commander Owen's report to Commodore Yeo relates, in part,

> I have obtained some idea of the fire arms on the Repetition Principle—the Swivels (which are placed in the Tops) have seven barrels—& throw 250 balls at each fire—They have one lock and the fire is communicated from barrel to barrel & they discharge successively at the Interval of one second—they load very quick—the balls are all perforated & and made up in cartridges for the charge—their boarders pistols have one lock and throw six balls—the muskets have two locks and throw twelve balls—eleven at one discharge and a reserve ball for the second lock.

The shocks from these arms is not greater than that from ones on the common construction & which must be attributed to the channel of fire passing through the aperture of each ball—On the 14th Commodore Chauncey has 12 swivels—50 musquets & 200 pistols of this description—more were daily expected.[47]

Owing to delays in getting out on the lake and to their evasive tactics, British and American squadrons skirmished but did not engage in a major battle on Lake Ontario in 1814. As a result, these novel weapons were not given a test in ship-to-ship combat. A similar machine gun, known as the Nock volley gun, was available on Royal Navy ships, but officers considered it unreliable and possibly dangerous because of the muzzle flash and recoil.[48]

Another weapon that made its appearance on US warships during the war was the gunade, a derivative of the carronade that was in general use along with long guns. The gunade was relatively lighter and smaller than a carronade; it was manufactured with trunnions (cylinders that were perpendicular to the bore and located on the centerline) to hold the gunade on its slide during firing. Its chief advantages were that it required a smaller gun crew and could be more easily loaded than a carronnade. The battery of the frigate *Constitution*, then under the command of Captain Charles Stewart, included thirty 24-pounder long guns, twenty 32-pounder carronades, and two shifting 24-pounder gunades. The adjective *shifting* refers to the fact that the gunades could be moved to wherever they were most needed during battle.[49]

Captain Stewart's innovative spirit was also evident in his design of a furnace for heating round shot. His ship was ready for sea, and he was waiting for the best weather window to leave Boston harbor. He described this device in letters sent to Secretary Jones just before his first cruise in *Constitution*. He proposed "only to use it against the enemies [*sic*] ships of such force as would render our safety precarious (if we cannot otherwise escape) by bringing them under our stern battery and firing a few red hot balls into their hull." The furnace, made of portable sheet iron, measured 3 feet long, 3 feet deep, and 18 inches wide. It would heat to red-hot 21 shot of 24 pounds in 20 minutes over a pinewood fire. He reported that its advantage was that it was not very expensive, would take up little room, and could be set up in the back part of the galley, where it would interfere with nothing. It had two grates made of bar iron, the upper to receive the round shot and the lower to hold the firewood. Below that there was a tin pan that fitted under the bottom grating to receive the ashes and coals. He recommended that the furnace be provided to all the frigates and gunboats. Jones responded that he would welcome a drawing and a model, which Stewart said he would provide.[50] Nothing further was discussed, but the furnace had already been built and Jones seems to have accepted the idea. *Constitution* put to sea from Boston on December 31, 1814, and slipped unnoticed through the British blockade.

Fulton's Naval Legacy

In the second year of the war, Secretary William Jones brought reform and new ideas to the navy's management and encouraged others to use their initiative and innovative ideas to assist the navy in its existential struggle with the Royal Navy. Robert Fulton was a major figure in offering his ideas and engineering skills to create new maritime weapons. Some of these failed, perhaps through lack of good execution; others nearly succeeded, as in the attempt to destroy HMS *Ramillies* on Long Island Sound. His finest hour was in the design, construction, and launch of *Demologos*, the world's first steam frigate. As one author ventured, in a counterfactual history essay, if *Demologos* had been launched in 1813 instead of late 1814, she might have caught HMS *Ramillies* unable to maneuver in one of the frequent summer calms on Long Island Sound. Had she done so, more steam warships would have been built, and the war might have ended differently.[51] However, the war ended before Fulton's steam warship was ready, Fulton died that same month, and many lives were spared by the advent of peace.

Similarly, with Secretary Jones's encouragement, the Chambers machine gun had been invented, ordered, and sent to ships in Chauncey's Lake Ontario squadron by July 1814 but never put to use. Whether the gunade would have assisted in winning a battle, it is impossible to say; however, we do know that the navy ordered many more for use in the fleet during the 1820s and 1830s.[52] Captain Charles Stewart's concept of a hot shot furnace for *Constitution* was not an original idea. The heating of shot for use in battle was of ancient vintage, especially in land warfare; however, the use of a hot shot furnace in frigates under way was unusual. There was always the danger of fire on board ship, as virtually everything was flammable. The loss of control of a red-hot round shot while loading and having it roll around a heaving deck would be a sailors' nightmare. Some commanding officers might not be eager to use a hot shot furnace, but Stewart was not that type. He was an excellent ship handler with considerable combat experience and full of self-confidence. Such an invention and the will to use it could make a difference in a difficult battle. The spirit of innovation brought out by the War of 1812 spurred the inventiveness of many citizens and contributed, in the popular phrase of that day, to the "annoyance of the enemy."

CHAPTER 9

Chauncey's War on Lake Ontario

At the outset of the War of 1812, the United States faced a hostile northern frontier stretching nearly from Quebec to Detroit, a distance of at least 735 miles. This was a heavily wooded, thinly populated area running along the St. Lawrence River and the northern shores of Lakes Ontario and Erie. These inland lakes were virtual inland seas; their waves could build into billows during a storm, and they were difficult to navigate for lack of accurate charts, low shorelines, and few discernable landmarks.

Building the Naval Base at Sackets Harbor

For Commodore Chauncey, who built a navy yard, barracks, and fortifications for the protection of the whole establishment at remote Sackets Harbor, at the east end of Lake Ontario, the logistical challenges were many. There were no nearby industries or good roads. He required hundreds of skilled shipwrights, sawyers, sailmakers, caulkers, riggers, lumberjacks, metalsmiths, and ordinary laborers. Most of the shipwrights and other maritime craftsmen traveled from New York City. The timber had to come from nearby forests, and pig iron for fastenings had to be hauled from distant forges. The naval personnel, supplies, and heavy guns for his vessels had to be transported by sloop or steamboat up the Hudson River from New York. They were off-loaded onto wagons and hauled from Albany up the Mohawk River to portages connecting with streams and rivers leading to Lake Onondaga, followed by another portage around the falls of the Oswego River. From the river, lake schooners took them the last fifty miles to Sackets Harbor, unless Commodore Yeo's vessels were blockading the ports. In that case, the cargoes would either wait for the opportunity to sail or be hauled by oxen or mules overland to Sackets Harbor by the coast road, which was about the same in mileage but much more expensive in terms of time and wages.

One of James Fenimore Cooper's nonfiction writings tells what this was like from the point of view of Ned Myers, a 20-year old seaman who volunteered to join Chauncey's lake squadron in September 1812. Ned was one of 140 sailors serving in the New York gunboat flotilla when Chauncey recruited them. According to Ned, they hated gunboat duty, so all joined up. As Cooper recorded, "When everything reached Oswego, all hands turned to, to equip some lake craft that had been bought for the service. These were schooners, salt droggers [freighters], of about sixty to eighty tons. All we did at Oswego, however, was to load these schooners, some six or eight in all, and put to sea. I went off in one of the first, a vessel called the *Fair American*. Having no armaments, we sailed in the night, to avoid John Bull's cruisers, of which there were several out at the same time."[1] They reached Sackets Harbor safely, and Myers soon found himself transferred to the brig *Oneida* for the attack on Kingston in November. Following this sortie, the squadron moored for the winter at Sackets Harbor.

By December, it was a foregone conclusion that the naval war on the northern lakes would come back to life after a winter of inactivity. Since neither Great Britain nor the United States had much in the way of an inland navy, most of the warships would have to be built near deep harbors on the shore of these lakes. While trading schooners were present on Lakes Erie, Ontario, and Champlain, some were modified for gunports and provided with 6- or 12-pounders, although they were not equipped with bulkheads for protecting the crew, nor would they handle well with heavier ordnance. In view of this, a great amount of natural and human resources would have to be found or created to provide a shipbuilding industry in areas of meager population, heavily wooded wilderness, and rough roads. The naval adversaries in this war faced enormous logistical problems. The events on Lakes Ontario and Champlain in 1813 provide ample evidence of how the naval commanders tried to overcome these obstacles (fig. 9.1).

As Lake Ontario began its annual winter freeze at Sackets Harbor, Commodore Chauncey could take satisfaction in having gained dominance on Lake Ontario by overmatching the Provincial Marine and taking some small prizes. Yet, he was very conscious of his overall responsibility as it pertained to Lake Erie as well. Surveying the scene, President James Madison had concluded that the only way to reconquer the Old Northwest was to build a US Navy squadron on Lake Erie to work in tandem with Major General William Henry Harrison's left division to recover Detroit and establish dominance on Lake Huron. Secretary Paul Hamilton had been impressed by the arguments of the Lake Erie merchant-trader Daniel Dobbins that the best place to build a navy was known locally as Presque Isle, Pennsylvania, where there was a well-protected natural harbor. As a first step, Hamilton appointed Dobbins to the rank of sailing master and sent him back to Presque Isle to commence building four gunboats.[2]

In December 1812, Chauncey made a western tour of inspection to personally visit Erie and then Black Rock, a small navy dockyard on the Niagara River adjacent to Buffalo.[3] He approved of Dobbins's chosen location but saw only a

Figure 9.1. Southeast View of Sacketts Harbour, US naval base, 1814. Painting by Thomas Birch. Lithograph by William Strickland. US Naval History and Heritage Command, Photograph NH 1524.

collection of shabby huts to shelter the workmen and their materials. He criticized the small size of the gunboats under construction, ordering two of them to be extended in length. He also ordered the building of proper quarters for these workmen and those who were to come. At Black Rock, he was no better satisfied. Several of the lake vessels that had been taken into the navy were in a dismantled condition and under repair. These were the sloop *Trippe,* the schooners *Amelia, Somers,* and *Ohio,* and the prize brig *Caledonia.* The Black Rock naval station was in a perilous location, about 1.5 miles north of Fort Erie on the opposite bank of the Niagara River. At maximum range, the British artillery was able reach the construction site with harassing fire. Without protection, the shipwrights had ceased working under this threat. Regardless, it was clear to Chauncey that these vessels would have to be completed by the spring thaw and hauled upriver to Buffalo before they would be clear of the British guns and able to sail westward to join the vessels being built at Erie.[4]

Chauncey anticipated that the British would soon make greater efforts to respond to his activity on both lakes. He wrote to Jones about what his spies and British deserters were reporting, such as preparations at Kingston to build a 36-gun ship, that 130 ship carpenters and 50 sailors had recently arrived in Kingston, and that about half of those carpenters were being sent on to York, where, as rumor had it, warships would also be built. Chauncey requested permission to start work on another ship to keep up with or get ahead of the British in the shipbuilding race that had commenced.[5]

The Royal Navy in Canada

As early as October 17, 1812, Governor General George Prevost had written to Lord Bathurst, the secretary of state for war and the colonies, stating his concerns about the inability of the Provincial Marine to contend with Chauncey's growing squadron.[6] Bathurst brought Prevost's request for reinforcements to the attention of Prime Minister Liverpool and his cabinet during meetings in early December. These discussions led to positive results for Prevost. On January 13, Bathurst informed him that two regiments of infantry and three hundred seamen would arrive on the first ships that could be sent to Quebec in the spring. From that point on, naval affairs in Canada were under Royal Navy control, subject to the approval of the governor general. Prevost went further, writing to Admiral Sir John Borlase Warren, commander of the North American station, requesting that he recommend officers for naval commands on the lakes. Warren cooperated by writing to John Croker, secretary to the Admiralty, on February 21 enclosing Prevost's letter. Within six weeks the Admiralty had prepared HMS *Woolwich*, a troopship, with the officers, seamen, and naval equipment that might suffice, at least in the early weeks of the campaign. The officer selected to command the lakes squadrons was Captain Sir James Lucas Yeo, who at age 30 had a distinguished record of service during the Napoleonic Wars.[7]

The Admiralty's instructions did not give Commodore Yeo an independent command to roam the lakes and destroy his enemy. In its letter of appointment, the mission was stated as follows: "The first and paramount object for which this Naval Force is maintained being the defense of His Majesty's Provinces of North America; we do hereby require and direct you in the employment thereof to cooperate most cordially with His Excellency the Captain General and Governor in Chief of the said provinces, not undertaking any operations without the full concurrence and approbation of him or the Commanders of the Forces employed under him; and on all occasions conforming yourself and employing the Force under your command, according to the Requisitions which you may from time to time receive to this effect, from the Governor or Commander of the Forces."[8]

The effect of this letter was to restrain Commodore Yeo from using his own discretion on certain occasions. He was to be fighting a defensive war against his American adversaries. In the case of Commodore Chauncey, who was similarly constrained, this led primarily to a campaign of maneuver on Lake Ontario. Each of the naval commanders had instructions to coordinate with his military counterpart. A successful strategy required the navies to protect the military supply lines and deliver troops where needed. The sooner one side could dominate the lake, the better chance its army would have of gaining the advantage in the war for control of the surrounding territory.

The principal naval events that took place on the lake in 1813 were characterized by cautious maneuvering interspersed with hit-and-run raids. Commodore Yeo's arrival at Kingston with Royal Navy officers and seamen signaled a major shift in naval strategy. Yeo took control of the vessels that were part of the British army's quartermaster general's Provincial Marine and placed them under the command of professional naval officers drawn from England.

Naval and Joint Operations on Lake Ontario

Commencing in April 1813, Commodore Chauncey and Major General Henry Dearborn launched amphibious attacks on York and Fort George. They succeeded in cutting British communications with Kingston, forcing the British to evacuate Fort Erie and retreat toward Burlington Heights. Taking advantage of the US squadron's absence, Prevost and Yeo attacked Chauncey's base at Sackets Harbor. This interrupted Chauncey's support of the American army. He then withdrew his squadron to Sackets Harbor for defense of the base, yielding control of the western end of the lake to the British. This enabled a British military recovery as the British won engagements at Beaver Dams and Stoney Creek and captured Brigadier Generals William Winder and John Chandler, forcing the American army to retreat to Fort George, which it occupied for the rest of the year. Following the completion of his new flagship, *General Pike*, Chauncey finally felt strong enough to contest the Royal Navy's dominance on the lake. He led his squadron out in early August. This commenced a campaign of maneuver and skirmish during which Chauncey lost two schooners (*Hamilton* and *Scourge*) in a sudden squall.[9] Another two (*Julia* and *Growler*) were captured as a result of failing to obey Chauncey's signals. Offsetting these losses, Henry Eckford and his shipwrights built the new war schooner *Sylph* in less than one month's time at Sackets Harbor. At 300 tons displacement and armed with four long 32-pounders and twelve long 6-pounders, she more than replaced the diminutive lake traders *Scourge* and *Hamilton*. On September 11, the American squadron overtook Yeo's ships in light air and fought a running battle off the mouth of the Genesee River. Chauncey's vessels were to windward, and their long guns did some damage, but there were few casualties.

Chauncey has been criticized for failing to disengage his schooners to allow his larger ships to use their speed to best advantage. He was in the habit of towing his armed schooners in order to have the use of their long guns. But this reduced his ability to deal harsh blows to Yeo's squadron. Again, on September 28, Chauncey's *General Pike* gained the weather gauge over the British and damaged, from a distance, Yeo's flagship, *Wolfe*, during the battle of Burlington Bay. Indeed, *General Pike* might have defeated *Wolfe* had not Commander Mulcaster thrust his own ship, *Royal George*, between them, thereby saving his commodore's flagship. Yet, this was another instance of Chauncey's reluctance to cut loose the schooners in tow so as to overtake and outmaneuver the enemy.[10] Perhaps, though, Chauncey had learned his lesson. On October 4, in the last significant lake action of the year, Chauncey's ships, casting off their tows, successfully overtook an escorted supply convoy en route to Kingston, capturing its cargo as well as 18 army and naval officers and 252 men of the de Watteville regiment.[11]

Chauncey vs. Perry: The Manning Issue

At length, with the supportive Secretary William Jones urging him on, Chauncey recovered lost ground during the summer of 1813. He was able to overcome logistical losses imposed by the Prevost-Yeo raid of early June, repair the slightly damaged *General Pike*, and order Henry Eckford's men to build the large schooner *Sylph*, which made it possible for the US squadron to regain dominance of the lake in late September. The major problem continued to be lack of experienced sailors. Chauncey wrote frequently of his need for more seamen and officers to man his growing squadron and to supply Commodore Perry with his manning requirements. Tension developed between the two commanders regarding the number and quality of sailors that Chauncey forwarded to Perry. Both of them needed the best seamen that could be obtained from recruiting and ships blockaded or under repair on the seacoast. Jones ordered seamen sent from the New York gunboat flotilla, from *Alert* and *John Adams* at the Brooklyn Navy Yard, and from *Constitution* and *Syren* at Boston.

In June, Jones informed Chauncey that Perry required 450 more men to man his squadron and that he was forwarding 120 seamen and 100 marines to Chauncey from *Syren*. In early July, Jones chided Chauncey for exaggerating the number of men he needed for his own squadron. Major General Harrison was pressing Perry to hurry his preparations to sail and needed his help at the western end of Lake Erie. On July 16, Chauncey sent Perry a group of 60 sailors led by the sailing master Steven Champlin, Perry's nephew. After Perry met them, he rashly responded that "the men that came by Mr. Champlin are a motley set, blacks, soldiers, and boys. I cannot think you saw them after they were selected. I am, however, pleased to see anything in the shape of a man." To which his nettled superior made a now famous rejoinder: "I regret that you are not pleased with the men sent you by Messrs. Champlain and Forrest, for to my knowledge a part of them are not surpassed by any seamen we have in the fleet, and I have yet to learn the color of a man's skin or the cut and trimmings of his coat can affect a man's qualifications or his usefulness. I have nearly 50 blacks on board this ship and many of them are amongst my best men."[12] Chauncey was ahead of his time in this respect, but another issue was bothering him. Perry had written separately to Secretary Jones that it might be better for him to be directly under Jones's direction since communications from Chauncey were slow to arrive and not conducive to preparing for battle. Chauncey quickly picked up on Perry's intent to request that his command be independent of Chauncey. It happened that Jones agreed with Perry in this regard but had not so informed Chauncey. These remarks incited Perry's resentment to the extent that on August 10, only one month before Perry's squadron engaged Barclay's, Perry requested that Jones reassign him. Jones perceived what was at stake and gave Perry the reprimand he deserved: that a change of commander under the circumstances was "inadmissible" and that it would result "in the most serious injury to the service and probably ruin to yourself." These remarks and others more complimentary induced Perry to climb down from his high horse. Jones concluded with the resounding, timeless message that "it is the duty of an officer . . . to sacrifice all personal motives and feelings when in collision with the public good."[13]

One month later, having augmented his ranks with some of General Harrison's troops, Perry met Commodore Barclay's squadron off the Bass Islands and fought to a complete victory, with many casualties suffered on both sides. This eliminated the British threat on Lake Erie and opened the way to Lake Huron. The military success longed for in Washington was achieved in the battle of the Thames, near Moraviantown, Ontario, where Harrison's army caught up with the retreating British and their First Nation allies. This resulted in the death of the Shawnee leader, Tecumseh, which demoralized and scattered his followers. Harrison's army now might have posed a threat to the western flank of the British outpost on Burlington Heights, yet his division comprised more Kentucky volunteer cavalry than US Army regulars. The Kentucky troops had signed on for only ninety days and were anxious to return home. Harrison felt that he had no choice but to withdraw from Moraviantown to Detroit. From there he sailed with his fifteen hundred regulars to Fort Erie, on the Niagara, and awaited further orders.[14]

Such was the result of good leadership and the harmonious collaboration between Commodore Perry's fleet and General Harrison's army to the north of Lake Erie. The same, however, cannot be said of Commodore Chauncey's relationship with General James Wilkinson and Secretary of War John Armstrong in the Lake Ontario region. Chauncey's inability to maintain dominance on the lake after the landings at York and Fort George and the enemy's raid on Sackets Harbor weakened Dearborn's army on the Niagara Peninsula. Had Chauncey's principal vessels been active, they might have prevented Yeo's support of Major General John Vincent's army and its counterattack, which pushed the US center division back to Fort George.

President Madison and Secretary Armstrong replaced the ailing Dearborn with Major General James Wilkinson, the most senior though least trusted general officer in the ranks. Armstrong and Wilkinson were both veterans of the Revolutionary War, as was Dearborn.[15] It became evident that their generation had outlived its usefulness, as would be seen in the debacle that took place during the St. Lawrence River expedition. Logistical difficulties played a role, but the failures of military leadership evident in lack of character, vacillation, and quarrels were equally to blame and would not be overcome until a younger generation of officers rose to the top.

The St. Lawrence Expedition

American strategy shifted eastward late in the season. Secretary of War Armstrong, Major General Wilkinson, and Commodore Chauncey had originally proposed attacking Kingston in order to sever British communications with Montreal and Quebec along the St. Lawrence River. This, however, depended on cooperation and coordination from Major General Wade Hampton's right-division army marching from Plattsburgh, New York, toward the St. Lawrence and joining Wilkinson's above Montreal. Why Armstrong put these two aging warriors in a tandem yoke is difficult to comprehend. Wilkinson and Hampton had served in the army at New Orleans, where they had quarreled in 1808–9.[16] Given that Armstrong knew of their enmity, it was unconscionable that he placed Wilkinson, who had seniority, in a position to give orders to the crusty Hampton, who had told Armstrong he would not take orders from anyone but Armstrong.

This plan was fated to fail because, among other things, the two generals shared such mutual distrust. This quickly led to conflicts in command and control. When Hampton marched from Plattsburgh, he chose an indirect route, cutting a road westward through New York's Adirondack forests and swamps and then marching northward along the Chateauguay River. Soon after his line of march joined the river, he ran headlong into a blocking army from Lower Canada led by Lieutenant Colonel Charles de Salabery and supported by Major General

Louis de Watteville.[17] Despite outnumbering the French Canadians, Hampton divided his force and suffered a defeat in confused fighting on October 26. He then retreated to Plattsburgh. This event occurred more than two weeks before Wilkinson was defeated at Crysler's Farm; in fact, Wilkinson's riverine expedition did not enter the St. Lawrence until October 30.

Commodore Chauncey had originally agreed to support the operation against Kingston. Wilkinson ordered Major General Jacob Brown to bring major elements of the army from Niagara to Sackets Harbor, where they would embark on army barges and the squadron's ships for the attack on Kingston. After learning that the British had reinforced the garrison and forts at Kingston, the ever-vacillating Armstrong opened the alternative of attacking Montreal. This was to be done by effecting a junction with General Wade Hampton's army, which would march northward from Plattsburgh. An angry Chauncey justly argued that it was too late in the season. Autumnal gales, then snow and freezing temperatures would soon arrive. The larger ships of his squadron could not play a supporting role in a river lacking adequate sea room and imperiled by rocky shoals and a swift current. Furthermore, Commodore Yeo's larger vessels would blockade the head of the St. Lawrence, possibly trapping the American squadron in the river's ice.

At that point, on October 27, Armstrong departed the scene, sensing that the expedition might well fail and that he was better off in Washington, where he should have been in any event. During the remainder of the campaign season, General Brown's army, under the sickly General Wilkinson's overall command, launched an amphibious expedition down the St. Lawrence, aiming to join Hampton's army and capture Montreal. To counter this threat, Commodore Yeo played his part by sending the schooners *Beresford* and *Sir Sidney Smith*, seven gunboats, and sixty bateaux to transport a "corps of observation" of more than one thousand troops to harass the US Army flotilla as they floated downstream. The British gunboats caught up and began to fire at the American flotilla, forcing Wilkinson's decision whether to land and fight or to ride over the Long Sault rapids to Montreal. Without unanimity in his war council, Wilkinson decided for the former. The Americans landed a force of 3,050, including artillery and cavalry, near a field on the north (left) bank owned by farmer John Crysler. The British army confronting them amounted to 1,149 in all branches, including 30 Mohawk warriors. Outmaneuvered and outfought, though superior in numbers, the US troops suffered 13 percent casualties. Wilkinson and his generals performed poorly that day, but there was no surrender—both sides stopped fighting from exhaustion at twilight. Wilkinson ordered his troops to withdraw across the river to American soil. He sent a message to Hampton, requesting that they join forces at St. Regis, at the junction of the St. Regis River and the St. Lawrence, but

Hampton refused owing to lack of supplies. Wilkinson ranted about Hampton when he heard of his retreat from the Chateauguay and his refusal to continue the campaign. With the operation ill-timed and poorly executed, Wilkinson's troops had suffered a humiliating defeat at Crysler's Farm and retreated to winter quarters in New York State, while Hampton marched back to Plattsburgh.[18]

Commodore Chauncey and General Wilkinson

In October 1813, the prolonged indecision that plagued Secretary Armstrong and General Wilkinson regarding whether to attack Kingston or launch a riverine expedition against Montreal proved to be a puzzle for the British commanders, who were to be on the defensive in either case. They had to be ready for either possibility. Commodore Yeo was concerned about how to position his squadron and gunboats. If he held back some vessels to protect Kingston, he would be less able to pursue the Americans in their descent on Montreal. On October 17, in a letter to Governor General Prevost, Yeo wrote that "it is with greatest reluctance that I divide the squadron . . . as I have a presentiment that Kingston is the place they will attack, particularly if they hear that we have divided our force—or they may take advantage of it and go up to York."[19] Thus, whether intended or not, the enemy was confused by US indecision.

Chauncey much preferred the attack on Kingston, in which his squadron would play a major role, conveying and protecting the army as it moved across the head of the St. Lawrence and then landed near Kingston. His ships would also provide cover for the troops as they landed. Chauncey anticipated capturing or destroying the British squadron if the attack were successful. Then the squadron likely could not be replaced in time to fight in the coming 1814 season, in which case Chauncey's Sackets Harbor base could be considered relatively safe. It was not until October 29 that Chauncey learned of Wilkinson's final decision to abandon the Kingston attack, which had been in the planning stage for four weeks. He wrote to Secretary Jones about his disappointment and the military disaster he feared would probably follow if the attack on Montreal were pursued. He promised Jones that he would protect the army's descent as far and as long as he could, but he deemed it unsafe for his vessels to remain in the river after November 1 because of ice formation.[20] Soon thereafter he informed Jones that the army had begun its downriver passage on November 5 and that the weather had been favorable until November 10. Since a heavy westerly gale with snow had blown in, he ordered the squadron out of the river, to proceed to Sackets Harbor.

After reprovisioning, Chauncey sailed for Fort George to embark General Harrison, his staff, and about eleven hundred troops to serve as protection for Sackets

Harbor. A strong easterly buffeted his ships and transport schooners, delaying the arrival of the squadron and Harrison's men until November 20. This ended the US Navy's operations on Lake Ontario in 1813, except for sending out the swift *Lady of the Lake* to check on the enemy's activities at Kingston harbor.[21] Regarding the future, Chauncey had considered the possibility of what would happen if he were unable to destroy Yeo's ships, either by fleet action or in not attacking Kingston. In this case, he wrote, "it would be necessary for us to build a sufficient number of vessels of an equal class—From the best information that I can get there is [*sic*] materials prepared at Kingston for three vessels—two of them are in some state of forwardness—one of these vessels is to be a frigate—the length of her keel . . . is 150 feet—a part of her frame is already raised—the other two are to be 20-gun ships or brigs."[22] These observations would lead Chauncey to request a major increase in his shipbuilding program in 1814.

Opening Moves on Lake Ontario, 1814

Despite this early warning, the US Navy's Ontario squadron was not first out on the lake in the spring of 1814. To explain this costly, untimely failure, we must explore several factors. The delay in preparing ships was not due to lack of intelligence on British construction plans. Chauncey let Secretary Jones know that he would need to match this pace or be blockaded in port with the British having a larger, more powerful fleet. The secretary and the commodore found that they had major logistical obstacles to overcome. Secretary Jones, on the other hand, was critical of the indecisive end of the 2013 campaign season, which in part could be blamed on Chauncey, who had withdrawn to Sackets Harbor for nearly two months after the British attempt to ravage the base and burn his new ship. Had Chauncey been more audacious, he could have distracted Yeo by sending his warships up the lake while depending on the military to defend his base, but this was not Chauncey's style. His caution had the effect of denying support to the American army at Niagara.

The danger of the British launching an attack across the ice during the coming winter was on Jones's mind. Chauncey tried to allay his concerns by describing how he had moored his ships at right angles to Navy Point so as to bring their guns to bear on the enemy if such an attack developed. Captain William Crane had arrived, and Chauncey put him in charge of the naval base during the time he planned to be absent at New York and Washington. As for other problems, Chauncey let Jones know that many of the men in the sloop of war *Madison* were ill, some so sick that he proposed detaching them from the service. The naval surgeon Walter W. Buchanan had been assigned to Chauncey's command in 1812 at the invitation of Chauncey, who was well satisfied with his performance.[23] Conditions on the lakes were difficult for seamen and marines, especially during the harsh winters. Being wet and cold on board unheated ships undermined the health of the seamen, who were required to remain on board. It was not unusual for 20 percent of the sailors and marines to be on the sick list. Marines who served ashore to protect the navy yard and were housed in barracks fared no better.[24] The secretary did not respond to the comments on seamen's health but did offer that he had arranged for additional guns to be sent to Sackets Harbor. He had ordered officers and enlisted from the frigates *Macedonian* and *John Adams* and Master Commandant Charles Ridgely's newly completed sloop of war *Erie* to be assigned to Chauncey's command.

One of the navy's problems in recruiting was competition from the army. The War Department offered a bounty to its recruits that the navy was not authorized to match. The officers and men in Commodore Chauncey's command so deeply resented this disparity that they petitioned the US Congress. Led by Master Commandant William M. Crane, the petitioners asserted that lake service had peculiar hardships; for example, items considered necessary for their comfort cost twice as much. Furthermore, the fixed pay of officers and the wages and rations of seamen had been reduced. With no privateers or merchant ships on the lake, there was no opportunity to benefit from prize money, and there was a marked difference between what was paid to soldiers and what was paid to seamen. Even the officers and seamen of the enemy were better paid. The petitioners stated that they had to live in a severe and unhealthy climate, and they hoped Congress would give them some compensation for these conditions. This petition was signed by Crane and twenty-four other commissioned, warrant, and noncommissioned officers. The petition and other influences finally did bring about a change. On April 18, 1814, Congress passed An Act concerning the pay of officers, seamen, and marines in the navy of the United States, which increased pay levels for all those except at the rank of captain and master commandant and guaranteed an additional 25 percent for those in service on the lakes as hardship pay.[25] No hint of official objection to the petitioners' unusual complaint came from the commodore, who may well have agreed with or even encouraged it.

Logistical Warfare: The British Attack on Oswego

By dint of much hard work and reinforcements from the North Atlantic squadron, Commodore Yeo and his new counterpart, Lieutenant General Gordon Drummond, were able to develop a raiding strategy aimed at preventing or delaying Chauncey's squadron from taking to the lake. They first considered another attack on Sackets Harbor but were informed that it was too well defended. Chauncey's frigate *Superior* had just been launched but had not yet been rigged. The British had the lake to themselves. Rather than blockade Sackets Harbor, Yeo and Drummond decided to raid Fort Oswego, Chauncey's major supply base. Under the circumstances, this was one of the most effective ways of slowing the US squadron's preparations. The British flotilla appeared off Oswego's defended shoreline early the morning of May 4 with nearly the entire squadron and 900 troops, including 350 Royal Marines. Opposing them were Lieutenant Colonel George Mitchell and Master Commandant Melancthon Woolsey and some 400 men of the Third Regiment of Artillery and 100 New York militia. Although outnumbered, the Americans put up a stiff resistance, forcing the British to make two failed attacks before the Americans had to abandon Fort Oswego. The British took away three trading schooners, seven heavy guns (32-pounders and 24-pounders), ordnance stores, naval stores, and provisions (800 barrels of flour, 500 barrels of pork, 500 barrels of bread) and destroyed the fort, outbuildings, and barracks. The defenders sank three 32-pounders as well as a large amount of cordage in the Oswego River before evacuating the fort.[26] The British attack on Fort Oswego made a serious dent in the American squadron's supply line, particularly heavy guns, although they were eventually replaced. In human terms, however, the action was less costly for the Americans than for the enemy. The British suffered 90 casualties, 64 killed and 26 wounded, as opposed to six Americans killed, 38 wounded, and 25 captured.[27]

In a skirmish that followed the raid on Oswego, the Americans turned the tables. Commodore Yeo's squadron had returned to sea after visiting Kingston to disembark his wounded, prisoners, and the captured supplies. The squadron returned to Oswego but saw nothing of interest, so Yeo sent a small contingent under Captain Stephen Popham, of the sloop of war *Montreal*, to look in at smaller lake ports farther east. Popham's flotilla captured one boat of a nineteen-boat convoy that was carrying heavy ordnance along the shore, heading for Sackets Harbor. With information gained about the others, Popham departed the squadron leading two gunboats and three cutters manned by 160 seamen and marines. Several hours later, Yeo reinforced Popham by sending Commander Spilsbury, of the sloop of war *Niagara*, and 60 men in two gunboats. Popham led the boats into Sandy Creek, where he thought the convoy might be hiding. He was right but unwary.

The American sailors, under Master Commandant Woolsey and Major Daniel Appling, protected by 130 infantry in the boats, had pulled about two miles up the meandering Sandy Creek. They were well armed and joined by 150 Oneida warriors, who had agreed to follow along the lakeshore. Meanwhile, Chauncey learned that the British had been sighted heading for Sandy Creek. He sent a troop of dragoons with artillery, a company of marines, and Captain Charles Ridgely and a party of naval infantry to reinforce Woolsey. The result was a successful ambush by the Americans and Oneidas from both sides of Sandy Creek. Popham survived, though he was wounded and captured. Of his party, 18 were killed, about 50 were wounded, and the rest were taken prisoner. All told, the British lost the services of 220 sailors and marines in this attempt to seize Chauncey's supplies. When the bad news arrived, Yeo was furious at Captain Popham's imprudence in taking his expedition up a narrow, winding, wooded creek. Yeo could ill afford to lose the crews of two sloops of war while trying to expand his squadron to confront Chauncey, whose frigate *Superior* was nearly ready for sea.[28]

The advanced planning of Woolsey and Appling and the fighting spirit of the infantry and the Oneida war party made it possible for the desperately needed guns, cordage, gunpowder, and round shot carried by the convoy to reach Sackets Harbor in early June. This coincided with Henry Eckford's launching of the 42-gun frigate *Mohawk* and the arrival of Captain John Smith and the crew of *Congress*. Smith had been scheduled to command *Mohawk* but had become ill and requested reassignment.[29] Captain Jacob Jones, formerly commander of *Macedonian*, assumed command. Aside from Chauncey, Jones was the senior captain at Sackets Harbor and stood next in line should anything happen to Chauncey. Most of Chauncey's needs in terms of men, rigging, guns, and ordnance stores had arrived for the completion of *Mohawk* and *Superior*. The squadron was nearly ready to sail.

Commodore Chauncey and General Brown

Two weeks after the skirmish at Sandy Creek, Brown wrote Chauncey directly, chiding him for his lack of communication regarding when the squadron would be ready to sail for the mouth of the Niagara River. Chauncey made haste to apologize, blaming the delay on his "extreme anxiety" about when his guns and other stores would arrive. But once they had, he promised to sail during the first week in July, but with the proviso that his first concern was Commodore Yeo's fleet and that he would have to watch its movements if his enemy remained near Kingston. If "Sir James" visited the head of the lake, the American squadron would be there, presumably to prevent the British squadron from supporting Drummond's army.[30] But this was far from what General Brown wanted to hear. Unfortunately for Brown and his left division, Chauncey was fixated on the safety of his base and did not trust it to the army and militia troops who had remained to protect it. It is apparent from hindsight that Chauncey may have been tortured by the inherent conflict in his standing orders.

In April 1813, Jones sent Chauncey orders on interservice relations, stating that "it is of primary importance to reconcile and harmonize the designs and movements of the combined forces so that the most perfect understanding and efficient concert may result from their mutual cooperation."[31] Yet, Jones ended by saying that Chauncey would be "the exclusive judge as to the timing, circumstances, and manner of employing that [naval] force." One year later, Jones reminded him that his mission was to attack, capture, and destroy the enemy squadron or closely blockade it in port; conversely, he was to cooperate with the US military, assisting in the transport of troops and supplies when they were vitally needed.[32] This was the situation the commodore faced in July 1814. In Chauncey's mind, this set up a conflict. The time was approaching when he could not do both missions simultaneously. The traumatic effects of this clash of duties became only too blatant in the days to come.[33]

A Tempestuous Summer

With little support available from the navy on Lake Erie, General Brown assembled his army at Buffalo, took Fort Erie, and waited for Commodore Chauncey to arrive at the mouth of the Niagara River. It would be a prolonged wait. By June 24, at Sackets Harbor, *Superior* was fully rigged and armed with crew on board, and Chauncey predicted to Jones that he would be ready to sail by July 1. He had received another letter from General Brown pleading to be informed by *express* when the squadron would sail. He asked Chauncey to arrive by July 10; if he could not arrive that day, Brown wanted to know when he could. The day he received Brown's letter, Chauncey replied that the new sloop of war *Mohawk* would be ready the first week of July, and then he would sail in search of Yeo's squadron, but he was careful to say that he would not appear off Niagara unless Yeo's ships led him there. On July 8, Chauncey wrote Brown again, ostensibly to pass on some military intelligence about British infantry and artillery moving to York and Fort George. In closing, Chauncey added that *Mohawk* was nearly ready and only needed some ironwork. As if by return of post, Brown replied from Queenstown, Ontario, on July 10, telling Chauncey that he thought Commodore Yeo would not fight and asking him to "for God's sake, let me see you," or at least to let him know what to expect from the US Ontario squadron. After this, a strange silence from Chauncey alarmed Secretary Jones, President Madison, and General Brown, whose troops had just defeated the British at the Chippewa

Bridge and would soon confront them again in the battle of Lundy's Lane on July 25. Just a day or two before the battle, Brown received a letter from Major General Edmund Gaines dated July 20 with the unwelcome news that although the American squadron was ready, Chauncey was ill and had refused to send the squadron out under Captain Jacob Jones, his second-in-command. Chauncey was bedridden with what many called "lake fever," a form of typhoid fever, known to have sickened sailors on both Lakes Erie and Ontario.

The commodore, in his anxiety, failed to communicate his illness to Secretary Jones, or perhaps he did not want to for fear of being relieved. Jones informed President Madison that he had not heard from Chauncey. Both knew that the battles at Niagara might depend on the navy's participation. Madison urged Jones to order Captain Decatur to set out for Sackets Harbor. If he found Chauncey unable to command, Decatur was to assume command himself. Fortunately for Chauncey, Decatur learned that the squadron had sailed when he reached Albany, and so he returned to New York. That, however, did not ameliorate the criticism aimed at Chauncey by Secretary Jones, contemporary writers, and since that time historians.[34]

A Failure to Communicate

Until July 25, Secretary of the Navy Jones received no communications from Commodore Chauncey for more than two weeks and only one from Captain Jacob Jones, who explained briefly about Chauncey's sickness and that the squadron could not sail without *Mohawk* receiving some ironwork and blocks needed for her gun tackle. Jones resisted writing until 3 August, when he let the commodore feel the full weight of his anger and frustration. "I cannot withhold from you," he wrote, "the knowledge of the extreme anxiety and astonishment, which the protracted and fatal delay of the squadron in port has excited in the mind of the President. . . . If the gallant and able commander of our squadron was rendered incapable by disease, why did not the second in command, in whom national confidence also resides, lead it into action, or scour the lake so as to prevent or intercept the transportation of the enemy, or force his fleet to battle while we have the known and decided superiority?"[35] These and the other questions Jones posed must have shocked the commodore into full awareness of how the failure to communicate had affected his reputation in the capital and in the country at large. Moreover, he had embarrassed the secretary in front of his peers and the president, something not likely to be soon forgiven.

The historian Henry Adams did not adhere to General Brown's harsh critique; in fact he called the general mistaken in placing on Chauncey the entire blame for the failure to conquer Upper Canada. Brown thought of Chauncey as a sort of "naval Wilkinson," a rather denigrating comment. Adams wrote that Chauncey, although he might have delayed Drummond's army, could not have prevented their attacking Brown or stopped their advance.[36] Theodore Roosevelt was of the opinion that even without *Superior*'s guns, Chauncey would have overawed Yeo's squadron without a fight. He wrote that "his [Chauncey's] ideas of the purpose for which his command had been created were erroneous and very hurtful to the American cause. That purpose was not, except incidentally, the destruction of the enemy's fleet, and if it was, he entirely failed to accomplish it. The real purpose was to enable Canada to be successfully invaded, or to assist in repelling an invasion of the United States. These services could only be efficiently performed by acting in union with the land forces, for his independent action could have little effect."[37] The Canadian naval historian Robert Malcomson provided a fair and thorough explanation of Chauncey's predicament, pointing out that he had not provided Brown with a date certain on which the squadron would be in sight off the Niagara River. He argued further that Brown had invaded the peninsula on July 3, without heeding Secretary Armstrong's advice not to move until Chauncey *actually* arrived. If this advice had been followed, Yeo's squadron would have disappeared over the horizon, and Chauncey's squadron would have been in place with guns ready to destroy Fort George.[38]

The commodore admitted having "apprehension that the enemy might receive large reinforcements at Kingston, and embarking some of the troops, make a dash at the Harbor and burn it with all my stores during our absence . . . my apprehension, it seems was groundless." For Chauncey, all revolved around logistics. He pointed out that ships in the Atlantic ports had much more protection in harbor and said that their needs there were met much more quickly than the needs of ships on the lake. His base was the only one within hundreds of miles on which he could rely, and he had only seven hundred troops to protect Sackets Harbor. He explained his delays as owing to his sudden illness but did not apologize. He closed by saying that he was "mortified in not succeeding in satisfying the expectations of the public" but that it would have been much more painful had he fallen short in other, more vital aspects of his duty.[39]

The major event that Chauncey was expecting finally came to pass. Commodore Yeo's new flagship, HMS *St. Lawrence*, with 104 guns, sailed from Kingston for the first time (except for sea and gunnery trials) on October 16. At 191 feet in length, 52 feet in beam, and 18 feet depth of hold and with a draft of only 12 feet, she instantly became the largest ship ever to float on the Great Lakes. A three-decker manned by six hundred seamen, she made a big difference in the number of guns and weight of metal that Yeo's squadron could throw in a major battle.[40] Chauncey's immediate thought was of the threat to Sackets Harbor, but he had little insight into the problems of his counterpart. Yeo came under immediate pressure to carry troops and supplies to General Drummond's army on the Niagara Peninsula, which was besieging Brown's army at Fort Erie. Governor General Prevost, on a visit to Kingston, pressed the case for Drummond, who had learned that the US Ontario squadron had landed General Izard near the Niagara with four thousand men and that the US Lake Erie squadron had disembarked a thousand troops from Detroit at Buffalo. Drummond had even told Prevost that should he be unable to defeat the Americans because of a lack of reinforcements, he would hold Commodore Yeo responsible.[41]

Hearing of the addition of *St. Lawrence* to Yeo's squadron, Chauncey withdrew his ships to Sackets Harbor and moored them in defensive positions around Navy Point. Across the lake, Prevost and Yeo disagreed about how to employ the flagship. General Drummond had requested transportation the Ninetieth Foot regiment and some artillery to assist in the siege of Fort Erie. Yeo demurred, not wanting to encumber his flagship, when Chauncey might sortie to challenge Yeo's newfound supremacy on the lake. Prevost persuaded Yeo to carry at least some troops and supplies to the hard-pressed general. This Yeo finally did with considerable reluctance. When Prevost next wrote to Lord Bathurst, his complaint about the lack of naval cooperation was similar to Brown's against Chauncey. He wrote that there had been a "struggle for ascendency on the water that has drawn forth from both sides a formidable array of vessels that could never have been anticipated on these inland seas, and the naval commanders have, I am afraid, in consequence, been led to consider themselves as directing squadrons which by a trial of strength were to decide the fate of the war, forgetting their necessary identity with the land force for the general identity of the common cause."[42]

The remainder of the 1814 campaign season for the lake squadrons was one of suspense but little fighting on Lake Ontario. The great naval battle for which many had wished did not occur. Instead, the summer had ended in a stalemate. Each squadron had increased its strength in ships, guns, and sailors during the year, but the thoughts of both adversaries were of preparing for the campaign season of 1815. It was common knowledge that commissioners for peace negotiations were meeting in Ghent, Belgium, but none knew when or how they would end.

Planning for an 1815 Campaign

In late October, Secretary Jones was nearing the end of his term of office. He had served for nearly two years in this arduous position, and as early as April 1814 he had written to President Madison about his situation, explaining that he had to return to private business to save himself from financial ruin. As a merchant, Jones had suffered from the embargo, trade restrictions, and the blockade during the war. He was fatigued from the cares of office. As navy secretary, Jones had performed well under the stress of organizing victories and suffering defeats not experienced even in Benjamin Stoddert's tenure during the Quasi-War or Robert Smith's in the course of the First Barbary War. In addition to his navy job, Jones had also taken on the additional responsibility of secretary of the treasury after Albert Gallatin resigned to become one of the peace commissioners. William Jones had become one of the president's most loyal and industrious cabinet secretaries. The president responded in two days, expressing "the sincerest regret which is much heightened by the considerations which produced it. The nature of these forbids any effort to divert you from your purpose, especially as it is qualified in the interval in carrying it into effect."[43]

Although Jones was not at that moment ready to resign, he felt that he should inform the president of his intentions. In September, he announced to Madison and others that he would serve until the end of the present session of Congress, November 30, 1814, if the president would allow him to take his leave.[44] Jones was burdened with the enormous disaster that had occurred at Washington on August 24–25, when a British army under Lieutenant General Robert Ross brushed away the American militias at the battle of Bladensburg and then burned the Capitol, the White House, and other public buildings, all within a space of twenty-four hours. And it was in obedience to Secretary Jones's reluctant order that Captain Thomas Tingey burned the Washington Navy Yard and the new ships awaiting completion to prevent them from falling into enemy hands.[45]

It was with all this in mind that Secretary Jones sought to protect, preserve, and deploy the navy he had nurtured for almost two years. In communications with Chauncey, they discussed the safety of the squadron at Sackets Harbor and preparations for the 1815 campaign season. It was evident from accounts of paroled prisoners of war and spies that the shipwrights at Kingston would augment Yeo's squadron by constructing large warships like *St. Lawrence*. There was little choice involved. The Americans would have to follow suit, and quickly, to avoid being, once again, last on the lake and the first to be blockaded. Yet, Jones wistfully speculated to Madison whether it would be worthwhile to continue the "War of Shipyards and Arsenals" on Lake Ontario. It might be more worthwhile, he suggested, to set up a large fortification at St. Regis, on the St. Lawrence, to cut transport of supplies, guns, and troops from Montreal to Upper Canada.[46]

Commodore Chauncey's response to Jones's request for what it would take to construct two first-rate ships and a 44-gun frigate at Sackets Harbor presents an excellent catalog of the conditions and materials needed for such a large project. There was adequate land and depth of water for them. Chauncey suggested that carronades rather than long guns would be preferable for the spar decks. He estimated that there would be enough timber locally for at least two of the ships, if not all three. He would need ninety-four guns and eight hundred seamen for each ship. Chauncey admitted that he would have to adjust his requirements as the enemy modified theirs. As for iron for round shot and ship fastenings, he estimated that some was available locally. Depending on the output of furnaces at Onondaga, Rome, and Utica, he should be able to count on about 400 tons of kentledge.

For building the ships, he would need the following mechanics (artisans): 600 ship carpenters, 60 ship joiners, 60 pairs or 120 sawyers, 75 blacksmiths, 25 block and pump makers, 10 spar makers, 15 gun-carriage makers, 10 armorers, and 5 tinsmiths. He would need to build a joiner's shop, a block maker's shop, a boat builders' shed, an armorer and tinsmith shop, a powder magazine, two wharves, and one ropewalk with all the machinery needed to lay a 24-inch cable. Many other, smaller items and devices would have to be manufactured at seaports, for example, cogs and pins for blocks and anchors, rudder pintles and braces, iron tillers, fids, hawse and scupper leads, pump chambers, galley bells, cannon locks, powder horns, match rope, magazine signal and battle lanterns, rockets, port fires, blue lights, canvas twine, bolt rope, and whatever shot and kentledge could not be furnished in the local vicinity, as well as bolt and bar irons, spikes, nails, and all the tools required in the various departments. The commodore recommended that all the heavy items be transported by boat to Albany before the Hudson froze. The roads west of Albany were generally good during late December and early February. The farmers who take produce to Albany were usually looking for goods to transport on the return trip toward the naval depot at Oswego. He hoped to be able to complete the ships and be ready to sail by the middle of May. His goal was to be the first squadron on the lake, with an advantage over the enemy.[47]

In his final letter to Chauncey, Jones assured him that the orders of the guns for the ships had been promptly dispatched, and he reported that the president had expressed his concern, especially on this subject. Jones acknowledged that he was concerned about the recruiting the many seamen needed, considering the popularity of privateering and the sailors' aversion to serving on the lakes. In one last expression of his respect for Chauncey, Jones wrote, "I cannot suffer this occasion to pass with bearing testimony to the talents, energy, judgment, and patriotism which you have displayed during your arduous command and stating my conviction that it could not have been in better hands."[48] This was high praise from Jones, who was not usually so gracious, considering the tension-filled days of July and the testy public letters published by General Jacob Brown. In any event, Commodore Chauncey had weathered that storm and was facing the future with optimism and with support from the administration.

CHAPTER 10

Macdonough's War on Lake Champlain

Just as remote as Lake Ontario from Washington, DC, Lake Champlain has a completely different physical configuration. It is oriented on a north-south axis, its waters draining northward into the Richelieu River on the Canadian border, a few miles north of Plattsburgh, New York. Founded in 1785, the town is located at the mouth of the Saranac River, on the western shore of Lake Champlain. Plattsburgh is about 175 miles from Sackets Harbor and only 60 miles from Montreal.

Lieutenant Thomas Macdonough, USN, arrived at Burlington, on the Vermont side of Lake Champlain, on October 8, 1812.[1] He had traveled from Portland, Maine, where he had briefly commanded a flotilla of gunboats. He was under orders from Secretary of the Navy Paul Hamilton to assume command of two old gunboats and other diminutive vessels that were under navy control.[2] Macdonough relieved Lieutenant Sidney Smith, a native of the region and a fellow veteran of the Tripolitan War, who had been serving as the navy's only lieutenant in service on the lake since 1810.[3] He had been primarily on patrol against smugglers from both sides of the border at the north end of Lake Champlain. Two days after Congress declared war, Lieutenant Smith wrote to Secretary Hamilton saying he had heard rumors of war and wondered whether any orders for him had gone astray. He mentioned that the last letter received from the department had taken three months to arrive, when it should have taken only seven days. Hamilton still paid almost no attention to the needs of the navy on Lake Champlain until September. Smith had only two deteriorating gunboats at his disposal, and they were aground near Vergennes, Vermont. At the urging of General Benjamin Mooers, of the New York State militia, Smith apparently had invested some of his own funds for repairs to these vessels. Meanwhile, the US Army had built several gunboats and purchased six lake sloops at Whitehall, New York. Lieutenant Smith, lacking other authority, cooperated with the army, providing transportation for troops and equipment from Whitehall to Plattsburgh.

Macdonough's first task was to pay a formal call on General Bloomfield. He sailed the twenty-two miles to Plattsburgh in the army sloop *President* and presented his orders to the general. After welcoming him to the lake, Bloomfield informed Macdonough that he would indeed be commanding the government's vessels, but under the US Army's control, according to Major General Dearborn, Bloomfield's superior. At this point, Macdonough had to assert himself and Secretary Hamilton's order to take command of the vessels on the lake. Here was a critical point: If there were to be harmony between the services on the lake, Macdonough had to be firm yet diplomatic. Eventually, Bloomfield acquiesced, for the time being, allowing Macdonough to inspect the vessels. When, a week later, Macdonough had his interview with Major General Dearborn at Greenbush, New York, he asserted his experience as a veteran of two wars and detailed what he proposed to do to strengthen—in effect create—a Champlain naval flotilla. Reluctantly, Dearborn acknowledged that as long as Macdonough supported the forthcoming invasion of Canada, he would transfer to him command of gunboats and several army sloops, with the exception of his favorite, *President*. Dearborn granted the guns, ammunition, and army personnel Macdonough requested for the flotilla but said that he would appeal to higher authority concerning the divided army-navy command on Lake Champlain.[4]

Among his first problems, Macdonough had to sort out the question of the military commanders in the Lake Champlain area. The man on the spot at the beginning of the war was Major General Mooers, a Revolutionary War veteran. He had family ties to the region and was well known to the state's governor, Daniel Tompkins. Mooers was commander of the Third Division of the state militia, including the units from Clinton, Essex, and Franklin Counties. Immediately in charge of US Army troops at Plattsburgh was Brigadier General Joseph Bloomfield, also a veteran of the Revolutionary War, who had been called into service from his job as governor of New Jersey. As a Regular Army brigadier general, Bloomfield outranked Mooers, who was a major general in the militia. At the top of this command structure was Major General Henry Dearborn, who as a result of his long service was the second-ranking senior officer of the US Army, junior only to Major General James Wilkinson. Although Dearborn lacked a distinctive military reputation, he had served in several major campaigns during the Revolutionary War and on General George Washington's staff in Virginia during the siege of Yorktown. Dearborn was secretary of war during the Jefferson administration, succeeded by Dr. William Eustis, President Madison's appointee, in 1809. In 1812 Eustis appointed Dearborn commanding general of the US Army and, concurrently, commander of the army's right division.

The US Army established two cantonments in the Champlain Valley, one at Burlington, Vermont, and the other at Plattsburgh. Of these the most important was at Plattsburgh, the nearer to the enemy. But Burlington was also important. Being farther away, it was better protected and closer to the sources of supply, and it was a rendezvous point for personnel coming from Boston and other points south and east. Burlington's Shelburne Bay was also a convenient stopping place for military and commercial vessels coming from Whitehall, New York, the closest port to Dearborn's headquarters. Commodore Macdonough's naval base was located on Otter Creek at Vergennes, about twenty miles south of Burlington.

At length, Macdonough was able to persuade Dearborn to transfer the sloop *President* to his command. The commodore's tasks in the winter of 1812–13 were to recruit seamen (including officers), repair or rebuild the vessels at his disposal, requisition sufficient guns and munitions for his vessels, train his flotilla for battle, and obtain knowledge of the enemy's naval strength and shipbuilding plans for the summer campaign. As he reported to Secretary Hamilton, "The enemy has at the Isle a[ux] Noix three gunboats carrying ('tis said) by several persons that have seen them, two 24-pounders each and about fifty men, three sloops of about eighty tons mounting six 6-pounders, and a 24-[pounder] each with about 50 men on board each sloop, and lately I am told they are fitting out a schooner to mount 12 to 14 guns and well-manned; however, were the vessels we now have armed to be manned, I think we should be able to cope with them." He then listed his three sloops—*President*, 8, *Growler*, 7, and *Eagle*, 7—and two gunboats carrying one long 12-pounder each. The three other sloops he had inherited from the army were too decrepit to be used except as transports.[5]

During his inspection of the area at Vergennes, Macdonough learned of the Monkton Iron Works, a valuable resource to have so close to his growing navy yard on Otter Creek. This company had been formed by a group of Boston businessmen in 1806. The iron ore was produced from bog iron in the immediate vicinity. Macdonough ordered three hundred tons of shot in December 1812, and before 1814 the ironworks had produced more than a thousand 32-pound round shot. Beyond this, the Otter Creek Falls were the site of eight forges, blast and air furnaces, rolling mills, a wire factory, a sawmill, and an abundance of timber. In a phrase, this was a perfect place for siting a navy yard.[6] When Secretary William Jones took over the Navy Department, he ordered Macdonough to do whatever was necessary to keep Lake Champlain under American control.

Macdonough was aware that in building his squadron he would be competing with Commodores Chauncey and Perry, on the other lakes, for available seamen and guns, as well as other supplies. He was junior to the others, so he pressed gently for his needs and did what he could with the sailors at his disposal. In his first letter to the new navy secretary, William Jones, Macdonough proposed to remove the quarterdecks from his sloops and in their place to build gunports on the main deck, thus nearly doubling the number of guns they could carry. When complete, the sloops would carry ten guns in gunports, five on each side, plus a long gun on a circle (pivot), centered forward of the mast. He remarked that he had only twenty seamen, enough to handle the sails but not enough to man the guns as well. He would need thirty more sailors or else he would have to borrow men from the army, who "are miserable creatures on shipboard." He asked that twelve to fifteen carpenters be sent from New York to mount the twelve 18- to 24-pounder carronades he had ordered. Jones immediately agreed to the alterations, sending the carpenters and enough swords (cutlasses) for each sloop. The sailors would be sent "in due time."[7]

A Difficult Summer on Lake Champlain

As Macdonough rebuilt his flotilla and accumulated supplies for the opening of the lake's sailing season, he learned more of the government's plan for the summer campaign. Essentially, it was a continuation of the strategy of 1812: a renewed effort to recover captured territory in the Northwest (Detroit and northern Michigan) through control of Lake Erie, to gain control of Upper Canada through control of Lake Ontario and the Niagara Peninsula, and to invade Lower Canada and capture either Kingston or Montreal by way of the upper Champlain Valley and the Richelieu (Sorel) River. Secretary of War John Armstrong ordered Major General Wade Hampton to command the right division of the army at Plattsburgh. Even before Hampton's arrival, several army regiments had been stationed at Burlington as well as at Plattsburgh after the demise of the attack on La Colle Mill in November 1812.

In June, Macdonough gave Lieutenant Smith command of the sloops *Growler* and *Eagle*, with the sailing master Jairus Loomis as helmsman. Smith's orders were to patrol the northern coast of the lake, being on the alert for any British vessels and smugglers of either country trying to evade authority. He told Smith explicitly not to venture into the mouth of the Richelieu River, which was north of "the line," the border between the United States and Canada. Smith, unfortunately, had other ideas. He had embarked an army captain and forty-one Maine and New Hampshire volunteers to serve as marines and went looking for trouble. British gunboats were out on the lake under oars, trying to lure the Americans into the river for a duel of sorts. Smith decided to enter the river, despite warnings from Loomis. The sloops started pursuing the gunboats; soon they were six miles downriver when they were caught in an ambush from both riverbanks. As the sloops attempted to tack, not only was the wind against them but the river narrowed, so that they could not turn back without grounding, and the two-knot current from the lake made it impossible to return. Nonetheless, the two sloops fought desperately for about four hours, until one sank and the other was subdued. All who survived, approximately one hundred, were made prisoners at Isle aux Noix.[8]

The question of Lieutenant Smith's motivations in disobeying Macdonough's orders has been variously answered by historians. Allan Everest merely suggests that Smith was "overeager." David Skaggs offers that Smith felt diminished when Macdonough was selected for the Champlain command instead of himself and wanted to "enhance his reputation" among his peers and at the Navy Department. Charles Muller describes Smith as being "impetuous and high strung" and suggests that he may have been overcome by the excitement of his first opportunity to fight on his own.[9] There is likely an element of truth in each of these judgments, but one might have expected a naval officer with thirteen years of service to have more self-discipline with his commanding officer's orders ringing in his ears.

Regardless, Smith had disobeyed Macdonough's direct order and paid the price, being imprisoned in Canada for a year before being paroled. In his favor, he attempted to escape, but the British recaptured him. After his release in 1815, Smith was subjected to a court of inquiry at Sackets Harbor on board the US brig *Jones* with Master Commandant Melancthon Woolsey presiding. The court was in a forgiving mood, stating magnanimously that "the general conduct of Lt. Sidney Smith on Lake Champlain was correct and meritorious. . . . Being satisfied by the testimony that Lt. Smith was deceived by his pilot, [we] are of the opinion that the sloops *Growler* and *Eagle*, when attacked by a superior force, were gallantly defended and that they were not surrendered until all further resistance had become in vain."[10]

The loss of the two sloops with their crews and armaments was a severe shock for Commodore Macdonough. He was furious with Smith for his bold indiscretion, which took from the command two-thirds of its strength and reflected the loss of several months' work in preparing for the campaign. It brought to Macdonough embarrassment in front of his army counterparts and Navy Secretary Jones. The commodore could not support the army's campaign until he could replace the sloops, costing both money and time. Further, the navy was now in no condition to defend the lake. This meant that the British could sail at will, which they did in short order.

Macdonough's report to the secretary listed his losses, which included, in addition to the sloops, "three experienced lieutenants, six midshipmen, three gunners, and seventy ordinary seamen—my guns are gone sir, and there is not a spare one on the lake—18 pounder carronades I think the best kind for these vessels as they are light and carry a greater quantity of grape shot than long guns of about the same weight and it is likely they will be used principally against small vessels with many men exposed in them, or against sloops. I should require also one thousand cylinders for the twenty guns which I calculate to mount on the two sloops, ten on each one."[11] Jones's response was unemotional. He encouraged Macdonough to redress the situation with as little delay as possible and offered him all possible assistance. He authorized him to purchase, arm, and equip two of the best sloops he could find and ordered Commodore Bainbridge to send twenty 18-pounder carronades from his yard in Boston. He authorized Macdonough to make other requisitions as needed from the navy agents John Bullus in New York and Amos Binney at Boston. He gave the commodore the authority to do whatever was needed, and he followed with a stout order: "You are to understand that upon no account are you to suffer the enemy to gain ascendency on the lake."[12] It would be nearly six weeks before Macdonough's flotilla was ready to take back control of the lake.

The British took early advantage of Macdonough's loss of *Growler* and *Eagle* by mounting an amphibious raid under the command of Lieutenant Colonel John Murray of the British army. Acting under the orders of Major General George Sheaffe, Murray was to create a diversion in favor of the army in Upper Canada by destroying public buildings, vessels, and stores on the western shore of Lake Champlain. He would have to avoid damaging private property and unarmed persons. He was ordered not to operate south of Plattsburgh unless he could do so without incurring undue risk. But he was also to reconnoiter the waters of the bay to discover the enemy's location and any shore batteries that might be an annoyance. Information gathering was an important part of the mission. This raid was to take no more than four or five days.

Murray departed Isle aux Noix on July 29 with about with one thousand soldiers in forty-seven bateaux and three galleys, in addition to seamen of HMS *Wasp* at Quebec under the command of Captain Thomas Everard, RN. The troops landed and destroyed the blockhouse, arsenal, barracks, and storehouses in Plattsburgh. Despite General Sheaffe's strict orders, Murray's men looted private homes and stole horses and carts to carry the purloined goods back to Canada. Lieutenant Daniel Pring, RN, and Captain Everard sailed south in HM sloops *Broke* (*Eagle*) and *Shannon* (*Growler*) to a position just off Burlington, where they bombarded the harbor and tried to lure Macdonough's unready vessels out for battle, but to no avail. They later sailed south to Whitehall, capturing eight commercial vessels that they found at waterfront communities along the way. All in all, this was an object lesson in the use of sea power for control of the lake that was not lost on Secretary of the Navy Jones. Macdonough received his promotion to master commandant on July 24 (fig. 10.1).

In June, the arrival in Burlington of Major General Wade Hampton from his command in Virginia signaled a new phase of the war. Hampton was under orders

Figure 10.1. Commodore Thomas Macdonough, USN, 1783–1825, commander of the US Navy Lake Champlain Squadron. Portrait by John Wesley Jarvis, 1815. New York City Hall Portrait Collection. Photograph by Glenn Castellano, Collection of the Public Design Commission of the City of New York.

from Secretary of War Armstrong to take command of the Sixth Military District and to coordinate operations with Major General Wilkinson. In this capacity Hampton was in charge of the troops encamped at Burlington and Plattsburgh. He was a notorious taskmaster in the training and disciplining of his troops, most of whom were new to soldiering and unused to discipline of any kind. The general was not pleased with the situation he found. Constrained because of Murray's raid and the navy's loss of control on the lake, he could not move his army without risk until Macdonough's sloops were replaced and armed and more officers and seamen arrived. He might well have growled impatiently at the commodore, asking when, if ever, he was going to provide an escort to deliver his army safely to Plattsburgh. Macdonough would be unable to answer such a question until early September. The officers, deckhands, and guns he needed arrived slowly, as they became available. Secretary Jones's attention had been diverted by the impending battle expected to take place imminently on Lake

Erie. Commodore Perry needed the same assistance with men and armaments as Macdonough, and the situation at Presque Isle was more urgent.

Finally, on September 6, Macdonough's rebuilt squadron, comprising the sloops *President*, 10, *Montgomery*, 9, and *Preble*, 8, four gunboats (one 18-pounder each), and two hired vessels, put to sea. The British flotilla moved into the lower lake as if to challenge the American squadron, but as soon as Macdonough's force appeared, they withdrew into the Richelieu River. Having cleared the lake, Macdonough escorted the army's four thousand troops, including infantry, cavalry, and artillery, from Burlington to the Plattsburgh cantonment. General Hampton, at a meeting with his senior officers, then asked whether Macdonough was ready to move and protect the army on its way north. Once again, the commodore made his position clear. He would move with the army but would not enter Canadian waters to assault Fort Isle aux Noix. This would be too risky and would imperil the entire squadron, making it impossible for him to maintain superiority on the lake. Hampton and his officers were unhappy, but with a divided command, they had to accept the commodore's position. With this settled, Hampton's expedition marched out of Plattsburgh on September 19, with Macdonough's vessels protecting the army's right flank as far as the Little Chazy River. This brought an end to their collaboration, as Hampton's army marched off to its destiny at the battle of Chateauguay six weeks later.[13]

For the rest of the year, Macdonough's squadron cruised the lake to discourage smuggling, which was a continuing annoyance as well as a valuable support to the enemy. When northerly winds swept down the lake, the British gunboats often appeared, remaining until Macdonough's lookout boats sighted them and chased them back over the line. On the opposing side, the British gradually increased their strength at Isle aux Noix, building storehouses, strengthening the fort, and building a drydock for repair of vessels. They brought in at least nine heavy galleys (gunboats) overland from the St. Lawrence that could be equipped with two large guns, a long 24-pounder in the bow and a 32-pounder carronade in the stern. To cope with this threat, Macdonough proposed to Secretary Jones that he be authorized to build twenty to twenty-five gunboats, each mounting similar armament, in preparation for the next summer's campaign. He also asked permission for leave to visit his family in Middletown, Connecticut, whom he had not seen in a year. Jones replied quickly, saying that preparations should be made to build fifteen galleys, of two types, similar to those being built at Washington and Baltimore for defense of the Chesapeake. He forwarded the plans and ordered naval and ordnance stores to be sent to Albany before the Hudson froze over. While he gave permission to the commodore to take leave, he cautioned that the visit "had better be made soon and as short as possible, as great exertions will be required to meet the enemy on the first opening of navigation."[14]

Among the drafts of seamen arriving at Burlington were two officers known to Commodore Macdonough, Lieutenants Steven Cassin and Robert Henley, both of whom had served with him in the Mediterranean. Of the two, the commodore selected Cassin to be his second-in-command. Leaving him in charge, during the winter Macdonough paid a visit to New York to hurry the New York Navy Yard commandant into sending him the men he needed at Vergennes and to meet with Noah Brown to confirm his willingness to travel north with his shipwrights to build the gunboats and other vessels needed. In the spring and summer of 1813, Brown and his New York–based shipwrights had completed the building of Commodore Perry's squadron at Presque Isle within the time constraints that allowed Perry to win the Battle of Lake Erie. Secretary Jones had no hesitation in engaging him to assist Macdonough.

The Approaching Storm in the Champlain Valley

At the outset, the British were known to have a superiority in gunboats at Isle aux Noix. In their correspondence, Macdonough and Jones both had accepted the necessity of building more gunboats. The question, posed by Jones, was whether the commodore should also build at least one ship in addition to the gunboats. One consideration was that it would take more seamen to man a flotilla of fifteen gunboats than a ship of 24 guns, and the ship's guns of varying calibers would be more powerful than the fewer and smaller guns of the gunboats. As Jones wrote, "The object is to leave no doubt of your commanding the lake and the waters connected, and that, in due time."[15]

As the spring thaw approached, Macdonough pressed Noah Brown and his shipwrights to accelerate their work, which they did, completing in thirty-five days the building of a new ship to be named *Saratoga* in honor of the Revolutionary War battle fought near Albany. At the same time, he repeatedly requested from the secretary and Commodore Bainbridge seamen and marines; if marines were not available, then soldiers who might be spared to act as oarsmen in the gunboats. In April, following the launch of *Saratoga*, the six gunboats—*Allen, Borer, Burrows, Centipede, Nettle,* and *Viper*—slid down the ways. Each was 75 feet long and able to mount a 24-pounder and an 18-pound long gun.

Time was of the essence. Spies and enemy deserters had brought Macdonough information on British activity at Isle aux Noix. Their shipyard was busy building gunboats as well as a ship. This convinced Macdonough that he would require a ship to be able to outgun his adversary. Fortunately, a civilian shipyard was building a steamboat about 120 feet in length not far from Vergennes. Secretary Jones was aware of this, and urged on by New York's Governor Tompkins, he suggested that Macdonough consider acquiring it for his squadron. The commodore accepted this idea but had strong arguments against using her as a *steamboat*. He considered dependence on propulsion machinery in a warship an extreme liability. Its moving parts were likely to wear out at the wrong moment, and there was no nearby source for spares or mechanics who could manufacture them. Another reason was that steamboats lacked speed. A commercial steamboat already on the lake could not make more than five knots, whereas an enemy gunboat could be rowed at six knots and with a stiff breeze and enemy warship under sail might cut through the water at seven or eight knots. Far better, he thought, to convert her to a schooner fitted out with 20 guns. In this light, he reminded Jones that he was still short three or four lieutenants and need 245 more deckhands for his growing squadron.

Not that the secretary needed reminding. He was inundated by requests from Commodore Chauncey for more men and guns for a frigate and a brig being built at Sackets Harbor. The secretary had already sent Chauncey the guns of the frigate *President*, then undergoing repairs at the New York Navy Yard. On Lake Erie, Captain Arthur Sinclair, who had replaced Master Commandant Jesse Elliott, was planning a war cruise on Lake Huron to cut British communications with their First Nation allies and traders in the Northwest. He needed a purser and replacements for men whose enlistments were expiring. The navy's needs were many and the resources few.

Skirmish at Otter Creek

An early test of strength for Macdonough and his new army counterpart, Major General Alexander Macomb, came in the form of an attack on the naval base at Vergennes.[16] Although the British naval commander Commodore Daniel Pring had not begun construction of *Confiance*, he struck as soon as the lake ice had cleared. Macdonough had expected an attack and was well aware that his vessels were not ready to contend with the British squadron. With the help of General Macomb's regulars and artillery and the local Vermont militia, he set up a defensive system around the harbor. On May 14, Pring's brig *Linnet*, the sloops *Broke* and *Shannon*, and thirteen gunboats took position two miles off Fort Cassin, at the mouth of Otter Creek, and commenced a bombardment. Pring's plan was to weaken the defenses and then land 130 Royal Marines and 60 sailors to burn the shipyard, blockhouse, and gunboats. The Americans put up a stiff resistance that discouraged any attempt to land. Fort Cassin's seven 12-pounders, manned by the army's artillerymen, and the navy gunboat division's 18- and 24-pounders forced the enemy to keep his distance. The US infantry and Vermont militiamen stood ready; as Pring wrote Yeo, "Every tree on the lake shore seems to have a Jonathan [Yankee] stationed behind it."[17] After an hour and a half, Pring's flagship signaled to cease fire, and they sailed away to their base at Isle aux Noix.[18]

While this standoff does not qualify as a battle won, it did signify that a good working relationship had been established between American naval and military leaders in the Champlain Valley. It also provided proof to the British that they had a worthy opponent whom they could disregard only at their peril. Macdonough's shipwrights were building vessels faster than Pring's in what would be a shipbuilding race virtually until the day of battle, about three months away. Under increasing pressure to move his squadron to the lake, Macdonough completed his preparations, got under way, and brought his squadron to anchor off Plattsburgh on May 29. Two weeks later he informed the secretary that he had confirmed news that the enemy's shipbuilders at Isle aux Noix had already laid the keel for a ship of 32 guns. He feared that this ship would outgun his flagship, *Saratoga*, so he requested permission to build another ship or brig to carry sixteen or eighteen long 18-pounders as soon as possible. On June 19, Macdonough learned that the Admiralty had sent partially constructed ship frames from English dockyards to speed up construction of ships on the lakes. Beyond that, according to the newspapers, troop reinforcements were coming from Europe, and "they would do much mischief, had they this ascendency."[19] As it happened, the ships in frame had no impact on the war. Only one set of frames actually reached the lakes. They were used to construct the 54-gun HMS *Psyche*, but she was not completed until after the war.

Smuggling at the Canadian Border

The British shipwrights at Isle aux Noix faced their own logistical problems. They needed timber from forests in Vermont, which was provided by neutral American landowners. This was part of a pattern of the enemy's dependence on American sources of supply. It was notorious that many New England citizens disagreed with the US government's war with Great Britain. The Federalist governors of these states had refused to permit their militias to perform national service when the Madison administration requested their participation. Beyond that, the peacetime smuggling operations that usually took place along the border from Maine to New York continued apace during the war. This reprehensible practice was, of course, condemned by more patriotic citizens as "trading with the enemy," and it undercut the central government's source of income, customs duties. It was costly in human terms as well. It meant that US citizens were pocketing money or bartering goods that supported the troops and sailors who were fighting against their fellow Americans. The British openly admitted that this was going on for their benefit.[20] The United States did not have enough customs inspectors, and those who were trying to do their jobs were often attacked or intimidated by the smugglers, both British and American. The local magistrates were subject to the same threats. In January 1813, General Pike, having caught a smuggler, observed that there was such a thirst for gain among the citizenry that he could find no court that would take cognizance of the transaction or the person concerned.[21]

Likewise, Commodore Macdonough had to deal with this challenge, for much of the smuggling took place on the lake. While guarding against British naval incursions, his sailors were under orders to arrest the smugglers and take possession of the goods. On June 29, Lieutenant Elie Vallette was patrolling along the Vermont shore in the gunboat *Burrows* when he captured a boat crewed by four Americans, one a navy deserter, towing two long logs, 80 and 85 feet long, intended to be spars for *Confiance*. About a week later, Macdonough sent Midshipman Joel Abbott and three others on a sabotage mission four miles behind enemy lines near Isle aux Noix. They discovered spars, which they hastily cut up before escaping without being noticed. In another such escapade, Lieutenant Valette intercepted men towing a raft of oak planking, 13,000 feet of ship's timbers, and naval stores on its way to Canada. He confiscated it and towed it back to Otter Creek for the use of Noah Brown's shipwrights. All of these amounted to a kind of logistical warfare, denying supplies needed by the enemy in preparing for battle.[22]

As it became clear that the British dockyard was close to completing its work on *Confiance*, Macdonough's correspondence showed his eagerness to add another vessel to his squadron. This meant that he had to get another approval from Secretary Jones, recruit more officers and enlisted for his crew, and press harder to acquire more guns, munitions, sailcloth, and provisions. At the same time, Jones, whose financial resources and patience were wearing thin, was reluctant to go this extra mile, despite the risk. He replied, mistakenly, that the squadron was already "greatly superior to the enemy." Finally, though, he gave in and authorized work to commence on building a brig. Jones ordered the navy agent John Bullus to forward the needed supplies, as well as nine long 18-pounders, and to make up the remainder with 32-pounder carronades. The testy Jones complained about the army's inability to close the passage to the lake with artillery and spoke bitterly about trying to hold the lake without the army doing its part: "It is therefore, in vain to rest exclusively upon our naval superiority, and I see no end to this war of Broad Axes."[23]

Status of Opposing Forces

The news of Emperor Napoleon's probable demise reached England in late 1813 and led those in authority, especially Lord Bathurst, secretary of state for war and the colonies, to turn their attention to the war in North America. After Napoleon's first abdication and banishment to Elba in March 1814, ships and troops became available to reinforce the British in Canada. Governor General Prevost had urgently requested additional seamen and military assistance from Lord Bathurst. In consultation with his government, the Duke of Wellington expressed the opinion that there was little use in sending more troops to Canada unless the Royal Navy controlled the lakes.[24] This Yeo had attempted on Lake Ontario, but he had not been able to induce the elusive Chauncey to do battle. In 1814, Yeo decided that the solution was to build larger ships, and of course he would need many more seamen to sail them. This had been a continuing problem on all the lakes, but Yeo tended to retain the most experienced hands for his own fleet on Lake Ontario. For him, Lake Champlain was a mere sideshow. In response to Prevost, Bathurst sent to Quebec hundreds more seamen, as well as about 2,600 troops sent by the Duke of Wellington's command in southern France, where they were no longer needed.

The Armies

By September 1, the British had increased their field army in North America to its largest point, a total of 34,000. This number includes troops assigned to defend the Niagara Peninsula, as well as units at York and Kingston and in Lower Canada. Those in Quebec assembled at Fort Chambly, outside Montreal, to prepare for an invasion of the Champlain Valley. The latter number varies considerably depending on which sources are used. According to the American historian Allen Everest, the most accurate number of troops involved in the attack on Plattsburgh appears to be 10,300 effectives, who marched out from Chambly. About 8,200 of these arrived at Plattsburgh, and the remaining 2,100 manned outposts from the border to Plattsburgh. However, the Canadian historian Donald Graves's accounting yields a more precise total of 11,349, less 136 enlisted on the sick list and 2,146 on detached service, leaving a total of 9,067 officers and enlisted men at Plattsburgh ready for duty. Those on detached service were posted at key points to protect communications with Canada and to protect river crossings and supply depots that had been established on the march south. Graves attacks the myth that the army was entirely made up of Wellington's Peninsular troops. At most, he states, only 29 percent, or 2,625 men, of the three brigades who fought at Plattsburgh were veterans of the Peninsular campaign. These brigades were led by three generals who had been among Wellington's most reliable officers: Major Generals Frederick Robinson, Thomas Brisbane, and Manly Powers.[25]

The force available to US Army Major General George Izard in the weeks before the battle of Plattsburgh totaled eight thousand officers and enlisted, but a strange disconnect occurred between the general and Secretary of War Armstrong that drastically weakened the army intending to defend Plattsburgh. In July, before Izard had heard about the buildup of British troops north of the border, he suggested to the secretary that he order Izard to detach a body of troops and march toward Ogdensburg, on the St. Lawrence, to threaten Kingston. This might have made sense in strategic terms, diverting Prevost's attention away from Plattsburgh and Lake Champlain; however, as the weeks passed, Izard received intelligence about the large British army assembling at Chambly, an obvious threat to Plattsburgh and the Champlain Valley route south. In late July, Armstrong ordered Izard to march with four thousand men not to Ogdensburg but to Sackets Harbor, there to board Chauncey's ships and to sail west to reinforce the American army fighting at Niagara. In view of the new threat from the north, Izard notified Armstrong that he and his troops would be needed more than ever at Plattsburgh. Armstrong did not reply, thus allowing his troop movement order to stand.

General Izard's army marched away on August 27, leaving General Macomb with 3,454 regulars to defend Plattsburgh. As it happened, Izard arrived at Niagara well after the crucial battles of Chippawa and Lundy's Lane and finally caught up with General Brown's army at Fort Erie. It would not have hurt Armstrong's overall plan to allow Izard to remain in place, given the impending invasion of American territory at Lake Champlain. To make up for his shortfall in troops, Macomb called on General Mooers to send for the New York State militia and asked Governor Chittendon of Vermont to provide units of the Vermont militia. Chittendon refused but did allow volunteers to go under the command of General Samuel Strong, of Vergennes. An estimated 2,200 volunteers showed up from Vermont, and 700 New York militia men answered the call to join with Macomb's army, giving him about 6,354 men by the time of the battle.[26]

The Navies

With the outfitting of *Eagle* at Vergennes on August 26, Commodore Macdonough's efforts to add a brig to his small squadron were realized just in time. *Eagle* sailed north to join the squadron, which on September 5 had anchored at Plattsburgh Bay inside Cumberland Point under the cover of Macomb's artillery batteries. From this position the squadron could protect the army's right flank from the British squadron. Macdonough's vessels were protected by land on three sides, exposed only to the south, from which Macdonough expected the enemy to approach. Since the British squadron's mission was to assist their army's attack, its new commodore, Captain George Downie, had to accept Macdonough's battle plan (table 10.1).

In 1814 Lieutenant Daniel Pring's was the first squadron on the lake after the thaw. He staged an attack at the mouth of Otter Creek, hoping to damage Macdonough's navy yard and block the mouth of the creek. Between these sorties, Pring increased the squadron's flotilla of gunboats and planned to build a frigate while continually pressing Commodore Yeo for more men. On the face of it, one would think that Yeo would have been pleased with these accomplishments and with Pring's aggressive attitude. The situation was complicated, however, by Yeo's resistance to Governor General Prevost's orders to reinforce Commander Pring at Isle aux Noix. Even though the commodore was considerably lower in rank and experience than the governor general, he was jealous of his senior's authority. He was behaving like the junior frigate captain he had once been rather than like the

TABLE 10.1
US Navy squadron strength, Lake Champlain, 1814

Vessel Type	Name	Commander	Guns	Crew
Brig	*Saratoga*	Macdonough	8 24-pounder long guns 8 42-pounder carronades 12 32-pounder carronades	250
Brig	*Eagle*	Henley	12 32-pounder carronades 8 18-pounder long guns	152
Schooner	*Ticonderoga*	Cassin	8 12-pounder long guns 4 18-pounder long guns 5 32-pounder carronades	115
Sloop	*Commodore Preble*	Budd	7 12-pounder long guns	45
6 gunboats (75′)	*Allen, Burrows, Borer, Nettle* *Viper, Centipede*		1 24-pounder long gun 1 8-pounder columbiad	210
4 gunboats (50′)	*Ludlow, Wilmer, Alwyn, Ballard*		1 12-pounder long gun	100

Sources: Used with permission from David Curtis Skaggs, *Thomas Macdonough: Master of Command in the Early U.S. Navy* (Annapolis, MD: Naval Institute Press, 2003), 119. See also John R. Grodzinski, *Defender of Canada: Sir George Prevost and the War of 1812* (Norman: University of Oklahoma Press, 2013), 257 (app. B); and Theodore Roosevelt, *The Naval War of 1812* (New York: Modern Library, 1999), 208.

senior commodore on the lakes.[27] Yeo prided himself on his independent naval command and was intensely focused on his war with Chauncey on Lake Ontario. And like Chauncey with Perry, Yeo retained the seamen he needed for the first-rate *St. Lawrence*, to the detriment of Pring's manning of *Confiance*. For the success of both squadrons, it would have been far better to nurture a cordial command relationship similar to Perry's with Harrison and Macdonough's with Macomb.[28] However, Yeo made things worse, ordering Captain Peter Fisher to relieve Pring in midsummer 1814. It was traditional protocol that a large frigate would be commanded by a post captain, with his higher rank and his temporary status of commodore. Fisher also assumed charge of the navy yard at Isle aux Noix and the construction of the *Confiance*. Pring became Fisher's second-in-command for a few weeks, until the time for battle neared. Then, with no advance notice, Captain George Downie arrived from Lake Ontario on September 1 with Yeo's orders to relieve Fisher, who was sent elsewhere. Pring remained as commander of the brig *Linnet*.

There was Downie, completely unfamiliar with the terrain, rocks, and shoals of Lake Champlain, surrounded by officers and enlisted whom he did not know, and under urgent orders to complete outfitting the 37-gun frigate *Confiance* for a battle that was only days away. Launched on August 25, at 147 feet in length, 37 feet in beam, she was considerably larger than *Saratoga*, outfitted with only 26 guns. *Confiance* had been built and launched in haste, and much remained to be done. The carpenters were still building the powder magazine as she sailed toward the prebattle rendezvous with the squadron. It was reported that the gun carriages and carronade slides were hard to work because of the rough-hewn deck and the oozing pitch, which slowed the guns as the crews returned them to battery.[29] Commodore Downie was under great pressure to complete the flagship because Prevost had ordered the army to march on Plattsburgh and wanted Downie's squadron and the army to conduct a simultaneous, mutually supporting attack on the American naval and land forces.

The American forces clustered close to the mouth of the Saranac River, opposite Cumberland Point, which sheltered the bay from the north and east. General Macomb's forts were positioned along the right bank of the deep, swiftly flowing river, atop the fortified earthen walls that had been built by General Izard and Major Joseph Totten. Macdonough carefully anchored his squadron along a north-south line, intended to prevent encirclement by Downie's vessels, which would be constrained by the shallower waters off Cumberland Point (table 10.2).

Macdonough ordered commanders of the four larger vessels to prepare spring lines connecting the stern to the bow anchor. They also set kedge and stern anchors, to be used if enemy gunfire destroyed the main anchor cable. In this way,

TABLE 10.2
Royal Navy squadron strength, Lake Champlain, 1814

Vessel Type	Name	Commander	Guns	Crew
Frigate	*Confiance*	Downie	27 24-pounder long guns 6 24-pounder carronades 4 32-pounder carronades 2 18-pounder long guns	325
Brig	*Linnet*	Pring	6 12-pounder long guns	125
Sloop	*Chubb*	McGhie	6 12-pounder long guns	50
Sloop	*Finch*	Hicks	6 18-pounder carronades 4 6-pounder columbiads 1 18-pounder columbiad	50
1 gunboat	*Wellington*		1 18-pounder long gun	41
3 gunboats	*Yeo, Prevost, Blucher*		1 24-pounder long gun	99
3 gunboats	*Murray, Drummond, Beckwith*		1 18-pounder long gun	99
4 gunboats	*Brock, Simcoe, Popham, Beresford*		1 32-pounder carronade	100

Sources: Used with permission from David Curtis Skaggs, *Thomas Macdonough: Master of Command in the Early U.S. Navy* (Annapolis, MD: Naval Institute Press, 2003), 120. See also John R. Grodzinski, *Defender of Canada: Sir George Prevost and the War of 1812* (Norman: University of Oklahoma Press, 2013), 257 (app. B); and Theodore Roosevelt, *The Naval War of 1812* (New York: Modern Library, 1999), 210.

a commander could shift position relative to the enemy to the right or left by winding, putting the spring on a windless. Or if enemy gunfire damaged one side of the vessel, the bow cable could be cut away, enabling the vessel to pivot its length on its stern anchor. This would enable the gunners to fire the unused guns from the undamaged side of the ship. Macdonough placed Robert Henley's brig *Eagle* first in line, to the northeast, his own ship *Saratoga* second, Stephen Cassin's schooner *Ticonderoga* next, and Charles Budd's sloop *Preble* last in line, to the south. The gunboats took position 40 yards inshore of the larger ships and were ordered to remain mobile, to dart between the larger ships to fire their guns, to prevent the enemy from trying to turn the flank of the squadron, and to attack the enemy's gunboats if they threatened.[30]

With the major exception of his flagship, *Confiance*, Commodore Downie's squadron was prepared. Prevost had given Downie to understand that the army would not be ready to attack until September 15, yet the impatient Prevost had jumped off nearly one week early, arriving at Plattsburgh on September 6 eager to go into battle even though his heaviest guns had not arrived. Every day thereafter the governor general prodded Downie to get under way, and each time Downie had to give him the same answer: *Confiance* was not ready for battle; in fact, she had not even had a sea trial to determine whether she was seaworthy or whether her crew was trained enough to face the severe test ahead. Downie had received little support from Commodore Yeo, particularly in his need for experienced seamen. As a result, he had a polyglot crew, many drawn from other ships

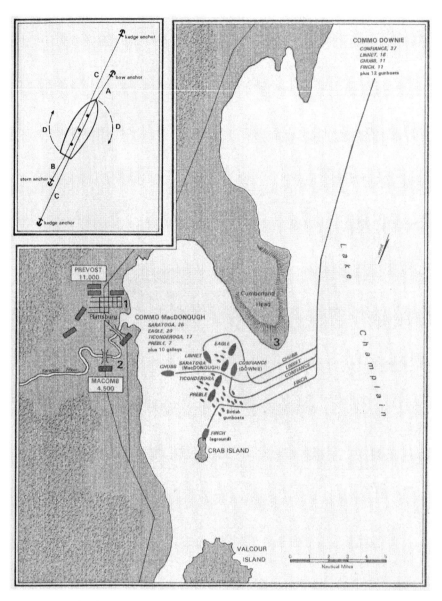

Map 10.1. Battle of Lake Champlain, 11 September 1814. Reprinted by permission from Craig. L. Symonds, *The Naval Institute Historical Atlas of the U.S. Navy*, Cartography by William J. Clipson, © 1995 (Annapolis, MD: Naval Institute Press).

in Quebec and soldiers with no seagoing experience to fill the gaps. They did not know one another or their officers and so they lacked the cohesion that makes men efficient under battle conditions (map 10.1).

The Battle of Lake Champlain

The British squadron needed a north wind to sail against the Richelieu River's current and into the lake. On September 11, at dawn, with the wind at his back, Downie got under way. By about eight o'clock he had arrived outside Cumberland Point. He boarded a gunboat and rounded the point to get his first look at the tactical situation, to see where Macdonough had anchored his vessels, and then returned to his squadron. He signaled his order of battle according to his enemy's anchored positions and rounded the point. Unfortunately for Downie, the wind failed him once they were inside Cumberland Point, upsetting his battle plan. This meant that they would have to fight at anchor and not in his preferred formation on the open lake, where his long guns would be more effective. The sloop *Chubb* ended up anchoring eastward of *Eagle*; the brig *Linnet* drifted to a position within range of *Eagle* and Macdonough's *Saratoga*; Downie conned *Confiance* toward a position opposite *Saratoga*; the sloop *Finch* followed next and anchored opposing the schooner *Ticonderoga* and the sloop *Preble*.

The battle commenced with *Chubb* firing a broadside while passing outboard of *Saratoga*. Macdonough himself fired the first gun from *Saratoga*, hitting *Confiance*'s bow, ricocheting down her main deck, killing several and destroying the ship's helm. The British gunboats, last in line, stood off *Ticonderoga* and *Preble*. Two broadsides from *Eagle* quickly shredded *Chubb*'s sails and rigging and wounded several, including her commander. The sloop drifted helplessly and soon surrendered; a US galley towed her out of the action.

After these first exchanges, all the guns roared over the narrow bay spewing acrid smoke, and the cries of the wounded shrilled over the general melee. The two flagships took a toll of the each other's crew as gunfire cut down rigging and spars and splinters flew. It is no exaggeration to say that the decks and scuppers ran red with the blood of the killed and wounded. In the end, Macdonough's leadership and carefully prepared spring lines won the day. He had been knocked down twice during the battle but regained his footing and ordered the sailing master to wind ship. This presented *Saratoga*'s undamaged larboard battery to the exhausted *Linnet* and *Confiance*. Macdonough continued to attack them both until they surrendered. One of the first officers to fall in *Confiance* was Commodore Downie, who was crushed by an upended gun. Henley's *Eagle* contributed to damaging both *Linnet* and *Confiance*, though he too had to shift position after *Eagle* was torn by their gunfire. Henley dropped anchor off the port quarter of *Saratoga* and recommenced firing on *Confiance* until she struck her colors. *Ticonderoga* and *Preble*, at the south end of the line, poured such devastating fire into *Finch* that she broke from her anchor and drifted toward Crab Island, where she surrendered to an island battery. Cassin's *Ticonderoga* had a violent struggle against four enemy gunboats trying to board her, but they finally yielded after being shattered. Budd's *Preble* suffered much damage and drifted ashore, finally out of the fight, much to Macdonough's dismay. The battle lasted about two hours, yielding a high casualty count: for the US squadron, 52 officers and enlisted killed and 58 wounded, for a total of 110; the British squadron suffered 54 officers and enlisted dead and 116 wounded, totaling 170. On board *Confiance*, 123 killed and wounded accounted for more than half of the ship's company, a complement of 300 sailors (including infantry acting as marines).[31]

Unexpectedly, the British army retreated shortly after Prevost learned the results of the naval battle. The army's artillery had commenced firing on Macomb's defenses as the naval engagement began, and Macomb's batteries answered in kind. Yet, Prevost delayed the infantry's primary assault until he could determine the course of the naval battle, though numerous skirmishes broke out through the town and at river crossing points. There had been a failure of understanding between Prevost and Downie. The commodore had expected support from the army's artillery as soon as he attacked Macdonough's squadron, but no British artillery were yet in position to assist. The governor general's expectation was that Downie's squadron would have to defeat the American squadron before he could commence a full-on assault against the formidable American defenses. When it became clear before noon that Macdonough had won the day, Prevost ordered his major generals to about-face and withdraw, taking or destroying as much of their supplies as possible. As he explained in his report to Lord Bathurst, he saw no purpose in unleashing an effusion of blood if the Royal Navy was unable to support his advance and occupation of American territory. His orders had been to take and hold as much territory as possible without his army being cut off and isolated in enemy territory. The example of General Burgoyne's predicament at Saratoga in 1777 may have been uppermost in his mind. Prevost concluded that without naval support he could not ensure his army's safety. At the expense of much muttered discontent and later public criticism, he ordered the artillery to cease firing and the army to immediately prepare to return to Canada.

Aftermath

By the end of autumn, Macdonough had repaired the battle damage of his squadron and sent it to winter quarters at Whitehall, New York. He was allowed a brief few weeks of home leave but was directed to return to his duty station in February to prepare the flotilla.[32] Rumors were flying about the British building more gunboats and larger vessels at Isle aux Noix, so he anticipated that he would have to fight another "war of Broad Axes," to use Jones's phrase.[33] Fortunately, for him and all concerned, the war ended with the ratification of the Treaty of Ghent.

Macdonough could feel well satisfied with his work. He had, by dint of tireless effort, built a shipyard at Vergennes, rebuilt the Lake Champlain squadron after a setback in 1813, and managed a logistical nightmare in recruiting sailors, ordering provisions, and requisitioning guns. He trained and disciplined his sailors, combatted enemy smuggling, nurtured friendships with his military counterparts in the army and militias, and finally, through inspirational leadership, destroyed the British squadron that threatened Lake Champlain, greatly aiding General Macomb's defense of Plattsburgh. General Prevost's withdrawal signaled the end of a major threat to the unity of the United States.

For his two and one-half years building and then leading the squadron to victory, Captain Thomas Macdonough received a commodore's share of the prize money ($22,807), a promotion to captain, the thanks of Congress and a gold medal struck in his honor, a tract of land on Cumberland Head (Point), a plot of land on Albany's Washington Square, a sword from the State of New York, a brace of pistols from Connecticut, and a sword and a gift of silver plate presented to him by Delaware's governor.[34] Likewise, the public, hungry for a sense of pride, acclaimed him as a hero in newspapers, articles, public dinners, and toasts. Macdonough was on his way to a brilliant career.

The War of 1812 did not end with the climactic Battle of Lake Champlain–Plattsburgh. But this battle did influence the opposing governments by demonstrating that the war could last a lot longer, and this became a matter that was concerning to both Britain and America. Neither nation could afford to carry on the war for another year. By sheer coincidence, the American repulse of the British attempt to occupy or destroy Baltimore occurred within days of the American victory on Lake Champlain. The American repulse of the British at Fort Erie, on the Niagara, followed soon thereafter. These reports shocked the British ministry of Lord Liverpool.

At that time, Lord Castlereagh, the foreign secretary, was managing negotiations for a peace treaty with American diplomats and preparing for a major settlement of European problems at the Congress of Vienna. Of these two diplomatic efforts, the Liverpool ministry considered the Congress of Vienna far more important in terms of a general European peace. After Liverpool's decision, Castlereagh pressured the British negotiators at Ghent to drop their harsh demands for adjusting the borders of the United States and Canada, creation of a Native American buffer state in the Old Northwest, and restriction of American fishing rights off the Maritime Provinces. At Vienna, the British diplomats wished to demonstrate that the American war was ending in their favor, or their military and economic power would be called into question. The British would have to show strength and resolve to achieve their ends at the congress. Thus, a compromise peace with the United States was the best option for the United Kingdom and the United States.[35]

While awaiting the results of these negotiations, Madison and his cabinet could not ignore the possibility of the war lingering into 1815. This would require more military and naval expenditures for a war-weary nation. The navy, for its part, considered it necessary to continue its shipbuilding competition on the northern lakes. This required selecting a new secretary of the navy to replace William Jones, whose efforts over two years had led to physical and financial exhaustion. His replacement, on an interim basis, was his chief clerk, Benjamin Homans, who could at least handle routine matters, while consulting with the new secretary of war, James Monroe, on major issues. President Madison ultimately settled on Benjamin Crowninshield, scion of the wealthy Salem, Massachusetts, merchant family, to lead the Navy Department.[36] Events on Lake Champlain were significant for the United States, but several months of war remained elsewhere, to which we must now turn our attention.

CHAPTER 11

In Defense of the Chesapeake Bay

In early 1814 the Royal Navy commenced an aggressive raiding strategy along the New England coast, bringing the conflict to America's shores in unexpected ways. None of the US Navy's warships were in play, since many either were bottled up in New York and New London or had sailed far out to sea and were unable to protect American harbors and ports. With most of the young nation's federal troops and sailors fighting in the Great Lakes region, the coastal states had to rely on their militias for defense. In addition, the New England states had resisted calls to use their militias for national defense since their Federalist majorities opposed the War of 1812 and refused to loan funds to the federal government. The British easily isolated offshore islands such as Nantucket and Martha's Vineyard, invaded the northern coast of Maine as far south as Castine, attacked Stonington, Connecticut, and burned twenty-seven vessels at Essex, on the Connecticut River— all without fear of serious opposition.[1] British raiding parties devastated the Chesapeake Bay region, and a small British army invaded and burned the most important buildings in Washington, DC. On occasion, local populations and militias put up a fight—specifically at Craney Island, near Norfolk, Virginia; St. Michaels, Maryland; and Stonington, Connecticut.[2] In the Chesapeake, a US Navy flotilla under the command of Commodore Joshua Barney, in collaboration with the Baltimore Committee of Safety, provided the only organized maritime defense.

The US Navy's Chesapeake Flotilla

The importance of naval readiness in manpower, supply, and construction is demonstrated by American preparations for the British threat in the Chesapeake. In July 1813, the veteran naval officer and privateersman Joshua Barney had suggested to Navy Secretary William Jones an alternative to the navy's sluggish gunboats: open, armed barges propelled by sail and oars. They could take advantage of the bay's shallow and often calm waters to attack British warships under the right conditions. Jones saw the wisdom of this advice and asked Barney to take charge of this project, offering him the rank of acting master commandant. He would be answerable only to Jones, in an independent command that would be called the Chesapeake Flotilla. Barney accepted the assignment and for the rest of the year supervised the building of the barges in Baltimore, using the navy agent James Beatty to purchase supplies and a network of merchants and boatbuilders he had known for decades. To man the flotilla, Barney recruited veteran merchant seamen who he thought would be in need of a job as long as the war lasted. But the availability of seamen depended in part on the Madison administration's sustained policy of restrictions on trade. As long as merchant ships could not sail, sailors did not get paid, so they went to find other employment in the flotilla's barges.

Eventually, Barney was able to build and man a flotilla of twenty-six barges (row galleys) built over a period of nine months and employing approximately a thousand seamen. Fifty officers and sailors would be assigned to each first-class barge, forty officers and sailors to the second-class barges.[3] The barges of Barney's flotilla, designed by William Doughty, chief constructor of the Washington Navy Yard, were of two different dimensions. Those Jones referred to as the first-class ones were 70 feet in length, double-masted, with a lateen (Mediterranean) rig, having a fixed rudder assembly aft the long gun at the stern. The second-class barges were 50 feet in length, single-masted, and lateen-rigged. Two sea trials showed them vulnerable to being swamped by large waves, so the builders added splashboards (or washboards) above the coaming to shield the cockpit from the waves. The barges were equipped with oars that the crews had to row from a standing position because of the height of the splashboards.[4]

Typical materials used for building and equipping the barges were listed in the inventory and cost record of building the row galley *Black Snake*, which Secretary Jones ordered to be the model for the flotilla barges. This inventory, containing eight categories, appears to be comprehensive. It includes the pine and white oak planks and white oak knees for structural support, pine masts and spars, cedarwood and canvas for awnings, ironwork, white lead paint and lamp black, naval stores, rope, cable, and small stuff, two anchors, leather to prevent wear and tear, blocks and sheaves, and canvas for sails. For armaments and gunner's stores, *Black Snake* carried one long 18-pounder and slide carriage, a cannon lock, a rammer and sponge, a powder horn, 80 round shot, 30 stands (cannisters) of grape shot, flannel cartridges, 3 flannel-lined powder chests, and other items. The barge also was equipped with one 32-pounder carronade and sliding carriage, a carronade lock, an elevating screw, a tompion, and many other items similar to those required for the long gun. For small arms, she carried 36 muskets, bayonets, cartridge boxes with belts, 1,800 musket balls with filled cartridges, and 150 flints; for hand-to-hand fighting, the barge carried 30 boarding pikes and 40 cutlasses.

Other categories, too numerous to itemize, included master's stores, boatswains' stores, carpenter's stores, and cook's stores (utensils). The value of all this, not including the shipwrights' labor, was approximately $5,300.[5]

Each barge would be manned by a sailing master, commanding one master's mate, one gunner, one boatswain, one steward, and one cook. Ten able seamen and thirty-four ordinary seamen would be assigned to the first-class barges and eight able seamen and twenty-six ordinary seamen to the second-class barges. Master's mates, gunners, and boatswains received monthly pay of $20; stewards and cooks, $18; able seamen, $12; and ordinary seamen, $10, with the same rations and privileges as sailors elsewhere in the US Navy. These men were to be shipped (i.e., signed up) for twelve months, for barge duty only and were not to be drafted for any other duty.[6] According to Jones's orders, the barges were intended for use in the upper part of the Chesapeake Bay, from the Potomac River north to the Patapsco River, and primarily for the defense of Washington DC, and Baltimore. Although some were retained for the Potomac Flotilla, Jones assigned the majority to Barney for the defense of the upper bay, especially Baltimore. Barges were more suitable for these waters than for the lower bay, where the longer fetch and access to the Atlantic made for higher seas.

During the spring and summer of 1813, the British raids concentrated in the upper part of the Chesapeake Bay to stir fear and terror among the residents and to try to divert US troops from the Canadian border to protect the Baltimore-Washington area. While they succeeded in raising alarms along the Chesapeake littoral, they had no success in diverting US troops from Canada. The state militias would have the burden of defending the coastlines. But the Royal Navy had another objective: to survey and sound the major rivers of the bay's Western Shore, particularly the Potomac, the Patuxent, and the Patapsco, for possible expeditions toward Washington and Baltimore. It became apparent to most American leaders observing the enemy's operations in the bay that if the war extended into the 1814 campaign season, these major cities would pay a heavy price if left undefended.[7]

After the return of Rear Admiral George Cockburn to the Chesapeake Bay in February 1814, Americans learned that the Admiralty had recalled Admiral Warren from his post as commander of the North Atlantic station and replaced him with Vice Admiral Sir Alexander Cochrane. Cochrane was a scion of an aristocratic Scottish family with strong Royal Navy connections.[8] Sir Alexander was a valuable officer in this command. He had served as a lieutenant on the North American station during the American Revolution and had been present when General William Howe occupied Philadelphia. He knew much of the coast and had a special reason for disliking Americans: his brother, Major Charles Cochrane, of the British army, who had served with Colonel Bannistre Tarleton's Raiders, had been killed while serving under General Cornwallis during the siege of Yorktown in 1781. In March, Vice Admiral Cochrane arrived in Bermuda, where he met with Admiral Warren for their change of command. At about the same time, Secretary Jones was in communication with Commodore Barney concerning his progress in building the flotilla and recruiting seamen. He reminded Barney of his orders: "We have 80 or 90 men belonging to the barges and gunboats here [Washington Navy Yard], but the Potomac must not be left without protection. We shall expect you to keep the enemy below the Potomac, and then the whole force can unite. The enemy has a strong desire to destroy this place and will assuredly make the effort for that purpose, your force is our principal shield, and all eyes will be upon you."[9] For a command vessel, Jones again provided Barney with the sloop *Scorpion*, which he had used in 1813, and the schooner *Asp*, to serve as quarters for his officers and a transport for the supplies needed by the flotilla. Barney mentioned that five barges being built near St. Michaels at Perry Spencer's shipyard were nearly completed. He provided the names of fourteen men whom he had recruited as sailing masters to command the barges. He advised Jones that he had seen the new sloop of war *Erie* anchored off Annapolis and worried that Master Commandant Charles Ridgely's eagerness to get to sea would place him in danger as "the season is past and the enemy concentrated near the entrance of the bay in such a manner as to defeat all prospects of escaping."[10] Ultimately, Ridgeley returned *Erie* to Baltimore's protected harbor. In April, Secretary Jones sent him and several members of his crew to Sackets Harbor to reinforce Commodore Chauncey's growing squadron. Ridgely then took command of the new brig *Jefferson* on Lake Ontario.

The Flotilla's Operations

Commodore Barney's flotilla sailed from Baltimore on April 14 on a sea trial in which he discovered that the smaller, 50-foot barges shipped water excessively. He twice returned to Baltimore to make changes in the form of added splashboards to their upper works to divert waves that washed over the bulwarks of the barges. This done, and after hiring more seamen, Barney set sail once again, commanding in his flagship *Scorpion* and accompanied by gunboats *No. 137* and *No. 138* and twelve barges. Also at this time, Jones promoted Barney to the rank of captain in the Flotilla Service of the United States and provided his senior barge commanders, Solomon Rutter and Solomon Frazier, with an acting lieutenant's commission.[11] They were well known as Eastern Shore seamen who supported the Madison administration. Recruiting went well until seamen learned that the

Madison administration had reversed itself and repealed the Non-Importation Act in mid-April. Most able-bodied seamen wanted employment on seagoing ships, hence recruiting efforts for the barge flotilla became more difficult. Another factor that depressed the number of available seamen was, according to Barney, pressure from local leaders of the Democratic-Republican and Federalist parties to prevent men from enlisting for fear of not being able to vote in the next election.[12] The election was still many months away, on October 1, 1814, and Barney assured the men that they would be back in time to vote.

While Commodore Barney was organizing his flotilla, Rear Admiral Cockburn sent his officers to search the islands of the lower bay for an ideal place to set up barracks and a supply depots for the summer campaign. They found what he wanted on Tangier Island, located on the eastern side of the bay, opposite the mouth of the Potomac River. The Admiralty had informed Cockburn that its plans for a vigorous summer campaign included the establishment of a Corps of Colonial Marines, slaves willing to risk running from the masters with their families. These refugees and their families would be made welcome on board British vessels and ultimately would be given the opportunity to settle freely in other places in British North America, including the Caribbean. Vice Admiral Cochrane issued a proclamation to this effect on April 2, 1814, before he had left Bermuda for the Chesapeake. The burden of supporting the "refugees" would fall on Cockburn, who would have to dedicate a transport ship to their needs and deliver those who wished to join the Colonial Marines to Tangier Island, where barracks, storehouses, and parade grounds would be built for military training.[13]

Rear Admiral Cockburn was under pressure because of the shortage of supplies and the small number of ships at his disposal for guarding the Virginia Capes, searching for American vessels anxious to escape the bay, and harassing the American militias, as well as his need for men of various specialties to build the cantonment on Tangier Island. He was aware that the Americans were building a small boat flotilla but apparently did not know when or where they would appear. He wrote from HMS *Albion* in Tangier Bay on May 9 that he already had sent 151 refugees to Bermuda and retained 38 male refugees on Tangier as soldiers, 13 as laborers, and 27 women and their children. Cockburn waxed eloquent when writing of the qualities of former slaves who had volunteered as soldiers: "Those whom . . . I have enlisted as soldiers are getting on astonishingly and are really very fine fellows, and I think whenever you arrive you will be pleased with them. They have induced me to alter the bad opinion I had of their whole Race & now I really believe these we are training will neither show want of Zeal or Courage when employed by us in attacking their old Masters."[14]

Having heard about British intentions to occupy Tangier Island and having only HMS *Albion* there at anchor, Barney planned to sail his flotilla down the bay and into Tangier Sound. Sailing south and through Hooper's Strait into Tangier Sound, behind the wetland islands and out of sight from the wider part of the bay, he could stealthily approach Tangier Island; then he would attack whatever structures were being built, terrify the inhabitants, and evade the movements of *Albion* and her boats by keeping to the shallower waters. It might have been possible, if all went well, for him to join to up with the US naval gunboat flotilla at Norfolk.[15] If that were to happen, it would be based on the presumption that Admiral Cockburn's officers had been unwary and that Federalist spies would not have provided Barney's location and intentions. Furthermore, Barney would have been exceeding his orders, which was not unheard of in earlier times. Barney himself had said that he would "be governed by events." Secretary Jones had designated the flotilla as a defensive force for the upper bay. At most, Barney was to proceed south to the Potomac and join up with the Potomac Flotilla to defend both Washington and Baltimore. That was the plan; however, as often happens in war, weather and then the enemy intervened. In this case, events did indeed govern Barney.

The Action off Cedar Point

Barney's flotilla set sail on May 24 with *Scorpion*, thirteen barges, gunboats *No. 137* and *No. 138*, the row galley *Vigilant*, and what Barney called a "lookout boat," the pilot schooner *Shark*. He had left behind eleven barges, for lack of seamen to man them, and the schooner *Asp*. He was unhappy about some of his second-class barges because they still shipped too much water and could not carry enough provisions. He wrote that gunboats *No. 137* and *No. 138* "are both such miserable tools I do not know what to do with them, they cannot carry anything but their own armament . . . and they sail so bad that I am afraid to trust them out of my sight ahead or astern."[16] The US Chesapeake Flotilla made its first contact with a flotilla of British barges off St. Jerome's Creek, on the Western Shore between the Patuxent and Potomac Rivers.

On June 1, Captain Robert Barrie in his gig and several ships' launches were searching for bay craft hidden in the streams and inlets of the St. Mary's County coast at St. Jerome's Creek when Barney's flotilla set sail from the Patuxent River, heading south with a following wind. The two flotillas sighted each other about the same time and prepared for battle. As they drew closer, Barrie recognized that he was outgunned and made a signal for assistance from HMS *Dragon*, his flagship, which was following some miles to the south. As they closed, Barney's larger barges fired their long guns, but they were out of range. Unluckily for Barney, the wind then shifted from northerly to southwesterly, favoring the British flotilla and *Dragon*. Seeing that he could well be overtaken, Barney signaled a retreat to the Patuxent, inside Cedar Point, where he could take shelter under a windward shore. As Barney saw that his sluggish supply boat, gunboat *No. 137*, was about to be captured, he signaled an attack on the British van. There was a brief skirmish, the leading enemy barges gave up the chase, and No. 137 was soon safe in friendly hands. Barney led his squadron farther into the Patuxent River. Captain Barrie ordered his now reinforced squadron to blockade the mouth of the river. The stage was then set for the next stage of the drama. As each side took advantage of events as they developed, Barney's flotilla became trapped in the Patuxent, and the British then committed themselves to inducing him to fight or following him into narrow, uncharted, and shallow waters where the US Navy barges would have the advantage. On the other hand, for every mile of river the British gained, the closer they drew to the nation's capital at Washington. From June 1 on, this was no longer a battle of 74s and frigates but one of barges, schooners, ships' launches, and landing parties. From Barney's point of view, it was a war of diversion and delay. The longer he could divert the enemy's attention from their major targets, Washington and Baltimore, the more time the defenders would have to prepare.

It was by chance that Commodore Barney's flotilla became trapped in the Patuxent River. According to Captain Barrie of *Dragon*, Barney and his flotilla were heading for Hooper's Strait when they came into sight on June 1.[17] There would still have been a battle, but it would have taken place on the eastern side of the bay instead of inside the Patuxent River. Barney had not disclosed to Secretary Jones his intent to visit Tangier Island. If he had, there would probably have been an immediate rejoinder or reprimand, as such an attack had not been part of Jones's instructions to Barney. His flotilla could have been destroyed or widely dispersed without having done anything to protect Washington or Baltimore. It was perhaps fortunate for the Americans that Barney was in the Patuxent. His tactics of withdrawal and defensive fortification at St. Leonard's Creek frustrated Captain Barrie, whose lighter vessels suffered damage as well as lives lost. Had there been a more active secretary of war and a well-thought-out plan for defending the national capital, Barney's delaying tactics might have led to a different outcome. Barney's strategy kept a good number of British vessels, six in all (two frigates, a gun brig, and three schooners) tied down blockading his "flotilla in being," in the lower Patuxent, when they might have been doing more damage elsewhere (map 11.1).[18]

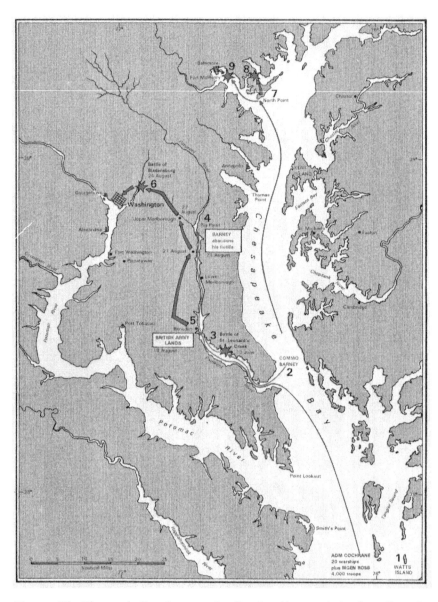

Map 11.1. The Chesapeake Bay, Summer 1814. Reprinted by permission from Craig. L. Symonds, *The Naval Institute Historical Atlas of the U.S. Navy*, Cartography by William J. Clipson, © 1995 (Annapolis, MD: Naval Institute Press).

The First and Second Battles of St. Leonard's Creek

Commodore Barney next led his flotilla up the Patuxent and into St. Leonard's Creek, a winding creek that led eastward into heavily wooded Calvert County. He reported that he had moved two miles up the creek and moored his barges in line abreast across the creek and prepared for battle. He had been pursued by the frigate *Loire* and the brig *Jaseur* and their launches. In the first battle of St. Leonards' Creek, on June 8–10, Barney's three boat divisions drove down on the British, firing as they came within range. Barney's force then withdrew to their moorings. The British then attacked upstream with Congreve rockets and were beaten back, with one American barge lost. Barney requested that Secretary Jones send supplies and military reinforcements. Jones responded the next day and sent a company of marines with four light 12-pounders on carriages. For the next ten days, the two sides called for reinforcements and calculated their next moves. Jones ordered that *Asp* be loaded with provisions and sent from Baltimore to the South River. From the port of London Town they could be sent overland to St. Leonard's Town. Jones was concerned about how Barney could remove himself from the trap at St. Leonard's Creek. He suggested that the barges could be lightened and hauled on a set of wheels by oxen over the four miles from St. Leonard's to the bay or, in a more difficult haul, from the upper Patuxent across to the South River, some fifteen miles to the north. Barney deemed both of these escape routes impracticable. He knew the British would learn of the attempts long before they could be accomplished, as local planters would have informed the British. The locals blamed Barney for bringing the British up the Patuxent, where they burned many farms and took tobacco, livestock, and other property. As Barney wrote to Jones, "I am convinced that within four hours after we prepare to begin transportation, the enemy will be informed of our intentions by the people of this district who are all disaffected."[19]

Deserters from British ships brought Barney word that a major expeditionary force on board transports would soon arrive from Bermuda. Secretary Jones scented a new possibility, namely, that the British were using the Patuxent blockade and reinforcements to "serve as a mask [or screen] for a rapid movement upon this City of Baltimore." Jones had hit upon the crux of the British strategy, although Admiral Cochrane had yet finally to decide upon it. At this point, Barney and Jones agreed that the flotilla must break out of St. Leonard's Creek and head for the upper Patuxent River in the hope of further delaying the British. On June 26, in the second battle of St. Leonard's Creek, with the help of army, Marine Corps, and flotilla land-based artillery (some with hot shot) and a full-scale push by the flotilla with guns blazing, Barney and his barges broke out of the creek and moved upriver toward Upper Marlboro. Expecting to be pursued, the enemy's rocket barges, launches, schooners, and two frigates retreated south to Point Patience, where their 74-gun flagship was anchored and could provide covering fire.[20] The first and second battles of St. Leonard's Creek caused the British delay and some irritation, as this was only the second serious naval resistance they had faced in the Chesapeake since the battle of Craney Island the year before. Rear Admiral Cockburn wrote to Vice Admiral Cochrane that "my public letters will inform you of all our late operations and how sharply and unexpectedly Jonathan has exerted himself in putting forth his Marine Armaments in this bay and how much I have been puzzled to cut and contrive to meet him at all points and cause all his effort to recoil on himself."[21]

Granted a temporary respite from battle, Barney accepted an invitation from Secretary Jones to visit Washington at the end of June to discuss the flotilla's strategies for the future. Jones was not convinced that Washington would be the enemy's next major target, though he was also obliged to protect Baltimore. Rear Admiral Cockburn had divided his fleet, sending one squadron to the mouth of the Potomac, while the other was to remain in the Patuxent until Admiral Cochrane's arrival. With the Chesapeake flotilla bottled up and lying at Benedict, on the west bank of the Patuxent River, there was nothing that Barney could do to assist the defense of the Potomac. There was little way out of the predicament except a farther retreat to Nottingham and ultimately as far up as Queen Anne's Town, where the river became too shallow for navigation. Barney scuttled gunboats *No. 137* and *No. 138* at St. Leonard's Creek as being of no more use. He ordered the barges' masts, rigging, and kentledge off-loaded before the second battle so that the British could not see barges moving behind the wetlands. Lieutenant Solomon Rutter loaded the spars and other equipment for transport to Hunting Creek, a few miles to the north.[22]

The British Invasion of Maryland

In early August, a large convoy of twenty-two ships, including transports, frigates, the 74-gun *Tonnant*, and Admiral Cochrane's 74-gun flagship, *Royal Oak*, entered the Chesapeake and headed for an anchorage off Tangier Island. These transports carried about thirty-five hundred troops who had recently served in Spain and France, as well as Royal Marines, artillery, infantry equipment, and a mountain of provisions for the troops. Rear Admiral Cockburn's long-awaited reinforcements had arrived. Secretary Jones received the news on August 19, the same day as Commodore Barney. The two exchanged views on what should happen next. As Jones wrote, "Appearances indicate a design on this place [Washington], but it may be a feint, to mask a real design on Baltimore; if, however, their force is strong in troops, they may make a vigorous push for this place." He advised Barney to move his vessels as high up as Queen Anne's and to leave a competent officer and a few men with orders to destroy the flotilla if the British landed and advanced toward him.[23] He ordered Barney to take his remaining men with their small arms and march toward the Washington Navy Yard, where he would meet Captain Samuel Miller, his company of Marines, and an artillery battery of three 12-pounders and two long 18-pounders to join with local forces at Bladensburg for the defense of the capital.[24]

The Potomac Flotilla

Other aspects of the maritime defense of Washington illustrate the stressful situation that enveloped Secretary Jones and Commodore Thomas Tingey at the Washington Navy Yard. Once the British troops landed at Benedict under the leadership of General Robert Ross on August 19, it was apparent to most sentient observers, if not to Secretary of War Armstrong, that Washington would be their objective. As early as February 1813, Jones had created the Potomac Flotilla, which was quite unlike what Barney's Chesapeake Flotilla would become during the year. In addition to three gunboats attached to the navy yard, Jones ordered the cutter *Scorpion*, herself a former gunboat (*No. 59*), to be sent to Washington under the command of Master Commandant Arthur Sinclair. They were to cruise south of the Potomac to seek out and destroy the smaller craft of the British fleet, mostly schooner tenders. One month later, he assigned Lieutenant Edmund Kennedy to this command and sent Sinclair, who was due to be promoted to captain, to Sackets Harbor to join Commodore Chauncey's Lake Ontario command. Jones then added a newly purchased schooner, *Asp*, though he restricted Kennedy's flotilla to patrolling just outside the mouth of the Potomac.

Kennedy's orders were to defend the Potomac. If the British ascended the river, he was to retreat gradually as far as Fort Warburton (Fort Washington), just below Alexandria, and cooperate defensively with the fort at that point. To man the flotilla, Jones had to order some seamen from the sloop of war *Adams*, commanded by Charles Morris, then under major repairs at the navy yard, until that ship was ready for sea. She was unable to depart the bay until January 18, 1814. But months before he left, Morris provided Secretaries Armstrong and Jones with an outline of a defensive plan in the event that the British threatened Washington via the Potomac.[25] Meanwhile, the Potomac Flotilla did not fare well. As Barney's need for men and gunboats grew, Jones sent gunboat *No. 137* and *Scorpion* to join that flotilla. Curiously, Secretary Jones made no effort to duplicate Barney's flotilla in the defense of Washington. Perhaps this was because of a shortage of manpower or a lack of funds to build additional gunboats or barges, or perhaps it signaled a tacit admission that a flotilla, no matter how well led, would be futile in the face of what the Royal Navy could send up the Potomac.

In his report, Morris anticipated that the enemy would probably send a squadron of six frigates and perhaps a 74-gun ship of the line. Since no effective resistance could be made on water, he recommended establishing powerful batteries at Greenleaf Point and Windmill Point, sinking hulks in at least two places, and constructing a water battery at Fort Warburton. Finally, he would place gunboats, scows, and galleys at the narrowest portion of the Eastern Branch of the Potomac. This was as good a suggestion as he could make, but very little was done to follow through, and Captain Morris was not there when the time came. His was another destiny. He had sailed into the Atlantic eight months earlier and would end up burning his ship to prevent its capture at Hampden, Maine.

A British Army Torches Washington

After the rout of the American militias at Bladensburg, the invasion and burning of Washington was achieved by General Robert Ross's British army.[26] With one exception: the Washington Navy Yard. Even after the British army's arrival in Washington, the navy yard was as yet unscathed. But as it was one of America's largest industrial facilities, the secretary of the navy was not about to allow it to be pillaged and burned by the enemy. As a question of honor as much as practicality, the navy had to burn its earliest and largest navy yard to keep its machinery, gunpowder, and newly built ships from falling in to enemy hands. Secretary William Jones had been much in conversation with the president and other members of the cabinet about preparations for defending Washington and what should be done if the British succeeded in invading Washington. He had already given permission to Thomas Turner, the navy auditor, to remove the papers of the Navy Department by wagons gathered by Mordecai Booth, Commodore Tingey's clerk.[27] This was a prescient act for which all naval historians should be eternally grateful. This saved not only the navy accountant's papers but also the secretary's extensive correspondence, including orders sent and reports received from most of the navy's officers, ships, and stations before and during the war. With the Capitol and the White House already in flames, it would be only a matter of time before the enemy troops descended on the navy yard with its valuable cache of timber, canvas, cordage, and explosives.

Considering this probability at twilight on August 24, Secretary Jones ordered Commodore Thomas Tingey to decide when and how the yard was to be destroyed.

Likewise, it was Secretary Jones who ordered Master Commandant John Orde Creighton to take charge of blowing up the bridge extending from the navy yard across the Eastern Branch. It was later found to be unnecessary because the British came into Washington on the Bladensburg Road. But giving the order to burn the navy yard must have been heartrending for Tingey, the man who more than anyone else from its beginning in 1799 had made this naval factory what it was.

By afternoon on August 24, the city of Washington was in chaos, with citizens, leaving on horseback and wagons, taking their cherished belongings with them. Citizens were particularly affected by the sight of wounded survivors of the battle walking or stumbling through the streets in their flight from Bladensburg. It was clear that the British would be coming. Captain Tingey had removed from the navy yard as much as could be done by wagons and small boats.[28] When the enemy troops were within half a mile of the yard, Tingey ordered the powder trains to be torched in the buildings and ships, including the new frigate *Columbia*, the sloop *Argus*, and the hulks of the old frigates *New York*, *Boston*, and *General Greene*, which had served their country in the Quasi-War and the Tripolitan War. The only vessel not burned was the schooner *Lynx*, which he spared because she was far down the wharf. Tingey loaded and sent the three remaining gunboats, *Nos. 70*, *71*, and *140*, toward Georgetown, and with Creighton and others of his staff he stepped into his gig and sailed for Alexandria. The fate of the gunboats, however, was that both *No. 70* and *No. 71* were found partially burned, while gunboat *No. 140* survived but was looted by local citizenry.[29]

The flames and explosions of the navy yard conflagration were both astonishing and frightening to witnesses, as if they were not frightened enough already at the arrival of more than three thousand enemy troops. Even worse was the burning of a privately owned ropewalk that erupted in an immense cloud of black smoke and probably toxic gases. The British torched the ropewalk even though they had been told it was private, not navy, property. Such buildings were about a half mile in length and filled with cordage, hemp, and tar, which burned with a vengeance. When asked why they had destroyed this private property, owned by Ringgold, Chalmers, Heath and Company, the British answered that most likely it would have been used by the navy anyway.[30] Weeks after these devastating events, Commodore Tingey gave an accounting to Congress of the navy yard's losses.

The Ransoming of Alexandria

As Captain Morris had predicted, a small Royal Navy squadron under Captain Sir James Alexander Gordon was under way up the Potomac partially as a diversion and partially as a stopgap measure to withdraw at least a portion of the British army should it suffer a reversal at Washington. Since that did not occur, Gordon halted his progress at the Alexandria waterfront on August 28 and threatened destruction of the town unless the citizens opened their warehouses and surrendered everything that Gordon's ships could carry away. Furthermore, he insisted, should anyone offer resistance, the town would be put to the torch. The town fathers abjectly consented as they had no means of armed resistance.[31] Gordon ordered twenty-one vessels to be seized and loaded with prize goods from warehouses, including 16,000 barrels of flour, 1,000 hogsheads of tobacco, 150 bales of cotton, and five thousand dollars' worth of wine and sugar. The enemy were ready to leave by August 31, but owing to contrary winds they could not get under way until September 4.[32]

The US Navy had one opportunity to punish the departing enemy. As soon as Secretary Jones heard of General Ross's army landing at Benedict, he wrote to three of his senior officers, Commodore John Rodgers, Commodore Oliver Hazard Perry, and Captain David Porter, ordering them to immediately abandon their present tasks and report to him at Washington to assist in the defense of the capital. At that time Rodgers, the most senior, was supervising the completion of his new frigate, *Guerriere*, at Philadelphia. Perry, by then promoted to captain, was in New York heading a court of inquiry into Porter's loss of *Essex* in the Pacific. He was eventually to take command of the new frigate *Java*, under construction at Baltimore. All three of these men, along with their crews, gathered at Baltimore, where Commodore John Rodgers, at the behest of his old friend Major General Samuel Smith, assumed command of the naval defenses of Baltimore. By the time they arrived at Baltimore, it was too late to save Washington, but Secretary Jones ordered Rodgers to bring his comrades in arms to Alexandria to make the British departure as difficult as possible. Stripping Baltimore of several hundred sailors who had been put under his command, Rodgers divided his sailors and marines into three groups. Rodgers himself would organize a group to prepare fireships to attack the rear guard of Captain Gordon's convoy. Porter organized a battery of guns to be emplaced along the right bank of the Potomac near the "white house," a structure of the old Belvoir plantation. Perry, at the suggestion of Acting Secretary of War James Monroe, organized a battery to be placed on the left bank of the Potomac, at Indian Head in lower Charles County.

The result of these improvised decisions made but little impact on Gordon's squadron. Rodgers's crew, sixty men in four barges, launched three fireships on September 3, but owing to a lack of wind and alert enemy guard boats, the fireships did not touch the British ships. Porter's battery (three 18-pounders, two 12-pounders, six 6-pounders, and two 4-pounders) did some damage, forcing the British to spend the better part of two days destroying Porter's guns. However, the battery's guns did "considerable damage" to the mortar sloops (bomb ships) *Erebus* and *Devastation* before being beaten off. Porter's 18-pounders might have done more damage had all of them been on carriages. General John Hungerford, of the Virginia militia, provided some 4- and 6-pounder guns and infantry to help delay the British. The battery, including some volunteer infantry from the hinterlands, suffered fourteen dead and thirty-two wounded. Gordon's squadron suffered seven killed and thirty-five wounded during its Potomac expedition.[33] Perry's battery at Indian Head, one long 18-pounder and several 6-pounders, was too small to be effective and ran out of ammunition after firing a few rounds; however, it did slow by one day the squadron's return to the mouth of the Potomac. Waiting there, eager for Captain Gordon's return, was Admiral Cochrane with a fleet of 74-gun ships, many frigates and transports, ready to sail for their next target, Baltimore.[34]

The Maritime Defense of Baltimore

While still in the Washington area, Commodore Rodgers received a short, alarming letter from General Samuel Smith. Smith was concerned that Rodgers and Porter had left Baltimore so precipitously. They had taken with them six hundred sailors and marines in answer to Secretary Jones's urgent request for assistance in opposing the British squadron at Alexandria. Smith was in the midst of preparing for a British thrust at Baltimore when Rodgers departed. When Smith heard from Rodgers that he had departed to send fire ships against the British ships, he sent the following curt note:

> Sir: I have recd. Yours & regret that the idea of setting fire to two frigates Should induce the Government to detain so large and so efficient as yours from our Aid, because although you come at the time the British are before us, your Station is not Assigned, and in the meantime, the Sloops of War intended to defend the Western Branch [of the Parapsco] are not prepared—if we are attacked on that side we are not defended, it is our Weak Point, I am persuaded you can do no good where you are—you may even cause the burning of Alexandria—What has become of the Ammunition secured in the Chapel, in haste, yours, S. Smith, Major General.[35]

Smith's letter was, in effect, a recall of Rodgers to Baltimore as quickly as he could come, bringing his marines and sailors with him. Rodgers, for good reasons, was caught owing services to both Secretary Jones and General Smith at a time of crisis. Of course, Rodgers had to respond immediately to the secretary's request to come to Washington because Gordon's squadron was already at Alexandria and there would be little time to set Jones's fireships plan in motion. But

Smith, who was in charge of the defense of Baltimore and had been preparing for months, was also Rodger's close friend of many years. Rodgers answered Smith the same day writing,

> Would to God! It was in my power to return to Baltimore immediately, as I am well assured that our seamen would be of more service there than they are likely to be here. There are now however 500 encamped at Snowden's [plantation] ready to march to Baltimore. The rest are here and in the vicinity of Alexandria so that you may calculate on having the whole detachment except about 80 who are on the Virginia side with Captain Porter. . . . I can assure you I have a deep interest in the welfare of Baltimore and am satisfied that I shall be with you with 7/8 of my force should the enemy attack you.[36]

Secretary Jones saw that his orders conflicted with General Smith's regarding Rodgers's assignments. He admitted to Rodgers that he was "really embarrassed between the desire of affording you the opportunity of effecting either the destruction or injury of the enemy and the dread of an attack on Baltimore before you shall have reached that place."[37] But he granted Rodgers the discretion to spend two or three more days on the Potomac before returning to Baltimore. If an attack there seemed imminent, Jones would notify him.

Following his abortive attempt to burn Gordon's ships, Rodgers returned to Baltimore the evening of September 7 and resumed his post as commander of the naval forces on the Baltimore station. He referred to his command as a brigade, in two regiments, one under Captain Porter, commanding the seamen and marines of the late frigate *Essex* and those of Rodgers's ship *Guerriere*, and the other under Captain Perry, commanding the officers and seamen of the Chesapeake Flotilla. When Perry returned from Indian Head, he was fatigued and sick, partly as a result of the illness he had endured on Lake Erie, so the actual leadership of the flotilla fell to Lieutenant Rutter under Rodgers's overall direction. Rodgers personally supervised the placement of naval batteries on Hampstead Hill, which overlooked the approaches to Baltimore from North Point. Using 300 sailors and 175 marines from his ship *Guerriere*, the Chesapeake Flotillamen, as well as the First Marine Artillery of the Union, Rodgers placed and manned 120 guns facing the probable direction of a British attack. General Smith added to this the far more numerous troops of the Maryland, Virginia, and Pennsylvania militias. Together they comprised an estimated 15,000 soldiers, sailors, marines, and volunteers arrayed at Hampstead Hill during the crucial three days of battle, September 13–15, 1814.

Other naval batteries were located to protect the river approaches to Fort McHenry on Whetstone Point. Flotillamen under the direction of Sailing Master Solomon Rodman manned the recently constructed water battery in front of Fort McHenry. Their guns were 36-pounders salvaged from the French ship *L'Eole* in the Chesapeake Bay not many years before. At the Lazaretto battery, opposite Fort McHenry's north side, Lieutenant Rutter took charge of three long 18-pounder guns and eleven barges armed with long 8- and 12-pounder guns and 18-pounder gunades. On the southwest side of Fort McHenry, Sailing Master John Webster commanded fifty flotillamen in charge of Fort Babcock's six 18-pounders. Lieutenant Henry Newcomb's battery of ten 18-pounders at Fort Covington and Lieutenant George Budd, stationed at Fort Lookout with seven 18-pounders, covered the west side of the fort, overlooking the Ferry Branch of the Patapsco River. The new frigate *Java* and the sloops of war *Erie* and *Ontario*, all undermanned, were anchored with spring lines in the Northwest Branch, off Fells Point, to cover the northerly approach in case the British were able to out-flank Rodgers's Bastion. The flotillamen had placed stationary naval defenses, mast and chain booms at Fort Point and sunken vessels to block the channel be-tween Lazaretto Point and Whetstone Point.[38]

Admiral Cochrane's Chesapeake Expedition sailed for Baltimore on Septem-ber 8, having welcomed back Captain James A. Gordon's Potomac squadron and its convoy of plunder from Alexandria. For those who were observing the fleet, comprising fifty warships of all types, nothing like it had been seen on the bay since Admiral Richard Lord Howe had brought an even larger fleet up the bay in 1777 to land troops at the head of the Elk River for his attack on Philadelphia. The heaviest and largest ships of Admiral Cochrane's fleet were the four ships of the line HMS *Tonnant*, *Dragon*, *Albion*, and *Royal Oak*. They and the troop trans-ports could not ascend the Patapsco River, as their deep keels could not pass over the shoals at the river's mouth. They anchored off North Point, approximately twelve miles from Baltimore, and supplied launches to land the troops and sailors for the naval infantry brigade. The smaller frigates, brigs, and mortar sloops could sail up the Patapsco to as close as two miles from Fort McHenry. Those that could come closest were the mortar sloops, armed with 10- and 12-inch mortars, whose heavy shells could be launched high in the air to explode either over Fort McHenry or on contact, throwing heavy chunks of iron with great impact.

The Battle of Baltimore was not a long-drawn-out affair, but lasted only four days, punctuated by several dramatic events. The enemy ships arrived at North Point on September 11. The troops landed during the dark early hours of Septem-ber 12. All told, these units amounted to 4,760 officers and enlisted, including two battalions of Royal Marines (1,300 men) and a naval brigade (600 men) from the various ships of the fleet. When they were formed up, General Robert Ross and Rear Admiral Cockburn rode in the vanguard with the light infantry.

In the late morning, during the first skirmish, a sniper's bullet hit Ross in the chest, a fatal wound as it turned out. Colonel Arthur Brooke took his place, but afterward things were never the same for the troops. A veteran of the Peninsular Campaign, Ross had been an admired leader, much loved for his courage and considerate personality. Brooke, not so well known, had led battalions but not armies in battle. Yet, at this point the army was his to command, and with this first skirmish the battle of North Point had begun. The battle was hard fought on both sides. General John Stricker led Baltimore's army of roughly 3,000 men, made up of the Third Militia Brigade, the First Maryland Rifle Battalion, three Pennsylvania volunteer companies, two Maryland volunteer companies, and one artillery battery of four 6-pounders. In a battle lasting most of the afternoon, Stricker held firm at first, then gave ground slowly, and finally withdrew to the entrenchments on Hampstead Hill shortly after 3:00 p.m. Brooke's infantry did not pursue; they stayed to bind up their wounds, bury their dead, and take stock of the situation. They had suffered 39 killed, including their beloved general, and 251 wounded. It now remained for Colonel Brooke to consult with Admirals Cockburn and Cochrane.

September 13 began overcast and misty, with the usual humidity and heat. It was the Royal Navy's turn to try Fort McHenry's strength, but it took most of the day for six frigates to work their way up the shallow river. The afternoon brought torrential rain, wind, and thunderstorms. Ahead of the frigates, the fleet's five mortar sloops with their shallower keels pulled to within shelling distance of two miles and let loose with a barrage that lasted the rest of the day and late into the night. One of them, *Erebus*, was equipped with Congreve rockets. The effect of these weapons was more psychological than lethal. Their aim was imperfect, they might go wildly off course but could cause fires, and the sight and sound of their plunging arcs could be fearsome.

As the enemy ships drew closer, the fort's water battery and the Lazaretto guns opened fire, forcing the frigates and mortar ships to withdraw to a safer distance. The French 36-pounders had a devastating effect as they ricocheted across the water and slammed into the hulls of those ships. The 18- and 12-pounders from the Lazaretto and the barges also had a telling effect. Meanwhile, the British army drew itself up before Hampstead Hill, which bristled with gun emplacements and entrenchments. Colonel Brooke tried a maneuver to the north side of the hill, thinking to outflank the batteries, but the Baltimore troops moved in parallel to refuse their left flank. Brooke was stymied and wrote to Admiral Cochrane for assistance, asking if the navy could outflank Fort McHenry on the west side, co-ordinated with an army attack at Hampstead Hill. Cochrane did not reply directly but rather gave Cockburn a thinly disguised warning for Brooke: "You are on no account to attack the enemy unless you are positively certain of success."[39] Cochrane also advised Cockburn that the fleet would not be able to render further assistance and that he was concerned that a failed attempt on Baltimore would "be only throwing the men's lives away and prevent us from going on other services."[40] Brooke decided, after a council of war, that under such conditions he could not be positive of success. He ordered the army to return to the fleet at North Point.[41]

Cochrane, meanwhile, unaware of Brooke's decision, had ordered a coordinated attack, telling Captain Charles John Napier to organize a barge attack into the Ferry Branch. This took time to organize. It was about 10:00 p.m. when Napier set out with twenty barges, *Erebus*, and *Euryalus* to attack Batteries Babcock and Covington, to the west of the fort. This plan went awry in the rain-filled night, with eleven barges getting separated and heading for the Lazaretto. Thus weakened, Napier continued with his remaining force, but the flotillamen at these batteries were alert, discovered the barges, and fought them off. Napier returned to the fleet, having heard nothing of the British army at Hampstead Hill. The Battle of Baltimore had ended.

The British Expedition Departs

Having had to withdraw, not to say retreat, from Baltimore, Admiral Cochrane had determined to return to Halifax to make repairs to his fleet and rest his troops. In his ensuing letter to the First Lord of the Admiralty, the admiral averred that the decision to attack Baltimore had not been his preference but said that he had reluctantly consented to the plan because of General Ross's eagerness to get on with it (likely at Admiral Cockburn's urging). Cochrane thought, in retrospect, that it would have been more advantageous to proceed with his original plan of attacking Rhode Island.[42] Cochrane had also been uneasy about attacking Washington once Barney's flotilla was destroyed, but Cockburn had persuaded Ross that it could be easily done, and so it was. Despite their success, Vice Admiral Cochrane apparently never completely forgave Rear Admiral Cockburn for ignoring his suggestion that the expedition return to its ships instead of attacking Washington.[43]

After the setback at Baltimore, Cockburn considered the expedition a military failure. He was impatient of the delays, which the army had spent organizing on Tangier Island, and criticized both General Ross and Admiral Cochrane for being indecisive. He thought that these delays had given Baltimoreans time to prepare their defenses. Cochrane, however, considered the Baltimore action to have been a "demonstration" of the type that Lord Bathurst and others felt would discourage the Americans and cause them to lose confidence in their ability to resist. Writing to the First Lord of the Admiralty, Cochrane explained that if he had had two thousand more troops, he might have outflanked the enemy's works, but with the troops that he had, this could not have been done without risk of being cut off from retreat by "the numerous militia the enemy had assembled."[44]

By early October, most elements of the Chesapeake fleet had sailed to Bermuda for refit, under the direction of Rear Admiral Cockburn, while Vice Admiral Cochrane took his division to Halifax. A few frigates and smaller vessels remained in the bay under the temporary control of Rear Admiral Pulteney Malcolm in his flagship *Royal Oak*. Cockburn was due to return to the Chesapeake to relieve Malcolm until Captain Robert Barrie in *Dragon* returned to assume command of the winter squadron. But Barrie had let it be known that he was not anxious to be left in charge of the naval rear guard in the Chesapeake for another winter.

CHAPTER 12

Hostilities in the Seaboard South

As Washingtonians sadly set about repairing the tremendous damage inflicted on the capital and Baltimoreans celebrated their defensive victory, the British admirals were anxious to begin their next campaign before the peace negotiations at Ghent ended. They hoped and expected to conclude the American war with a flourish that would bring not only peace in North America but security for the Canadian provinces and their First Nation allies in the west. The strategy, as planned in the spring of 1814, included a direct attack on the Gulf Coast and diversionary strokes at Charleston and southern Georgia to draw American defensive forces from the principal target, New Orleans. If the British could obtain control of the Mississippi River, they would be in a position to manipulate the US government and trade in the center of the continent until or unless a settlement favorable to Great Britain could be made at the peace table.

The Southern Strategy

The original source of the British southern strategy of 1814 may have been Admiral John B. Warren, Cochrane's predecessor, who addressed the subject in a letter to Lord Melville in 1812. But Cochrane too was a strategic thinker and had the aim of subjugating the southern and Gulf coasts with the aid of the Creek and Seminole tribes, who disliked the land-hungry Americans. These plans were thoroughly thrashed out in London during the spring of 1814. Lord Melville optimistically expected to send seven thousand troops for the New Orleans expedition.[1] When this proved to be unfeasible because of the cost and the continuing need for troops in Europe, Cochrane wrote suggesting that he could accomplish his plan with three thousand men. The Admiralty found that number to be so reasonable that they provided even more: about fifty-three hundred infantry plus artillerymen, sailors, and marines, in all totaling about ten thousand men.[2] While Cochrane prepared a fleet to sail for a rendezvous with troopships at Negril Bay, Jamaica, he ordered Cockburn to take charge of a diversionary attack on the southern Atlantic coast from North Carolina to Fernandina, Spanish East Florida. Cockburn's principal point of attack was to be at St. Marys in order to take control of the American intercoastal trade. This trade extended from Cumberland Bay between the Sea Islands and the mainland all the way to Charleston. He hoped that the attack would draw American troops away from New Orleans, Mobile, Pensacola, and Apalachicola on the Gulf Coast, where his amphibious forces would focus their attention.

For various reasons, Admiral Cockburn arrived late at his new base on Cumberland Island, Georgia. The Admiralty had cut back on the number of troops available for Cockburn's operation in order to meet the needs in Canada and at New Orleans. For his diversionary operation, Cockburn had to round up Royal Marines and black Colonial Marines from available ships and bring them from Bermuda to Cumberland Island. Although he had sent ships to strengthen the blockade on the South Carolina coast, the operations he had planned there never took place, perhaps for reasons related to the weather.

Naval Defenders of the Seaboard South

The US Navy vessels stationed on the shores of the seaboard South were, of necessity, of shallow draft and capable of being sailed or rowed, depending on the wind and the current. The barrier islands were essentially sandbars, penetrated by occasional inlets, protecting a series of inland sounds. If a vessel drew 10 feet or less, it could sail in the sounds between ports and be safe from enemy warships and dangerous seas. At first, the British were unfamiliar with these sounds and inlets and tended to avoid them. The seaboard inhabitants, however, were knowledgeable about the sounds, shoals, and inlets and therefore good pilots for coastal voyaging. Plantation owners along the coast requested navy gunboats and schooners for the protection of their properties. But Secretary of the Navy William Jones wanted southern defenses limited to gunboats and barges (row galleys) at Wilmington, Charleston, Savannah, and St. Marys. The barges generally measured 48 feet on the keel and 9 feet in beam, were half-decked, allowing for storage lockers. and could be rowed remarkably fast, with twelve oars on a side. They were armed with an 18- or 24-pounder carronade and small arms. The navy gunboats were heavier and could mount larger guns, but they were less agile under oars and slow under sail.[3] The two naval commanders in charge of the southern naval stations were Captain John Dent at Charleston and Captain Hugh Campbell at Savannah. As one of the navy's younger captains, Dent was of the same cohort as Captain James Lawrence, born in the early 1780s, joining the navy in 1798 as a midshipman and serving in the Quasi-War with France under Captain Thomas Truxtun in the frigate *Constellation* when she defeated *L'Insurgent*. Following that duty, Dent served as first lieutenant under Commodore Edward Preble in the frigate *Constitution* and was her acting captain for a time in early 1804, when Commodore Edward Preble had to go ashore at Valletta, Malta, for several days.[4] Dent later served as commanding officer of the brig *Scourge*, the schooner *Nautilus*, and the sloop of war *Hornet*. He married into a Charleston family and was in command of the Charleston naval station at the outset of the War of 1812. One distinguishing feature of Dent's command was his tendency to mete out harsh punishments on board his ships, frequently exceeding the twelve lashes customarily applied to shipboard malefactors, for which Secretary Jones took him to task.[5]

At Charleston, Captain Dent found himself bombarded by requests from local citizens for help to protect trading vessels in the coasting trade, particularly for those carrying rice, which was much needed for the citizens of the city. The Royal Navy had three brigs patrolling the coast to interdict that trade, and Dent at first lacked the fast-sailing schooners or brigs to counter the blockade. In October 1812 he had requested that Secretary Hamilton provide a fast-sailing schooner with ten or twelve guns and remarked that local shipowners might be able provide one through the state government's purchase or a loan.[6] Less than a month later Hamilton gave his assent, and Dent reported that he had purchased two schooners. One, recently built but not yet launched, would carry fourteen guns and ninety men and would be called *Carolina*; the other, *Ferret*, would carry eight 6-pounders and one long 12-pounder on a circle. He also had at his disposal a schooner-rigged gunboat (*No. 166*), *Alligator*, stationed at Beaufort, South Carolina, and the former Baltimore privateer *Nonsuch*, which Dent had bought for the navy at Charleston in December 1812. The schooner *Carolina* would perform superbly two years later, in the defense of New Orleans.

As Dent acknowledged to Secretary Jones in early 1813, he had need of officers (a lieutenant commanding for the schooner and eight midshipmen for the barges) and seamen to complete the complements of the schooners and barges, as well as a purser for *Carolina*. His men had no proper hospital, and the house of the naval surgeon had recently burned down, destroying his surgical instruments and medicines. Jones, however, was resistant to the many demands for men on southern stations; in fact, he sent out orders to reduce the number of gunboats in service and place them in ordinary, essentially taking them out of service until urgently needed. He believed it was a waste of funds to maintain partially manned gunboats. He constantly chided his commanders to economize in order to have funds to support his building of oceangoing sloops of war.

The British blockading vessels drew too much water to use the intercoastal channels, so they too used barges or launches with oarsmen to patrol the coastal waters. They operated in barge groups manned by up to 150 men from the larger ships. Dent found it useful to escort trading vessels in convoy with several barges to combat these flotillas and to prevent interruption of service. Often, he had to shift seamen from the schooners to man the barges, though he occasionally was able to borrow troops from the army for this duty.[7] In January 1814, Secretary Jones authorized five more barges to be built at Charleston, designed along the lines of the second-class (50-foot) barges used by Joshua Barney in the Chesapeake. He ordered Dent to arm them with 12-, 18-, or 24-pounder long guns, though he preferred 18-pounders. During 1812 and 1813 the Royal Navy had only a small division of vessels on blockade of Charleston, such as a sloop of war, a brig, and a schooner, but beginning in August 1814 they increased strength to a frigate, several sloops of war, a brig, and a tender off Charleston and two brigs stationed between Savannah and St. Marys.

Captain Hugh George Campbell had charge of the navy's gunboats and barges on the Georgia station. He, like Dent, had risen to his rank by virtue of service during the Quasi-War with France and the Barbary Wars in the Mediterranean. But Campbell, born in 1760, was of an older generation. Of Irish extraction and known as "Old Cork," he was a South Carolinian who at age 15 joined the crew of the schooner *Defence*, of the South Carolina navy, during the American Revolution. Later, he served as a sailing master in the US Revenue Cutter Service schooner *Eagle*, and when she was taken into the navy during the Quasi-War with France in 1799, Master Commandant Campbell sailed as her commander. He became a friend of William Jones, who was in those days a merchant in Charleston. His highly successful war record in *Eagle* earned him the command of the frigate *General Greene*, and later, during the Tripolitan War, he commanded the frigate *Constellation*.[8] By the time of the War of 1812, Captain Campbell was in his early fifties, a wise old salt with a game leg, probably the perfect person to have in charge of the Savannah naval station. He had a strong reputation as an excellent blue-water commander with a shrewd way of handling men unaccustomed to strict discipline, as many young enlisted and their officers were (fig. 12.1).

Campbell's responsibilities required him to keep a close watch over the Sea Islands and St. Marys, overlooking the waters of Fernandina Sound, where Spanish territory began and US sovereignty ended. It was a perfect place for foreign ships to meet smugglers intent on avoiding US customs to bring finished goods into Georgia and along the intercoastal network of channels to Savannah and other towns. In early 1813, he commanded twelve gunboats, the 18-gun sloop *Troup*, and six barges from Charleston. Yet, being short of seamen, this was a weakly manned force. At Jones's order, Campbell decommissioned six of the gunboats, keeping six at St. Marys, and laid up four barges at Savannah. This left some gaping holes in the protection of the Georgia coast. The British ships could

Figure 12.1. American gunboat. Painting by Lewis Victor Mays. Used courtesy of Sara Louise Hessler.

easily interrupt the communications and trade between St. Marys and Savannah by entering St. Andrew or St. Simon Sound.[9]

The Royal Navy was not the only enemy facing Campbell and his sailors. Autumn hurricanes could wreak havoc with southern shipping, as happened in September 1813. Three gunboats (*Nos. 62, 161,* and *164*) sank, four others were blown inland on storm surge, and it took many days of work to extract them from the wetlands. The guard/receiving ship *Troup* was apparently damaged, and Jones ordered her to be dismantled, her crew to be distributed among the remaining gunboats.

Throughout the ensuing months, the British ships played cat and mouse with the US gunboats and trading vessels. When the larger British ships detected a coasting ship in the intercoastal waterway, they would move faster in the same direction until they came to an inlet and then send their boats across the bar to intercept the ship before the gunboats could catch up. Sometimes the gunboats and an enemy ship's boats would engage in a firefight. Gunboat *No. 160* was escorting several vessels from Savannah to St. Marys on October 6, 1814, when they were confronted with a night boat attack in St. Andrew Sound. The Royal Navy ships had sent in ten boats and a sloop tender, with two hundred men in all. The enemy boats were able to capture *No. 160* and four merchant vessels, but not before suffering twenty killed and wounded, compared with the American loss of just three wounded. Rather than taking the American sailors prisoners, they marooned them on a sandbar in danger of being drowned by a rising tide. The American sailors were ultimately rescued.

Rear Admiral Cockburn Invades Georgia

As difficult as his situation was, Captain Campbell reported that his convoy system was effective. Despite losses and the sickliness of his crews, he had, over several months, been able to protect $6 million worth of property in the inland water trade. He reported that one of his convoys included as many as eighty-eight vessels. Campbell's worst nightmare came to pass when Rear Admiral Cockburn's squadron arrived and landed on Cumberland Island during early January 1815. Some of Cockburn's ships arrived ahead of the flagship and took immediate action. Captain Kenelm Somerville, of the frigate *Thames*, took possession of the island and sent a body of six hundred troops to the Georgia mainland, where they captured an American battery at Point Pete, and then occupied St. Marys. After Cockburn arrived on January 14 with about one thousand more troops, he sent his boats on a raid up the St. Marys River and sent several ships to strengthen the blockades off Savannah and Charleston. This was the beginning of a British occupation that did not end until March 17. As US gunboats and barges were useless against such a powerful force, Captain Campbell gathered up as many vessels as he could and retreated up the Savannah River. He was most concerned that Savannah itself would be a target of the British.

But that was not to be; the British had other objectives. One was to draw off as many American troops as possible from the defense of the Gulf Coast as part of the offensive against New Orleans. The other was to weaken the economy of the region by inducing slaves to flee from their plantations, as they had in Maryland and Virginia. Cockburn failed of his first objective owing to bad timing. The finale of the Battle of New Orleans had occurred on January 7, three days before the British arrived on Cumberland Island.[10] Jackson's army had defeated General Pakenham's regulars at great cost to the British, and the long-negotiated Treaty of Ghent had been signed on December 24. The ratifications had yet to be exchanged, so the peace was not definitive, but it was near at hand. Cockburn's second objective was coming to fruition on Cumberland Island. He had let it be known through proclamation and word of mouth that since Cumberland Island was now British territory, any slaves who chose to leave their masters would be considered free when they reached the island. Those who wished to join the Colonial Marines would be welcomed and provided with uniforms, weapons, and training. Their families were expected to accompany them. Others would be transported to British possessions and would be free to settle in either Halifax or Trinidad. Approximately 1,483 escaped slaves gained refugee status after arriving at Cumberland Island during the eight weeks of British occupation.[11] Admiral Cockburn made his headquarters at Dungeness, an enormous five-story house built on a plantation owned by the descendants of General Nathaniel Greene, who had been granted the property by the state of Georgia after the American Revolution.[12]

Cockburn fortified the residence with an entrenchment with a large breast-work and built a long pier. He expected to stay for a lengthy period to take in prize goods from his blockading squadron and to attack Savannah and Charleston from this base. These expectations were cut short by the news in February that the Treaty of Ghent had been ratified; however, the liberation of the slaves brought problems in terms of how to deal with large numbers of men, women, and children as refugees, feeding them and initially clothing them, for this was their expectation. He tried to persuade them to work for pay so as to take care of their own needs. Eventually, as the news of peace spread, the angry plantation owners demanded the return of their slaves, which he refused. The governor of Georgia accused the admiral of theft. When slaves from Spanish Florida showed up, Cockburn accepted them despite a protest from the governor of East Florida. The admiral asserted that they had come of their own free will and were now subjects of Great Britain, which had prohibited slavery. This he continued to do, and he refused to acknowledge the peace until he was officially informed that treaty ratifications had been exchanged. On March 1, Cockburn received Admiral Cochrane's orders to cease operations. The Treaty of Ghent went into effect on February 17. The Royal Navy finally evacuated Cumberland Island on March 18.[13]

The Creek War

At this point, having dealt with Admiral Cockburn's diversionary stroke, our attention shifts to the Gulf Coast and the internal conflicts that brought Major General Andrew Jackson and his troops into the Lower South. The US Navy had very few assets on the Gulf Coast, and those it had were stationed at New Orleans. In effect, the Royal Navy had open access to ports and harbors along the coast from Apalachicola to Pensacola, with the cooperation of Spanish authorities who exercised rather weak control of their West Florida possession. From western Georgia and Florida to the Mississippi Territory (the future states of Alabama and Mississippi) lived a diverse population of Seminole, Creek, Chickasaw, and Choctaw Native American tribes, slaves, free blacks, and runaways, as well as white settlers from the neighboring states of South Carolina and Tennessee. During the period 1796 to 1817, this territory experienced a surge in population as white new-comers arrived seeking more fertile lands. The Native Americans who tradition-ally lived in the area considered this migration a disturbing and troublesome in-terruption of their lives.

In this thinly populated but rapidly growing area lived a number of British traders and Native American agents who maintained contact with British govern-ment and commercial representatives in the Bahamas and Jamaica. Some of the traders had intermarried with tribal members and had considerable influence among the natives. With the onset of war, British authorities depended on these traders as sources of information, and by providing weapons and promises of pro-tection, they hoped to turn the tribes into British allies against the United States. The Creeks, especially those in the northern part of the territory, were vulnerable to this type of approach. They had been exposed to the visits of the Shawnee chief Tecumseh and his brother Tenskwatawa, the Prophet, in 1811, when they were urging Native American warriors' alliance against the Americans, who were in-vading their hunting grounds and destroying their way of life. The older of the Creek chiefs counseled against this uprising, but the younger, more warlike Red Sticks, as they called themselves, adopted this stance and staged attacks on white settlements in Tennessee, Kentucky, and Mississippi in 1812 and 1813. The role of the Red Sticks at the battle of Burnt Corn and their massacre of settlers at Fort Mims, north of Mobile, drew national attention and brought about invasions from the border states of Tennessee and Georgia that began the Creek War.

These attacks alarmed frontier communities in the Old Southwest and pro-voked them to send armies to suppress the Red Sticks. Foremost were Andrew Jackson, a general of the Tennessee militia, and US Army Major Generals Thomas Pinckney and Thomas Flournoy. During the winter of 1813–14, Jackson led a body of Tennessee militia into the Creek territory, what today is north-central Alabama, and defeated the Red Sticks in several encounters. Jackson, though, suffered losses and was short of food and men. But he was determined to finish the campaign and called on Governor Blount of Tennessee to send five thousand of the state's militia, and General Pinckney assisted by sending the Thirty-ninth US Infantry. With these reinforcements, Jackson and Brigadier General John Coffee scored a major victory on March 28, 1814, at the battle of Horseshoe Bend. Jackson then imposed a punishing treaty on the Creeks, including even those who had been allied with him. The Treaty of Fort Jackson took away half of the Creeks' traditional lands (33,000 square miles) and set the stage for lasting Creek hostility, opening the door for British inducements.[14]

Anticipating trouble from the British on the Gulf Coast and covetous of Span-ish Florida, Congress authorized the occupation of West Florida in February 1813. Secretary of War Armstrong issued orders to ranking major general James Wilkinson, already stationed at New Orleans, to capture and occupy Mobile and all territory up to the Perdido River. Wilkinson organized an expedition and with the cooperation of the New Orleans naval station commander, Captain John Shaw, loaded troops on flatboats and sailed to Mobile under gunboat escort. The Spanish garrison was weak and ill-prepared to defend itself. Within three days, the Spanish surrendered Fort Charlotte, and Mobile became US territory. This, for the US Congress, was a decision taken with alacrity and carried out swiftly by the military and naval units available, an exception to the rule for the War of 1812. The step showed foresight, for Mobile was a logical place for the British to capture if the target was New Orleans and the plan was to attack along the Gulf Coast from the east.

From early in the war, Governor Cameron, of the Bahamas, had been sending intelligence reports to his superior, Earl Bathurst, concerning unsettled conditions among the Creeks and other Native Americans of the Gulf Coast and the likelihood that they could be encouraged to make war on American settlements in the region. He had contacts with Spanish and British trading companies who had remained in Spanish territory after the American Revolution. He had recommended a plan to arm the Native Americans, many of whom did not have muskets, ammunition, or powder, and to provide for them if war broke out. These ideas had become part of the overall strategic plan to end the war that Bathurst and Admiral Cochrane were discussing in 1814. When the news of Jackson's defeat of the Creeks at Horseshoe Bend reached Bathurst, he decided that the time had come to execute this plan and take advantage of the discontent among the native tribes.[15] Admiral Cochrane sent Captain Hugh Pigot in HMS *Orpheus* with instructions to land officers to communicate with the Creek chiefs and assess their mood, obtain information on American military, and land arms if needed. He also sent a small squadron under Captain William S. Percy, of HMS *Hermes*, to test the strength of Fort Bowyer, at the entrance to Mobile Bay. Pigot's men reported that the Spanish were worried that the Americans would attack Pensacola. Percy found that Fort Bowyer was well defended; indeed, he lost his ship after grounding and coming under fire from the fort on September 13. Percy returned with his smaller squadron to Pensacola. When Jackson's agents reported that the British had landed at Pensacola at the request of the Spanish governor, he marched to Pensacola and demanded capitulation. The British withdrew, except for a small rear-guard unit that blew up Fort Barrancas and Fort Santa Rosa as Jackson's troops attacked on November 7, 1814. As a result of the Americans' strategic moves—the capture of Mobile, the strengthening of Fort Bowyer, and the capture of Pensacola—they had preempted Earl Bathurst and Admiral Cochrane's plans for the British army, which otherwise might have attacked New Orleans overland and from the east and north via Pensacola, Mobile, and Baton Rouge.[16]

The Navy's Defenses

Well before the attack on Washington, the British high command had determined that one of the most valuable targets for them would be New Orleans.[17] In mid-September, Vice Admiral Cochrane had withdrawn his forces after the failed attack on Baltimore and was preparing to attack Rhode Island when he received new orders from the Admiralty. He immediately canceled his plans to sail for New England in order to prepare for operations in the Gulf of Mexico. New Orleans was a valuable piece on the strategic chessboard. Situated as it was, whoever controlled the port city could regulate or tax the river trade. If the city could be captured and held, other concessions might be wrung from the bankrupt US government, or under the threat of destruction the city could be ransomed. With wealthy citizens, warehouses full of cotton bales, and barrels of sugarcane, the enemy could sail away with a small fortune.

Since Thomas Jefferson's purchase of the Louisiana Territory from Napoleonic France in 1803, the only semblance of the US government in the territory was the US naval station. The city was approximately one hundred miles from the Gulf by river, but there were other means of access through a web of shallow tidal creeks or bayous. Naval officers assigned to command at New Orleans had to contend with this situation and were to find that their worst dreams coming true. In late 1814 the Gulf Coast became a major theater of war when the British aimed a thrust at New Orleans and the Gulf Coast.

The navy had established its station at New Orleans in 1806, when Captain John Shaw was assigned to command forces there. Succeeded by Master Commandant David Porter for the brief period 1808–10, Shaw was ordered back to New Orleans in time to participate in the suppression of a slave rebellion in early 1811. Shaw's personality and projects gave the New Orleans naval station its character during the first eighteen months of the war. The problems he faced would prove to be typical of those endured by Master Commandant Daniel Patterson, Shaw's successor. On February 3, 1812, Shaw reported to Secretary of the Navy Paul Hamilton that he had some four hundred men under his command distributed among two brigs of war and a dozen gunboats.[18] Six months later an August hurricane did severe damage, leaving the naval station devastated and several gunboats driven ashore or otherwise damaged.

The residual force at New Orleans was made up of two brigs and a small collection of older, Jeffersonian-era gunboats. Some had even been stationed at Baton

Rouge and Natchez. It took almost four weeks for news of the declaration of war to reach New Orleans, and when it did, Shaw immediately replied to Hamilton that his vessels were inadequate to guard "the extensive portion of the coast assigned to them for protection, and I may add, particularly of the islands and City of New Orleans."[19]

The brig *Syren* was armed with sixteen 24-pounder cannons, two 12-pounders, and sixty men. Slightly less impressive was the brig *Viper*, which carried twelve 12-pounder cannons, two 6-pounders, and sixty men. Neither *Syren* nor *Viper* was present at the Battle of New Orleans. Secretary Jones had ordered them to sea to attack British convoys or take targets of opportunity, but they were eventually captured by British blockaders. The half-dozen gunboats still seaworthy at New Orleans were a varied collection of shallow draft vessels, rigged as either schooners or sloops, carrying but two cannons and a variety of small arms. Although the gunboats were well suited for navigating the shallow waters of the Mississippi delta and among the bays and islands of the Gulf Coast, their design did not suit them well for pursuit and attack offshore. The primary peacetime duties assigned to the New Orleans station commander included the enforcement of embargo laws, the capture of smugglers, and the protection of American commerce from the harassments of British and French warships, privateers, and pirates.

The force under Shaw's command was too small for the many obligations imposed on it. It was impossible for these few vessels to guard all the multiple water routes through bays and bayous of the delta country simultaneously. The most the navy could do was to station its vessels in locations where pirates and smugglers usually sailed or anchored. One of these rendezvous was in Lake Barataria, several miles west of the Southwest Pass. It frequently occurred, however, that the gunboats were no match for the swift schooners that participated in the smuggling trade.

Perhaps the most fortunate event for the navy at New Orleans during 1812 was Secretary Hamilton's authorization for purchase of a merchantman capable of being fitted out as a warship. The owner, J. H. Laurence & Company of New York, offered her for sale to the government at New Orleans on July 4, 1812. She was purchased, taken into the navy in September, and given the name *Louisiana*. Captain Shaw immediately commenced fitting her out, but acquisition of the ship placed new demands on items in short supply, such as gunpowder. As she was being prepared to carry sixteen long 24-pounders, *Louisiana* would need almost all of what Shaw had in the station's magazine.[20]

When William Jones took over as navy secretary in 1813, he let Shaw know that he considered the New Orleans station to have been extravagant and wasteful, and though Shaw protested that such was not the case, he made no headway in getting additional resources. One of Shaw's favorite projects was the construction of a "blockship" at his improvised navy yard on the Tchifoncta River near Lake Ponchartrain. Had it become a reality, this floating fortress might have been quite useful in defense of New Orleans, but Jones was skeptical. Finally, by October Jones had had enough of the testy Captain Shaw. He ordered Master Commandant Daniel Patterson to take command at New Orleans and instructed Shaw to settle his accounts with the Navy Department before he could receive a new command.[21] Before he relinquished command of the station, Shaw wrote to Patterson urging particular vigilance with regard to the eastern approaches to New Orleans along the Gulf Coast and across Lake Borgne. This prescient warning Patterson took to heart and repeated in a letter to Major General Andrew Jackson on September 2, 1814.[22] Shaw closed by stating that he was "truly mortified" at being unable to turn over to Patterson a naval force that could provide an honorable defense of New Orleans.[23]

This change of command coincided with major shifts in the European war, which in turn would bring greater military pressure to bear on the United States. As this situation developed, Patterson adjusted to the demands of his new post. Secretary Jones strongly impressed him with the necessity of strictly managing his accounts "to check the enormous expenditure and waste which has hitherto marked the Naval Service on that Station."[24] He also ordered Patterson to make a detailed report on the progress of the blockship and advised him that if any gunboats were too decayed for use, he would replace them with large barges similar to those used in the Chesapeake Bay flotilla. He promised to send plans so that Patterson could build them at New Orleans; but although the plans eventually arrived, Jones failed to authorize the building of the barges before it was too late.

Patterson swiftly obeyed these orders but soon found himself running toward the same reefs that had threatened Shaw. Having made his tours of inspection, Patterson began to complain of the insufficient number of seamen, too few vessels, inadequate supplies, and the need to complete the blockship.[25] He also advised Jones that letters received from Jamaica mentioned that the British were preparing light draft vessels "for an expedition against this country" and said that he hoped he would have by then "sufficient forces to afford a reasonable prospect of success."[26] The secretary acted to put an end to this carping. He wrote that Patterson had ordered too many supplies, that men could not be stripped from northern stations and sent to New Orleans, and that the blockship, so highly regarded by Shaw, was a "worthless hulk." Jones directed that all construction cease and that the Tchifoncta shipbuilding establishment be broken up.[27]

Patterson must have winced when Lieutenant Daniel Dexter discovered extensive rot in the gun deck of *Louisiana* and after a survey pronounced her unfit for the naval service. Fortunately, she remained in commission long enough to take part in the Battle of New Orleans.[28] Patterson informed Jones of *Louisiana*'s condition and urged him to authorize the building of galleys or barges. In June, disturbing news arrived from Pensacola: the British were sending arms to the Creek Indians and had landed men and supplies. He fully expected an attack on Mobile and an attempt on New Orleans during the winter.[29]

Patterson's expectations were only too accurate. In September, the British mounted an attack on the approaches to Mobile, but they were shocked at a severe repulse from Fort Bowyer that destroyed one British ship and damaged three others in the process.[30] General Jackson had requested the assistance of Patterson's naval force in defending Fort Bowyer, but Patterson had respectfully declined, pointing out that they would be of better service at New Orleans.[31] The navy had a more immediate use for its gunboats and the recently arrived 14-gun schooner *Carolina*. Secretary Jones had sent Master Commandant John D. Henley in this vessel to help Patterson suppress piracy on Lake Barataria.[32] Patterson's raid on Barataria came off successfully, but there was no time to waste in celebration (map 12.1).[33]

The Battle of Lake Borgne

By December 12 a large British expeditionary fleet had anchored east of New Orleans, near Cat Island in the Mississippi Sound. The fleet included Admiral Cochrane's flagship, HMS *Tonnant*, 74; HMS *Plantagenet*, 74; HMS *Royal Oak*, 74; HMS *Vengeur*, 74; HMS *Seahorse*, 28; HMS *Armide*, 38; HMS *Rota*, 28; HMS *Sophie*, 26; HM brig *Carnation*, 18; HMS *Aetna*, 10; HMS *Meteor*, 10; HMS *Herald*, 20; HM schooner *Pygmy*, 10; and many others serving as troop transports and escorts. The ships and transports drew too much water to advance within sixty miles of the city. The British would have to use oar-propelled barges to approach through shallow Lake Borgne. Patterson ordered Lieutenant Thomas ap Catesby Jones, commanding five gunboats and two tenders, *Alligator* and *Seahorse*, to keep watch on the enemy's movements and to defend Pass Christian, at the mouth of Lake Borgne. If threatened, Jones was to drop back on the strait known as Les Rigolets, adding his guns to those of Fort Petites Coquilles, which guarded the entrance to Lake Ponchartrain.

Jones had to improvise. Cochrane's plan of attack was to send ships' boats loaded with sailors and infantry across Lake Borgne and then through Bayou Bienvenue and Bayou Mazant, following the channels as far as possible. From there the troops would have to slog through the swamp to the firmer ground on the left bank of the Mississippi where the Villere plantation was located, six miles below New Orleans. This was to prove a time-consuming and difficult route. But first the British had to

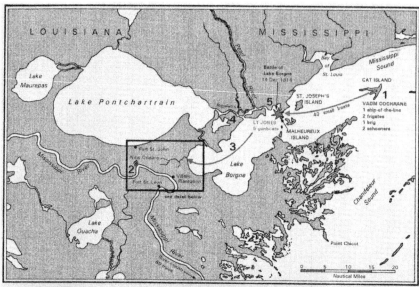

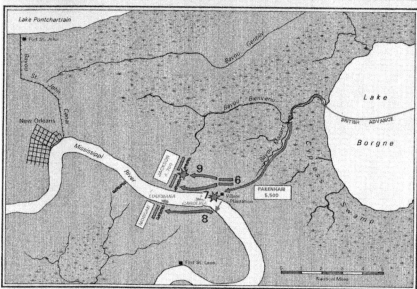

Map 12.1. Lake Borgne and Battle of New Orleans December–January, 1814–1815. Reprinted by permission from Craig. L. Symonds, *The Naval Institute Historical Atlas of the U.S. Navy*, Cartography by William J. Clipson, © 1995 (Annapolis, MD: Naval Institute Press).

contend with Jones's gunboats, which he had deployed across the approach to Lake Borgne. The battle was joined on December 14. Faced with little wind and an un-favorable tide, Jones aligned his boats as best he could for mutual defense, in a line abreast with antiboarding nettings drawn up by the rigging. Armed with long guns and carronades as well as cutlasses, pikes, and side arms, the Americans faced an attack of forty-five barges and some 1,200 enemy. In a two-hour battle, the British boats prevailed, but at a cost of 17 killed and 77 wounded. Jones, who had 182 men and 23 guns, suffered 6 killed and 35 wounded, himself included. While the British gained access to Lake Borgne, the sacrificial battle won valuable time for General Jackson and Commodore Patterson, allowing them to strengthen defenses and call for more reinforcements for New Orleans.[34]

Faced with a battle that could mean the loss of a major seaport and give the enemy access to the nation's central river system, Patterson then had to readjust his meager forces to meet the British on the Mississippi. Working closely with Jackson, Patterson prepared *Carolina* and *Louisiana* to harass the British forces that had invaded the Villere plantation. This field was a sodden piece of ground, subject to flooding, with no natural cover to use for protection from either the enemy or the weather. The British troops had to be delivered to that site by barges, which made dozens of round-trips by rowing to the fleet anchorage to pick up men and ordnance for the battlefield. The on-scene commander, British Major General John Keane, commandeered the Villere plantation house as his head-quarters and waited for reinforcements. Meanwhile, Jackson's troops, militia, volunteers, and slaves were put to work building defensive works along the Ro-driguez Canal, which ran perpendicular to the river from the cypress swamp, on Jackson's left flank.[35]

USS *Louisiana* and USS *Carolina* on the River

By December 23 some fifteen hundred British soldiers had arrived. Jackson de-cided to attack while the numbers were still in his favor. In the night action that followed, Jackson's troops attacked from the cypress swamp, on the British right, while Patterson's *Louisiana* and *Carolina* fired on the British lines at almost point-blank range from anchorages on the river. This was followed by Jackson's stealthy attack from the swamp, which was a fever-pitch melee for which the British were unprepared, yet they still put up a good fight.

Three thousand more British troops and their artillery arrived on Christmas Day, led by General Sir Edward Pakenham, who as senior officer had taken over command from Major General Keane. Two days later, the British guns were posi-tioned to destroy *Carolina*, which had constantly harassed the enemy encampment with grape and round shot. The British artillerymen dealt out hot shot, which had been heated in a field furnace. One of the rounds penetrated *Carolina's* hull and started an unquenchable fire that consumed and blew up the schooner, though not before most of the crew escaped with two of the ship's guns. *Louisiana's* crew pulled her upriver and out of harm's way.[36]

Patterson ordered two of *Carolina's* officers, Lieutenants Ortho Norris and Charles Crawley, and their gun crews to serve naval batteries in Jackson's line.[37] He sent Lieutenant Francis de Bellevue and his marines to man two gun batteries (totaling nine guns) on the right bank of the Mississippi, where lines had been built to prevent the British from outflanking Jackson's lines.[38] Pakenham's next move was a reconnaissance in force on December 28, when he marched his army to within a half mile of Jackson's line, but they were forced to turn back in the face of heavy and accurate fire from Jackson's artillery and *Louisiana's* guns. Concerned that *Louisiana* might suffer *Carolina's* fate, Patterson then hauled her out of range upriver and transferred some of her sailors and two 12-pounder guns from *Louisiana's* unengaged side to the batteries on the right bank, where they could enfilade the next British attack.[39] General John Morgan and his weakly armed Louisiana militia were posted, widely dispersed, just south of Patterson, protecting his right flank. Meanwhile, reinforcements had continued to strengthen Jackson, whose troops swelled to four thousand on the front line, with a thousand men held in reserve.

Battle at the Rodriguez Canal

The climax of the Battle of New Orleans took place on January 8, 1815. A British reinforcement of two thousand men arrived on January 6 under the command of General John Lambert, bringing the strength of available British troops to seventy-seven hundred. This determined the timing of Pakenham's main assault. In an effort to outflank Jackson's lines on the Rodriguez Canal, he ordered Colonel William Thornton to cross the Mississippi with six hundred men in flatboats to move up the right bank, attack Morgan's troops, and capture Patterson's guns. They nearly succeeded, but Thornton's timing was thrown off by the swift river currents, carrying them downstream and upsetting Pakenham's planned coordination. The impatient Pakenham refused to wait for Thornton and began his assault on Jackson's fortified line. This failed utterly, as his troops, falling under a rain of rifle and cannon fire, were unable to scale the mud-and-timber wall protecting the American troops and batteries.

Generals Pakenham and Gibbs were wounded fatally, and Keane severely, while their troops suffered hundreds killed and more than twelve hundred wounded. At about the same time, however, Thornton, on the right bank. was able to surprise Morgan's troops and overrun their position. Patterson's men, suddenly exposed, spiked their guns and retreated upriver. This enabled Thornton to capture the position, clear the guns, and threaten to rake Jackson's right flank. At that moment, General Lambert, who had been in charge of the troops held in reserve, assumed command in the midst of mass confusion and flight. He called Thornton back to support the main army in its distress. Patterson immediately recaptured his guns and harassed the British as they withdrew. In reporting to Secretary Jones, Patterson gave high praise to Henley, who, despite his wounds, had commanded a battery of two 24-pounders on the right bank.[40]

At the end of the battle there was neither a surrender nor a peace parley. Generals Jackson and Lambert exchanged notes and agreed to a day's truce. They arranged for care of the badly wounded British and agreed to provide an accounting of the missing, who presumably were prisoners of war. Then the two sides exchanged prisoners of war. It is likely that during all this time General Lambert was awaiting news from the naval flotilla that Admiral Cochrane had sent some days before to attack Fort St. Philip, at the Plaquemine Turn on the lower Mississippi. Five Royal Navy ships, brigs, and mortar vessels bombarded the well-prepared fort for nine days.[41] The fort's defenders gave back in equal measure and were well supported by boats from New Orleans bringing supplies, ammunition, and fuses for the fort's huge 13-inch mortar. Unable to pass or destroy the fort, the flotilla gave up and sailed downriver on January 18. On the same day, Lambert ordered his troops to begin a stealthy retreat to their boats. So passed the last opportunity for the British to gain a victory at New Orleans.

US Navy Contributions to the Battle of New Orleans

In conclusion, Lieutenant Jones's gallant stand with five gunboats against forty-five barges from the British fleet was a model of duty performed and bravery in a vital delaying action. In retrospect, this could have been just the beginning and not the end of the battle of Lake Borgne. Three times as many gunboats, augmented by barges such as those belatedly authorized by Secretary Jones, could have bedeviled and imperiled the British waterborne attack on the New Orleans bayous.[42] A stout blockship, strategically located, might have lured the British into a costly attack, diminishing their resources for an invasion. The rest of the navy's participation in the Battle of New Orleans was stirring.

The officers and men of *Carolina* and *Louisiana* performed essential and valuable services by harassing the British lines night and day with accurate cannon fire. Major Daniel Carmick's marine detachment joined vigorously in the battle, manning a battery on the right bank of the Mississippi. Carmick himself was severely wounded by a British rocket. Two officers from *Carolina* served batteries with their men on the right bank after the British destroyed their ship with red-hot shot.

The root of the navy's main problem at New Orleans lay in the weakened financial condition of the nation. The British commercial blockade had strangled the US income stream, and the antiwar New England states had refused financial assistance to the nation. Secretary of the Navy Jones, who had also been appointed secretary of the treasury, must have been overwhelmed by these burdens. While Jones may have had a blind spot where New Orleans was concerned, it is clear that Master Commandant Patterson and his officers and men played a vital supporting role in the victory at New Orleans with the resources they had on hand.[43] It is ironic that the one US naval station that was truly suited for a gunboat navy had only five at the time of its greatest need.

The Second Battle of Fort Bowyer, Alabama

General Andrew Jackson's victory at New Orleans on January 8, 1815, and the withdrawal of the British army by the end of January gave the British another opportunity to strike at Fort Bowyer. General Jackson was aware of this possibility. In fact, Admiral Cochrane had not given up hope of making another attack on New Orleans, this time by land. He attempted to persuade General Lambert, who was supportive but hesitant. To do this, they would have to capture Fort Bowyer and Mobile and then march from Mobile to Baton Rouge. From there they could stage an attack on New Orleans from the north. The question was whether their Native American allies would help. In the event, the British landed about 1,000 men on the sandy shores near Fort Bowyer, unopposed, moved in their heavy guns, positioned two bomb sloops, and demanded that the fort surrender.[44] Colonel William Lawrence, in charge of the fort, had only 375 men and lacked provisions and water. The US Navy was in no condition to offer support. Its gunboats had been captured, and there were no larger vessels at hand. Jackson had left Mobile and the fort with too few men. After a three-day siege, on February 11 Lawrence surrendered the fort. Before any further action could be taken, news of the ratification of the Treaty of Ghent arrived. Cochrane and Lambert withdrew their forces, but not before leaving guns and supplies for their Creek, Seminole, and black allies to protect the British-built fort at Prospect Bluff, near Apalachicola.[45] This marked the end of the British dream of seizing New Orleans and exerting control over the Mississippi River system to wrest concessions from the United States.

CHAPTER 13

Sailors' Life and Work

To understand the experience of men who sailed and fought at sea more than two hundred years ago is to be transported to a most unfamiliar environment. The difficulty of surviving in wooden ships where modern comforts were unknown was daunting. It was not uncommon for temperatures between a ship's decks to descend to freezing or below, or they could swelter in tropical heat to over 100 degrees without ventilation. Ships' decks could be leaky, with seawater surging about, soaking clothing and bedding on the decks below. Some of the daily tasks that sailors were ordered to perform, such as swabbing the decks, were harmful to their health.[1]

Men slept in canvas hammocks swung between bulkheads and deck-supporting stanchions, with perhaps only 10 inches of space between hammocks. Privacy was virtually unknown. Ships' pursers provided enlisted men not with uniforms but with "slops" made of woolen or cotton. Food after a few weeks at sea became nearly rotten and filled with vermin. Drinking water was often unclean and spoiled from being kept in aged wooden casks. Medical care and medicines were primitive and often inadequate; ships' sick bays lacked antiseptics and anesthetics. Patients were attended by navy doctors ranked as naval surgeons or surgeon's mates, some of whom were well educated, while others were uninformed about the real needs of the human body as we know them today. At shore stations such as New Orleans, St. Marys, or Charleston, where much of the sailors' work involved working through swampy areas in barges or schooners, the men were exposed to insect bites that spread malaria and skin diseases, to say nothing of snakes and alligators.

On large ships, crowded with several hundred young to middle-aged men living in the closest of quarters, taut discipline applied with an iron hand was essential. Failure to obey the orders of an officer or petty officer usually brought swift punishment. Brutal beatings applied with a cat-o'-nine-tails across a man's back could rip the skin off his bones and take months to heal. A sailor's life as it was then seems miserable to us dwellers of the modern age, yet many survived, though no doubt it was a "survival of the fittest." This was even more true for those sailors who were captured and held in British prisons and prison ships. Yet despite the hardships, there was something about life at sea that drew men to it, whether it was the beauty of the dark blue sea tossing whitecaps on a sunny day or the excitement of fighting the elements, the ship rising and plunging in a gale. Many seamen had a longing for adventure and the unknown that life on a farm or in a shoemaker's shop could not satisfy, and once such a person went to sea, he might make it a career or at least an occasional cruise of three to four months.

The decision to enlist in the navy might be taken lightly or only after failing at some other occupation. Normally, a potential recruit would go not to a naval recruiting office but to a ship's rendezvous, temporarily located at a waterfront pub. There the recruiting officer, accompanied by a fife and drum, tried to tempt the prospect with promises of steady pay, prize money, an enlistment bounty, and probably a drink to sign on for the next cruise. In a few cases, however, manipulation by a recruiting officer might work a hardship not only on the recruit but on his family.

The Families

A petition sent to Secretary of the Navy Hamilton by Jane Singer, a Philadelphia housewife, shows how such hardships could happen. She wrote to obtain the release of her husband, a baker, who, having become inebriated, was "incapable of knowing what he did" and the marine recruiting officer "took advantage of his intoxication when he persuaded him to enlist and . . . he had not recovered from effects of liquor when he took the oath before the magistrate." Mrs. Singer said she was left with two small children and no means of providing for their support or maintenance. She would willingly sacrifice some of her furniture to procure a substitute in place of her husband. She pleaded for the secretary of the navy to direct the commanding officer of the station to discharge her husband upon her providing a substitute. She provided the supporting signatures of three Philadelphia citizens to get the secretary's attention. One of them was Tench Coxe, a former assistant secretary of the treasury under Alexander Hamilton, in 1791, and later commissioner of revenue. It is not known how Mrs. Singer's case was resolved, but the circumstances are similar to those of other underhanded recruiting practices known in many countries over the years.[2]

In another case, the wife of a missing sailor obtained help from a friend, Henry Hedley, to write to Secretary Hamilton to ascertain the whereabouts of her husband, Patrick McDonnough or McDonald—she was unsure which it was. He had entered service on board one of Commodore Stephen Decatur's ships. Mrs. McDonnough said that her husband had written letters to her in the past but that she had not heard from him for more than nineteen months. A sailor who said he had known her husband told her that he had died on board USS *Constitution* and been buried in Washington on about April 23 of the previous year. Mrs. McDonnough was very distressed by this news and wanted to know the truth. She had written to the secretary of war but had not received an answer. Apparently, she had visited several navy ships in an effort to find her husband. She knew that he had spent three years as a marine and two as a seaman under Decatur. She had even placed ads in newspapers and visited the New York navy agent's office to seek word of him. Research established that the story was authentic—a seaman named Patrick McDonough had died on May 11, 1812, when his ship was in Washington to have her hull cleaned.[3] In this sad case, the commanding officer may be faulted for failing to notify the seaman's wife of his death, which he no doubt would have done if her husband had been an officer, but a sailor's status was such that what would be a normal courtesy in a later period was, regrettably, often left undone.

After Signing On

When the War of 1812 began, some ordinary seamen joined the navy because they were deprived of other seagoing employment. Merchants expected the British Royal Navy to soon send ships to blockade American seaports. Many shipowners decided not to risk their ships, so they paid off their crew and left them to shift for themselves. As described in James Fenimore Cooper's *Ned Myers*, the title character was but one sailor among many who found himself unemployed and had to decide what to do. In his as-told-to autobiography, 20-year-old Ned recalls that he and his shipmate Bill Swett were in New York without a ship. They visited Governors Island to meet a captain of the artillery, who gave them a letter of introduction to navy lieutenant Edward Trenchard at the New York (Brooklyn) Navy Yard, who duly swore them in and had them sign on to serve in the US Navy. In Ned's words, this is what happened next:

> Swett got a master's mate berth, and I was offered the same, but was too much afraid of myself to accept it. I entered the navy, then, for the first time as a common Jack. This was a very short time before the war was declared and a large flotilla of gunboats was getting ready for the New York Station. Bill was put on board of *No. 112* and I was ordered to *No. 107*, Sailing Master Costigan. Soon after, we were all employed in getting the [US frigate] *Essex* ready for sea, and while thus occupied the Declaration of War actually arrived. On this occasion, I got drunk for the second time in my life. A quart of whiskey was started into a tub, and all hands drank to the success of the Conflict.[4]

Officers often shared the discomforts of the enlisted men. Captain John Cassin had been appointed commander of the Norfolk Shipyard after working for some years for Commodore Tingey at the Washington Navy Yard. Born in 1760, Cassin belonged to the older generation of officers. In August 1812, he wrote the following letter describing his arrival at his post in Norfolk:

> I have the honor to inform you of my arrival at this place on Sunday last after a very disagreeable passage of ten days, heavy gales and rainy weather and I am very unwell, but by the assistance of Dr. Schoolfield, I am much better. I caught a violent cold in the river followed up by going into the house which is too small entirely for my family and on the first night we had 18 inches of water in the cellar when I was compel'd to call all hands to pump or bail the ship out. I shall be compel'd to partake of your liberal instructions as it respects my quarters by making two small wings & kitchen to the house, my office is too small and under the hospital; whenever they wash it the water runs all over me, books, and everything. I find we are in want of everything to make it like a Navy Yard.[5]

Conditions for sailors stationed on the Great Lakes during the winter could be discouraging. They were very isolated from civilization, at the edge of an enormous lake in the midst of a wilderness of deep forests and rough roads, far from friends and relatives. The following letter from an anonymous midshipman, probably in his early to mid-teens, illustrates the effects of service on Lake Ontario:

> Most Esteemed Uncle, I wrote you on the 10th Ultimo and also on the first Instant, informing you of my have [*sic*] been attacked with the fever . . . operations of an offensive nature are suspended here for the season. 'Tis exceedingly cold and every article we have to pay the most extravagant prices for 'tis reported we are going to build two ships and a brig. I hope it may be true, for if I am allowed an opinion, I conceive it to be of more importance that our forces on the lakes should be strengthened than on the Ocean. 'Tis also reported that our prize agent J. N. Heard is coming on to pay us our prize money. I know not whether 'tis correct, would to God it may be so. You may judge how much we have the need. The Como. has given the men one dollar apiece to celebrate Christmas and there are not five Officers who have money sufficient to take their letters from the post office.[6]

There was indeed a shortage of funds leading to slow payment of salaries; in fact, it was felt by more senior officers as well. Army personnel were better paid and had enlistment bonuses until the secretary of the navy realized why his commanders were having trouble finding recruits. A group of officers in Commodore Chauncey's command petitioned Congress, and an increase in pay was passed by an act of Congress in April 1814, as mentioned in an earlier chapter.

The Great Guns

The guns of a heavy frigate ranged from 9-pounder long guns to 42-pounder carronades. The weight of the shot determined the size of the gun, as round shot was of different diameters and required different amounts of gunpowder, depending on the desired range of the weapon. For example, a 24-pounder long gun weighed 5,824 pounds, almost 2.5 tons, and could fire a round shot 1,200 yards. The heaviest battery carried in the ship was thirty 24-pounders on the gun deck, though sometimes a captain would substitute some shorter and lighter 32-pounder carronades, which had more destructive power but a shorter range, about 500 yards. The lighter battery carried on the spar deck was made up of twenty 18-pounder long guns.

The heaviest battery was placed on the gun deck, and the lighter guns on the spar deck, to avoid shifting the ship's carefully calculated center of gravity in relation to the theoretical metacenter, which determined the ship's buoyancy. The higher the added weight, the less stable the ship was when the wind caused her to heel from one side to the other. This could cause a severe problems with steadying the ship and would throw off a gunner's aim. If a ship was top-heavy, as was the case with the first American 74s (*Washington*, *Independence*, and *Franklin*), she could heel so far over that her leeward gunports, if open, would flood with seawater, another dangerous situation.

These "great guns," as they were called, did not always fire round shot. To spread more damage to an enemy ship's crew, the gunner's mates would load cannister and grape shot of small diameter, which would spread its pellets like a shotgun. To damage enemy sails and cut rigging, they would load chain shot or double-headed shot. To cause more mayhem, a cannon could fire langrage, a random assortment of sharp-edged metal. To fire a large gun required a gun crew of about eight hands. The guns were mounted on a carriage or a slide equipped with ring bolts, blocks, and rope that ran through blocks bolted to each side of the gunport. The crew loaded the gun with powder, ball, and wad and rammed it all back in the gun barrel. Then they would haul the carriage into the gunport, and the gun captain would use a slow match to ignite powder in the primer, which in turn fired the charge in the gun. As the gun fired, it would recoil backwards, and then the crew would use a long-handled worm (a spiral twist of metal) to extract any burning matter and then use a sponge to swab the bore. The loading process would begin again. Gun crews would have to practice this exercise over and over until they could meet the captain's standard for rapid, accurate fire.

A standard measure of firing rate was three minutes from fire to fire; if it could be done in less time without a mistake, the captain would be pleased. But there could and would be mistakes. For example, on recoil the gun carriage might run over the foot of a crewman if he were in the way. Or if the gun barrel were not sufficiently cleared of burning material, the next round of powder might explode prematurely, causing a fire on the gun deck. Or if a gun's tube were used once too often, it might weaken and explode, wounding or killing many of the crew.

All in all, a naval engagement was a very bloody business, the object of which was to disable the enemy's ship by killing and wounding as many of its crew as possible and cutting its rig to bring down its masts, spars, and sails. Often, flying splinters would wound or kill members of the crew. Naval surgeons often found wounds from splinters especially difficult to heal because of infection. The following is an excerpt from the log of the frigate *Constitution* after the August 1812 battle with *Guerriere*, describing the damage to Old Ironsides and her crew:

> Our loss sustained during the action in Killed and Wounded 14. Seven of which were killed, among the latter William S. Bush, Senior Lieutenant of Marines, and among the latter Lieutenant Charles Morris dangerously, and Mr. Aylwin Sailing Master, slightly; one of the Seamen of the number Killed, Robert Brice lost his life through want of precaution in sponging his Gun, being blown from the Muzzle of the piece, our standing and running rigging much cut, and One Shot through the Fore Mast, one through the Main Mast, and one through the heel of the Fore Top Gallant Mast, and the Starboard Cross Jack yard arm cut away, as also the Spare Top Sail Yard in the Main chains, and the band for the slings of the Main Yard broken, our spanker Boom, and Gaff Broken by the Enemy, when foul of our Mizzen Rigging, at 11 AM the First Cutter returned with the Master finding it impracticable to get the Prize in tow, having been obligated by the drift of the Wreck to slip the Hawser, during the night keeping at a convenient distance from a different Tack to receive the prisoners, and knotting and splicing the Rigging and getting the Ship clear for action; our sails also being much cut through with the Enemies Shot.[7]

Keep in mind that *Constitution* won this battle, having a larger, heavier ship with 150 more men and a more powerful gun battery in terms of broadside throw weight (692 lb. vs. 581 lb.). It is perhaps not surprising that *Guerriere*'s losses were significantly higher, with twenty-three dead and seventy-six wounded. *Constitution*'s gunners dismasted *Guerriere* and fired thirty round shot into her hull, leaving her an unmanageable wreck.[8] *Constitution*'s commander, Captain Isaac Hull, removed Captain James Dacres and his crew, provided medical care to the wounded, and took them to Boston as prisoners of war.

Discipline and Punishment

Considering the dangerous, frightening work demanded in battle, success depended a great deal on how well a crew was led and disciplined. The largest American frigates, when fully manned, carried 450 men: 12 commissioned officers, 25 warrant officers, 36 petty officers, 320 seamen, and 57 marines. Over all these men stood the commanding officer, whose authority was unquestionable. When a ship of this size left port for a cruise of three months or more, a crew of this many men required careful oversight, frequent inspections, gunnery drills, and rigid discipline. It was a community of men of many different backgrounds, ages, and experiences living and working in close proximity. The captain was responsible for the safety of the ship and crew; the secretary of the navy charged him with carrying out the ship's mission. The officers reported to him, just as the lower-ranking warrant officers and petty officers reported to the senior officers. The senior lieutenant of the six who were carried in the ship's complement was the first lieutenant. He carried out the duties of the executive officer in today's navy. If the commanding officer died in battle or was too sick to command, the first lieutenant succeeded him, if only temporarily.

A properly disciplined crew reflected the captain's personality. Ideally, if he had earned the respect of the crew through his command presence, physical courage, quick reactions in moments of crisis, fairness in judgments, and moral courage, he could draw on that respect and his orders would be followed to the letter. Lesser commanders, owing to some failing or flaw, might not be so fortunate. Met with a failure to follow their orders, some commanding officers might use excessive punishments for trivial offenses, fail to follow through in seeing that duties were faithfully performed, or blame others for his own failures to act. The navy had a long list of punishments that commanders and other officers could use to enforce discipline.

In 1800, Congress passed An Act for the Better Government of the Navy of the United States. This act came to be known as the Articles of War, governing standards of conduct, identifying violations of naval law and corresponding punishments. The articles described the administrative duties of commanding officers, specified the rules for navy courts, and established a formula for distributing prize money. Captains of all vessels were required to read the articles to their assembled crews once a month.[9] Punishments were in order for the following offenses: drunkenness, swearing, theft, negligence, desertion, cowardice, disaffection, insubordination, and mutiny. If a person was guilty of one or more of these offenses, he could be fined, confined in irons, suspended from the service, or flogged. The captain could also use other traditional punishments, such as reduction in rank, stoppage of rations, and the wearing of a badge of disgrace. A principal, frequent punishment was flogging.

The Articles of War permitted up to a dozen lashes on sailors guilty of misdemeanors that did not require a court-martial. The lashing was done by with the knotted end of a "starter" of rope "well laid on" or the infamous cat-o'-nine-tails applied to a sailor's bare back by a boatswain or master-at-arms. This method of physical punishment lasted in the navy until 1850, when a reform-minded Congress abolished flogging. More severe punishments required the convening of a court-martial. Twelve of the most serious offenses, considered capital crimes, could receive a death penalty. These included disobeying a lawful order in time of battle, deserting or inducing others to desert, providing intelligence to an enemy, receiving information from an enemy and not informing one's superior officer, acting as a spy for the enemy, attempting or making mutiny, threatening or striking a superior officer, and committing murder in a public ship or vessel of the United States.[10]

Captain Thomas Truxtun, a veteran of the American Revolution and later commander of the frigate *Constellation*, was considered by many to have set a high standard of discipline in the early US Navy. Truxtun believed there were essentially three behavior groups in the navy: "The great majority of seamen who were well-disposed or at least neutral in behavior; a second group who were always willing to participate in misbehavior and minor anti-social acts, given the opportunity and malevolent leadership; and third, a small minority of trouble makers, ill-disposed persons who must constantly be controlled by fear to prevent them from infecting the whole ship's company if the reins of discipline are too relaxed."[11] Thus discipline flowed from examples set at the top. The character of the navy's most respected commanders—Commodores Truxtun, Edward Preble, John Rodgers, and Charles Stewart, for example—was what influenced this hierarchy and its leadership style. One of the critics of "Old Navy" discipline has pointed out that during this time one of the problem areas was among the junior officers, many of whom came from the more affluent families of the middle Atlantic states. Although well educated by tutors or private academies, they were unused to discipline, and some were prideful in the extreme. This led to quarrels and bad behavior. Their differences were occasionally settled by dueling, though this was frowned upon officially. It has been estimated that dueling caused the deaths of thirty-three naval officers between 1798 and 1843. And as James Valle wrote, "They [junior officers] could usually evade being punished for offenses that would send an [*sic*] enlisted men to the gratings [flogging]; but let them incur the wrath of a senior officer, and they might find themselves summarily dismissed from the service or living under a regimen of petty harassment designed to elicit a resignation."[12]

Blacks in the US Navy

Sailors of the early navy were of diverse ethnicity, racial origin, and nationality. American citizenship was not a requirement. The maritime world was a subculture all its own, partly owing to the harsh conditions of the work, the long voyages, the difficulty of communication, and an idiomatic seafaring vocabulary derived from centuries of tradition. This was the one vocation in which white, brown, and black worked together, because it was essential for the mission. In the merchant service in 1810, a survey of crew lists from Philadelphia, one of the busiest ports, showed that of 2,524 seamen, 378, or 15 percent, were of African American descent. By 1812 African Americans made up 17 percent, similar to their percentage in Baltimore.[13] At Providence, Rhode Island, the numbers of African American seamen was even higher, 20 percent, in a city where blacks were only 8 percent of the city's population. The situation was similar all along the coast. At the time, there was a demand for seaman and the supply was limited. On board ships racial distinction was less important than rank and social class. This is not to say that prejudice was absent. It was generally accepted that black seamen messed together, as did petty officers, warrant officers, and commissioned officers. But there were opportunities as well. White and black sailors did the same work and generally received the same pay, and promotions were possible.

In the US Navy, black sailors served on most ships during the frequent naval wars of the early nineteenth century despite the personal stricture of Secretary of the Navy Benjamin Stoddert against admitting "negroes and mulattoes" to the service. While Congress prohibited the enlistment of blacks as marines, there was no such law against enlisting them in the navy. The fact was that the navy had trouble recruiting seamen during the Quasi-War with France. Many of Stoddert's commanders had to delay sailing or to depart without having a full complement, in which case Stoddert expected them to sail with 10–15 percent less than the full complement.[14]

By the War of 1812, the demand for sailors was so high and the supply of experienced free black sailors so ample that naval commanders went ahead and enlisted them.[15] Some officers brought black slaves with them as servants and had them added to the ship's muster roll, expecting them to perform ship's work as well as to tend to their owner's needs. Black sailors' assignments aboard ship were not limited to stewards and cooks; rather, they filled the billets any ordinary or able seamen would fill, including as members of gun crews when at battle stations. The historian Christopher McKee estimated that blacks, both slave and free, constituted 15–20 percent of the navy's enlisted men and served in crews that were integrated and that approximately half of the enlisted were foreign nationals, of which three-quarters were British.[16] In a more recent work, McKee revised his estimates. He states that during the War of 1812 sailors of color—almost exclusively men of African or mixed-ethnicity descent—amounted to 9–10 percent of the navy's enlisted force and that the percentage may have been as high as 20 percent on the Great Lakes.[17] It is also notable that the navy did not differentiate in its record keeping between white and black sailors. This impartiality has made it difficult for historians to identify who were the black seamen on the navy's muster rolls, yet sufficient anecdotal evidence exists to tell us about how many there were and what they did.[18]

Cooper's *Ned Myers* provides an example of black sailors on board *Scourge*, one of the schooners in Commodore Chauncey's squadron. Ned was captain of a 6-pounder gun and makes mention that five of his gun crew were black sailors. They had named the gun Black Joke and referred to themselves as "Black Jokers." On a sultry night in early August 1813, the ships and the schooners of the squadron were under sail but becalmed. As Ned recalled, the captain had told them to sleep by their guns in case of an action that night with the nearby British squadron. While asleep they were struck by a sudden thunderstorm, and a blast of wind caught the schooner with her sheets cleated down. In an instant, Ned was up and called for the jib sheet to be loosened, but it was too late. The schooner was already on her beam ends and taking on water. As she went down, she took several crew with her, including the captain. Ned saved himself by jumping off the stern and found a boat floating astern. He climbed aboard and saved several shipmates, including the captain's steward, a mulatto from Martinique. He looked for his Black Jokers, but they had disappeared, all drowned, as was the schooner's powder boy, a black named Philips. Another he saved was a mulatto named Ebenezer Duffy, the cook. Ned and his shipmates were taken on board the schooner *Julia*, which had lived to sail and fight another day. Interestingly, he mentions seven men of color from one small schooner of the squadron. The crew numbered forty-five in all; the blacks on board made up about 15 percent, a percentage in line with recent estimates of the number of black sailors on Lakes Ontario and Erie.[19]

American Sailors as Prisoners of War

One of the risks all sailors took was possibly becoming prisoners of the enemy if their ship were captured. Depending on the location of the action, they could be sent to Melville Island prison in upper Halifax Bay if they were taken prisoner on the Great Lakes, or if taken on the Atlantic they could be sent to a prison or prison ship (hulk) in England. The most likely prison for American sailors, whether navy seamen or privateersmen in the War of 1812, was Dartmoor Prison in Devonshire, a remote, desolate, and unpopulated area of the West Country. This was probably not the worst place to end up. That would have been in a prison ship, where men were held in close confinement, poorly fed, if at all, and deprived of medical care. Malnutrition and disease were commonplace in such hulks, as was death at an early age.

One such prisoner was Ned Myers. *Julia*, the schooner that rescued Ned, was trapped along with the schooner *Growler* when they failed to respond to a signal from the commodore. After making a run through the British fleet in an effort to escape, Ned and his shipmates escaped injury but were captured. The British seamen boarded, made them prisoners, and took them on board *Royal George*. They sailed to York, where the prisoners were made to march under guard to the St. Lawrence River. There they were put into boats to pass over the rapids on the Long Sault. They ultimately arrived at Quebec, where the guards ordered them on board *Lord Cathcart*, a prison ship in Quebec harbor.

From there, Ned and his eight shipmates were sent to the frigate HMS *Surprise*, 32, for a voyage to Halifax. On arriving, the were placed in irons on board the transport *Regulus*, which then sailed to Bermuda. There they were taken on board *Asia*, 74, Admiral Warren's flagship, for investigation and then on board Captain Thomas Hardy's 74-gun *Ramillies* for more questioning from the captain himself. Ned recalled that he was nervous because he was worried that his Halifax family background would be discovered; it may have been, but nothing untoward happened. *Ramillies* escorted transports containing several hundred French prisoners back to Halifax. Ned and the other "lakesmen," as he called them, found themselves taken under guard and marched to the Melville Island prison, where they joined about twelve hundred other American prisoners.

Ned's life as a prisoner at Melville prison was not terribly harsh. It was not a very secure or well-guarded facility, though he spent much of his time plotting to escape and did so on two occasions, each time being recaptured. Since Ned knew the landscape around Halifax, he and his companions had an advantage other prisoners did not, so they were able to lead their pursuers on a merry chase. At one point, they formed a large conspiracy and attempted to dig their way out,, with the help of one John Crowninshield, a privateer officer from Massachusetts who had commanded the schooner *Diomede*. The prison guards discovered the plot before it could be executed. Several hundred prisoners, including Crowninshield, received extra punishment by way of transatlantic transportation to England's Dartmoor Prison, there to remain until beyond the war's end.

American Sailors at Dartmoor

During their long war with Napoleonic France, the British found they had no adequate prison facility to accommodate the thousands of French and other prisoners whom they captured. They decided to construct a prison complex at Princetown, on the desolate moors of Devon, called HM Prison Dartmoor. It was completed in 1809. After the War of 1812 began, they added American prisoners, both white and black, who were mostly privateersmen, navy seamen, and impressed American merchant seamen who refused to work on British warships once the war began. During this time, the Dartmoor Prison population rose to approximately 6,000. This reflects Britain's burden in terms of a nearly unsustainable prisoner-of-war population from captures after French naval and military defeats. By 1812, there were more than 52,000 French imprisoned in Britain, including 12,000 from French privateers. By 1814, some 14,500 Americans had joined the prison population, sent to Stapleton, near Bristol, as well as Dartmoor. By the end of the war, fully 100,000 prisoners of many nations inhabited land prisons, prison ships, depots, and camps in Scotland, Wales, and the West Country, as well as at Portsmouth. Overcrowding and poor living conditions resulted in prison riots, sometimes between French and American sailors, at other times between black and white American sailors. There was tension outside the prisons too, as civilians objected to scarce, expensive food being delivered to the hated prison facilities.[20]

HM Prison Dartmoor was (and is) a massive structure, built of granite with outer walls eighteen feet high containing three concentric walls and housing the prisoners in several different barracks-like structures, but without the cells one might expect. The British restricted all the Americans to berthing in prison unit 4. This put them living in as close proximity as they would have had in a typical 74-gun ship. Two Royal Navy officers, Captains Isaac Cotgrove and Thomas Shortland, were in charge of the prison. British militia troops were there to reinforce general discipline and to prevent escapes, but the prisoners were allowed to set up their own forms of governance and rules enforcement.[21]

As the historian Jeffrey Bolster has pointed out, there was a curious symbiotic relationship between the African American and white American sailors within the prison. Although they messed separately, they mingled in various ways, as they did on ships. Occupying the top or loft floor of prison block 4, the blacks staged their own entertainments—musical performances, plays, pugilistic dancing, wrestling, fencing, and boxing matches—in which some white sailors occasionally took part. Most fascinating to white sailors were the blacks' evangelical religious rites.

In many American cities and towns of any size, the free black population was accustomed to holding its own elections as an informal kind of community event. The black sailors at Dartmoor did the same. Usually the largest, strongest, most charismatic sailor became the acknowledged leader, or "king." The leading example was Richard Crafus of Boston. Commonly called "King Dick," at six feet three he towered over the typical sailor of his day. who was on average only five feet six. He was the acknowledged leader of the black sailors and intimidated the others. He had his supporters and enforcers and ruled over all in prison block 4, despite being the leader of an ethnic minority of the sailors. The arrival of black sailors at Dartmoor was gradual, beginning with 24 brought in along with 226 white sailors in April 1813. But by the end of the war in 1815, Dartmoor Prison contained 6,560 Americans, of whom 1,174 were African Americans. Lest this be considered all of the American prisoners of war held in British confinement, the current estimate is 20,000, with 8,000 confined at Melville Island and the rest in prisons and hulks in the British Isles.[22]

The Dartmoor Massacre, an event remembered by many naval veterans of the war and those familiar with the history of American maritime prisoners at Dartmoor, occurred in April 1815.[23] On February 17, the United States Senate ratified the Treaty of Ghent. As the news of peace arrived at the prison, the inmates grew impatient to be released, but it was weeks before the needed amount of shipping arrived. In addition, black prisoners made it known that they would not board ships headed for southern US ports. By April, impatience and restlessness had grown among the Americans, both white and black. On April 4, all it took to produce a riotous protest was the distribution of hard tack instead of soft bread. On April 6, as the men assembled in the prison yard, Captain Shortland, sensing that a plot to escape was in progress, sounded the alarm and called for the militia to stand ready with their muskets. The prisoners taunted the soldiers and threw stones. The soldiers, perhaps without orders, fired a volley and then continued firing at will as the prisoners tried to get out of the yard. The captain, a lieutenant, and the hospital surgeon got the soldiers to cease firing. Seven Americans were killed outright, and sixty were wounded, thirty seriously. Afterwards, a joint Anglo-American commission agreed that the captain had been justified in calling out the guard and for the initial shooting. The British government paid reparations to the families of the dead and pensions to those who were wounded. For Americans this final, tragic episode is a hateful memory that has haunted the histories of the war ever since.[24]

Sailors' Casualties and Mortality

In what may be considered Secretary William Jones's farewell letter, he wrote in dismay to President Madison in October 1814 stating that the US Navy had an aggregate force of slightly more than 12,000 officers and enlisted men. Of that total only 450 remained in service on the ocean, while 3,250 were in service on the northern lakes. Otherwise, he described 6,512 sailors as being on "harbor defense," meaning those in the five remaining frigates—*Congress* at Portsmouth, *Constitution* at Boston, *President* at New York, the newly constructed *Guerriere* at Philadelphia, and *Constellation* at Norfolk—and the sloop *Hornet* at New London. There were three vessels at sea, the sloops *Peacock* and *Wasp* and the brig *Siren*, whose crews amounted to 450. The captured crews of *Argus*, *Frolic*, and *Rattlesnake*, 405 sailors, languished in British prisons, and about 1,200 sailors were serving at southern naval stations from North Carolina to New Orleans.[25]

Seafaring during the War of 1812 was a dangerous profession. The risks to life and limb were many, even when not in combat. That being the case, it may be surprising that studies show that only a small proportion of the navy's seamen were killed in action or died from wounds, disease, drowning, or accidents on board ship. In comparison with the navy's approximately 10,600 on duty in 1814, an estimated 700 had died during 1812–14 from combat-related deaths, 300 from disease, and 100 from accidents of all sorts. Figures for the Marine Corps show that six officers and 335 marines died in the War of 1812. As a proportion of all those who served during the war, the loss of navy and Marine Corps personnel is close to 10 percent.

Although not part of the navy, privateers did much the same work in attacking and capturing British merchantmen and occasionally fighting Royal Navy vessels. Since privateering was a primarily a patriotic business, it was not under the control of a government naval establishment. There was no overall administration of the privateers' operations. Federal and state authorities required the issuance of the commission or letter of marque and required the owners to obtain a surety who was not one of the owners to post a five-thousand-dollar bond to assure a privateer commander's good behavior.

Courts of admiralty determined whether privateer captains had captured legitimate prizes, the evaluation and sale of the prizes, and the distribution of the proceeds. As in the navy, there was plenty of risk involved if they were overtaken by a British man of war or a British privateer, and it was always possible that a privateersman could end up in a British prison or prison ship. When a privateer captured a prize, it would have to take off its crew, replace them with a prize crew, and order them to sail to the nearest American port for adjudication. There was always a chance of the Royal Navy recapturing the prize before it reached the United States, in which case the prize crew would probably end up in Dartmoor.

More than 150 years ago, Lieutenant George F. Emmons, USN, compiled a list of War of 1812 privateers that has stood the test of time. He found 521 privateers and listed them alphabetically and by port of origin.[26] The numbers of men involved varied according to the size of the vessel and whether it was a true privateer or an armed letter-of-marque trading vessel that had a dual mission, to trade the goods it carried and to capture enemy merchantmen. Usually the letter-of-marque vessel carried fewer men in its crew; however, Lieutenant Emmons's list does not distinguish between privateers and letters of marque.

To estimate the number of men who sailed in privateers and letters of marque requires positing an average crew such ships might have carried. Taking Baltimore's privateering as an example, in only the first four months of the war the city produced forty-one privateers manned by 3,000 officers and seamen. The average crew size was 71 men per vessel, usually 300-ton schooners. Letter-of-marque traders rarely carried more than 40 men, whereas larger privateers often carried many more men so that they could provide prize crews. Thomas Boyle's privateer *Chasseur*, for example, carried 148 on his first cruise and 150 on the second. *Chasseur*, however, was one of the largest privateer schooners, at more than 320 tons and measuring more than 115 feet in length.[27] To estimate the number of men who shipped on all American privateers, if we conservatively estimate an average of 70 per vessel, we arrive at approximately 36,470. Of these, the British Admiralty records state that the Royal Navy captured 228 American privateers, carrying 906 guns and 8,974 seamen. If Dartmoor contained 6,000 American mariners, this means that 2,974 were held captive at Melville Island and elsewhere in the United Kingdom; almost all of those at Melville Island, except for the 405 US Navy sailors mentioned by Secretary William Jones, were privateersmen.[28] Aside from these conclusions, there is no very accurate way of commenting on the mortality and casualties suffered among those Americans who served on board privateers. Unfortunately, there was no centralized record keeping in existence for privateersmen during the years 1812–15.

As a matter of naval logistics, manpower was as essential to the United States as ships, sails, provisions, rigging, guns, and gunpowder. Experienced officers and seamen, especially able seamen, made the difference between success and failure of a ship's mission. The harsh conditions under which they lived and worked were the same regardless of nationality or ethnic origin. Reliable, patriotic sailors were in many respects responsible for the navy's successes and its survival against their British enemy, which had deeper resources from which to draw. Those who entered the navy had to accept risks to life and limb that could as well occur in a storm at sea, in a broadside-to-broadside engagement, or while imprisoned at Melville Island or at HM Prison Dartmoor. Despite its underfunded and small international standing, the nation's navy sustained American honor in a war of two and one-half years. This was achieved through the frigate victories of 1812, the Lake Erie success of 1813, holding the line on Lake Ontario, the victory on Lake Champlain in 1814, the navy's support of General Andrew Jackson's army at New Orleans, *Wasp*'s taking of *Frolic*, and *Hornet*'s captures of *Pelican* and *Penguin*.

And then there were the losses. On the Atlantic, *Chesapeake* and *President* were both captured. *Constellation* was blockaded at Norfolk throughout the war. *United States* and *Macedonian* were blockaded at New London for the last eighteen months of the war. *Essex* suffered defeat in the Pacific off Valparaiso, and *Congress* was blockaded at Portsmouth, New Hampshire. The Royal Navy defeated the smaller vessels *Nautilus*, *Viper*, *Vixen*, *Argus*, and *Siren*. Yet, it was never a question of an overall American victory, more a matter of survival against superior numbers and larger ships. With the benefit of good luck and fortunate timing, these several victories enabled US diplomats to achieve a status quo ante bellum position in negotiating the Treaty of Ghent in 1815.

By that time, few of the sixteen original War of 1812 ships, brigs, and schooners were left. The US Navy had started the war with a small professional cadre of officers and enlisted, trained through experience in the Quasi-War with France and the Barbary Wars. Yet, as a result of years of financial neglect the navy's shore establishment was sorely lacking in logistical preparations for a confrontation with Britain's Royal Navy. The navy's small size and its lack of 74-gun ships, together with the fact that it was led initially by Navy Secretary Paul Hamilton, a man lacking in maritime background and experience, meant that the US Navy commenced the war at a serious disadvantage. The explanation for this must be sought in the financial philosophy of the Democratic-Republican Party, which governed the United States during the twelve years that preceded the War of 1812. It is to that era we will turn, however briefly, before examining the cumulative effects of the British commercial and naval blockade and its role in the War of 1812.

CHAPTER 14

War Finance and the Blockade

The US economic system in 1812 in effect evolved from the Jeffersonian Democratic-Republican philosophy of a decentralized government with no direct taxation and was generally supportive of the wishes of the agrarian interests of the nation in the South and West, as opposed to the Federalists' centralized government, reflecting the interests of the large business-owning class that invested in industry, finance, and mercantile shipping communities of the major seaports in the middle Atlantic and northeastern states. After the formation of President George Washington's administration in 1791, these two groups gradually evolved into political parties aligned with their economic philosophies. That of the Federalist party dominated the decade under the administrations of President George Washington and the single-term administration of President John Adams. Under Washington, the financial concepts of Alexander Hamilton, secretary of the treasury, held sway. Hamilton established the nation's first national bank, assumed the states' debts, and established a system of credit favored by business leaders and industrialists, who were looked upon as the new republic's wealthy, urban-based elite.

Gallatin, No Friend of the Navy

Opposing Hamilton's views on finance, the Swiss-born Albert Gallatin was a foremost Republican voice in Congress, an indefatigable opponent of national debt whose voice during the next decade helped shape the nation's economy in a way that favored agrarian and mercantile interests but left the country ill-equipped to deal with a major war when it came. In foreign affairs, Federalists favored friendly relations with Great Britain and opposed postrevolutionary France, which since 1789 had drifted increasingly leftward in reaction to centuries of monarchical rule. The Jeffersonian Republicans, on the other hand, looked with sympathy on the French republicans in their struggle against the reactionary British Hanover dynasty and other royal families in Europe.

Finally, Federalists and Republicans differed significantly regarding the necessity of establishing permanent military and naval institutions. Republicans disavowed the need for a standing army and navy, believing that their mere existence would bring involvement in unnecessary wars, and at great expense. In military policy, the Federalists followed Washington's advice that "to be prepared for war is one of the most effectual ways of preserving peace."[1] Under Washington's administration, the peacetime army was expanded from fewer than 1,000 to more than 5,400 by 1801. After the American Revolution, the Confederation government disestablished the Continental Navy and had sold its warships by 1785. Nearly ten years later, however, in response to the dangers posed to American merchantmen by the Barbary States, President Washington proposed the building of six frigates. All six were completed by 1800, and several saw action during the Quasi-War with France. Benjamin Stoddert, the first secretary of the navy, commissioned other warships as well, and by the time President Thomas Jefferson assumed office in 1801, the navy had grown to thirteen frigates, with six 74-gun ships of the line planned for construction.[2]

With the Republicans ascendant in Congress and the presidency, changes in national policy were on the horizon. As secretary of the treasury, fiscal hawk Albert Gallatin replaced Alexander Hamilton, whom he had opposed for years in Congress. As Henry Adams wrote, "What Hamilton was to Washington, Gallatin was to Jefferson, with only such difference as circumstances required . . . the government was, in fact, a triumvirate almost as clearly defined as any triumvirate of Rome. During eight years this country was governed by these three men, Jefferson, Madison, and Gallatin, among whom Gallatin represented the whole political influence of the great Middle States, not only held and effectively wielded the power of the purse, but also was avowedly charged with the task of carrying into effect the main principles on which the party had sought and gained power."[3]

Gallatin tried to carry out his version of Jefferson's philosophy—that America could stand aside from events in Europe, follow its own political development, and reduce armaments to nothing more than was needed to enforce domestic peace. Further, he believed that capital was best left in the hands of its citizens, government could be one of plain common sense, and natural self-interest should be the rule in foreign commerce. With particular reference to the reestablishment of the navy in 1798, it can at least be said that although Gallatin opposed its rebirth, he did not advocate its abolition once it was created, though he did his best to make sure it operated with a minimum of expense during his terms as secretary of the treasury. Therein lies the crux of the problem, for despite the potential for war between the United States and Great Britain after the *Chesapeake–Leopard* affair of 1807, the majority of congressional Republicans failed to respond in a timely manner to the navy's prewar needs.[4]

In 1801, Gallatin's driving intent was to pay off the principal and interest on the national debt as quickly as possible. He then estimated the national debt at

$38 million, with an annual balanced budget of $9.8 million. He calculated that if he held expenditures for civilian, military, and naval needs at $2.6 million per year, he could provide $7.2 million for payment of principal and interest. The army would have to get along with $930,000, and the navy with $670,000, per year. He estimated that at that rate the nation would be able to eliminate the national debt in eight years. That was, of course, assuming that no extraordinary events or needs would develop to throw off his optimistic projections. Only a month later he had to revise his figures upward, but he was still able to balance the budget at $10.6 million (see table 14.1).

The financial highwater mark for Jefferson's administration was 1805–7. Gallatin's experiment to eliminate the national debt by then had come within eight years of reaching its goal. By keeping expenditures low while enjoying increasing income from customs duties, ship registrations, and export licenses, the Treasury was reaping annual surpluses that Gallatin applied to eliminating deficits and reducing the national debt. In fact, he even suggested that the US revenue was doing so well that the federal government might begin increasing the navy, a thought that would have been anathema to him ten years earlier.[5]

The turning point occurred in June 1807 with the shocking aftereffects of the *Chesapeake–Leopard* affair, which was perceived as a stain on national honor. Commodore Barron's inability to respond to the threats of HMS *Leopard* and his bending to the will of the British commander, allowing him to muster USS *Chesapeake*'s crew and to remove four seamen, claiming they were British deserters, brought on an international incident. Had Jefferson wished it, a war with Great Britain might have been the result that very year. The president instead decided to experiment with economic sanctions in his attempt to persuade the Crown to

TABLE 14.1
US governmental expenses, 1802–1811 (US dollars)

Year	Civil	Military	Naval	Total
		Expense		
1802	1,462,928	358,988	915,561	3,737,477
1803	1,841,634	944,957	1,215,230	4,001,821
1804	2,191,008	1,072,015	1,189,832	4,452,855
1805	3,768,597	991,135	1,597,500	6,357,282
1806	2,890,136	1,540,420	1,649,641	6,080,197
1807	1,697,896	1,564,610	1,722,064	4,984,570
1808	1,423,283	3,196,985	1,884,067	6,504,335
1809	1,195,803	3,761,108	2,427,758	7,384,669
1810	1,101,144	2,555,692	1,654,244	5,311,080
1811	1,367,290	2,259,746	1,965,566	5,592,602
Total	18,939,719	19,245,656	16,221,463	54,406,838

Source: Henry Adams, *The Life of Albert Gallatin* (Philadelphia: J. B. Lippincott, 1880), 293.

withdraw its hurtful legislation on neutral shipping and cease its impressment of seamen from American ships.[6] He had already set a precedent by requesting the passage in April 1806 of the Non-Importation Act, forbidding importation of certain popular items, in response to the British judicial decision forbidding trade with ships that had "broken voyages." This referred to American ships that had indulged in illegal trade with the British and French West Indies and then disguised the fact by putting into an American port and obtaining a clean bill of lading before sailing to England.[7]

Britain's response to Napoleon's promulgation of the Continental System in the Berlin Decree of 1806 was the Crown's order in council of November 1807, aimed at preventing neutral ships from trading with any ports under French control. The United States was neutral regarding the warring powers of Europe and was trading with both Britain and France. These new regulations placed the United States in a vice, as it were, between the two largest naval powers in Europe. American merchant ships were under the threat of being captured and treated as prizes by both France and Britain. This provided the context for President Jefferson's decision to declare an embargo, withdrawing American trade from Europe altogether.

Jefferson's Embargo, or "The O Grab Me Act"

Jefferson's embargo, signed on December 22, 1807, was based on his parochial view that by prohibiting American merchants from trading with Britain and her colonies, the United States could slow British imports and exports to the point that the Crown would have to yield to American pressure on the issues in question. He did not take into sufficient consideration that Great Britain had other sources of raw materials and other markets into which it could sell. Furthermore, the Royal Navy's shortage of seamen during the long war with imperial France would not permit its yielding on impressment of seamen. This was not a negotiable issue. The paradox was that American consumers, producers, and merchants were hit doubly hard because the order in council also aimed to cut off American trade, except with Britain. The same was true of Napoleon's Milan Decree, except that neutral ships could trade with France only. The embargo also pinched off the flow of America's customs receipts, the main source of government revenue. Concurrent with this was the inflation of American prices owing to shortages of imported manufactures of all types.

There was irony in Gallatin facing Jefferson's adamant position on the embargo. For most of his career as a legislator and public servant he had, as a good

Republican, opposed the government's intervention into the lives and business of its citizens. As Gallatin wrote to Jefferson on December 18, 1807, "In every point of view, privations, sufferings, revenue, effect on the enemy politics at home &c., I prefer war to permanent embargo."[8] He now found himself having to carry out the terms of a blatant exercise of executive power, preventing ships from sailing, sending foreign ships away in ballast rather than carrying cargoes, depriving men of their incomes, all in the interest of President Jefferson's experiment, which he had opposed. There was considerable resistance to and evasion of the new law; to oppose this, federal officers had to use force and confiscation, give orders to the Revenue Marine, and even request the help of the navy's gunboats and other small vessels. In Gallatin's mind, going to war was a better alternative, but as secretary of the treasury his job was to enforce the embargo or resign, something he was not then prepared to do.

During the years 1801 to 1811 the US Treasury had some good years, such as 1805, when customs receipts reached $12 million, with a surplus of $4 million. Generally, though, naval and military expenditures increased, not only because of the ongoing costs of the navy's war with Tripoli but also because of the war scare produced by the *Chesapeake–Leopard* affair. In attempts to reduce these costs, Gallatin continually urged Secretary of the Navy Robert Smith to reduce his budget. To some degree this had been accomplished by decommissioning ships and discharging seamen on their return from the Mediterranean. The frigates *Boston, Chesapeake, Congress, Constellation, New York, President*, and *United States* were laid up in ordinary at the Washington Navy Yard as they returned from their Mediterranean service. Of these, *Chesapeake, Congress, Constellation, President*, and *United States* were recommissioned and repaired in 1811–12. *Constellation* was extensively rebuilt in 1812. The others were considered too rotten and worn out to be recommissioned.[9]

Before James Madison's assumption of office, several changes took place. First, Congress repealed the embargo, and second, it replaced the embargo with a revival of the Non-Importation Act, with the proviso that the president could proclaim resumption of trade with either France or Britain if one or the other ceased violating the rights of neutrals. Third, a coalition of Republicans and Federalists in Congress managed passage of an act to repair and refit those naval ships judged worthy of service. There was an awareness that war with either Britain or France was a distinct possibility, yet Congress could still not bring itself to add new warships to the navy despite the need. When at last President Madison realized that neither Britain nor France would yield on the question of neutral rights, despite some hopeful moments that Britain might revoke its orders in council, he delivered a message to Congress on June 1, 1812, asking for a decision on whether and against whom war should be declared. The congressional declaration of war against Great Britain came on June 18.

Probably the last thing Gallatin wanted was to preside over the Treasury Department during a war that would destroy his earlier dreams of paying off the national debt and developing his adopted nation with the financial resources he had so carefully husbanded. Yet he continued to do his duty. When he submitted his budget for 1813, six months after the declaration of war, revenues were about the same, at $12 million, but the combined military ($13 million) and naval expenses ($8 million) had increased to $21 million—from $2,588,635 in 1805. The difference would have to be made up from loans from affluent, patriotic individuals and internal taxes from everyone else. As the war proceeded into 1813 and 1814, the nation's deficits and debt increased significantly as the naval and commercial blockade's interdiction of trade began and the regulations of the Non-Importation Act continued to exact a toll.[10]

The Bank of the United States—Failure to Recharter

One of the most valuable institutions established during the Washington administration was the Bank of the United States. According to Alexander Hamilton's bill to charter such a bank, the bank would collect taxes and regulate trade. Although creation of a bank of the United States was not specifically included among the Constitution's powers delegated to Congress, neither was it forbidden. Hamilton contended that it was one of the implied powers related to those delegated to Congress regarding the powers to tax and regulate trade. The bank's charter provided that it would expire in twenty years and its duration could be extended at that time. The due date for extension fell on March 4, 1811.

According to Gallatin, the bank had performed well, providing surplus funds for the Treasury as well as interest for its stockholders. During earlier debates in Congress in 1808 and 1810, when extension was considered, there had been little opposition to its passage, but this was postponed. Yet, in early 1811 a chorus of complaints arose from the advocates of state banks. The delay in reconsidering the bank's extension had provided an opportunity for its enemies to organize. The state banks, especially those in Massachusetts, Pennsylvania, Maryland, Virginia, and Kentucky, represented local interests longing for extensions of credit and the availability of specie. One of the bank's vulnerabilities was that a majority of the its stockholders were British, especially Baring Brothers & Company; another was that the bank's origin was Federalist, as were many of the bank's American participants. This aroused the opposition of Republican ideologues, who objected to the British as profiteers and viewed the bank's existence as a corruption of the Constitution. Finally, there were those in Congress who disliked Gallatin's lingering influence as a foreigner holding high office in the US government. Defeating the bank was their way of striking at him. Apparently, what few of these opponents considered was the potential utility to the United States of the bank's resources if war were to break out. In mid-February 1811, the bank's friends were unsuccessful in both the House and the Senate, where Madison's vice President, George Clinton, an anti-Madisonian Republican, cast the tie-breaking vote. In the years to come, several of the bank's former enemies would regret their votes.

The Nation and the Navy in a Pinch

During the first six or seven months of the war, the Royal Navy blockade of French ports on the Atlantic and the Mediterranean prevented the Admiralty from imposing a strict naval and commercial blockade on the American coast. Admiral Sir John B. Warren's available ships were mostly based at Halifax and barely outnumbered the ships and other vessels of the US Navy. Many American commercial vessels were able to sail back to their home ports before the full force of the war could be felt in American markets and government coffers. From 1808 to 1811 the Jeffersonian embargo restrictions had reduced income from trade, much of which was with England. For example, the value of imports fell by 60 percent in only one year, 1807–8, and exports fell by 80 percent during the same period. After 1809, when Madison's Non-Importation Act and Macon's Bill No. 2 went into effect, American felt the pain of further reductions. Net customs revenue fell from more than $12 million to about $8.9 million in 1811. This last figure was 90 percent of all the government's income for 1812. There was also, without doubt, a loss of income because of smuggling at sea and at border crossings from the northeastern states into Canada.[11]

Financial Impact of the Blockade

As a result of the increasing effectiveness of the blockade, customs receipts plummeted to $6.8 million during 1813 and experienced a further decline to $4.7 million in 1814. At the same time, the US national debt had skyrocketed to $63.5 million by the end of 1814 and was estimated to be $119.7 million or higher in 1815.[12] Since Congress had refused Gallatin's request to extend the life of the Bank of the United States, his only recourse for funding the war would be solicitation of loans from wealthy individuals such as John Jacob Astor, Stephen Girard, and David Parish and the issuance of treasury notes at a discount. Congress, after a year and a half of war, finally found the courage to authorize a direct tax on land, a duty on imported salt, and excise taxes on stills, retailers, auction sales, sugar, carriages, bank notes, and other negotiable paper as the war extended into a third year.[13]

The navy's difficulties stemmed from parsimonious budgeting, a timid secretary of the navy, and congressional unwillingness to commit to war preparations on a broad front before 1811. In that year Gallatin estimated the navy's normal expenses at $1.9 million, with several ships in ordinary. In December 1811, Secretary Paul Hamilton responded to a question from the chairman of the Naval Committee of the House of Representatives as to how much it would cost to put the navy on a war footing. He reported that it would cost an additional $3 million to ready all the navy's vessels for active duty, manned and ready for sea, thus making the navy's projected annual expense about $5 million for 1812. After entering the war, Congress was more willing to grant increases, so Gallatin provided a considerable increase for the navy's 1813 budget. For its wartime expenses, he allowed the navy $4.9 million, to which he added $3 million to begin construction of four 74-gun ships and six frigates, as contained in a late request from Secretary Paul Hamilton before his departure from office.[14]

The prime beneficiary of this increase in the navy's budget was the new secretary of the navy, William Jones. He was a Revolutionary War veteran, a former congressman from Philadelphia, and a seagoing merchant who was thoroughly familiar with naval matters. It is curious that it was Jones who volunteered to succeed Albert Gallatin as acting secretary of the treasury only a few months later, loyally committing himself to holding two of the most difficult positions in Madison's cabinet simultaneously for the next nine months.

Peace Negotiations

In March 1813, the arrival of an offer from Tsar Alexander I of Russia to mediate an end to the Anglo-American War introduced a sea change in Madison's cabinet. The president did not hesitate to accept the offer but then had to decide whom to send as a commission to negotiate the terms of a peace agreement. John Quincy Adams, the American minister to Russia, would necessarily lead the delegation. Madison selected the Federalist senator James Bayard and then was faced with Albert Gallatin's request to be a third commissioner. This was a delicate moment, as Madison considered Gallatin the most valuable member of his cabinet and nearly indispensable as a shrewd adviser, not just on government finance but on political matters as well. Nonetheless, the cosmopolitan Gallatin would be equally valuable on the US negotiating team. He was also anxious to escape the toils of office and had formed a strong dislike of fellow cabinet member

Secretary of War John Armstrong. Madison, however, did not want to lose Gallatin and persuaded him that his departure from the cabinet would be only temporary. He would appoint an interim secretary of the treasury and asked Gallatin to return when the peace negotiations were at an end. Gallatin embarked for Russia in May after handing over his portfolio to William Jones.[15] The Senate, however, in an act of spite, rejected Gallatin's appointment as one of the peace commissioners, claiming that the two offices were incompatible.[16]

In late 1813, a ship arrived delivering a letter from the British minister of foreign affairs, Lord Castlereagh, offering Madison direct negotiations instead of a mediated peace. The president accepted the offer and finally named his peace commissioners. They included John Quincy Adams, James Bayard, Henry Clay, Jonathan Russell, and Albert Gallatin. Six months later, Treasury Secretary William Jones wrote to the president saying that he had expected Gallatin to return to the United States in November to reoccupy his office at the Treasury. As this had not happened, Jones's workload had become such that he was not even able to attend to the important business of his own department. Consequently, he requested that the president relieve him of the task of leading the Treasury Department for the sake of the administration and his own peace and reputation.[17] On February 8, 1814, Madison reappointed Gallatin as a member of the Peace Commission, and on the same day he named George W. Campbell, a senator from Tennessee, as acting secretary of the treasury. Campbell, after serving only six months at a most difficult time, resigned in October 1814, when he was succeeded by Alexander J. Dallas.

The severe budgetary pinch persuaded Secretary Jones that he would have to slow the construction progress of the 74-gun ships at Portsmouth, Boston, and Philadelphia. In April 1814 he wrote to Captain Isaac Hull,

> I have to request that you will postpone any further contracts or purchases on that account [*Washington*, 74] until further orders. It has become necessary to reduce the expenditure as much as possible in the eastern section of the union owing to the fiscal operations of the government in that quarter and to the artificial obstruction to the credit and circulation of the paper of the government as well as of the Banks of the Middle States. The inconveniences attending the transmission of specie from the latter to the former to meet the expenditures would not derive an equivalent advantage by the immediate preparation of all the equipment for the 74. A temporary suspension is deemed necessary until the current of exchange shall redeem its circulation.

He urged Hull in the meantime to proceed to finish the hull, masts, spars, gun carriages, water casks, and blocks. The launching took place on June 22, 1814, but the ship did not sail until after the end of the war.[18] Months later, after the battle of Bladensburg, the devastating raid on Washington, and the Battle of Baltimore, there was no change except for the worse. Jones was distraught about the financial situation of the Navy Department. As he wrote to the president, "I am destitute of Money in all quarters. Seamen remain unpaid and the recruiting service is at a Stand. I have none for the most urgent contingent cases. If the salvation of a city depended upon the prompt transportation of a body of our seamen, I have not a dollar. In some cases articles contracted for or purchased are withheld until funds appear to meet them. We are all apprised of the unpleasant cause, but it is our duty to make known to you the consequences."[19] However, the war continued, and the navy and other departments had to make do with what little funds could be found.

After the Fire

For Secretary Jones as well as many others living and working in Washington during the autumn of 1814, it must have been a dismal time. Everywhere were reminders of the August raid on the capital—the smell of charred timbers, the remains of the burned Capitol and the White House (no longer white), the destruction of the navy yard, and the businesses bankrupted that depended on employed government shipyard workers. Although the cleanup had begun, the rebuilding of government buildings and morale would take time. Congressmen finally returned to Washington from their recess to undertake a lengthy investigation into what had gone wrong. President James Madison arranged for Congress to meet at Blodgett's Hotel, at 7th and E Streets NW, until a newer temporary structure could be made available.

Among Secretary Jones's immediate concerns was the condition of the navy yard during the weeks after the fire. According to Commodore Tingey's report,

> The buildings destroyed by the fire from the frigate, etc., were the mast shed and timber shed, the joiners' and boat builders shops and mould loft; the medical store; the plumbers' and smiths' shops and block makers' shop; the saw mill and block mill, with their whole apparatus, tools and machinery; the building for the steam engine, and all the combustible parts of its machinery and materials; the rigging loft; the apartments of the master and boatswain of the yard, with all of their furniture; the gun carriages makers' and painter's shops with all the materials and tools therein at the time. . . . Also the hulls of the old frigates *Boston*, *New York*, and *General Greene* [sheer hulk].[20]

There was nothing of immediate practical use left except Commodore Tingey's official residence at the foot of 8th Street SE. Secretary Jones submitted a detailed report on the Navy Department's activities during the British raid to Congressman Richard M. Johnson (D-KY), chairman of the Select Committee to Inquire into the Causes of the British Attack on Washington and Alexandria.[21]

Secretary Jones had confidentially informed President Madison in April that his personal finances were in disarray because of the collapse of maritime trade—he had suffered the loss of a new ship—and he would have to resign his office by December 1.[22] In September, Jones wrote that "the circumstances which induced me to explain to you on 25th April last . . . having gathered irresistible strength by the lapse of time, I now respectfully tender my resignation of the office of the Secretary of the Navy, the acceptance of which is subject to your decision at any time between this and the first day of December next."[23]

Planning for the 1815 Campaign

As his term as secretary of the navy neared its end, Jones was reflective when he thought about the next season's naval campaign. Although it was common knowledge that peace talks were taking place at Ghent, Belgium, no one could know whether there would be peace, a truce, or continued war. The Royal Navy was already building the next generation of warships on Lake Ontario.[24] Their lead ship was HMS *St. Lawrence*, a first-rate ship of 102 guns whose force threatened to overthrow the balance of naval power on that lake. Another ship, temporarily referred to as "Frigate B," was scheduled to be assembled from prefabricated frames that had been shipped from England at great trouble and expense.

The increased activity at Kingston had triggered alarm in Commodore Chauncey. His immediate answer was to recommend building three 80-gun frigates that each would carry 94 guns and be manned by eight hundred seamen, if they could be found. For Jones the logistical challenges seemed overwhelming. He expected the British to build two frigates over the winter, and he told the president, "As the naval context on Lake Ontario has become a warfare of dockyards and arsenals it may be well to examine with candor the relative capacity, resources, and facilities of the combatants to attain their respective objects within the time limited." He continued to describe the advantages that had accrued to the British since the European war had diminished the need for so many Royal Navy ships in Continental waters. Jones expected that seamen and ships' stores would be sent to Canada in more than adequate numbers, and the enemy knew that US supplies of both were very limited, so all the British had to do was continue to build and outwait their naval opponents on the lakes. Jones figured that the naval service had at its disposal no more than twelve thousand seamen in aggregate, of which seven thousand would be required on the lakes. This calculation left only five thousand for duty on the Atlantic and to protect seaports, bays, sounds, and harbors stretching from Maine to Louisiana.[25]

After listing the problems he faced, Jones recommended that a better balance between fighting on the lakes and on the open sea be made possible by establishing a military choke point on the St. Lawrence where the river narrows at St. Regis, New York. He offered to move some of his larger guns from Sackets Harbor to St. Regis to command the river. This would prevent enemy supplies and men from reaching Kingston and points farther west. This proposal had been advocated before in the cabinet but had not been put into effect. If it worked, Jones argued, he could transfer many of his sailors to the Atlantic to complete the complements of ships capable of breaking the blockade. He also seemed ready to fall back on a fleet of twenty schooners that he proposed building, although this seems unrealistic given the financial condition of the navy. He admitted that these thoughts were only speculations brought on by the distress of the moment. Nonetheless, the plan to build these ships for Lake Ontario would continue if Chauncey thought he could do it, and Jones promised to hire both Henry Eckford and the Brown Brothers to do the work, combining the construction teams that had built the squadrons for Lakes Erie, Ontario, and Champlain in 1813 and 1814.

Commodore Chauncey's response to Jones seems fairly optimistic in terms of his ability to overcome the logistical difficulties involved in building the three ships Jones had in mind; however, Chauncey urged that it would be more feasible to build two first-class ships and one 44-gun frigate. Even so, the materials he needed would have to be shipped from New York to Albany before ice closed off the water route. This would make it possible to transport the heaviest timbers and ordnance overland from Albany to Sackets Harbor between December 15 and February 15, before the roads became choked with mud and impassible. He would require 600 ship carpenters, 60 joiners, 60 pairs of sawyers, 75 blacksmiths, and 25 block and pump makers, among other artisans, as well as a ropewalk with all its machinery so he could manufacture his own heavy 24-inch cables. Various other commodities would have to be manufactured at the seaports. He believed that if these needs could be fulfilled, he could have two of the ships ready by May 15. On the basis of reports from his intelligence agents, Chauncey predicted that the British would have their own problems in ship construction, since they lacked the necessary timber (especially oak), guns, stores, and artisans. He too endorsed the idea of an American army building a fortification on the St. Lawrence to interdict transport from Montreal to points west.[26] He did not consider the likely result of such an action: a British invasion of American soil at that point to remove this threatening blockage of their enemy's all-important link to the lakes and their seaports.

In Secretary Jones's last letter to Chauncey, he recommended that the commodore visit the navy agent John Bullus in New York to check on the progress of orders sent to strengthen the squadron at Sackets Harbor. He mentioned that a committee made up of Governor Tompkins, Captain Decatur, and Robert Fulton had consulted on the wisdom of building a variant of Fulton's steam frigate *Demologos* on Lake Ontario. Their unanimous opinion was that its design was not appropriate for the open waters of the lake. Fulton concurred, saying that further design changes would be necessary in that event. Jones asserted that it would be difficult to find enough seamen willing to sign up for the lakes ships and that privateers, with their available berths, would compete with the navy for sailors because of an unhealthy environment on the lakes, better pay on privateers as prize money, and easier discipline. In his farewell to Chauncey, Jones wrote, "I cannot suffer this occasion to pass without bearing testimony to the talents, energy, judgment, and patriotism which you have displayed during your arduous command and stating expressly my perfect conviction that it could not have been in better hands." This was high praise coming from Jones, who was not generous with compliments to his senior officers. This was especially so because Chauncey was one of the few naval officers who could have lost the war in a single day had he made a wrong decision with respect to the Lake Ontario squadron.[27]

The Legacy of William Jones

As secretary of the navy, William Jones made an indelible contribution to the US Navy during the War of 1812. He was a tireless, dedicated executive who came to the job with nearly perfect credentials. Secretary Jones's legacy can be seen in the efficient and detailed way he handled the commanding officers under his control. He expected them to use their ships as commerce raiders and not to seek combat with enemy warships unless it was unavoidable. The death of Captain James Lawrence and the loss of *Chesapeake* in the action with *Shannon* only reinforced this mandate. Commanders were to prepare their ships to stay at sea as long as possible, given the threat of meeting Royal Navy blockaders in the areas near the coast. His ship commanders generally did not like him as well as they had former secretaries Robert Smith and Paul Hamilton, who treated their commanders in a more accessible and respectful way. Jones gave Captain Charles Stewart a sharp rebuke when he believed that Stewart had returned too early (after 90 days at sea) from a cruise in 1814. Stewart had left Boston on December 31, 1813, and returned on April 3, 1814, with a sprung lower mainmast and a crew sickened by typhus and scurvy, hoping for a quick repair and departure. Commodore Bainbridge, not a good friend of Stewart's, reported the unexpected arrival to Secretary

Jones and recommended a court of inquiry, to which Jones agreed.[28] Although the Bainbridge court returned a mild opinion of "mistaken judgment" on Stewart's part, the entire episode poisoned Stewart's relationship with Bainbridge and Jones.[29] The secretary, according to Christopher McKee, was apt to be haughty, reserved, and abrasive with his naval subordinates.[30] Though Jones was very knowledgeable about seafaring in general, he also pretended to know more about naval architecture than he actually did. The result in some cases became an embarrassment to the navy, as in Jones's insistence on reshaping the sheer plan of the 74s over the protests of Captain Isaac Hull. As a result, those ships' lower gunports shipped water and would have been useless in a stormy-seas engagement. Among Jones's favorites were Captains William Bainbridge, whom he had known in prewar years in the merchant service, and Isaac Chauncey, whose administrative and organizational skills he admired. His one flash of anger toward Chauncey occurred during July 1814, when the commodore failed to inform Jones and his army counterparts of how sick he was and could have ordered his second-in-command, Captain Jacob Jones, to take charge of the squadron. As a result, the squadron was unable to support the army's battles on the Niagara Peninsula at a crucial time.

In addition to steering the navy through its challenging operations during the War of 1812, William Jones's other major contribution was his suggestions for reforming the navy. He had a keen understanding of logistics, and what he had seen in his two years as secretary had convinced him that the navy's entire administrative system needed an overhaul. Over the fifteen years since its founding in 1798, the navy's traditionally loose structure had allowed corrupt practices to creep into the administration, such as sweetheart contracts, nepotism, navy agents' paying too much for goods, lack of inspections to ensure compliance with regulations, pursers' exploitation of sailors, promotion of officers by seniority instead of by merit, and commanders' rearranging the rigging of their ships without approval. His suggested reforms may well have been inspired by Captain Charles Morris's report to the House Naval Committee in January 1813.[31] Jones's actions are contained in his November 15, 1814, call for the establishment of a board of inspectors made up of three senior offers and two civilians well versed in naval affairs to assist the future secretaries in the handling of their exceedingly complex duties.[32]

The Board of Inspectors

The responsibilities of the board of inspectors covered nearly the whole gamut of naval organization and administration. In a lengthy report to the Senate of November 15, 1814, Jones noted that while the British system of civil regulation of the Royal Navy has its faults, "its regulations and instructions for service at sea . . . are excellent and afford much matter worthy of incorporation into our system, with such modification as the peculiar circumstances of the service may require." In regard to the ships of the American navy, he stated that "the character of the navy of any nation will be determined by its commercial and navigating enter-prise." He praised the classes of its ships, saying that "their form, construction, armament, and equipment have been tested by experience. Their classes, being few, and so uniform that without inconvenience, the masts, spars, and equipment of any one of a class, will serve indifferently for any other of the same class." As for the seamen, he recommended that some form of registration of all the seamen in the United States be created and kept in the several districts. Since sailors were by nature itinerant, it would be convenient for the Navy Department to be able to locate and call on these experienced individuals for service for a reasonable pe-riod should the need arise. The navy had no equivalent of the army's militia system, whereby men could be called upon for service in local areas. Jones in ef-fect suggested that the navy needed a kind of draft registration system to assure a supply of veteran seamen in a crisis. Finally, Jones urged the establishment of a naval academy with suitable professors to instruct naval officers in mathematics, experimental philosophy, the science and practice of gunnery, the theory of na-val architecture, and the art of mechanical drawing.[33]

For the convenience of Congress, Jones offered a draft bill that encapsulated his ideas for a reform of naval administration. To begin with, he stated that the office, duties, and powers of the secretary of the navy remained as established by law, except as noted in the act. The board of inspectors, three naval officers and two other judicious persons, would be appointed by the president of the United States. This board would have the power to establish the rules and regulations for its own proceedings, to employ such clerks and assistants as might be required, and to purchase books, maps, charts, plans, drawings, models, and stationery as the public interest required, with the president's approval. Other sections of the bill provided for the president to appoint a person skilled in the science and prac-tice of naval architecture to serve as the naval constructor and two assistant constructors. The constructor would be allowed one clerk to assist in the duties of his office. In addition, the president was authorized, with the advice and con-sent of the Senate, to appoint a paymaster of the navy, who would be required to provide bond with sureties for such sum as the president would direct. The board's inspectors would receive the pay and rations of a naval captain commanding a squadron on separate service plus $1,200 per year in lieu of house rent, fuel, and forage. The naval constructor would receive $3,000 per year; the assistant con-structors, $1,500; and the paymaster, $2,000.

The board's inspectors would have the general superintendence of the affairs of the navy, as delegated by the president of the United States, and would report to the secretary of the navy. They would have authority over all officers, agents, and personnel of the Navy Department and would furnish to the secretary all estimates of expenditure required by the various branches of the service. They would have the power to contract and purchase either directly or through navy agents. The naval stations of the United States were to be given specific boundaries or districts, commanded by a naval officers of rank, trust, and confidence. All requisitions made upon the agents had to be checked by the board or by an officer designated by the board before they were made effective. Payments and advances were to be made through the navy agents with the sanction of the secretary of the navy, the board, or a resident officer authorized by the board. The following general regulations were proposed:

The Board should establish general regulations for the conduct of its members in the discharge of the special and important trusts severally assigned to them by the secretary of the navy; and should digest and report to the department distinct regulations for the following objects:

1ˢᵗ Uniform regulations, establishing several classes of ships and vessels of the navy with tables of dimensions, proportions, number, quantity, quality, nature, and description of masts, spars, rigging, anchors, cables, armament, and equipment of all kinds, likewise for provisions and stores of every species for each class.

2ⁿᵈ Regulations for receiving, preserving, issuing, and strictly accounting for the expenditure of materials and stores of all kinds and in every department of the service, within the United States.

3ʳᵈ Regulations for surveying and authenticating the actual state and condition of all the ships and vessels of the navy, and of all materials and stores every species, reported to be decayed, damaged, or defective and for directing the repair, conversion, sale, or other disposition of the same, as the nature of the case may require.

4ᵗʰ A more perfect system of general regulations, for the naval service at sea and on the lakes.

5ᵗʰ General regulations for the flotilla, or force employed in harbor defense adapted to the peculiar nature of that service.

6ᵗʰ Uniform regulations for the navy yards, arsenals, and depots of stores and materials.

7ᵗʰ Regulations for the cruising ships of the navy, while in port; for the recruiting service, at sea and for officers of the navy while on shore, on duty, or on furlough in order to ascertain the actual state and local situation of all the officers.

8th A system of detailed regulations for the naval hospitals and the medical department of the navy, within the United States.

9th An entire and new system of regulations for the conduct of pursers in the navy, accurately defining their duties, securing a more strict accountability, limiting their emoluments by a fixed and reasonable standard, and protecting the seamen of the navy from undue advantages which may be practiced, with impunity, under the present system.

10th Regulations for ascertaining by examination the moral character and professional qualifications of all the officers of the navy below the rank of master commandant, classing them in the scale of their several merits and the pretensions of those who may be selected for promotion, as well as the candidates for warrant appointments in the navy.

All which regulations when approved by the president of the United States should be established and obeyed, until revoked by the same authority. The duties and details of the service proposed to be assigned to the several inspectors of the Board may be classed as follows:

1st class: the general correspondence of the Board and the preparation of all reports, estimates, and statements, required by the Department; and the communication of such propositions and information to the secretary of the navy, as the board may deem interesting; and also the general charge and direction of the flotilla service on the New Orleans station.

2nd class: Comprehending the general military correspondence of the Board with all the officers of the navy; the roll of all officers of the navy and records of their services, merits, and qualifications, to be kept on the files of the Board; and orders for courts of inquiry and courts martial, and the preparations of all the documents and statements connected with these objects. Also, the general charge and direction of the flotilla service on the Southern Station, viz: Georgia, South Carolina, North Carolina, and Norfolk.

3rd class: Comprehending the direction of ordnance and transportation; the general superintendence of foundries, laboratories, armories and other works connected with the naval ordnance department and the inspection and proof of arms, ammunition, &c. The direction of the transportation of all persons, stores, and provisions of the navy by land and water; and the general charge and direction of the flotilla service in the Patapsco, Delaware, and at New York.

4th class: Comprehending victualling and sustenance, including purser's, medical, and hospital stores; also general charge of the flotilla service on all the naval stations from New York eastward and on Lake Champlain.

5th class: Comprehending the supply of hemp, yarns, cordage, sail, duck, iron, and other metals, anchors, and all other equipment and materials, required for the service, except those which are included in the foregoing classes and in the Constructor's department; and also the general charge and direction of the service on Lake Ontario and the upper lakes.

The superintendence and direction of these five classes of objects would be distributed among the five inspectors.

The department of construction, under the direction of the secretary of the navy, and of the board of inspectors would prepare all drafts, plans and instructions for the building of all the vessels of the navy; construct the models, and when approved, direct, and superintend, under the control of the board of inspectors, the building and repair of the ships, vessels, boats, the formation of masts, spars, &c. and the contracting for, and procuring, all the materials of wood, and of copper, in pigs, belts, and sheets necessary for the supply of the navy; construct from the lines in the mould loft all the moulds requisite for the moulding and beveling of the timber in the forest, under the direction of skillful persons to be employed by the constructor for that purpose, and would superintend the construction of the wharves, ships, workshops, and engines, required in the building and repairing the ships of war.[34]

Secretary Jones ended his draft of this momentous reform bill with the understatement that "it is a copious subject which it is difficult to combine with brevity and perspicuity."[35] This work ultimately made the navy more systematic and accountable for its actions. Secretary Jones's proposal contains the seeds of the beginning of the modern naval bureaucracy in the United States. This is one of the legacies of the War of 1812, a short, painful learning period during which the US Navy came of age. From Jones's stated requirements, rules, and regulations grew the Board of Navy Commissioners, established in 1816. On the basis of Jones's draft bill the commissioners built the structure of the navy bureaus that within a century became virtual fiefdoms—the Bureau of Navigation, the Bureau of Naval Personnel, the Bureau of Ordnance, the Bureau of Naval Construction, and others. These endured and multiplied from the 1840s to the 1960s and promoted the increased red tape that tripped up the unwary who tried to breathe new life into a system that had become sclerotic by the end of World War II.

Two weeks before the end of his tenure as secretary of the navy, William Jones revealed where he stood on the issue of whether the navy of the War of 1812 deserved to have the rank of admiral available to its most competent senior officers. He had been prompted by a letter from the chairman of the Senate Committee on Naval Affairs on November 7 asking whether the grade of admiral should be created and whether brevet promotions should be permitted as well. In response, Jones said that although it would not be appropriate to create several grades of admirals as in the Royal Navy, it was timely to create at least the grade of rear admiral in the US Navy, leaving it to future generations to decide whether to create the grades of vice admiral and admiral. He also recommended allowing brevet promotions for meritorious service.

Three weeks later, Senator Charles Tait, speaking for the committee, explained to the Senate that although the US Army had established the grade of major general, the navy had no equivalent rank. A captain in charge of a squadron of naval ships was granted the temporary flag rank of commodore, but that was not considered the equivalent of the rank of brigadier general in the army, which was a permanent rank. He wrote that "the surest means by which you will probably induce the officers to qualify themselves for an admiral's command is to create that grade in the navy; thereby requiring in the same act great professional attainments and offering a reward for them." He offered two resolutions: he said that the committee considered it expedient to authorize officers above the grade of captain in the navy of the United States but inexpedient to confer naval rank by brevet.[36] Congress did not act to create the rank of rear admiral until 1861, awarding that promotion to Captain Charles Stewart, the last surviving War of 1812 commander, on the eve of the Civil War.

CHAPTER 15

Renewal of the US Navy

With the resignation of William Jones on November 30, 1814, there was about a month's vacancy at the top of the navy's leadership. Jones's chief clerk, Benjamin Homans, as acting secretary of the navy took charge of the routine paperwork and kept the Navy Department running while President Madison searched for a capable replacement for Jones. The man he selected, Benjamin Crowninshield, was the Salem-born son of Jacob Crowninshield, who headed the family's highly successful shipping business. Forty-three years old, Benjamin Crowninshield was about the same age as several of the navy's captains and well acquainted with the sea. By 1804 he had risen to the command of the family-owned armed schooner *America* and had taken her to the Far East and back in the spice trade.[1] By 1814 he had been elected twice to the Massachusetts Senate as a Democratic Republican, and he still held that seat when Madison offered him the post of secretary. Crowninshield's first reaction was to decline the offer, intimating that he was concerned about his health and too involved in the family business, but within two days he had changed his mind, as he wrote, "at the behest of his political friends and with the permission of his family" (fig. 15.1).[2]

Although it would not be known for two and a half months, owing to the inevitable delay of communications, the American and British commissioners at Ghent had come to agreement on a peace treaty on December 24, but each government would have to ratify its terms. The war would be declared at an end at that time. According to article 2, a schedule would allow for the news to travel to combatants, depending on their location: for those in the North Atlantic, 30 days; in the South Atlantic, 60 days; in the Indian Ocean below the equator, 90 days; anywhere else, 120 days.[3]

Meanwhile, the war continued unabated. At this time, the Battle of New Orleans was under way and would continue for another week. The US Navy squadrons on the lakes were in winter quarters at Erie, Sackets Harbor, and Whitehall, New York, while preparing for another summer campaign. Likewise, Commodore Yeo's Lake Ontario squadron lay frozen at anchor, stripped for winter weather at Kingston, Ontario. The lakes and the St. Lawrence were covered with snow, making this an ideal time for the British to transport needed provisions

Figure 15.1. Secretary of the Navy Benjamin Crowninshield, 1815–1818. Portrait by U. D. Tenney. Courtesy of Navy Art Collection, Washington, DC, US Naval History and Heritage Command, Photograph NH 54721-KN.

and supplies from Quebec and Montreal to Kingston. They also planned to establish a new navy depot at Turkey Point, on the north shore of Lake Erie, and to reinforce their small naval force on Lake Huron.[4]

Demobilization on the Northern Lakes

Although both Commodores Chauncey and Yeo had expected the war to continue into a third summer, their plans were interrupted by the news that peace had arrived. Chauncey had given orders for the construction of three large ships before spending several weeks in New York, leaving the naval base in the hands of Captain Jacob Jones. While in New York, he spurred contractors to fill his orders for supplies and transport and spent time with his family. He returned to Sackets Harbor on January 25 with his son John, a newly minted midshipman. By this time, construction had begun on two of the ships of the line, *New Orleans* and *Chippewa*, under the watchful eyes of the shipwrights

Henry Eckford and Adam and Noah Brown. On February 23, when he learned of the treaty ratification, Chauncey ordered work to cease and wrote to his former adversary to inform him of the good news. At that moment Yeo was returning from a tour of inspection at Long Point, Lake Erie, and Georgian Bay, Lake Huron. When he heard the news, Yeo closed down the work going on at Long Point but ordered the workers at Kingston to continue building the ships of the line *Canada* and *Wolfe*.

In late December rumors had reached Washington that the British were planning a winter raid on the navy's base at Whitehall, New York, where Commodore Macdonough had collected his squadron.[5] This news had a basis in fact. Major General Brisbane volunteered to Governor General Prevost that he would be pleased to lead such an expedition comprising seven thousand men and one thousand sleighs. Secretary of War James Monroe ordered alerts at Plattsburgh and Whitehall, and Acting Secretary of the Navy Benjamin Homans ordered Commodore Macdonough to return to Whitehall to make defensive arrangements in conjunction with Major General Macomb at Plattsburgh. Ultimately, Governor General Prevost, who had been circumspect about the expedition from the first, called off the raid on the basis of intelligence received about American defensive preparations. Prevost's successor, Commodore Sir Edward W. C. R. Owen, took command on March 22, 1815. After mature study of Canada's defenses, he continued the demobilization begun by Prevost and Yeo, but he also took care to provide for Canada's future defense in case of a need for remobilization.[6]

Secretary Crowninshield wrote to all commanding officers on February 14 to inform them of the anticipated treaty ratification, ordering them to lay their ships up in ordinary and provide for preservation in case of future need. He ordered Captain Arthur Sinclair to leave home and report to Erie, where he would attend to laying up and preserving the brigs *Lawrence* and *Niagara*. He had to keep in service those vessels that would best serve to maintain contact with US posts at Detroit and Michilimackinac on Lake Huron. Other vessels were to be sold.[7] At Sackets Harbor, Chauncey ordered all the converted merchant schooners to be sold, the navy-built vessels put in ordinary, and *New Orleans* and *Chippewa* housed over, in which condition they remained for many years. At Whitehall, Commodore Macdonough acknowledged the secretary's orders and informed him that he had dismantled the entire squadron and removed all guns, sails, ballast, powder, and shot and stored them. He advised that the vessels be whitewashed inside and out and allowed as much air circulation as possible. He also wanted them to be roofed over to keep them out of the sun. He ordered the sloops and galleys at Whitehall sold at auction. Inevitably, with time, the remaining vessels rotted and sank at anchor.[8] Only the lower hull of the former schooner *Ticonderoga*, raised in 1958, survives, albeit in very sad shape, under an open metal canopy for occasional visitors' interest.

Final Engagements at Sea

Captain Stephen Decatur's *President* was at New York awaiting a winter storm so that she could depart with her consorts *Hornet*, *Peacock*, and the schooner *Tom Bowline*. Their orders were to break through the blockade together and head for the South Atlantic, where they would rendezvous at the island of Tristan da Cunha. Of course, they had not counted on Decatur's earlier departure on January 14 and his early defeat. The rest of the squadron did not depart until January 23. They were to replenish at Tristan da Cunha and set course for the Indian Ocean and the East Indies. Due to a storm, *Hornet* became separated, but *Peacock* and *Tom Bowline* continued to the rendezvous, arriving on March 18. *Hornet* arrived on March 23. *Constitution*, with Charles Stewart in command, straining at her moorings, was ready to depart Boston with the next winter gale. She had returned in the early spring with a damaged lower mainmast that needed replacement and in need of seamen to replace those who were seriously ill.

USS Constitution *versus HMS* Levant *and HMS* Cyane

During *Constitution*'s lengthy stay in Boston, Captain Stewart had plenty of time to make sure that his ship was fully ready to go to sea. But two factors prevented him from leaving, one being a need for more seamen. On his return to Boston, some had departed since their enlistments had expired. To replace them, Stewart had to open a rendezvous and hope that he would not be asked to send some of his sailors to the lakes. The other issue was the more crucial matter of the blockade. During the war, the impressive battle record of the American 44s had persuaded the Admiralty to design some new frigates along the same lines. Two of these—*Leander*, 50, commanded by Sir George Collier, and *Newcastle*, 50, commanded by Lord George Stuart—had been completed and sent to blockade Boston for the specific purpose of capturing *Constitution*. To make triply sure, the Admiralty had assigned the *Acasta*, 40, a lighter, weatherly frigate under the command of Captain Alexander Kerr, to complete Collier's squadron. As the late fall weather worsened, *Newcastle* and *Acasta* sheltered at Provincetown, while Stewart, hearing that the coast was clear of enemy warships, set sail on December 17. Collier's *Leander* had been at Halifax when *Constitution* sailed and did not arrive to join its consorts until December 24. Stewart had a week's head start over his adversaries and made the most of it, heading south and then northeasterly toward Portugal. He doubled back, and off the Madeira Islands he discovered two British ship-sloops—*Cyane*, 32, and *Levant*, 20—sailing as rear guard of a south-bound convoy. In a remarkable night action, Stewart took on both ships. With skillful maneuvering, he managed to rake each sloop with his long 24-pounders while their carronades were out of range and did little damage to *Constitution*. Each British ship put up a stiff fight, finally surrendering when she was unable to maneuver and had taken many casualties. In the five-hour battle, Stewart's crew lost four killed and fourteen wounded; the combined loss for *Cyane* and *Levant* was twelve killed and twenty-eight wounded. Stewart put prize crews on both vessels and sailed for the Cape Verde islands. It was there, on March 8, that Collier's squadron, having tracked *Constitution* for more than two months, caught up just as Stewart was getting under way with his prizes. In the ensuing stern chase, with hazy visibility, Stewart worried that *Cyane*, last in line, would be over-taken, so he signaled her to tack to the northwest. None of the chasing ships took the bait but kept on after *Levant* and *Constitution*. After another hour or so, Stewart ordered *Levant* to tack, but to his surprise all three British ships tacked after *Levant*, leaving *Constitution* free to sail without further pursuit. This episode ended well for the US Navy. *Constitution* dropped her prisoners off at Maranhão, Brazil, and put in briefly at San Juan, Puerto Rico, where the captain received the welcome news that the ratifications had been exchanged and the war was over. On May 15, Stewart brought *Constitution* safely to New York, where he was met by news that his prize *Cyane* had arrived a month earlier, also unscathed.[9]

Pursuit and Capture of USS President

Although *Constitution*'s war was over, we must turn back the clock to summarize the remaining course of the naval war with respect to *President*, *Hornet*, and *Peacock*. Commodore Stephen Decatur Jr., we recall, had been rudely cut off from the war by being bottled up in the Thames River at New London. His ships *United States* and *Macedonian* had been relieved of their seamen and armament because of greater needs for them at Sackets Harbor and at New York. In May 1814, Secretary Jones ordered Decatur to take command of the frigate *President*, formerly Commodore Rodgers's command, while Rodgers received orders to take command of the newly built *Guerriere* at Philadelphia. Jones and Decatur had discussed the strategy of his forthcoming cruise. At this stage of the war, it made little sense to cruise the Atlantic, where the Royal Navy was looking for Decatur. Jones preferred that his ships strike where they might not be expected, in the distant Indian Ocean and the East Indies. After Decatur joined up with his squadron, comprising James Biddle's *Hornet* and Lewis Warrington's *Peacock*, he might be lucky enough to capture a convoy of East India Company ships.

Decatur filled his ship with the best men he could find and ordered provisions loaded on board for a cruise of several months. Meanwhile, the Royal Navy was preparing a dangerous reception for him when he departed New York. The long wait ended on January 14, when a northerly blizzard blew into New York, providing cover for Decatur's sortie. He had arranged with coastal pilots to mark with buoys the edge of the shoals, such as the Middle Ground, off Sandy Hook. Yet, as *President* moved swiftly through the lower harbor and into the marked area, she ran aground on that very shoal and pounded there for two hours, ripping loose some of her hull's copper sheathing and damaging the rudder housing. This was valuable time lost, for when *President* got under way from Sandy Hook, the storm had passed. With visibility improved, the offshore blockaders had returned to their stations and had no trouble identifying her.

From pursuit to battle was a matter of time, wind, sailing skill, and expert gunnery. The chase began at 5:00 a.m. on January 15, and the first exchange of shots occurred at 2:00 p.m., roughly nine hours later. To whom Decatur surrendered may be debated, whether HMS *Endymion* or HMS *Pomone*, but surrender he did at 9 p.m., after a seven-hour running fight. The British proudly brought *President* as a prize into Bermuda and then to England, where she was preserved for many years to demonstrate that the famed New York–built 44 was not invincible after all.[10]

USS Hornet *versus* HMS Penguin

Commodore Decatur had decided that *President* would depart New York alone, without the rest of his South Atlantic–bound squadron. The rest soon followed but escaped the blockade. Captain Warrington's *Peacock* and Captain Biddle's *Hornet*, in company with their storeships, *Tom Bowline* and *Macedonian*, sailed swiftly through the blockade zone and headed for the rendezvous at Tristan da Cunha. They expected to meet *President*, but unbeknownst to these officers, she had been captured. From this point they were on their own, still obligated to carry out their sailing orders as long as the war lasted.

Biddle arrived at bleak, inhospitable Tristan on March 23, but the enemy soon arrived in the shape of HMS *Penguin*, 20, under Commander James Dickinson. *Hornet* and *Penguin* were evenly matched in rig and armament, but *Hornet*'s gunnery was superior. During a sharp action of twenty minutes, Captain Dickinson was killed, and the command devolved on Lieutenant James McDonald, who carried on the fight, attempting to board *Hornet*. Unable to do so in the face of *Hornet*'s musketry, *Penguin* shook free of *Hornet* but lost her bowsprit and foremast.

McDonald then surrendered, as his ship was no longer maneuverable and faced continued broadsides from *Hornet*. *Penguin* suffered fourteen killed and twenty-eight wounded, while on board *Hornet* casualties were far fewer, with one killed and eleven wounded, including Biddle, who received a neck wound late in the battle.

While Biddle recovered from his wound and repaired the ship's damage, Warrington's *Peacock* arrived in company with the storeship *Tom Bowline*.[11] They waited three weeks for Decatur, but on April 12 they sailed for the Indian Ocean. Biddle ordered *Tom Bowline* to serve as a cartel, taking his *Penguin* prisoners to Rio de Janeiro, Brazil. Two weeks later, they had the bad luck to close with a large ship presumed to be an East Indiaman; however, she turned out to be the newly built HMS *Cornwallis*, 74. *Peacock*, the faster-sailing of the two Americans, fled to the east, so *Hornet* became the larger ship's target. *Cornwallis* turned out to be a persistent foe, countering every move *Hornet* could make. Finally, Biddle jettisoned all his stores, spare spars, and most of his guns and ammunition. Eventually, with a change of wind, *Cornwallis* fell far behind and gave up the chase. Biddle at length reached Salvador da Bahia, where he learned the war was over.[12]

USS Peacock *in the East Indies*

Despite British fears, no US Navy ships ventured into the Indian Ocean and Far Eastern seas until 1815; however, several American privateers were active in this broad area, namely, the ships *Hyder Ally*, 22, and *Jacob Jones*, 16, the schooner *Russell*, 6, from New Bedford, the schooner *Rambler* from Boston, and the schooner *Tamahanaka*, 16, which may have been a letter-of-marque trader. These vessels, operating independently, interrupted traditional trade routes and forced the Admiralty to deploy warships it would have preferred to keep in seas closer to home.[13] This was the situation until March 1815, when Captain Warrington's *Peacock* appeared on the scene.

Sailing around the Cape of Good Hope and into the Indian Ocean, Captain Warrington's *Peacock* surged eastward for weeks, encountering no prizeworthy ships until reaching Java. The Treaty of Ghent specified that warships east of the Cape of Good Hope and below the equator would have ninety days to receive the news of the exchange of ratifications.[14] The deadline for Warrington and his crew was May 18. Any prizes taken after that were illegal. We know Warrington received news of Decatur's surrender of *President* when he found a letter addressed to him at the islands of Saint-Paul and Amsterdam in the southern Indian Ocean, 500 kilometers distant from Antarctica. These islands were on the route of merchantmen sailing for southern Australia. The mail drop was most likely on

Amsterdam Island, the larger and more visited of the two islands because of its protected harbor. On June 13, as *Peacock* neared Java, Warrington took his first prize, *Union*, an East India Company ship carrying a cargo of spices, opium, saffron, raw silk, and five thousand dollars in gold. He burned the prize and continued to the Sunda Strait. This happened nearly a month after the prize-taking deadline, although Warrington supposedly did not know that. This was the beginning of troubles that were to haunt him and the Navy Department for years.

Once in the Sunda Strait, between Sumatra and Java, Warrington captured *Venus*, a British merchant ship traveling in ballast carrying only mundane cargo, but hidden in a pork barrel was six thousand dollars in cash. Not burning *Venus*, Warrington planned to use her as a cartel, which he definitely needed after capturing *Brio de Mar*, another British ship sailing in ballast but carrying a few casks of wine and about nine thousand dollars in cash, on May 29. On the next day, *Peacock*, under British colors, approached Anjier, a British settlement, where he was visited by some officials brought out by the East India Company brig *Nautilus*, 14, flying no colors. On discovering that *Peacock* was an American warship, Lieutenant Charles Boyce, the commander of *Nautilus*, then hoisted his colors and informed Warrington that their two countries were at peace. Warrington demanded that Boyce lower his colors if that was true. Boyce refused, at which point *Peacock* fired its guns, *Nautilus* responded with a broadside, and the battle began. After fifteen minutes, with Boyce and his first lieutenant severely wounded, *Nautilus* hauled down its ensign. *Nautilus* suffered six killed and seven wounded in the action. Immediately thereafter, the master intendant went ashore to obtain the proof of peace that Warrington demanded. Apparently satisfied with the documentary evidence, Warrington gave up *Nautilus* to British control, transferred his prisoners, and departed from Sunda Strait on July 2.[15] *Peacock* and *Nautilus* had fought the last battle of the War of 1812, but the American captain would have much to answer for after his return to the United States four months later.[16]

Word of Warrington's actions in the East Indies spread to Great Britain and the United States before he arrived at his home port. The British accused him of knowingly taking prizes after learning of the Treaty of Ghent and its deadline for taking prizes in distant seas. Further, the owners of the ships and their cargoes used that argument as the basis for demanding restitution from the United States for their losses. The Navy Department supported Warrington in a court of inquiry held in May 1816. The British shifted their ground to Admiralty court at the suggestion of Secretary of the Navy Crowninshield. Represented by the Baltimore law firm of S. Smith and Buchanan, the owners and insurers of *Union*, *Venus*, and *Brio de Mar* sued the United States for restitution of their properties, and surprisingly, the Court for the Southern District of New York agreed. As a matter of equity, the US Congress would have to pay restitution even though the Navy Department rejected the claim that Warrington had violated the treaty.[17]

Some historians, such as Theodore Roosevelt, have accused Warrington of inhumane conduct, particularly with his violent bombardment of the East India Company brig *Nautilus* after being been told about the establishment of peace more than four months before the action.[18] Warrington's position was that he believed this was but a ruse and wanted to see proof of the treaty and its ratification. The military historian John R. Elting's view is realistic: "Naturally, Warrington's conduct has been much deplored,—but utterly alone on hostile seas— there was no reason why he should trust his enemy or spare him humiliation."[19]

Warrington and crew had been at sea for six months, since leaving New York, except for a brief stop at Tristan de Cunha. He did not return to New York until October 30, another four months. He had done a remarkable job of sustaining the ship, his crew, and himself. This was a good example of naval leadership and self-reliance. He had to provide his own logistics, except for provisions from *Tom Bowline*, to maintain *Peacock* out of range of a friendly port, and he used the supplies and cash taken from his three prizes to sustain the crew for the final four months of his return voyage.

The Board of Navy Commissioners

While Captains Stewart, Decatur, Biddle, and Warrington were fighting their last War of 1812 battles, Congress began to act on Secretary Jones's recommendations for reform of the navy. Mindful of their need for professional advice, the House Naval Committee established a Committee on Naval Reform under the chairmanship of William Reed. He sent out Jones's recommendations in a circular letter to all the navy's captains, asking them for their frank views and welcomed anything they wished to add. It was generally understood that although the relatively dysfunctional organization of the service had held up, there were several weak points.

One of these was at the apex of the bureaucratic triangle. There simply were not enough staff members in the department to keep track of everything the secretary wanted done. Since delegation of authority, except in matters such as record keeping, was not an option, the secretary was swamped with work. He not only had to issue operational orders but he had to follow up with administrative acts to ensure that ships received the supplies they needed. With regard to matters of supply, there was little supervision of the navy agents, who did the purchasing via contracts with commercial firms and industrialists, who controlled the means of production. As a result, bills were overpaid or contracts were not fulfilled because enforcement was lacking; there had been much wastage, and funds had been poorly spent. A third major weakness was the tendency of commanding officer to make unauthorized changes to the ships under their command. This offended Jones's principle of uniformity in design and strict attention to classification of the navy's ships, their rig, and ordnance. With the support of the ranking officers of the navy and Congress, the internal structure of the navy had to be changed.

In the hands of Congress, William Jones's board of Inspectors became known as the Board of Navy Commissioners, made up of three captains selected by the secretary, the senior of whom would serve as president of the board.[20] They would report to the secretary of the navy. Their responsibilities included oversight of all the material requirements of the navy. They were allowed to have two well-established civilian specialists, such as the senior clerk of the department and the navy constructor, to handle technical matters, and a secretary of the board, as well as number of civilian functionaries to handle paperwork and messenger duties.

The secretary of the navy would represent the navy to Congress and report to the president of the United States. The secretary would control the operational aspects of the navy, advised by the commissioners. In actual practice, many of the future secretaries came to the office without much knowledge of the naval profession. Many were attorneys or businessmen unaccustomed to managing a growing military bureaucracy and had to learn on the job, leaning heavily on the president of the board.

Early in the board's existence, its first three officers—Captains John Rodgers, Isaac Hull, and David Porter—disagreed with Secretary Crowninshield regarding how much control the secretary should exert over the board. The law establishing the board was not sufficiently clear about whether Crowninshield's "ministerial duties" included controlling information about the movement of naval forces and the distribution of naval personnel. The commissioners wanted to require the secretary to share such information with them. Crowninshield appealed to President Madison.[21] All business halted for three weeks in May 1815 while President Madison pondered the issue. Madison's sage opinion came down on June 12, 1815.[22] He pointed out that the board was attached to the secretary's office, not to the president's. The navy secretary had been appointed by the president and therefore was organically part of his administration. The board's ministerial duties were to be supervised by the secretary of the navy. The board could be considered neither independent of the secretary nor a power unto itself. President Madison's opinion made a fair distinction in terms of civil-military relations. It firmly reinforced civilian control of the navy and put an end to the controversy.[23]

One of the board's signal accomplishments was a complete rewrite of the the navy rules and regulations, last issued in 1802. The new version detailed the responsibilities of officers—noncommissioned officers, warrant officers, and officers in charge of the shore establishment. The requirements for paperwork expanded; in addition to the usual reports and receipts, the number of forms required for accounting purposes, especially related to contracting, multiplied.[24]

Another major event of the immediate postwar period was congressional support for the building of a larger navy, or as it was called in 1816, the "gradual increase of the navy," to the tune of an additional $1 million a year for eight years to the navy's budget for that purpose.[25] This was intended to fund the building of nine 74s, twelve new 44-gun frigates, and three steam frigates (then called "steam batteries"). All this was a new departure, the building of a major naval force in peacetime. This phenomenon is explained by the navy's surge in popularity thanks to its performance during the War of 1812 and to the postwar recovery of the nation's treasury. A severe recession in 1819 slowed the progress of this massive building program, but it continued partially because of the desire for a respectable navy and a determination to be prepared for eventualities.

All Things Naval Considered

The purpose of this study is to demonstrate the importance of logistics for the US Navy in the War of 1812. Logistics were important in all the far-flung campaign areas, and it was as true for the British forces as it was for the American. Those in charge had to have a proper grasp of logistics in order for the navy's operations to succeed. Logistics included all the elements of naval war except the fighting—administration, communications, finance, shipbuilding, acquisition of timber, hemp, and sailcloth, recruitment, training, supply (requisitions, provisions, and material), transportation, ordnance (guns, powder, related equipment), medical necessities, and competent leadership.

The US Navy's survival after two and one-half years of war was remarkable. For one thing, the navy had been well founded. It had its traditions, centered on the stout little navy of the American Revolution. The Continental Navy, opposing the British Royal Navy of the mid- to late eighteenth century, had come into being for some of the same reasons that the War of 1812 navy had fought for: to be able to conduct its own operations free from interference of an overweening naval power and to protect its nation's merchant ships from being devoured by larger and better-armed blockaders from the imperial motherland. One of the strengths of the young US Navy and its predecessor was its adoption of the fighting traditions of the Royal Navy. It was Congressman John Adams himself who wrote the rules and regulations of the American navy, based on those of the Royal Navy. Many of the captains of the Continental Navy had served as junior officers in the Royal Navy and had brought its fighting traditions with them. One of the lessons learned in that earlier war was that of self-sufficiency. It is true that the French navy had come to the rescue of the United States, and this had taught the American captains and congressmen the value of sea power—what the power of a maneuverable body of ships and seamen could contribute in coordination with a land campaign. In the aftermath of the Revolutionary War at sea, when the new republic was feeling its way in the world, its leaders discovered the truth of what Commodore John Paul Jones had written to Robert Morris in 1776: "Without a Respectable Navy, alas America."[26]

The road to a respectable navy was long and winding, but in the 1790s the first steps were taken: the building of the first six frigates began when it became apparent that America's merchant marine needed protection. The challenges came in the Mediterranean from the corsairs of the Barbary regencies. This threat had barely passed when the warships and privateers of the French Directory interrupted US trade with the Caribbean. This truly brought the message home to the Federalists in Washington.

From the late 1790s, navalists began to build the infrastructure of a new US navy. They needed to provide a logistical base for all that followed. To build the new 44-gun frigates, shipwrights needed the hardest timbers, carved from the live oaks that spanned the littorals of the seaboard South. Spurred on by the new secretary of the navy, Benjamin Stoddert, men surveyed, designed, and built the navy yards that eventually stretched from Gosport, Virginia, to Washington, Philadelphia, New York, Boston, and Portsmouth, New Hampshire. These would become the first government-owned industrial establishments, with dedicated artisans and veteran sailors to construct everything a ship needed to provide for sailors and marines who had to live, fight, and die for their country's honor on the high seas and freshwater lakes. They provided a logistical base on which to build the navy.

To man these frigates and smaller vessels, there had to be many naval rendezvous, where men could be hired to serve during long cruises. To keep order and maintain discipline of the hundreds of men in these ships, there had to be a system of rules and regulations, with appropriate punishments for miscreants unaccustomed to naval discipline. In time these regulations became known as the "rocks and shoals" on which enlisted men and even officers would run aground from time to time. And, of course, an officer corps had to be selected by the secretary of the navy, with the help of congressmen, who never ceased to favor the sons of important constituents. These young men would be designated as midshipmen. It would be up to the commanding officers of the navy's ships to separate the wheat from the chaff—the strong men from the weak, the trustworthy from the untrustworthy—

in order to form a disciplined officer corps. There was no official naval academy in the early days to provide an elementary seagoing education. It was another thirty years before a naval academy was established. Usually, the candidates for a midshipman's birth had a fair secondary education, but they had to show competence in mathematics, which was usually obtained from tutors or private schools. Although the US Army's military academy was established in 1802, the US Navy, in the words of Captain Charles Stewart, believed the best school for officers was "on the deck of a ship."[27]

A review of the previous chapters brings forward the significance of logistics to the performance of the US Navy in the War of 1812. Despite having a well-trained officer corps and well-trained enlisted men, most of whom had served in the two previous naval wars, the navy simply did not have enough ships of the right types to contend with the Royal Navy. Secretary Jones believed in 1814 that even if more ships were built for the lakes squadrons, there would be difficulty finding enough seamen to fight them. This was not a secret. In the years leading up to the declaration of war, numerous pronaval congressmen had pointed this out. When the questions of adding ships to the navy arose, the opposed congressmen inevitably brought up the question of costs, despite the obvious contradiction of facing a probable war with Great Britain without the essential weapons to oppose the Royal Navy.

Secretary Hamilton's survey of the various naval stations showed inadequate powder supplies just months before the war. Much of the gunpowder in storage at Boston Navy Yard had been neglected, left unturned and unmixed. Powder in that condition loses its potency. Reports from station commanders mentioned the lack of hand weapons and ammunition, including round shot for gunboat crews, and an insufficient number of men healthy enough for service. In May 1812, tests of the gunpowder from the frigate *United States* showed it to compare favorably with powder stored at Gosport Navy Yard, much of which also showed insufficient potency.

The advent of war had a stimulating influence on the American ordnance industry, as demand from both military and naval sources brought new business to these entrepreneurs in powder-making firms and iron foundries. Particularly useful for the navy were the powder factories, such as the Bellona factory, near Newark, New Jersey, and several in Maryland outside Baltimore. As for iron foundries, the navy had two principal sources for its guns and round shot, Henry Foxall's Columbia Works, at Georgetown, Maryland, and Samuel Hughes's Principio Ironworks, near Havre de Grace, Maryland. During Admiral Cockburn's raid on Havre de Grace in 1813, his sailors and marines completely destroyed the ironworks's boring machinery and spiked or blew up forty-five guns ranging from 32-pounders and 24-pounders to carronades and smaller-caliber weapons. Fortunately for the navy, Foxall's business was able to make up for the loss of Principio.

The war's stimulus also brought forth inventors offering new weapons to the navy. Secretary Jones, looking for any advantage, encouraged these efforts. Significantly, Robert Fulton's mechanical genius applied to maritime affairs introduced the first steam warship, *Demologos*, and mines that he called "torpedoes," used against the Royal Navy on Long Island Sound and on Chesapeake Bay. He also experimented with an underwater cannon, the predecessor of modern steam torpedoes, and a primitive submarine that interested Presidents James Madison and Thomas Jefferson, but Fulton died before he could develop these concepts further. Tests of Joseph G. Chambers's multibarrel machine gun proved so interesting to Secretary Jones and Commodore Chauncey that Chauncey adopted it for use on Lake Ontario in 1814.

The long-range debilitating effects of the blockade were manifold in their logistical impact. They interrupted the coastal commerce, which the US Navy depended on for timely delivery of live oak from the Georgia barrier islands and coastal swamps. This delayed the completion of the American 74s until the end of the war. Deliveries of extremely heavy cargoes, such as 18-, 24-, and 32-pounder long guns and carronades, had to be transported by ox-drawn wagons slowed by bad roads rather than risk capture at sea. The interruption of intercoastal deliveries of grain, rice, and other supplies worked a hardship for seaport populations and caused disruption of financial markets. Finally and most telling, the cutting off of imports drastically reduced a source of government income from customs duties and drove the US government to near bankruptcy in the latter months of the war.[28]

There is a controversy about the effectiveness of the British blockade against the United States compared with its blockade of France during the Napoleonic Wars. The war against France lasted much longer, as did the blockade, and it was more effective than its counterpart against the United States—so goes the argument.[29] The counterargument, published more recently, is that the Royal Navy blockade off the American coast was definitely effective, especially in 1814. The latter argument has a more convincing statistical basis in terms of the blockade's financial impact on the United States Treasury.[30] Nevertheless, the United States just managed to sustain the war into 1815 as the treaty negotiators at Ghent were completing their work. If one asks what if, it is safe to say that had the war continued through another year, the United States might have had to sue for peace. Of course that did not happen, and owing to a unique turn of events in the battles of Baltimore, Plattsburgh, Lake Champlain, and New Orleans, many Americans believed that the United States had actually won the war. Instead, the country had a narrow escape, primarily as a result of a national determination to keep on fighting despite the cost. Both the American military and naval services and many civilians made essential sacrifices and contributions that brought the war to an honorable conclusion, which both sides believed they deserved and had won.

After William Jones took up the post of secretary of the navy in January 1813, he made it his business to reform the navy according to his principles of efficiency. Captain Charles Morris's suggestions closely aligned with his superior's ideas about dealing with matters or supply, better control of navy agents, improved accountability in purchases, and insisting that commanding officers refrain from altering ship rigging and ordnance carried. While it was difficult to accomplish all these things during the conduct of the war, Jones took the opportunity in the month before he resigned to outline his proposed reforms. One of the most obvious needs was an adequate staff for the secretary of the navy, as well as a source of professional advice on technical matters that threatened to overwhelm the overburdened secretary.

Gradual Increase of the Navy

The navy's harsh experiences and a few brilliant victories during the War of 1812 created the environment for change and improvement, along with the desire to strengthen the navy in material ways. For example, the navy had been forced to innovate and to create the means of fighting the war on the northern lakes, which for the most part succeeded. It hoped in this way to be better prepared for future conflicts and to enlarge the navy in order to carry out its responsibility. The navy's widely perceived successes during the war fortified the cause of the nationalist Republicans, such as Henry Clay and John Calhoun, who advocated strengthening all aspects of national defense. This included building coastal forts and increasing the number and sizes of the navy ships. In 1822, the navy purchased the sidewheel steamer *Seagull* for service under Commodore David Porter's command in the Caribbean.[31] The next purpose-built steam warship, *Fulton II*, was launched and commissioned in the Brooklyn Navy Yard in 1837, commanded by Matthew Calbraith Perry.[32] With the recovery of the Treasury Department, larger budgets were voted for defense. As time went by, with the recession of 1819 and the diplomatic reduction of Anglo-American tensions, the urgency to complete this program waned, but the principle of naval preparedness remained the goal, and the senior officer veterans of the War of 1812 were there to ensure that they had not fought in vain.

Chapter 1 · The Resources for Naval War

1. Tim McGrath, *Give Me a Fast Ship: The Continental Navy and America's Revolution at Sea* (New York: NAL Caliber-Penguin Group, 2014); George C. Daughan, *If By Sea: The Forging of the American Navy from the Revolution to the War of 1812* (New York: Basic Books, 2008).

2. Secretary of War to House of Representatives, "Construction of Frigates under the Act of March 27, 1794," *American State Papers: Naval Affairs*, 1:6.

3. Charles O. Paullin, *Paullin's History of Naval Administration, 1775–1911* (Annapolis, MD: Naval Institute Press, 1968,), 147.

4. David Curtis Skaggs and Gerald T. Altoff, *A Signal Victory: The Lake Erie Campaign, 1812–1813* (Annapolis, MD: Naval Institute Press, 1997), 60–61.

5. John A. Huston, *Sinews of War: Army Logistics, 1775–1953* (Washington, DC: US Army Center of Military History, 1988), vii–viii.

6. Henry R. Eccles, *Logistics in the National Defense* (Newport, RI: Naval War College Press, 1997), 21–22.

7. Huston, *Sinews of War*, 669–78.

8. Michael J. Crawford, "U.S. Navy Petty Officers in the Era of the War of 1812," *Journal of Military History* 76, no. 4 (Oct. 2012), 1035–52.

9. Secretary of the Navy Benjamin Crowninshield to John W. Eppes, Chairman, Ways and Means Committee, House of Representatives, 8 Feb 1815, *American State Papers: Naval Affairs*, 1:363–64.

10. Christopher McKee, *A Gentlemanly and Honorable Profession: The Creation of the U.S. Naval Officer Corps, 1798–1815* (Annapolis, MD: Naval Institute Press, 1991), 331–37.

11. Gordon S. Brown, *The Captain Who Burned His Ships: Captain Thomas Tingey, USN, 1750–1829* (Annapolis, MD: Naval Institute Press, 2011), 58–63.

12. Secretary of War Henry Knox, report to Congress, "Construction of Frigates under the Act of March 27, 1794," communicated to the House of Representatives, 29 Dec. 1794, *American State Papers: Naval Affairs*, 1:6–7.

13. Frederick C. Leiner, *Millions for Defense: The Subscription Warships of 1798* (Annapolis, MD: Naval Institute Press, 2000), 177–83.

14. Michael A. Palmer, *Stoddert's War: Naval Operations during the Quasi-War with France, 1798–1801* (Columbia: University of South Carolina Press, 1987), 10–14, 233–36.

15. Acting Secretary of the Navy Samuel Smith to Captain Richard Dale, 20 May 1801, in US Office of Naval Records and Library, *Naval Documents related to the United States Wars with the Barbary Powers: Naval Operations Including Diplomatic Background from 1785 Through 1807*, ed. Dudley W. Knox, 6 vols. (Washington, DC: GPO, 1939 44), 1:465–69, hereafter cited as Knox, *Naval Documents related to the United States Wars with the Barbary Powers*.

16. Commo. Preble to J. M. Mathews, US Consul at Naples, 19 Mar. 1804, in Knox, *Naval Documents related to the United States Wars with the Barbary Powers*, 3:506.

17. Spencer C. Tucker and Frank T. Reuter, *Injured Honor: The Chesapeake–Leopard Affair, June 22, 1807* (Annapolis, MD: Naval Institute Press, 1996), 189–211.

18. Brian Lavery, *Nelson's Navy: The Ships, Men, and Organization, 1793–1815* (Annapolis, MD: Naval Institute Press, 1989), 43–48. See also Rif Winfield, *British Warships in the Age of Sail, 1793–1817: Design, Construction, Careers, and Fates* (London: Chatham, 2005), 65.

19. Capt. Richard Byron, RN, to VAdm. Herbert Sawyer, RN, 27 June 1812, in *The Naval War of 1812: A Documentary History*, ed. William S. Dudley, 4 vols. (Washington, DC: GPO, 1985–2021), 1:157–60.

Chapter 2 · Paul Hamilton's Ordeal: The Onset of War, 1809–1812

1. Biography of Governor Paul Hamilton, South Carolina Digital Library, University of South Carolina, Columbia, http://sciway.net/hist/governors/phamilton.html.

2. Christopher McKee, *A Gentlemanly and Honorable Profession: The Creation of the U.S. Naval Officer Corps, 1794–1815* (Annapolis, MD: Naval Institute Press, 1991), 9–27.

3. Gordon S. Brown, *The Captain Who Burned His Ships: Captain Thomas Tingey, USN, 1750–1829* (Annapolis, MD: Naval Institute Press, 2011), 99–115.

4. Secretary Paul Hamilton to Col. Morton Waring, 1 Oct. 1810, "SC Governors— Paul Hamilton, 1804–1806," SCIWAY, http://sciway.net/hist/governors/phamilton.html.

5. Ronald Hatzenbuehler and Robert Ivie, *Congress Declares War: Rhetoric, Leadership, and Partisanship in the Early Republic* (Kent, OH: Kent State University Press, 1983), 92–113.

6. Hamilton to Commo. John Rodgers, 22 June 1812, in *The Naval War of 1812: A Documentary History*, ed. William S. Dudley, 4 vols. (Washington, DC: GPO, 1985–2021), 1:48–49, hereafter cited as *Naval War*.

7. James Madison, Third Annual Message, 5 Nov. 5, 1811, "Presidential Speeches," UVA Miller Center, millercenter.org/president/speeches.

8. "Increase of the Navy," report from the Naval Committee, House of Representatives, 17 Dec. 1811, *American State Papers: Naval Affairs*, 1:247–48.

9. Hamilton to Capt. Hugh G. Campbell, 8 Apr. 1812, and Campbell to Hamilton, 25 Apr. 1812, in *Naval War*, 1:90.

10. John K. Mahon, "Florida," in *James Madison and the American Nation, 1751–1836: An Encyclopedia*, ed. Robert Rutland (New York: Simon & Schuster, 1994), 147–48; James G. Cusick, *The Other War of 1812: The Patriot War and the American Invasion of Spanish East Florida* (Gainesville: University Press of Florida, 2003).

11. Gene A. Smith, *For the Purposes of Defense: The Politics of the Jeffersonian Gunboat Program* (Newark: University of Delaware Press, 1995), 94–113.

12. Spencer C. Tucker, *The Jeffersonian Gunboat Navy* (Columbia: University of South Carolina Press, 1993), 82–102.

13. Donald R. Hickey, *The War of 1812: A Forgotten Conflict*, Bicentennial Edition (Urbana: University of Illinois Press, 2012), 36–37.

14. Lt. Col. Franklin Wharton to Capt. John Hall, USMC, 4 May 1812; MCdt. Samuel Evans to Hamilton, 8 May 1812; Hamilton to Selected Officials, 6 May 1812; Wharton to Hall, 10 May 1812; and Evans to Hamilton, 22 May 1812, in *Naval War*, 1:103–17.

15. An Act Establishing Navy Hospitals, 26 Feb. 1811, ch. 26, 3 Stat. 650. Soon after the federal government moved to Washington in November 1800, medical services and supplies were provided for the navy yard there from an apothecary shop at the corner of Pennsylvania Avenue and 9th Street, where the Washington Naval Hospital was later built. See Rodger Streitmatter, "History of the Old Naval Hospital," http:/oldnavalhospital.org /History_Streitmatter.html.

16. Harold D. Langley, *A History of Medicine in the Early U.S. Navy* (Baltimore: Johns Hopkins University Press, 1995), 167–73.

17. Surgeon Edward Cutbush to Hamilton, 21 June 1812, in *Naval War*, 1:141–42.

18. Cutbush to Hamilton, 6 July 1812, in *Naval War*, 1:184–85.

19. Rodgers to Hamilton, 3 June 1812, in *Naval War*, 1:119–22.

20. Capt. Richard Byron, RN, to VAdm. Herbert Sawyer, RN, 27 June 1812, in *Naval War*, 1:157–60.

21. Commo. Rodgers's Journal (extract), USS *President*, 23 June 1812, in *Naval War*, 1:154–57.

22. Capt. Isaac Hull to Hamilton, 2 July 1812, in *Naval War*, 1:160–61.

23. Hull to Hamilton, 21 July 1812, in *Naval War*, 1:161–65.

24. Hull to Hamilton, 28 Aug. 1812, in *Naval War*, 1:231–33; Tyrone G. Martin, *A Most Fortunate Ship: A Narrative History of Old Ironsides*, rev. ed. (Annapolis, MD: Naval Institute Press, 1997), 143–65.

25. *Documents Relative to the Investigation, by Order of the Secretary of the Navy, of the Official Conduct of Amos Binney, United States Navy Agent at Boston, upon the Charges made by Lieutenant Joel Abbot and Others. Published by the Accused* (Boston, 1822); *Naval War*, 1:466n.

26. Hamilton to Navy Agent Amos Binney, 8 Sept. 1812, in *Naval War*, 1:466–67.

27. Commo. Stephen Decatur to Hamilton, 8 June 1812, in *Naval War*, 1:122–24.

28. William H. J. Manthorpe, "Jacob Jones, A Hero of the War of 1812: Neglected by History," *Pull Together: Newsletter of the Naval Historical Foundation* 52, no. 1 (Winter 2012–13): 9–14. See also Kevin D. McCranie, *Utmost Gallantry: The US and Royal Navies at Sea in the War of 1812* (Annapolis, MD: Naval Institute Press, 2011), 45–47. Jones's *Wasp* had returned from Europe in July; he received orders from Hamilton to sail independently in search of an enemy brig off the Delaware coast but exceeded his orders by sailing into enemy waters off Halifax before returning to the Delaware River on 11 September.

29. MCdt. Jacob Jones to Hamilton, 24 Nov. 1812, in *Naval War*, 1:580–83.

30. Capt. James Lawrence to Secretary William Jones, 19 Mar. 1813, in *Naval War*, 2:70–71.

31. Journal of Midn. David Feltus, USS *Essex*, 12 Dec. 1812, in *Naval War*, 1:626–27.

32. David F. Long, *Nothing Too Daring: A Biography of Commodore David Porter, 1780–1843* (Annapolis, MD: Naval Institute Press, 1970), 76–77.

33. Rodgers to Hamilton, 17 Oct. 1812, in *Naval War*, 1:535–36. See also John H. Schroeder, *Commodore John Rodgers: Paragon of the Early American Navy* (Gainesville: University Press of Florida, 2006), 119–20.

34. Rodgers to Hamilton, 4 Sept. 1812, and Rodgers to Hamilton, 2 Jan. 1813, in *Naval War*, 1:450–51 and 2:5–6.

35. First Secretary of the Admiralty John W. Croker to Station Commanders in Chief, circular, 10 July 1813, in *Naval War*, 2:183–84.

36. Lt. Glen Drayton to Hamilton, 8 Feb. 1813, in *Naval War*, 2:41–43 and 43n. After his brig's capture, MCdt. Reed died of illness while in captivity in Jamaica.

37. John R. Elting, *Amateurs to Arms! A Military History of the War of 1812* (1991; reprint, New York: Da Capo, 1995), 21–54.

38. Lt. Melancthon Woolsey to Hamilton, 26 June and 4 July 1812, in *Naval War*, 1:277–81.

39. Lt. Col. A. H. Pye to Gov. Gen. George Prevost, Report of the Provincial Marine, 7 Dec. 1811, in *Naval War*, 1:268–73.

40. Gov. Tompkins to Navy Agent John Bullus, 13 July 1812, and Bullus to Hamilton, 16 July 1812, in *Naval War*, 1:281–83.

41. Hamilton to Capt. Isaac Chauncey, 31 Aug. 1812, in *Naval War*, 1:296–301.

42. Woolsey to Chauncey, 5 Sept. 1812, in *Naval War*, 1:305.

43. Purser Samuel Anderson to Hamilton, 8 Oct. 1812, in *Naval War*, 1:322–24; Peter l. Bernstein, *The Wedding of the Waters: The Erie Canal and the Making of a Great Nation* (New York: Norton, 2005), 174–79.

44. Lt. Thomas Macdonough to Hamilton, 20 Dec. 1812, in *Naval War*, 1:370–71.

45. On 3 April 1809 Hull wrote Secretary of War William Eustis recommending that the United States build "armed vessels" on Lake Erie. Lt. Col. James Grant Forbes, *Report of the Trial of Brig. General William Hull commanding the Northwestern Army of the United States by a Court Martial held at Albany on Monday 3rd January 1814 and Succeeding Days, taken by Lt. Col. James Grant Forbes* (New York, 1814), app. 1, pp. 28–29.

46. Lt. Jesse Elliott to Hamilton, 9 Oct. 1812, in *Naval War*, 1:328–31; MGen. Isaac Brock to Prevost, 11 Oct. 1812, in *Naval War*, 1:331–33.

47. Chauncey to Hamilton, 6, 13, and 17 Nov. 1812, in *Naval War*, 1:343–51.

48. Hamilton to Burwell Bassett, 13 Nov. 1812, in *Naval War*, 1:570–77; Capt. Charles Stewart to Hamilton, 12 Nov. 1812, *American State Papers: Naval Affairs*, 1:278–79.

49. McKee, *Gentlemanly and Honorable Profession*, 10–11.

50. J. C. A. Stagg et al., eds., *The Papers of James Madison, Presidential Series*, vol. 5, *10 July 1812–7 February 1813* (Charlottesville: University of Virginia Press, 2004), 534–35 and 535n1.

Chapter 3 · William Jones's Challenge: A Two-Front Naval War

1. Secretary of the Treasury Albert Gallatin to James Madison, 7 Jan. 1813, in *The Papers of James Madison, Presidential Series*, ed. J. C. Stagg et al., vol. 5, *10 July 1812–7 February 1813* (Charlottesville: University of Virginia Press, 2004), 557–58 and 558n1.

2. Jones and Clark Papers, 1784–1816, American Business Records, Historical Society of Pennsylvania, Philadelphia.

3. "Notes made by Secretary of the Navy Jones, . . . ," 28 Feb. 1813, William Jones Papers, U. C. Smith Collection, Historical Society of Pennsylvania; William S. Dudley, ed., *The Naval War of 1812: A Documentary History*, 4 vols. (Washington, DC: GPO, 1985–2021), 2:54–55 and 54n1 (duties of the chief clerk), hereafter cited as *Naval War*.

4. Benjamin Homans to Secretary William Jones, late March 1813, in *Naval War*, 2:55–56.

5. Lt. Charles Morris to Congressman Langdon Cheves, 9 Jan. 1813, in *Naval War*, 2:20–24.

6. Jones to Congressman Burwell Bassett, 2 Feb. 1813, in *Naval War*, 2:24–25.

7. William Jones to Eleanor Jones, 23 Jan. 1813, William Jones Papers, in *Naval War*, 2:34–35.

8. To James Madison from MGen. David Mead, Pennsylvania Militia, 29 Aug. 1812, Founders Online, National Archives, https://founders.archives.gov/Madison/03-05-02-0166, originally published in Stagg et al., *Papers of James Madison, Presidential Series*, 5:219–21.

9. Commo. Isaac Chauncey to Secretary Paul Hamilton, 1 Jan. 1813, in *Naval War*, 2:406–7.

10. Denys W. Knoll, *Battle of Lake Erie: Building the Fleet in the Wilderness* (Washington, DC: Naval Historical Foundation, 1979), 6–20.

11. Chauncey to Hamilton, 8 Jan. 1813, and Chauncey to Lt. John Pettigrew, 9 Jan. 1813, in *Naval War*, 2:407–10 and 410–11.

12. Chauncey to Secretary William Jones, 20 and 21 Jan. 1813, in *Naval War*, 2:417–19.

13. John R. Grodzinski, *Defender of Canada: Sir George Prevost and the War of 1812* (Norman: University of Oklahoma Press, 2013), 10–25.

14. Grodzinski, *Defender of Canada*, 50–56.

15. Lt. Col. A. H. Pye to Gov. Gen. George Prevost, Report of the Provincial Marine, 7 Dec. 1811, in *Naval War*, 1:268–73.

16. Patrick A. Wilder, *The Battle of Sackett's Harbour, 1813* (Baltimore: Nautical & Aviation Publishing, 1994), 17–18.

17. Lt. Melancthon Woolsey to Hamilton, 25 Aug. and 5 Sept. 1812, in *Naval War*, 1:295, 305 (quotation).

18. *Madison*, launched 26 November 1812, measured keel 112', beam 32'6", and hold 11'6", displaced 580 tons, and carried twenty-four 32-pounder carronades.

19. Grodzinski, *Defender of Canada*, 95–97; Frederick C. Drake, "Commodore Sir James Lucas Yeo and Governor General George Prevost: A Study in Command Relations, 1813–1814," in *New Interpretations in Naval History: Selected Papers from the Eighth Naval History Symposium*, ed. William B. Cogar (Annapolis, MD: Naval Institute Press, 1989), 156–57.

20. Robert Malcomson and Thomas Malcomson, *HMS Detroit: The Battle for Lake Erie* (St. Catherine's, ON: Vanwall, 1990), 20–28.

21. MCdt. O. H. Perry to Hamilton, 28 Nov. 1812, in *Naval War*, 1:354.

22. Chauncey to Perry, 20 Jan. 1813, in *Naval War*, 2:422.

23. Chauncey to Jones, 21 Jan. and 18 Mar. 1813, in *Naval War*, 2:218 and 431–32.

24. Grodzinski, *Defender of Canada*, 110.

25. Grodzinski, *Defender of Canada*, 100–106.

26. Jones to Chauncey, 8 Apr. 1813, in *Naval War*, 2:433–35.

27. Chauncey to Jones, 16 Feb. 1813, Chauncey to Noah Brown, 18 Feb. 1813, and Chauncey to Jones, 22 Feb. 1813, in *Naval War*, 2:424–30.

28. Chauncey to Jones, 29 May 1813, and Perry to Chauncey, 12 June 1813, in *Naval War*, 2:479–80.

29. Commo. O. H. Perry to Jones, 19 June 1813, in *Naval War*, 2:481–82; David Curtis Skaggs, *Oliver Hazard Perry: Honor, Courage, and Patriotism in the Early U.S. Navy* (Annapolis, MD: Naval Institute Press, 2006), 59–77.

30. Skaggs, *Oliver Hazard Perry*, 84–85.

31. Perry to Chauncey, 27 July 1813, in *Naval War*, 2:529–30.

32. Chauncey to Perry, 30 July 1813, in *Naval War*, 2:530–31.

33. Jones to Perry, 18 Aug. 1813, in *Naval War*, 2:533–34.

34. David Curtis Skaggs and Gerard T. Altoff, *A Signal Victory: The Lake Erie Campaign, 1812–1813* (Annapolis, MD: Naval Institute Press, 1997), 85–86.

35. MGen. Procter to Noah Freer, British Military Secretary (to Gov. Gen. Prevost), 6 Sept. 1813, in *Naval War*, 2:554; Skaggs and Altoff, *Signal Victory*, 108.

36. Prevost to Commo. Robert Barclay, 21 July 1813, in *Naval War*, 2:545–46.

Chapter 4 · From Lake Erie to Lake Huron

1. David Curtis Skaggs, "Joint Operations during the Detroit–Lake Erie Campaign," in *New Interpretations in Naval History: Selected Papers from the Eighth Naval History Symposium*, ed. William B. Cogar (Annapolis, MD: Naval Institute Press, 1989), 126–29. Skaggs states that it is reasonable to credit the army with providing roughly 40 percent of Perry's sailors and marines.

2. David Curtis Skaggs and Gerald T. Altoff, *A Signal Victory: The Lake Erie Campaign, 1812–1813* (Annapolis, MD: Naval Institute Press, 1997), 101–3.

3. Usher Parsons, *Surgeon of the Lakes: The Diary of Dr. Usher Parsons, 1812–1814*, ed. John C. Fredriksen (Erie, PA: Erie County Historical Society, 2000), xv.

4. Parsons, *Surgeon of the Lakes*, 40–51.

5. Commo. Robert Barclay to MGen. Procter, 9 Aug. 1813, in *The Naval War of 1812: A Documentary History*, ed. William S. Dudley, 4 vols. (Washington, DC: GPO, 1985–2021), 2:547–48, hereafter cited as *Naval War*; Robert Malcomson and Thomas Malcomson, *HMS Detroit: The Battle for Lake Erie* (St. Catherine's, ON: Vanwall, 1990), 87.

6. Spencer Tucker, *Arming the Fleet: U.S. Navy Ordnance in the Muzzle-Loading Era* (Annapolis, MD: Naval Institute Press, 1989), 124–27.

7. The question why Master Commandant Elliott's *Niagara* did not closely engage *Queen Charlotte*, his assigned opponent, has been fiercely argued for two hundred years. Perry at first praised his second-in-command for assisting in the battle by bringing the smaller schooners into action but overlooked Elliott's failure to bring up *Niagara* to support Perry's *Lawrence*. Elliott's supporters later argued that Perry's orders for his commanders to keep vessels in strict line of battle order took precedence. Perry's friends and shipmates maintained that Elliott purposely delayed, taking advantage of *Lawrence*'s weakened condition, hoping for an opportunity to save the day by moving into battle at the last moment and gain credit for the victory. The controversy ultimately divided the officer corps into two camps and indirectly led to the 1819 duel between Stephen Decatur Jr. and Captain James Barron. Decatur had been a close friend of Perry's; Elliott supported the disgraced Barron and was his second in the duel. It seems that Elliott had transferred his hate

from Perry to Decatur for taking Perry's side and for Decatur's role in Barron's court-martial in 1807. See David Curtis Skaggs, *Oliver Hazard Perry: Honor, Courage, and Patriotism in the Early U.S. Navy* (Annapolis, MD: Naval Institute Press, 2006), 122–42 and 218–44; and Skaggs and Altoff, *Signal Victory*, 137–58.

8. Usher Parsons, MD, *The Battle of Lake Erie: A Discourse, delivered before the Rhode Island Historical Society* (Providence, RI: Benjamin T. Albro, 1852).

9. Malcomson and Malcomson, *HMS* Detroit, 113; Skaggs and Altoff, *Signal Victory*, 151–52.

10. The name *Durham boat* became associated with this boat type because of its use by the Durham Ironworks, of Durham, Pennsylvania, for hauling freight on the Delaware River. In Canada, such boats were more commonly referred to with the French word *bateau*, plural *bateaux*. In general use on the Great Lakes and the St. Lawrence and Mohawk Rivers, they varied in size and shape depending on local custom, but normally they were about 30 feet in length, 8 feet in breadth, flat-bottomed, with a shallow draft, and straight-sided except for curvature where the sides met at the stem and stern. They were used for heavy freight and could carry a number of men when necessary, but they usually had a crew of three. They were often named for places where they were used, such as Schenectady (NY) Boats.

11. Commo. O. H. Perry to Secretary William Jones, [28 Sept. 1813], [29 Sept. 1813], and 7 Oct. 1813, in *Naval War*, 2:569–70; John R. Elting, *Amateurs to Arms! A Military History of the War of 1812* (1991; reprint, New York: Da Capo, 1995), 111–12; Skaggs, *Oliver Hazard Perry*, 128–29.

12. Jones to Perry, 29 Sept. 1813, in *Naval War*, 2:577.

13. Commo. Isaac Chauncey to Jones, 13 Oct. 1813, in *Naval War*, 2:578–79.

14. Capt. Jesse Elliott to Jones, 5 Jan. 1814, in *Naval War*, 3:373–74. Here Elliott provides a description of what happened: "On the morning of the 29th [Dec.] the Enemy . . . 2000 strong, crossed the Niagara river at the mouth of Scigocerdus Creek at Buffalo (one mile below Black Rock) and with little opposition marched to the Village of Buffalo, succeeded in taking it from the Militia and at 8 in the morning committed it to flames, together with two of the prize vessels, the *Little Belt* and *Chippawa*, and the sloop *Trippe* that had driven on shore some time previous in a gale of wind. LT [John] Packet with 12 men whom I had left in charge of these vessels for the purpose of securing the rigging and other apparatus, have succeeded in effecting their escape, and I expect will be here [Erie] in the morning."

15. Commo. Sir James Yeo to Gov. Gen. Prevost, 11 Dec.1813, in *Select British Documents of the Canadian War of 1812*, ed. William Wood, 3 vols. (Toronto: Champlain Society, 1920), 3, pt. 1:33–35.

16. Lt. Gen. Gordon Drummond to Prevost, 21 Jan. 1814, in *Naval War*, 3:375–76.

17. Drummond to Prevost, 3 Feb. 1814, in *Naval War*, 3:378.

18. Prevost to Drummond, 8 Jan. 1814, in *Naval War*, 3:379–81.

19. Drummond to Prevost, 28 Jan. 1814, in *Naval War*, 3:382–83.

20. Lt. Col. Ralph H. Bruyeres, Royal Engineers, to Prevost, 23 Jan. 1814, and Capt. Ralph Bullock, British Army, to Captain Robert Loring, British Army, 26 Feb. 1814, in *Naval War*, 3:382–84.

21. Chauncey to Elliott, 1 Apr. 1814, in *Naval War*, 3:417–18.

22. Skaggs and Altoff, *Signal Victory*, 167–70.

23. Commo. Arthur Sinclair to Jones, 27 Apr., 2 May, and 6 May 1814, in *Naval War*, 3:449–51, 453–57. These letters indicate that Elliott was out of his depth in commanding a

naval station; he was better suited to serving as a senior lieutenant carrying out a commander's orders, as had been the case when he worked under Chauncey on Lake Ontario.

24. Jones to Sinclair, 7 Apr. 1814, in *Naval War*, 3:419–20.

25. Parsons, *Surgeon of the Lakes*, 65. Purser Hambleton departed 8 March 1814 for leave and later joined Perry's new ship the frigate USS *Java* then under construction at Baltimore.

26. Sinclair to Jones, 2 May 1814, in *Naval War*, 3:452–53.

27. Secretary of War John Armstrong to James Madison, 1 May 1814, in *Naval War*, 3:459.

28. Sinclair to Jones, 27 May 1814, in *Naval War*, 3:503–4.

29. Jones to Sinclair, 1 June 1814, in *Naval War*, 3:513–14.

30. Col. Thomas Talbot, Middlesex Militia, to MGen. Phineas Riall, British Army, 16 May 1814, in *Naval War*, 3:484–85.

31. Col. John B. Campbell to Armstrong, 18 May 1814, in *Naval War*, 3:486–87.

32. Donald E. Graves, *And All Their Glory Past: Fort Erie, Plattsburgh, and the Final Battles in the North, 1814* (Montreal: Robin Brass Studio, 2013), 297–98; George F. G. Stanley, *The War of 1812: Land Operations* (Ottawa: Macmillan, 1983), 279–80; Ernest A. Cruickshank, "The County of Norfolk in the War of 1812," in *The Defended Border*, ed. Morris Maslow and Wesley B. Turner (Toronto: Macmillan, 1964), 233–35: "Mathias Steele, who was agent for Col. Nichol, made an affidavit in which he stated that altogether twenty dwelling houses, three flour mills, three saw mills, three distilleries, twelve barns, and other buildings were destroyed by the invaders and that they shot all the cows and hogs they could find, leaving their bodies to rot on the ground" (234).

33. Remaining at Erie, under the command of Lt. Edmund P. Kennedy, were the vessels *Porcupine, Somers, Amelia, Lady Prevost*, and the unrepaired prizes *Detroit* and *Queen Charlotte*.

34. Surgeon Parsons's journal names vessels in company as of 17 July, omitting *Hunter*, and states that one of the supply vessels (probably *Hunter*) was sent back to Lake Erie. See Parsons, *Surgeon of the Lakes*, 79–83.

35. Barry Gough, *Fighting Sail on Lake Huron and Georgian Bay: The War of 1812 and Its Aftermath* (Annapolis, MD: Naval Institute Press, 2002), 88–90.

36. Lt. Col. Robert McDouall to Drummond, 17 July 1814, in *Naval War*, 3:562–63.

37. Sinclair to John H. Cocke, 3 Sept. 1814, as quoted in Parsons, *Surgeon of the Lakes*, 87n121; and Sinclair to Jones, 9 Aug. 1814, in *Naval War*, 3:568–70.

38. Elting, *Amateurs to Arms!*, 273–81.

39. Sinclair to Jones, 9 Aug. 1814, in *Naval War*, 3:568–70.

40. McDouall to Midn. Worsley, 28 July 1814, enclosed in Sinclair to Jones, 3 Sept. 1814, in *Naval War*, 3:575.

41. Sinclair to Lt. Daniel Turner, 15 Aug. 1814, in *Naval War*, 3:570–71.

42. Sinclair to Jones, 28 Oct. 1814, and Turner to Sinclair, 1 Nov. 1814, in *Naval War*, 3:646–47 and 647–48.

43. Lt. Edmund Kennedy to Jones, 8 July 1814, in *Naval War*, 3:543. Kennedy enclosed a letter from General Jacob Brown stating that he had taken Fort Erie and "would wish your whole force to move down & take a position near the fort where the vessels can continue with perfect safety & form a very desirable support to our rear."

44. Jones to Kennedy, 13 July 1814, in *Naval War*, 3:544–45.

45. Jones to Kennedy, 19 July 1814, in *Naval War*, 3:545–46.

46. Maj. Gen. Brown to Armstrong, 25 July 1814, in *Naval War*, 3:553.

47. Kennedy to Jones, 15 Aug. 1814, in *Naval War*, 3:589–90.

48. Sinclair to Jones, 5 Dec. 1814, in *Naval War*, 3:674. See also Charles E. Brodine Jr., "'A Gallant and Valuable Officer': The Naval Career of Thomas Holdup Stevens, 1809–1841," in *The Battle of Lake Erie and Its Aftermath: A Reassessment*, ed. David Curtis Skaggs (Kent, OH: Kent State University Press, 2013), 177–216, 189.

Chapter 5 · Sailors, Privateers, and Munitions

1. Nicole Eustace, *1812: War and the Passions of Patriotism* (Philadelphia: University of Pennsylvania Press, 2012), 36–39.

2. Capt. Stephen Decatur Jr. to Secretary William Jones, 18 Feb. 1813, in *The Naval War of 1812: A Documentary History*, ed. William S. Dudley, 4 vols. (Washington, DC: GPO, 1985–2021), 2:428–29, hereafter cited as *Naval War*. Decatur was evidently writing on behalf of William Henry Allen, commander of the *Argus*. Decatur had known Allen from their service in the Mediterranean, and Allen had served as a lieutenant on the frigate *United States* under Decatur's command. Decatur, in effect, became Allen's patron and mentor, and by writing to Jones he was acting in Allen's best interest. See Ira Dye, *The Fatal Cruise of the* Argus: *Two Captains in the War of 1812* (Annapolis, MD: Naval Institute Press, 1994), 113–19.

3. The brig *Argus* departed New York for European waters on 18 June 1813. Despite having a relatively new crew, Allen made a swift voyage to France carrying Minister to France William H. Crawford. He carried out a spectacular series of captures before being defeated in battle by HM sloop of war *Pelican* on 14 August.

4. Commo. Isaac Chauncey to Jones, 18 Mar. 1813, in *Naval War*, 2:429.

5. Commo. William Bainbridge to Jones, 27 Apr. 1813, in *Naval War*, 2:429–30.

6. Linda Maloney, *The Captain from Connecticut: The Life and Naval Times of Isaac Hull* (Boston: Northeastern University Press, 1986), 33–34.

7. *Annals of Congress*, 4th Cong., 2nd sess., 229–30; Henry Adams, *The Life of Albert Gallatin* (Philadelphia: J. B. Lippincott, 1880), 170.

8. Faye M. Kert, *Privateering: Patriotism and Profits in the War of 1812* (Baltimore: Johns Hopkins University Press, 2015), 80 (table 3.2), 149–56 (appendix). Kert advises that sources and dates are incomplete.

9. Kert, *Privateering*, 104–6, 197; Ron Joy, *Dartmoor Prison: A Complete Illustrated History*, 2 vols. (Devon, UK: Halsgrove, 2002); Brian Cuthbertson, *Melville Prison and Deadman's Island* (Halifax, NS: Formac, 2009).

10. Jerome R. Garitee, *The Republic's Private Navy: The American Privateering Business as Practiced by Baltimore during the War of 1812* (Middletown, CT: Wesleyan University Press, 1977).

11. An Act Concerning Letters of Marque, Prizes, and Prize Goods, 26 June 1812, in *Naval War*, 1:169–70.

12. MCdt. Oliver H. Perry to Secretary of the Navy Paul Hamilton, 3 Sept. 1812, in *Naval War*, 1:447–49.

13. *Liverpool Packet*, formerly a slave-trading vessel named *Black Joke*, had been captured by the British in 1811 for breaking anti-slavery laws. See Kert, *Privateering*, 113–17.

14. Testimony of George W. Burbank, 6 Mar. 1813, Marine Barracks, Charlestown Navy Yard, in *Naval War*, 2:33–34.

15. The name Bellona was not unusual for a powder manufacturer. Bellona was the name of the Roman goddess of war and over the centuries was used in many different contexts in the literary arts and sculpture. Thus, the naming of the Bellona Powder Works in Maryland follows this tradition, as did the one in New Jersey.

16. After a brief career as one of the proprietors of the Bellona Powder Mill in Belleville, New Jersey, John Pine Decatur returned to the military. He was commissioned as a captain of the Fifth Company of the Essex Squadron of Cavalry on 11 May 1812 and eventually rose to the rank of lieutenant colonel, although he finished the War of 1812 as a major. Decatur continued his career in the navy, serving as naval storekeeper in the Brooklyn and Portsmouth navy yards.

17. "The Irish and the Powder Mill," *The Irish of Belleville, New Jersey*, http// irishofbellville.blogspot.com/2015/06.

18. Kim Burdick, "Gunpowder Industry," The Encyclopedia of Greater Philadelphia, http://philadelphiaencyclopedia.org/archive/gunpowder-industry/.

19. "Baltimore Bellona Gunpowder Manufactory. The proprietors have commenced manufacturing and offer for sale Gunpowder of a superior quality, and refined Saltpetre. LEVERING," *Federal Gazette*, 5 Dec. 1801.

20. An Act to Incorporate the Bellona Gunpowder Company of Maryland, *Archives of Maryland*, vol. 192, *1799–1819* (1820), pp. 1625–26, Maryland State Archives, Annapolis; *Maryland Gazette*, 13 June 1810; *Baltimore Patriot*, 6 June 1816.

21. Scott Sheads, "Baltimore Bellona Gunpowder Manufactory (1801–1856)," *Maryland in the War of 1812* (blog), https://Maryland1812.wordpress.com/category/manufactories; Daniel D. Hartzler, *Arms Makers of Maryland* (York, PA: George Shumway, 1977).

22. Arlan K. Gilbert, "Gunpowder Production in Post-Revolutionary Maryland," *Maryland Historical Magazine* 52, no. 3 (1957): 187–202.

23. Spencer Tucker, *Arming the Fleet: U.S. Navy Ordnance in the Muzzle-Loading Era* (Annapolis, MD: Naval Institute Press, 1989), 22–23.

24. "The powder supplied for the Navy previous and during the War was manufactured at the Baltimore mills [Bellona Gunpowder Mills], also by Decatur at Frankford [Philadelphia] and Belleville [New Jersey], and by Dr. Ewell at Washington, of the amount so manufactured we cannot form any idea." DuPont Company letterbook, 1829–31, 117, in DuPont Company Records, 1802–1902, Acc. 500, Series 1, Vol. 786, Hagley Museum, Wilmington, DE.

25. Ewell was a graduate of the University of Pennsylvania, where he specialized in chemistry. He wrote the first textbook on chemistry published in the United States, became a physician, and briefly served as an army surgeon. He resigned and gained an appointment as a naval surgeon in 1807. The public dispute with former chief clerk Charles Goldsborough over gunpowder testing led ultimately to his forced resignation from the navy in May 1813. See Harold D. Langley, *A History of Medicine in the Early U.S. Navy* (Baltimore: Johns Hopkins University Press, 1995), 210–11.

26. Thomas Ewell to James Madison, 10, 20 Jan., 15 Apr., 21 May, and 27 July 1813, Founders Online, National Archives, https://foundersarchives.gov, originally published in *The Papers of James Madison, Presidential Series*, ed. J. C. A. Stagg et al., vol. 4, *5 November 1811–8 July 1812* (Charlottesville: University of Virginia Press, 1999). President Madison did not respond to any of these letters.

27. Catalano was the Sicilian navigator who piloted Decatur's raid into Tripoli harbor in 1804, resulting in the burning of the frigate *Philadelphia*. As a reward for his services, Catalano was brought to the United States and appointed a sailing master attached to the Washington Navy Yard. He also performed duties as acting gunner of the yard, which explains why he was involved in the testing of Ewell's gunpowder.

28. Gordon S. Brown, *The Captain Who Burned His Ships: Captain Thomas Tingey, USN, 1750–1829* (Annapolis, MD: Naval Institute Press, 2011), 81–82.

29. Angelo I. George, "Central Kentucky Gunpowder Factories," *Journal of Spelean History* 20, no. 2 (Apr.–June 1986): 32–33.

30. Capt. Samuel Evans to Hamilton, 8 May 1813, in *Naval War*, 1:105–6. If left unmoved in storage for months on end, gunpowder (a combination of potassium nitrate, sulfur, and charcoal) modified itself, with the heavier potassium nitrate particles, which were 75 percent of the mixture, filtered gradually to the bottom of the container, whether a keg or a barrel. If the powder were exposed to the air or dampness, it would lose much of its power as a propellant. C. F. Eckhardt, "Charley Eckhardt's Texas," "Keep Yer Powder Dry!," *Texas Escapes Online Magazine*, www.texasescapes.com.

31. Capt. John Dent to Hamilton, 4 June 1813, in *Naval War*, 1:128–30.

32. Capt. Thomas Tingey to Hamilton, 9 July 1812, in *Naval War*, 1:188–89.

33. Bainbridge to Hamilton, 5 June 1812, in *Naval War*, 1:130.

34. General Helms, a veteran of the Revolutionary War, had been a four-term congressman from New Jersey. He was appointed navy agent in Tennessee by the Madison administration in 1811.

35. Hamilton to Gen. William Helms, 8 July 1812, and Capt. John Shaw to Hamilton, 27 Oct. 1812, in *Naval War*, 1:387 and 1:418.

36. Benjamin Homans, Memorandum for Jones, n.d., probably Mar. 1813, in *Naval War*, 2:56.

37. Tucker, *Arming the Fleet*, 25–26.

38. Brian Lavery, *Nelson's Navy: The Ships, Men, and Organization, 1793–1815* (Annapolis, MD: Naval Institute Press, 1989), 37–57.

39. When *Essex* returned from duty in the Mediterranean in 1806, she was ordered decommissioned and "laid up in ordinary" in the Washington Navy Yard along with others. In January 1809, with the Jeffersonian embargo at an end, Congress ordered the *immediate* deployment of four frigates, including *Essex*, to protect American trade. See Brown, *Captain Who Burned His Ships*, 112–13.

40. Capt. David Porter to Hamilton, 14 Oct. 1812, in *Naval War*, 1:527–28. Porter protested to Hamilton that *Essex*'s main battery was primarily dependent on carronades, for which he had developed an "insuperable dislike"; he thought *Essex* was slow for a frigate of her size. In an earlier letter to Hamilton he described the possibility of being trapped in a situation very like the one that occurred later at Valparaiso. Porter to Hamilton, 23 Sept. 1812, NA, RG 45, Captains' Letters (CL) to the Secretary of the Navy, vol. 3,

no. 68. For the reference to Captain Smith's request, see Brown, *Captain Who Burned His Ships*, 184n20.

41. Hamilton to Porter, 31 Oct. 1811, NA, RG 45, Letters Sent by the Secretary of the Navy to Officers, Ships of War, 8:54–55. See also David F. Long, *Nothing Too Daring: A Biography of Commodore David Porter, 1780–1843* (1970; reprint, Annapolis, MD: Naval Institute Press, 2014), 60–61.

42. Lt. Charles Ludlow to Hamilton, 9 July 1812, 187–88, and 29 Sept. 1812, in *Naval War*, 1:503–4.

43. Hamilton had written to Chauncey, "You are at liberty to purchase, hire or build in your discretion, such others and of such form & armament, as may in your opinion be necessary: to take from the yard under your command, from the *John Adams*, and the gunboats, cannon, carriages, shot, powder, small arms and every other munition of war . . . to order upon this [Lakes] service any of the officers or men of the *John Adams* or on the New York Station." Hamilton to Chauncey, 31 Aug. 1812, in *Naval War*, 1:297–98.

44. Thomas Tingey to Hamilton, 13 June 1812, in *Naval War*, 1:132 and n. 1.

45. Howard Chapelle, *The History of the American Sailing Navy* (New York: Bonanza Books, 1949), 282.

46. Geoffrey M. Footner, *Tidewater Triumph* (Centreville, MD: Tidewater, 1998), 84–90.

47. Secretary of War James McHenry to Capt. Samuel Nicholson, 16 Mar. 1797, James McHenry Letterbook, Papers of the War Department, 1784–1800, ardepartmentpapers .org//s/home/item/56875.

48. Tucker, *Arming the Fleet*, 60.

49. According to his biographer, Jane B. Donovan, Foxall, a devout Methodist all his life, probably was introduced to Morris through Methodist connections in the Philadelphia area. Donovan, *Henry Foxall: Industrialist, Methodist, American* (Nashville: New Room Books, 2017).

50. Tucker, *Arming the Fleet*, 61.

51. Donovan, *Henry Foxall*, 70–72. Friend's Orebank and Keep Tryst were in use producing iron as early as 1763, when they were sold to the Scottish merchant-developer John Semple. *Keep Tryst* was a Scottish variant of *Keep Trust*, his family's motto. Semple went bankrupt, and the properties ended up in the hands of the Revolutionary War general Richard Henry Lee, who eventually sold them to the government at President Jefferson's request. See David Curtis Skaggs, "John Semple and the Development of the Potomac Valley, 1750–1773," *Virginia Magazine of History and Biography* 92, no. 3 (July 1984): 282–308, which provides the larger context of colonial industry in Virginia and Maryland.

52. Donovan, *Henry Foxall*, 105–7.

53. Tucker, *Arming the Fleet*, 117–18.

54. RAdm. Cockburn to Adm. Sir John Borlase Warren, 3 May 1813, in *Naval War*, 2:341–44 and 344n1.

55. Donovan, *Henry Foxall*, 158–59.

56. Ralph Eshelman, Scott Sheads, and Donald Hickey, *The War of 1812 in the Chesapeake: A Reference Guide* (Baltimore: Johns Hopkins University Press, 2010), 104; Joshua Barney to Jones, 14 Apr. 1814, NARA, RG 45, Miscellaneous Letters Received by the Secretary of the Navy (MLR), vol. 3, no. 40.

57. Donovan, *Henry Foxall*, 147–48, 157.

Chapter 6 · The British Blockade of 1813–1814

1. Jonathan R. Dull, *The French Navy and the Seven Years' War* (Lincoln: University of Nebraska Press, 2005), 136–38, 224–26.

2. David Syrett, *The Royal Navy in European Waters during the American Revolutionary War* (Columbia: University of South Carolina Press, 1998), 166–68.

3. Nicholas A. M. Rodger, *The Command of the Ocean: A Naval History of Britain, 1649–1815* (New York: Norton, 2004), 464–65, 528–29; Brian Lavery, *Nelson's Navy: The Ships, Men, and Organization, 1793–1815* (Annapolis, MD: Naval Institute Press, 1989), 300–305.

4. Wade G. Dudley, *Splintering the Wooden Wall: The British Blockade of the United States, 1812–1815* (Annapolis, MD: Naval Institute Press, 2003), 7–34.

5. Kevin D. McCranie, *Utmost Gallantry: The U.S. and Royal Navies at Sea in the War of 1812* (Annapolis, MD: Naval Institute Press, 2011), 9–12.

6. "A list of American Privateers taken and destroyed by His Majesty's Ships and Vessels on the Halifax Station," in *The Naval War of 1812: A Documentary History*, ed. William S. Dudley, 4 vols. (Washington, DC: GPO, 1985–2021), 1:225–26, hereafter cited as *Naval War*.

7. Adm. Sir John B. Warren, RN, to John Wilson Coker, Esq., 29 Dec. 1812, in *Naval War*, 1:649–50.

8. Lords Commissioners of the Admiralty to Warren, 26 Dec. 1812, in *Naval War*, 1:633–34.

9. First Lord of the Admiralty [Robert Saunders Dundas, 2nd Viscount Melville] to Warren, 26 Mar. 1813, in *Naval War*, 2:78–79.

10. Secretary William Jones to Commo. Hugh G. Campbell, 26 Feb. 1813, in *Naval War*, 2:52–54d.

11. Capt. Jacob Lewis to Jones, 27 Feb. 1813, in *Naval War*, 2:40–41.

12. Jones to Lewis, 23 Apr. 1813, in *Naval War*, 2:106–7.

13. Jones to Nicholas Fish, 15 May 1813, in *Naval War*, 2:107–8.

14. Jones to Campbell, 20 Feb. 1813, in *Naval War*, 2:52–54.

15. Lt. Johnston Blakeley to Jones, 8 Apr. 1813, in *Naval War*, 2:88–89.

16. Jones to Sailing Master Thomas Gautier, 22 June 1813, in *Naval War*, 2:151–53.

17. Manuel Eyre to Jones, 9 May 1813, and Jones to Eyre, 12 May 1813, in *Naval War*, 2:113–20.

18. Jones to Thomas Leiper, Chairman, Philadelphia Flotilla Committee, 16 Sept. 1813, in *Naval War*, 2:232. *Northern Liberties* was apparently the brainchild of the famous Revolutionary War naval commander Gustavus Conyngham, a Philadelphia notable who was a member of the flotilla committee. The origin of the gunboat's name is that of an early (1790s) northern suburb of Philadelphia.

19. Jones to Committee of Underwriters of Baltimore, 18 Feb. 1813, in *Naval War*, 2:330–32.

20. Captain Charles Gordon to Jones, 13 Mar. 1813, in *Naval War*, 2:331–32. The tenor of Gordon's letter intimates that he wrote at the suggestion of Senator Smith, who had been given command of the defense of Baltimore by Governor Levin Winder.

21. Jones to Gordon, 15 Apr. 1813, in *Naval War*, 2:348–50.

22. Gordon to Jones, 29 May 1813, in *Naval War*, 2:351–52.

23. William L. Calderhead, "Naval Innovation in Crisis: War in the Chesapeake, 1813," *American Neptune* 36 (July 1976): 206–21.

24. Captain Joshua Barney to Jones, 4 July 1813, in *Naval War*, 2:373–76.

25. Jones to Barney, 20, 27 Aug., 2 Sept. 1813, in *Naval War*, 2:377–81.

26. Secretary of the Navy Benjamin Stoddert to the House of Representatives, 29 Dec. 1798, *American State Papers: Naval Affairs*, 1:65–66.

27. Howard Chapelle, *The History of the American Sailing Navy* (New York: Bonanza Books, 1949), 171–73; Commo. William Bainbridge to Secretary Paul Hamilton, 14 Apr. 1812, in *Naval War*, 1:91–92.

28. Hamilton to Burwell Bassett, 13 Nov. 1812, in *Naval War*, 1:571–73. Hamilton relied on Captain Charles Stewart's letter of 12 November to substantiate his argument. See Capt. Charles Stewart to Hamilton, 12 Nov. 1812, American *State Papers: Naval Affairs*, 1:278–79. This letter was cosigned by Captains Isaac Hull and Charles Morris.

29. Jones to Senator Samuel Smith, 22 Feb. 1813, in *Naval War*, 2:45. Senator Smith was then chairman of the Senate Naval Committee.

30. Jones to Commanders of Ships Now in Port Refitting, circular, 22 Feb. 1813, in *Naval War*, 2:48.

31. Richard Eddy, "Defended by an Adequate Power: Joshua Humphreys and the 74-Gun Ships of 1799," *American Neptune* 51, no. 3 (Summer 1991): 173–94.

32. Jones to Navy Constructor William Doughty and Amos Binney, 8–9 Feb. 1813, in *Naval War*, 2:44.

33. Jones to George Harrison, 5 Mar. 1813, in *Naval War*, 2:46. The nautical phrase "to a cleat" means in landsmen's language "to the last inch," a cleat being a device for securing a line.

34. Linda Maloney, *The Captain from Connecticut: The Life and Naval Times of Isaac Hull* (Boston: Northeastern University Press, 1986), 214–15.

35. Virginia S. Wood, *Live Oaking: Southern Timber for Tall Ships* (Boston: Northeastern University Press, 1981), 24–25.

36. Wood, *Live Oaking*, 40–43.

37. Jones to Capt. Isaac Hull, 30 Apr. 1813, in *Naval War*, 2:94–95. As Jones wrote, "I cannot but express my regret that so great a deficiency in the timber at Portsmouth should be discovered at this late period, particularly as the transportation by water is almost entirely cut off by the enemy."

38. Maloney, *Captain from Connecticut*, 215.

39. Jones to Hull, 10 Aug. 1813, in *Naval War*, 2:196–97.

40. Jones to Bainbridge, 28 Apr. 1813, in *Naval War*, 2:93–94; Maloney, *Captain from Connecticut*, 213–14.

41. Hull to Jones, 3 Nov. 1813, in *Naval War*, 2:268–69.

42. Maloney, *Captain from Connecticut*, 230–31.

43. Lt. Edward McCall to Hull, 7 Sept. 1813, in *Naval War*, 2:235–37; Joshua Smith, *Battle for the Bay: The Naval War of 1812* (Fredericton, NB: Goose Lane Editions, 2011), 75–91.

44. McCranie, *Utmost Gallantry*, 141–42, 305n43; William M. P. Dunne, "'The Inglorious First of June': Commodore Stephen Decatur on Long Island Sound, 1813," *Long Island Historical Journal* 2, no. 2 (Spring 1990): 201–20.

45. Commo. Stephen Decatur Jr. to Hamilton, 28 Dec. 1812, in *Naval War*, 1:638.

46. Warren to Lords Commissioners of the Admiralty, 11 Nov. 1812, in *Naval War*, 1:566–69.

47. Donald R. Hickey, *The War of 1812: A Forgotten Conflict*, Bicentennial Edition (Urbana: University of Illinois Press, 2012), 113–14.

48. The licenses were called "Sidmouths" after the British prime minister and chancellor of the exchequer (1801–4) Henry Addington, 1st Viscount Sidmouth, who enacted the license system as a way to encourage neutral American trading vessels to support the British war effort against Napoleon.

49. Justice Joseph Story in The *Julia*, Appeal from the Circuit Court for the District of Massachusetts, 12 US 190; https//supreme.justia.com/cases/federal/us//12/181.

50. Jones, circular, Naval General Order, 29 July 1813, in *Naval War*, 2:205–6.

51. Secretary Hamilton sent identical letters to Commodores Rodgers, Bainbridge, and Decatur dated 9 Sept. 1812. Each commodore was to command a squadron of three vessels made up of his flagship, another frigate, and a brig. To Commodore Bainbridge were assigned Captain Porter's *Essex* and Captain Lawrence's *Hornet*. As they were in different ports, it was difficult to synchronize their movements. Porter had just returned from a cruise and needed to repair and resupply. Bainbridge ordered him to get under way as soon as possible and rendezvous with him at one of several locations.

52. David F. Long, *Nothing Too Daring: A Biography of Commodore David Porter, 1780–1843* (Annapolis, MD: Naval Institute Press, 1970), 109–74.

53. Barry Gough, *Britannia's Navy: On the West Coast of North America, 1812–1914* (Vancouver: University of British Columbia Press, 2016), 41–47.

54. Long, *Nothing Too Daring*, 164–65.

55. Commo. David Porter to Jones, in *Naval War*, 3:730–47. See also David G. Farragut, *Some Reminiscences of Early Life* (extract), in *Naval War*, 3:748–59.

Chapter 7 · Managing the Navy Department

1. William Jones to Burwell Bassett, Chair, Naval Committee, House of Representatives, 4 Feb. 1813, *American State Papers: Naval Affairs*, 1:285–86.

2. Instructions from the Secretary of War to the Agents, Superintendents, Constructors, and Clerks of the Yards, for building the frigates of the United States, 27 Dec. 1794, *American State Papers: Naval Affairs*, 1:7, www.memory.loc.gov.

3. Christopher McKee, *A Gentlemanly and Honorable Profession: The Creation of the U.S. Naval Officer Corps, 1794–1815* (Annapolis, MD: Naval Institute Press,1991), 174–77.

4. Leonard D. White, *The Jeffersonians: A Study in Administrative History, 1801–1829* (New York: Macmillan, 1956), 290–92; Capt. Edward Preble to Joseph Barnes, US Consul, Naples, 1 June 1804, in US Office of Naval Records and Library, *Naval Documents related to the United States Wars with the Barbary Powers: Naval Operations Including Diplomatic Background from 1785 Through 1807*, ed. Dudley W. Knox, 6 vols. (Washington, DC: GPO, 1939–44), 4:140–41, hereafter cited as Knox, *Naval Documents related to the United States Wars with the Barbary Powers*. Preble had named Abraham Gibbs, John Broadbent, and George Dyson as navy agents at Palermo, Messina, and Syracuse and requested that Consul Barnes name these merchants as vice consuls. He stated, "The above-named agents whether

they are consuls or not, will receive consignments of every American cargo, and all the business of the navy department."

5. Preble, Order Book, May 1803–June 1805, Library of Congress, as printed in Knox, *Naval Documents related to the United States Wars with the Barbary Powers*, 4:122.

6. *Documents Relative to the Investigation, by Order of the Secretary of the Navy, of the Official Conduct of Amos Binney, United States Navy Agent at Boston, upon the Charges made by Lieutenant Joel Abbot and Others. Published by the Accused* (Boston, 1822), 60–61. See William S. Dudley, ed., *The Naval War of 1812: A Documentary History*, 4 vols. (Washington, DC: GPO, 1985–2021), 1:466, hereafter cited as *Naval War*.

7. McKee, *Gentlemanly and Honorable Profession*, 350–71.

8. Samuel Brown Papers, 1797–1805, Account Book, 18 June 1803, Massachusetts Historical Society, Boston, http://www.captainsclerk.info/lucky%/bag/bag/html./. Samuel Brown (1753–1825) was a prominent Boston merchant during the late eighteenth and early nineteenth centuries who dealt with navy agents regarding products and services needed by the navy's ships moored or under repair in Boston.

9. US Naval Institute staff, *Naval Regulations of 1802* (Annapolis, MD: Naval Institute Press, 1970), 25–27. This edition, embellished with notes by Professor H. R. Skallerup, is based on an original used by Commodore Edward Preble, now in the Nimitz Library, US Naval Academy.

10. Knox, *Naval Documents related to the United States Wars with the Barbary Powers*, 3:40.

11. Commo. Rodgers to Jones, 2 Jan. 1813, in *Naval War*, 2:5.

12. Capt. Stephen Decatur to Jones, 10 Mar. 1813, in *Naval War*, 2:51–52.

13. David F. Long, *Sailor Diplomat: A Biography of Commodore James Biddle, 1783–1848* (Annapolis, MD: Naval Institute Press, 1983), 50–51. Tristan da Cunha is a remote island group about midway between Capetown, South Africa, and Uruguay on about the same latitude. The schooner *Tom Bowline*, commanded by Lieutenant B. V. Hoffman, had been purchased for the navy in Portsmouth, New Hampshire, in late 1814 in preparation for *Hornet* and *Peacock*'s cruise to the East Indies.

14. Capt. James Lawrence to Jones, 19 Mar. 1813, in *Naval War*, 2:70–72.

15. Adm. Albert Gleaves, *James Lawrence, Captain, United States Navy, Commander of the Chesapeake* (New York: Dutton, 1904). Gleaves reveals that Lawrence, whose wife was pregnant and living in Massachusetts, would have much preferred command of *Constitution*, which was then refitting and unlikely to depart Boston until late 1813. Instead, Lawrence felt he had to accept command of *Chesapeake*, whose refit was nearly complete, even though he had enjoyed only about two months' duty ashore.

16. Jones to MCdt. William Crane, 16 Apr. 1813, in *Naval War*, 2:103–4.

17. Frederick C. Leiner, "The Squadron Commander's Share: Decatur vs. Chew and the Prize Money for the *Chesapeake*'s First War of 1812 Cruise," *Journal of Military History* 73 (Jan. 2009): 69–82.

18. Jones to Commanders of Ships now in Port Refitting, circular, 22 Feb. 1813, in *Naval War*, 2:48. Jones stated: "Our great inferiority of naval strength does not permit us to meet them [the blockaders] on this ground without hazarding the precious germ of our national glory—we have however the means of creating a powerful diversion, and of

turning the scale of annoyance against the enemy. It is therefore intended to dispatch all our public ships, now in port, as soon as possible, in such positions as may be adapted to destroy the commerce of the enemy."

19. Capt. P. B. V. Broke to Capt. Thomas Bladen Capel, Senior Naval Officer, Halifax, 6 June 1813, and Lt. George Budd to Jones, 15 June 1813, in *Naval War*, 2:126–34.

20. Jones to William Bainbridge, 30 June 1813; Bainbridge to Jones, 16 July 1813; and Jones to Bainbridge, 1 Aug. 1813, in *Naval War*, 2:164–67.

21. Jones, circular, 22 Feb. 1813, in *Naval War*, 2:48–49.

22. William M. P. Dunne, "'The Inglorious First of June': Commodore Stephen Decatur on Long Island Sound, 1813," *Long Island Historical Journal* 2, no. 2 (Spring 1990): 201–20; David Syrett, *Admiral Lord Howe: A Biography* (Annapolis, MD: Naval Institute Press, 2006), 133–39.

23. Journal of Minister to France William H. Crawford, in *Naval War*, 2:217–19.

24. Kevin D. McCranie, *Utmost Gallantry: The U.S. and Royal Navies at Sea in the War of 1812* (Annapolis, MD: Naval Institute Press, 2011), 130–37.

25. Jones to William Henry Allen, 5 June 1813, in *Naval War*, 2:141–42.

26. Ira Dye, *The Fatal Cruise of the* Argus: *Two Captains in the War of 1812* (Annapolis, MD: Naval Institute Press, 1994), 276–90. Sources disagree on the number of ships *Argus* stopped or captured. I have accepted the number 19 as stated in *Naval War*, 2:217; Dye states 20, but his text names only 19, and McCranie states 21 but names only 9.

27. *Naval Regulations issued by Command of the President of the United States of America, January 25, 1802* (1802; reprint, Annapolis: Naval Institute Press, 1970), 16–17.

28. Journal of James Inderwick, 12–14 Aug. 1813, in *Naval War*, 2:220–22. Lieutenant Allen was not doing well after his amputation. Dr. Inderwick requested assistance from Dr. Magrath, the head surgeon at Mill Prison Hospital, in Plymouth. Magrath ordered the lieutenant taken to the hospital, but his wound was not healing and had become septic. Allen became restless, delirious, went into shock, and died the night of 18 August 1813. He was buried in Plymouth with full military honors.

29. Dye, *Fatal Cruise of the* Argus, 280.

Chapter 8 · Naval Innovation and Inventions

1. Nicole Eustace, *1812: War and the Passions of Patriotism* (Philadelphia: University of Pennsylvania Press, 2012), 115–21.

2. Fulton received financial and other assistance in France from Barlow, who had previously served as consul to the Barbary States, in 1795–1797. http://www.unc.edu/depts /diplomat/item2012/01/06/ca/sommers_barlow.html; Peter P. Hill, *Joel Barlow: Diplomat and Nation Builder* (Washington, DC: Potomac Books, 2013); Cynthia Owen Philip, *Robert Fulton: A Biography* (New York: Franklin Watts, 1985), 85–137.

3. Alex Roland, *Underwater Warfare in the Age of Sail* (Bloomington: University of Indiana Press, 1978), 114.

4. Robert Fulton to Thomas Jefferson, 28 July 1807, Founders Online, National Archives, Early Access document from the Papers of Thomas Jefferson, https:/founders .archives.gov/documents/Jefferson/99-01-02-6050.

5. Jefferson to Fulton, 16 Aug. 1807, Founders Online, National Archives, https: /founders.archives.gov/Jefferson/03-02-02-0203; Dumas Malone, *Jefferson and His Time*, vol. 5, *Jefferson the President, Second Term, 1805–1810* (Boston: Little, Brown, 1974), 451, 503–6.

6. "Use of the Torpedo in the Defense of Ports and Harbors," US Senate, 11th Cong., 2nd sess., *American State Papers: Naval Affairs*, 1:211–27; *Annals of Congress*, 11th Cong., 2nd sess., 583–84.

7. John H. Schroeder, *Commodore John Rodgers: Paragon of the Early American Navy* (Gainesville: University Press of Florida, 2006), 80–82.

8. See Paul Hamilton, "Experiments on the Practical Use of the Torpedo," in Hamilton to Joseph P. Varnum, Speaker, House of Representatives, 12 Feb. 1811, *American State Papers: Naval Affairs*, 1:234–44.

9. Robert Livingston to Secretary Paul Hamilton, 7 Dec. 1810, *American State Papers: Naval Affairs*, 1:237–39.

10. Fulton to Hamilton, 22 June 1812, in *The Naval War of 1812: A Documentary History*, ed. William S. Dudley, 4 vols. (Washington, DC: GPO, 1985–2021), 1:146–47, hereafter cited as *Naval War*.

11. Philip, *Robert Fulton*, 296.

12. *Annals of Congress*, 12th Cong., 2nd sess., 1168.

13. Fulton to William Jones, 8 May 1813, original sold at auction to unknown buyer, copy held by Donald G. Shomette. Email from Shomette to Dudley, June 25, 2018, in author's possession.

14. Philip, *Robert Fulton*, 296–97.

15. Sailing Master Elijah Mix to James Madison, 8 Apr. 1813, Founders Online, National Archives, https://founders.archives.gov/documents/Madison/03-06-02-0175; J. C. A. Stagg et al., eds., *Papers of James Madison, Presidential Series*, vol. 6, *8 February– 24 October 1813* (Charlottesville: University of Virginia Press, 2008), 182–83.

16. Jones to Capt. Charles Gordon, 7 May 1813, in *Naval War*, 2:354–55.

17. RAdm. Cockburn to Adm. James B. Warren, 16 June 1813, in *Naval War*, 2:355–56 and 356n; Roland, *Underwater Warfare in the Age of Sail*, 121.

18. Capt. Jacob Lewis to Jones, 28 June 1813, in *Naval War*, 2:161 and nn. 1 and 2.

19. Warren to John W. Croker, First Secretary of the Admiralty, 22 July 1813, and enclosure, and Capt. Thomas Hardy to Warren, 26 June 1813, in *Naval War*, 2:162–63.

20. General Order No. 87 of Admiral Sir John B. Warren, *San Domingo* in the Chesapeake, 19 July 1813, in *Naval War*, 2:164.

21. Memorandum of an Agreement between Robert Fulton and Samuel Swartwout, 22 July 1813, Gilbert H. Montague Collection of Robert Fulton Manuscripts. Manuscript Division, New York Public Library, Astor, Lenox, and Tilden Foundations.

22. Philip, *Robert Fulton*, 301–2; Commo. Stephen Decatur Jr. to Fulton, 9 Aug. 1813, in *Naval War*, 2:212.

23. James Tertius De Kay, *The Battle of Stonington: Torpedoes, Submarines, and Rockets in the War of 1812* (1990; reprint, Annapolis, MD: Naval Institute Press, 2013), 32, 81.

24. According to Commodore Decatur, Penny had been hired as a pilot to guide a group of torpedoists into the waters of Gardiner's Bay, where they planned to ambush *Ramillies* and *Orpheus*. See Decatur to Jones, 30 Sept. 1813, NA, RG 45, CL, 1813, vol. 6, no. 30; see also *Naval War*, 2:247n.

25. Adm. Sir Thomas Hardy, RN, to Maj. Benjamin Case, US Militia, commanding at Sag Harbor, Long Island, 24 Aug. 1813, in *Naval War*, 2:246–47 and 246n. This account confirms a column published in the *Easthampton Star*, 24 Sept. 1998, by Michelle Napoli, "What's in a Name, Penny's Sedge Island." See also Joshua Penny, *The Life and Adventures of Joshua Penny, a native of Southold, Long Island, Suffolk County, New York . . .* (Brooklyn, NY: Alden Spooner, 1815).

26. John Mason, son of George Mason, was a merchant and investor and had been the federal superintendent of Indian trade from 1807 to 1815. See Gerald Neuman and Charles F. Hobson, "John Marshal and the Enemy Alien: A Case Missing from the Canon," *Green Bag*, Autumn 2005, 1–2 and 2n.

27. Madison to Jones, 6 Sept. 1813, and Madison to Commissary of Prisoners John Mason, 23 Sept. 1813, in *Naval War*, 2:247–48.

28. Lewis to Jones, 20 and 28 June 1813, in *Naval War*, 2:113–14.

29. This is one of Fulton's earliest mentions of a steam-driven warship. See Fulton to Jefferson, 29 June 1813, Founders Online, National Archives, https:/founders.archives.gov /documents/Jefferson/03-06-02-0242, originally published in *The Papers of Thomas Jefferson, Retirement Series*, ed. J. Jefferson Looney, vol. 6, *March to 27 November 1813* (Princeton, NJ: Princeton University Press, 2009), 243–50.

30. Jefferson to Madison, 13 July 1813, Founders Online, National Archives, https:// founders.archives.gov/documents/Jefferson/03-06-02-0241, originally published in *Papers of Thomas Jefferson, Retirement Series*, 6:289–91.

31. Fulton to Decatur, 5 Aug. 1813, and Decatur to Fulton, 9 Aug. 1813, in *Naval War*, 2:210–12.

32. Decatur to Jones, 20 Dec. 1813, CL, NA, RG 45; Henry Adams, *History of the United States of America during the Administrations of James Madison*, vol. 2, *1809–1817*, Library of America (New York: Viking, 1986), 814; Donald R. Hickey, *The War of 1812: A Forgotten Conflict*, Bicentennial Edition (Urbana: University of Illinois Press, 2012), 264.

33. David B. Tyler, "Fulton's Steam Frigate," *American Neptune* 6 (1946): 253–74.

34. *Annals of Congress*, 13th Cong., 2nd sess., 627 and 1799–1803. Discussions were led by Senator John Gaillard, chair of the Senate Naval Committee, and Representative Lowndes, chair of the House Naval Committee. On 9 March 1814 Congress appropriated $500,000 to build, equip, and put into service floating batteries to attack enemy ships approaching the shores and waters of the United States. Ch. 21, 2 Stat. 104.

35. Tyler, "Fulton's Steam Frigate," 262–63.

36. Charles Beebe Stuart, *The Naval and Mail Steamers of the United States* (1853; reprint, Sacramento, CA: Andesite Press & Scholar Select, Creative Media Partners, 2018), 13–17.

37. Howard Chapelle, *Fulton's Steam Frigate: The Secret Weapon to End the War of 1812* (Tucson, AZ: Fireship, 2010), discusses the design history of *Demologos*. It is based on Chapelle's much earlier Paper 39, "Fulton's 'Steam Battery': Blockship and Catamaran," published in the Smithsonian Institution's National Museum of American History's Bulletin 240 (Washington, DC, 1966). In the introduction, he explains that it had been difficult to come to conclusions about *Demologos*'s design in the absence of Fulton's detailed plans. Historians and naval architects had only seen a copy of the sketch Fulton submitted to the US Patent Office and a wood engraving based on a sketch Fulton had shown to President Madison in 1813. It was only when Chapelle requested a folder of American ship

plans from the Royal Danish Archives at Copenhagen in 1960 that he found three drawings of *Demologos*, copied in 1817, along with drawings of USS *Princeton*, a screw sloop of war. From these drawings Chapelle proceeded to redraw the lines and build a model of *Demologos* for display at the Smithsonian.

38. Jones to Capt. David Porter, 8 Sept. 1814, SNL, MR II, vol. 11, NA, RG 45. Jones's order stated: "Sir, you will proceed to New York and take the command of the Steam Vessel of War now building at that place, under the direction of the Committee for Coast and Harbour defense for the Navy of the United States and expedite her equipment by all the means in your power. You will please observe that this vessel, even with the best economy will be very costly—that she is for a local and temporary purpose, and from her construction cannot be durable. Every part of her equipment will therefore be of the most plain and economical kind, & I rely upon your prudence and good management to limit the actual expenditures to that which may be required by absolute necessity."

39. Chapelle, *Fulton's Steam Frigate*, 56.

40. Stuart, *Naval and Mail Steamers of the United States*, 13–15.

41. Report of Commissioners Henry Rutgers, Samuel L. Mitchill, and Thomas Morris to Secretary of the Navy Crowninshield, 28 Dec. 1815, in Stuart, *Naval and Mail Steamers of the United States*, 155–59.

42. David F. Long, *Nothing Too Daring: A Biography of Commodore David Porter, 1780–1843* (Annapolis, MD: Naval Institute Press, 1970), 171, citing Porter to Jones, 29 Oct. 1814, NA, RG 45, CL, 1814, vol. 7, no. 37.

43. Fulton to Madison, 5 Nov. 1814, Founders Online, National Archives, https://founders.archives.gov/documents/Madison/03-08-02-0302, originally published in *The Papers of James Madison, Presidential Series*, ed. J. C. A. Stagg et al., vol. 8, *July 1814–1 February 1815* (Charlottesville: University of Virginia Press, 2015), 366–69. This letter also contains several remarkable paragraphs in which Fulton, having heard that Secretary Jones had submitted his resignation to Madison, offers himself as a successor to Jones so that he can devote his full time and the navy's resources to his projects for the period of one year. So far as is known, the president did not respond.

44. Report of Commissioners Henry Rutgers, Samuel L. Mitchill, and Thomas Morris to Secretary of the Navy Crowninshield, 28 Dec. 1815, in Stuart, *Naval and Mail Steamers of the United States*, 155–59.

45. Jones to Joseph Chambers, 27 Apr. 1814, in Tyrone Martin, "The U.S. Navy's Early Machine Guns," *Naval History Magazine* 28, no. 5 (Oct. 2014): 5.

46. Jones to Commo. Isaac Chauncey, 27 May 1814, quoted in Martin, "U.S. Navy's Early Machine Guns," 7.

47. Cdr. Charles Cunliffe Owen, RN, to Commo. Sir James Yeo, RN, 17 July 1814, in *Naval War*, 3:536–37.

48. The Chambers gun was apparently a variation of the multibarrel machine gun invented by Britain's James Wilson in 1779, manufactured by Henry Nock, and ordered for use in the Royal Navy. The "Nock guns," as they were known to Royal Navy officers, were rarely used because of the danger of muzzle flash setting off fires among highly flammable sails, rigging, and powder cartridges. The Nock gun, also known as the "volley gun," had seven barrels and fired all barrels at once with a huge recoil; the Chambers gun also had seven barrels but fired its balls in sequence.

49. Spencer Tucker, *Arming the Fleet: U.S. Navy Ordnance during the Muzzle-Loading Era* (Annapolis, MD: Naval Institute Press, 1989), 128–30. Tucker explains that the gunade was probably an amalgam of the carronade and the long gun.

50. Capt. Charles Stewart to Jones, 5 Dec. 1813, Jones to Stewart,14 Dec. 1813, and Stewart to Jones, 25 Dec. 1813, in *Naval War*, 2:292–93. There was no further correspondence on this matter.

51. Richard Paul Smyers, "Demologos—One Year Sooner," *Changing the Times*, updated 15 May 2011, http://wwwchangingthe_times.net/samples/NapWar/Demologos.htm.

52. Tucker, *Arming the Fleet*, 130.

Chapter 9 · Chauncey's War on Lake Ontario

1. James Fenimore Cooper, *Ned Myers; or, A Life Before the Mast*, ed. William S. Dudley, Classics of Naval Literature Series (Annapolis, MD: Naval Institute Press, 1989), 55–56.

2. Secretary of the Navy Hamilton to Daniel Dobbins, 15 Sept. 1812, in *The Naval War of 1812: A Documentary History*, ed. William S. Dudley, 4 vols. (Washington, DC: GPO, 1985–2021), 1:311, hereafter cited as *Naval War*.

3. Commodore Isaac Chauncey to Hamilton, 1 Dec. 1812, and enclosure, Chauncey to Major General Henry Dearborn, 30 Nov. 1812, in *Naval War*, 1:361–64.

4. Chauncey to Hamilton, 25 Dec. 1812, and 1, 8 Jan. 1813, in *Naval War*, 1:372 and 2:406–10.

5. Chauncey to Secretary of the Navy [Jones], 20 Jan. 1813, in *Naval War*, 2:417–18.

6. Robert Malcomson, *Lords of the Lake: The Naval War on Lake Ontario, 1812–1814* (Annapolis, MD: Naval Institute Press,1998), 36 and n. 28.

7. Lords Commissioners of the Admiralty to Commo. Sir James Lucas Yeo, RN, 19 Mar. 1813, and enclosure, in *Naval War*, 2:435–37. Yeo had been knighted by the prince regent of Portugal for arranging the transport of the Portuguese royal family to Brazil, and for success in attacking French Guiana, King George III had made him a Knight of the Bath.

8. Lords Commissioners of the Admiralty to Yeo, 19 Mar. 1813, in *Naval War*, 2:435–36.

9. Cooper, *Ned Myers*, 77–92. This is an "as told to" biography written by Cooper after meeting Myers by chance in New York City in 1843, thirty-seven years after they had first met as teenagers in the merchant ship *Sterling*.

10. See Theodore Roosevelt, *The Naval War of 1812* (New York: Random House, Modern Library, 1999), 137–41; Malcomson, *Lords of the Lake*, 204–7; Dudley W. Knox, *A History of the United States Navy* (New York: G. P. Putnam's Sons, 1936), 115; and John R. Elting, *Amateurs to Arms! A Military History of the War of 1812* (Chapel Hill, NC: Algonquin Books, 1991), 99–100.

11. De Watteville's regiment, a unit of about 1,455 mercenaries originally from Switzerland in British service, fought against France in the Napoleonic Wars. By the time of the War of 1812, the enlisted came from many different European countries, but the leader, Louis de Watteville, and his officers were all Swiss. Very experienced and well led, they were often used by the British as shock troops, as in the night assault against Fort Erie in August 1814. See Donald E. Graves, *And All Their Glory Past: Fort Erie, Plattsburgh, and the Final Battles in the North, 1814* (Montreal: Robin Brass Studio, 2013), 64–65, 375–76.

12. O. H. Perry to Chauncey, 27 July 1813, and Chauncey to Perry, 30 July 1813, in *Naval War*, 2:529–31.

13. Perry to William Jones, 10 Aug. 1813, and Jones to Perry, 18 Aug. 1813, in *Naval War*, 2:531–34. It is worth noting that in these urgent matters an exchange of letters between Perry and Chauncey took only three days, while an exchange of letters between Jones and Perry took eight days.

14. David C. Skaggs, *William Henry Harrison, and the Conquest of the Ohio Country: Frontier Fighting in the War of 1812* (Baltimore: Johns Hopkins University Press, 2014), 213–14.

15. By the end of 1812, Dearborn was aware that his performance had been disappointing. He wrote to President Madison to that effect, requesting that he be allowed "to retire to the shade of private life." See Dearborn to James Madison, 13 Dec. 1812, in *The Papers of James Madison, Presidential Series*, ed. J. C. A. Stagg et al., vol. 5, *10 July 1812–7 February 1813* (Charlottesville: University of Virginia Press, 2004), 503–5. Unfortunately, the president did not take the hint and retained him in service for another six months.

16. Donald R. Hickey, *The War of 1812: A Forgotten Conflict*, Bicentennial Edition (Urbana: University of Illinois Press, 2012), 141–42. Wade Hampton was a volunteer cavalry officer in South Carolina during the American Revolution. He transferred to the US Army in 1808 as a colonel and was promoted to brigadier general in 1809, when he was ordered to relieve Brigadier General James Wilkinson as commander of US Army units stationed at New Orleans. Wilkinson was accused of mismanagement when thousands of troops deserted or died of disease during his tenure. See also *American State Papers: Military Affairs*, 1:268–95; and Wilkinson to Madison, 20 Apr. 1811, in *The Papers of James Madison, Presidential Series*, ed. J. C. A. Stagg et al., vol. 3, *3 November 1810–4 November 1811* (Charlottesville: University of Virginia Press, 1996).

17. René Chartrand, "Watteville, Louis de," in *Dictionary of Canadian Biography*, accessed 15 Nov. 2018, http://www.biographi.ca/en/bio/watteville_louis_de_7E.html.

18. Donald E. Graves, *Field of Glory: The Battle of Crysler's Farm, 1813* (Montreal: Robin Brass Studio, 1999); Malcomson, *Lords of the Lake*, 212–24.

19. Yeo to Gov. Gen. Prevost, 17 Oct. 1813, in *Naval War*, 2:593.

20. Chauncey to Jones, 30 Oct. 1813, in *Naval War*, 2:594–96.

21. Chauncey to MGen. Wilkinson, 12 Nov. 1813, and Chauncey to Jones, 21 Nov. 1813, in *Naval War*, 2:597–600.

22. Chauncey to Jones, 8 Oct. 1813, in *Naval War*, 2:591.

23. Harold D. Langley, *A History of Medicine in the Early U.S. Navy* (Baltimore: Johns Hopkins University Press, 1995), 219–21. Dr. Buchanan had joined USS *Ganges* as a naval surgeon during her first cruise in the Quasi-War with France in 1798.

24. Chauncey to Jones, 7 Mar. 1814, in *Naval War*, 3:401.

25. 3 Stat. 136 (18 Apr. 1814); Chauncey to Jones, 7 Mar. 1814, and Jones to Chauncey, 18 Apr. 1814, in *Naval War*, 3:401–2.

26. Yeo to First Secretary of the Admiralty [John W. Croker], 9 May 1814, in *Naval War*, 3:477–78.

27. Lt. Gen. Gordon Drummond to Prevost, 7 May 1814, and Lt. Col. George Mitchell, USA, to MGen. Jacob Brown, USA, 8 May 1814, in *Naval War*, 3:468–70 and 474–77; Malcomson, *Lords of the Lake*, 272–73.

28. Maj. Daniel Appling, USA, to BGen. Edmond P. Gaines, USA, 30 May 1814; Cdr. Stephen Popham, RN, to Yeo, 1 June 1814; and MCdt. Melancthon Woolsey to Chauncey, 1 June 1814, in *Naval War*, 3:508–12. These letters contain the after-action reports of the leaders in the battle of Sandy Creek.

29. Captain John Smith (1780–1815) joined the navy as a midshipman from South Carolina in 1799. Though never reaching the heights of fame of some of his cohort, he served reliably and was promoted regularly during the Quasi-War with France and the First Barbary War. When *Congress* was blockaded at Portsmouth in1814, Secretary Jones gave Smith his choice of command: *Java*, under construction at Baltimore, or *Mohawk*, at Sackets Harbor. Smith was taken ill as soon as he arrived at Sackets Harbor. Jones granted his request for a change of orders and assigned him to supervise construction of the ship of the line *Franklin* at Philadelphia; however, his illness was fatal, leading to his death in August 1815 at the age of 35.

30. Brown to Chauncey, 21 June 1814, and Chauncey to Brown, 25 June 1814, in *Naval War*, 3:526–28.

31. Jones to Chauncey, 8 Apr. 1813, in *Naval War*, 2:433–34.

32. Jones to Chauncey, 20 July 1814, in *Naval War*, 3:551.

33. Brown to Secretary of War Armstrong, 7 June 1814, in *Naval War*, 3:525; Richard V. Barbuto, *Niagara, 1814: America Invades Canada* (Lawrence: University Press of Kansas, 2000), 112–14; Elting, *Amateur, to Arms!*, 181–82; Malcomson, *Lords of the Lake*, 286–87.

34. William S. Dudley, "Commodore Isaac Chauncey and U.S. Joint Operations on Lake Ontario, 1813–1814," in *New Interpretations in Naval History: Selected Papers from the Eighth Naval History Symposium*, ed. William B. Cogar (Annapolis, MD: Naval Institute Press, 1989), 139–55.

35. Jones to Chauncey, 3 Aug. 1814, in *Naval War*, 3:556–57.

36. Henry Adams, *History of the United States of American during the Administrations of James Madison*, vol. 2, *1809–1817*, Library of America (New York: Viking, 1986), 929.

37. Roosevelt, *Naval War of 1812*, 201–2.

38. Robert Malcomson, *Warships of the Great Lakes, 1754–1834* (Annapolis, MD: Naval Institute Press, 2001), 288–92.

39. Chauncey to Jones, 10 Aug. 1814, in *Naval War*, 3:585–86.

40. Curiously, of all naval historians, Theodore Roosevelt takes little notice of the 102-gun *St. Lawrence* in his *Naval War of 1812*. Considering her size and the immense efforts Commodore Yeo's command expended in constructing, manning, and arming this line-of-battle ship, Roosevelt does not even refer to her as being under construction. He mentions her presence on the lake only once, and then, mistakenly. In every other case of a potential battle or matchup he goes to much trouble detailing the number of guns, the ship tonnage, and the size of the crew of each ship. Perhaps he held it to be of no interest because *Superior* and *St. Lawrence* never met in battle. Malcomson, *Warships of the Great Lakes*, 112–16.

41. Drummond to Prevost, 15 Oct. 1814, as quoted in Malcomson, *Lords of the Lake*, 305; see also n. 68.

42. Prevost to Secretary for War and the Colonies Earl Bathurst, 18 Oct. 1814, in *Naval War*, 3:627–29. See also Malcomson, *Lords of the Lake*, 305–9.

43. Jones to Madison, 25 Apr. 1814, https://founders.archives.gov/documents/Madison /03-07-02-0394; and Madison to Jones, 26 Apr. 1814, https://founders.archives.gov /documents/Madison/03-07-02-0395.

44. Jones to Madison, 11 Sept. 1814, https://founders.archives.gov/documents/Madison /03-08-02-0816.

45. Gordon S. Brown, *The Captain Who Burned His Ships: Captain Thomas Tingey, USN, 1750–1829* (Annapolis, MD: Naval Institute Press, 2011), 129–33.

46. Jones to Madison, 26 Oct. 1814, in *Naval War*, 3:631–36.

47. Chauncey to Jones, 5 Nov. 1814, in *Naval War*, 3:637–39.

48. Jones to Chauncey, 30 Nov. 1814, in *Naval War*, 3:670–71.

Chapter 10 · Macdonough's War on Lake Champlain

1. David Curtis Skaggs, *Thomas Macdonough: Master of Command in the Early U.S. Navy* (Annapolis, MD: Naval Institute Press, 2003), 63–36.

2. Thomas Macdonough to Secretary of the Navy Hamilton, 14 and 26 Oct. 1812, in *The Naval War of 1812: A Documentary History*, ed. William S. Dudley, 4 vols. (Washington, DC: GPO, 1985–2021), 1:324–27, hereafter cited as *Naval War*.

3. From Plattsburgh, New York, Sidney Smith had begun as a midshipman on 26 July 1800 and become a lieutenant on 7 March 1807. He had served in USS *President* during the Quasi-War with France, for brief tours in *President*, *New York*, *Congress*, and *Constitution*, and in the brig (bomb ketch) *Vengeance* under Lieutenant William Lewis, in Commodore John Rodgers's Mediterranean squadron, in 1805. In 1807 he was fifth lieutenant on board *Chesapeake* during the *Chesapeake–Leopard* incident and gave testimony during the court-martial of Capt. James Barron. See US Office of Naval Records and Library, *Naval Documents related to the United States Wars with the Barbary Powers: Naval Operations Including Diplomatic Background from 1785 Through 1807*, ed. Dudley W. Knox, vol. 6 (unnumbered), *Personnel and Ships' Data, 1801–1807* (Washington, DC: GPO, 1944), www.history.navy.mil/registers-of-the-navy/1801-1807.html. See also Spencer C. Tucker and Frank T. Reuter, *Injured Honor: The Chesapeake–Leopard Affair, June 22, 1807* (Annapolis, MD: Naval Institute Press, 1996), 155.

4. Charles G. Muller, *The Proudest Day: Macdonough on Lake Champlain* (New York: John Day, 1960), 65–70.

5. Macdonough to Hamilton, 20 Dec. 1812, in *Naval War*, 1:370.

6. Allan Everest, *The War of 1812 in the Champlain Valley* (Syracuse, NY: Syracuse University Press, 1981), 147.

7. Macdonough to Secretary William Jones, 22 Jan. 1813, in *Naval War*, 2:424–25. Jones's response is briefly annotated on the reverse of the letter.

8. Everest, *War of 1812 in the Champlain Valley*, 108–9.

9. Everest, *War of 1812 in the Champlain Valley*, 109; Skaggs, *Thomas Macdonough*, 69; Muller, *Proudest Day*, 132–33.

10. Muller, *Proudest Day*, 343. Sidney Smith was promoted to the rank of master commandant on 28 February 1815 and remained on the Navy List until 1827. He died in May 1827 at age 45 in Plattsburgh, New York, while "awaiting orders." See Knox, *Naval Documents related to the United States Wars with the Barbary Powers*, vol. 6 (unnumbered), *Personnel and Ships' Data, 1801–1807*; and *Register of Officers of the U.S. Navy and Marine Corps, 1815*, www.navy.history.mil/register-of-officers/1815.html.

11. Macdonough to Jones, 4 June 1813, in *Naval War*, 2:490–91. The cylinders Macdonough requested were intended for canister shot; they were cylindrical tins filled with ball shot, which scattered on being fired.

12. Jones to Macdonough, 17 June 1813, in *Naval War*, 2:513.

13. Skaggs, *Thomas Macdonough*, 77; Everest, *War of 1812 in the Champlain Valley*, 126–27; Muller, *Proudest Day*, 150–51.

14. Macdonough to Jones, 23 Nov. 1813, and Jones to Macdonough, 7 Dec. 1813, in *Naval War*, 2:603–4.

15. Jones to Macdonough, 28 Jan. 1814, in *Naval War*, 3:393–95.

16. Macdonough to Jones, 14 May 1814, in *Naval War*, 3:480–81; Everest, *War of 1812 in the Champlain Valley*, 149–50.

17. Skaggs, *Thomas Macdonough*, 95. The term *Jonathan* was then widely used by the British military to denote an American, especially a New Englander. It is derived from a term of abuse used by Royalists against Puritan rebels during the English Civil War.

18. Cdr. Daniel Pring, RN, to Lt. Col. William Williams, British Army, 14 May 1814, in *Naval War*, 3:481–82. This letter contains Pring's after-action report and a surprisingly accurate summary of the intelligence gathered by Pring's command on the growing strength of Macdonough's squadron.

19. Macdonough to Jones, 29 May, 11 and 19 June 1814, in *Naval War*, 3:504–6.

20. H. N. Muller, "'A traitorous and diabolical Traffic': The Commerce of the Champlain and Richelieu Corridor during the War of 1812," *Vermont History* 44 (1976): 78–96.

21. Everest, *War of 1812 in the Champlain Valley*, 95; Donald E. Graves, *And All Their Glory Past: Fort Erie, Plattsburgh, and the Final Battles in the North, 1814* (Montreal: Robin Brass Studio, 2013), 371; John R. Grodzinsky, *Defender of Canada: Sir George Prevost and the War of 1812* (Norman: University of Oklahoma Press, 2013), 163; J. J. Little, *Loyalties in Conflict: A Canadian Borderland in War and Rebellion, 1812–1840* (Toronto: University of Toronto Press, 2008), 43–48.

22. Muller, *Proudest Day*, 254–56; Everest, *War of 1812 in the Champlain Valley*, 152; Skaggs, *Thomas Macdonough*, 106–7.

23. Jones to Macdonough, 5 July 1814, in *Naval War*, 3:509.

24. J. C. A. Stagg, *The War of 1812: Conflict for a Continent* (New York: Cambridge University Press, 2012), 145–46.

25. Graves, *And All Their Glory Past*, 370–71.

26. John R. Elting, *Amateurs to Arms! A Military History of the War of 1812* (1991; reprint, New York: Da Capo, 1995), 256.

27. Graves, *And All Their Glory Past*, 34.

28. Grodzinski, *Defender of Canada*, 166–67, 191, 239.

29. Graves, *And All Their Glory Past*, 368–69; Everest, *War of 1812 in the Champlain Valley*, 164–65.

30. Skaggs, *Thomas Macdonough*, 125–26, 133.

31. Macdonough to Jones, 13 Sept. 1814, and Pring to Commodore Sir James Yeo, 12 Sept. 1814, and enclosure, Lt. James Robertson to Pring, 12 Sept. 1814, in *Naval War*, 3:612–16.

32. Acting Secretary of the Navy Homans to Macdonough, 27 Dec. 1814, in *Naval War*, 3:682. In this letter Homans writes at the direction of President Madison, ordering

Macdonough to return immediately to Lake Champlain to ascertain the condition of the squadron and send any intelligence on the state of British preparations to renew hostilities.

33. Macdonough to Secretary of the Navy Crowninshield, 18 Jan. and 6 Feb. 1815, in *Naval War*, 3:684–86. Macdonough wrote that reports of British preparations to attack were untrue but that he had taken defensive measures to protect the flotilla, in any event. The winter was mild, and the lake was not completely frozen. On 6 February, he wrote that adequate men were on hand to maintain the fleet but that if an early spring operation were needed, additional officers, carpenters, sailmakers, and others would be required. He intended to proceed to the steam frigate in New York, *Demologos*, which he had been ordered to command. He respectfully requested that he not be sent back to the lake's command in the ensuing summer.

34. Skaggs, *Thomas Macdonough*, 146–47.

35. Andrew Lambert, *The Challenge: America, Britain, and the War of 1812* (London: Faber & Faber, 2012), 380–401.

36. President James Madison to Crowninshield, 23 Dec. 1814, Founders Online, National Archives, https://founders.archives.gov/documents/Madison/03-08-02-0395, originally published in *The Papers of James Madison, Presidential Series*, ed. J. C. A. Stagg et al., vol. 8, *July 1814–1 February 1815* (Charlottesville: University of Virginia Press, 2015), 464. This letter extended the invitation to serve as secretary of the navy, which Crowninshield declined. Madison must have issued a second invitation or Crowninshield quickly changed his mind and replied in another response not yet found.

Chapter 11 · In Defense of the Chesapeake Bay

1. Reginald Horsman, "Nantucket's Peace Treaty with England in 1814," *New England Quarterly* 54 (1981): 180–98; Jerry Roberts, *The British Raid on Essex: The Forgotten Battle of the War of 1812* (Middletown, CT: Wesleyan University Press, 2014); Frederick Drake, "Castine, Maine," in *The Encyclopedia of the War of 1812*, ed. David Heidler and Jeanne Heidler (Santa Barbara, CA: ABC-Clio, 1997), 84–85; Wikipedia, s.v. "The Battle of Hampden," accessed 18 Feb. 2019, en.wikipedia.org/wiki/battle_of_hampden; Bonnie Stacy, "Historical Perspective: Martha's Vineyard during the War of 1812," *Edgartown Times*, 26 June 2012.

2. John M. Hallahan, *The Battle of Craney Island: A Matter of Credit* (Winchester, VA: St. Michael's, 1986); Roger Morriss, *Cockburn and the British Navy in Transition: Admiral Sir George Cockburn, 1772–1853* (Columbia: University of South Carolina Press, 1997), 89–100; Walda DuPriest-Brandt et al., *We Are One: The War of 1812 at St. Michaels, Maryland* (St. Michaels, MD: Commissioners of St. Michaels, 2013); James Tertius De Kay, *The Battle of Stonington: Torpedoes, Submarines, and Rockets in the War of 1812* (1990; reprint, Annapolis, MD: Naval Institute Press, 2013).

3. Secretary of the Navy Jones to Acting MCdt. Joshua Barney, 2 Sept. 1813, in *The Naval War of 1812: A Documentary History*, ed. William S. Dudley, 4 vols. (Washington, DC: GPO, 1985–2021), 2:380, hereafter cited as *Naval War*.

4. Donald G. Shomette, *Flotilla: The Patuxent Naval Campaign in the War of 1812* (Baltimore: Johns Hopkins University Press, 2009), 40–53.

5. Shomette, *Flotilla*, 407–10.

6. Jones to Barney, 20 and 27 Aug. 1813, in *Naval War*, 2:376–78.

7. Morriss, *Cockburn and the British Navy in Transition*, 89–96.

8. Captain Thomas Cochrane, 10th Earl of Dundonald, Sir Alexander's nephew, gained fame as a bold frigate commander in the Napoleonic Wars and in later years as the commander of the Chilean navy in the Latin American Wars of Independence.

9. Jones to Commo. Barney, 18 Feb. 1814, in *Naval War*, 3:34–35.

10. Barney to Jones, 1 and 25 Mar. 1814, in *Naval War*, 3:35–37.

11. Jones to Barney, 14 Apr. 1814, in *Naval War*, 2:54–55. This letter contained a reference to "the Commissions for yourself and officers," which were delivered to Barney on 27 April. Barney's commission was not approved by the Senate until 18 October, and it was not delivered to him until the following year, on 16 February. See Barney to Secretary of the Navy Benjamin Crowninshield, 18 Feb. 1815, in *Naval War*, 2:355.

12. Barney to Jones, 4 Apr. 1814, in *Naval War*, 3:54–55.

13. VAdm. Alexander Cochrane to Rear Admiral George Cockburn, 8 Apr. 1814, in *Naval War*, 3:60–61.

14. Cockburn to Cochrane, 9 and 10 May 1814, in *Naval War*, 3:61–66.

15. Shomette, *Flotilla*, 75.

16. Barney to Jones, 11 May 1814, in *Naval War*, 3:58–59.

17. Capt. Robert Barrie to Cockburn, 1 June 1814, in *Naval War*, 3:77. See also Cockburn to Cochrane, 25 June 1814, in *Naval War*, 3:115.

18. Barney to Jones, 1 Aug. 1814, in *Naval War*, 3:181–83.

19. Barney to Jones, 16 June 1814, in *Naval War*, 3:101–2.

20. Joshua Barney to Louis Barney and to Jones, both dated 27 June 1814, in *Naval War*, 3:123–28.

21. Cockburn to Cochrane, 25 June 1814, in *Naval War*, 3:115–17.

22. Acting Lt. Solomon Rutter, Flotilla Service, to Commo. Joshua Barney, 3 July 1814, in *Naval War*, 3:143–44.

23. Shomette, *Flotilla*, 353–58, contains an update of the underwater archaeological work done by Donald Shomette and his associates. His earlier work, *Tidewater Time Capsule: History Beneath the Patuxent* (1995), provides more detail on the search for the flotilla and the investigation of the "Turtle Shell" wreck, probably Barney's flagship, *Scorpion*.

24. Jones to Barney, 19 and 20 Aug. 1814, in *Naval War*, 3:186–88.

25. Capt. Charles Morris to Jones, and Jones to Morris, 18 July 1813, in *Naval War*, 3:370–72.

26. George Robert Gleig, *A Narrative of the Campaigns of the British Army at Washington, Baltimore, and New Orleans . . . in the Years 1814 and 1815* (Philadelphia: M. Carey and Sons, 1821), 113–41; Mary Barney, ed., *Biographical Memoir of the Late Commodore Joshua Barney . . .* (Boston: Gray & Bowen, 1832), 267.

27. Captain's Clerk Mordecai Booth to Commo. Thomas Tingey, 22 Aug. 1814, in *Naval War*, 3:202–5.

28. Booth to Tingey, 24 Aug. 1814, in *Naval War*, 3:208–13.

29. Gordon S. Brown, *The Captain Who Burned His Ships: Captain Thomas Tingey, USN, 1750–1829* (Annapolis, MD: Naval Institute Press, 2011), 117–34; Spencer C. Tucker, *The Jeffersonian Gunboat Navy* (Columbia: University of South Carolina Press, 1993), 136.

30. Anthony S. Pitch, *The Burning of Washington: The British Invasion of 1814* (Annapolis, MD: Naval Institute Press, 1998), 137–38.

31. Charles G. Muller, *The Darkest Day: The Washington-Baltimore Campaign during the War of 1812* (Philadelphia: University of Pennsylvania Press, 1963); Pitch, *Burning of Washington*; Steve Vogel, *Through the Perilous Fight: From the Burning of Washington to the Star Spangled Banner; Six Weeks That Saved the Nation* (New York: Random House, 2013).

32. Pitch, *Burning of Washington*, 174.

33. Commo. David Porter to Jones, 7 Sept. 1814, and Commo. John Rodgers to Jones, 9 Sept. 1814, in *Naval War*, 3:251–55 and 256–58.

34. Capt. Oliver H. Perry to Jones, 9 Sept. 1814, in *Naval War*, 3:256; David Curtis Skaggs, *Oliver Hazard Perry: Honor, Courage, and Patriotism in the Early U.S. Navy* (Annapolis, MD: Naval Institute Press, 2006), 160–61; John H. Schroeder, *Commodore John Rodgers: Paragon of the Early American Navy* (Gainesville: University Press of Florida, 2006), 135.

35. MGen. Samuel Smith to Rodgers, 2 Sept. 1814, in *Naval War*, 3:262–63.

36. Rodgers to Smith, 1 Sept. 1814, in *Naval War*, 3:261–62.

37. Jones to Rodgers, 4 Sept. 1814, in *Naval War*, 3:250.

38. Scott S. Sheads, *The Chesapeake Campaigns, 1813: Middle Ground of the War of 1812* (New York: Osprey, 2014), 23–24; Sheads, *The Rockets' Red Glare: The Maritime Defense of Baltimore* (Centreville, MD: Tidewater, 1986), 6–18.

39. Cochrane to Cockburn, 13 Sept. 1814, quoted in Capt. James Pack, *The Man Who Burned the White House: Admiral Sir George Cockburn, 1772–1853* (Annapolis, MD: Naval Institute Press, 1987), 205. Cochrane's letter was given to Lieutenant James Scott, Cockburn's aide, who personally delivered it to Cockburn. James Scott, *Recollections of a Naval Life* (London: Richard Bentley, 1834), 334–35.

40. Cochrane to Cockburn, 13 Sept. 1814, in *Naval War*, 3:277–78.

41. Col. Arthur Brooke to Cochrane, 13 Sept. 1814, in *Naval War*, 3:279.

42. Cochrane to First Lord of the Admiralty [Robert Saunders Dundas, 2nd Viscount Melville], 17 Sept. 1814, in *Naval War*, 3:289–91.

43. Cochrane chose to ignore the usual protocol after the troops' victorious return. Instead of allowing Lieutenant Robert Scott, Cockburn's aide-de-camp, to deliver the dispatches in person to Lord Bathurst, Cochrane chose Captain Wainwright, of HMS *Tonnant*. Normally, when a junior officer was chosen to deliver such dispatches, he received a promotion to the next higher rank. The same reward would not be forthcoming for a post captain. See Pack, *Man Who Burned the White House*, 199–200; and Morriss, *Cockburn and the British Navy in Transition*, 105–6.

44. Cochrane to First Lord of the Admiralty, 17 Sept. 1814, in *Naval War*, 3:289–91.

Chapter 12 · Hostilities in the Seaboard South

1. First Lord of the Admiralty [Robert Saunders Dundas, 2nd Viscount Melville] to VAdm. Cochrane, 29 July 1814, National Library of Scotland, Edinburgh, MS 2574, folio 146.

2. Donald Hickey, *Glorious Victory: Andrew Jackson and the Battle of New Orleans* (Baltimore: Johns Hopkins University Press, 2015), 105. Agreement on the number of British "troops" for the Gulf Coast expedition is elusive. Some estimates are as high as fifteen thousand, but this number may include many who contributed to the mission but

did not participate in the actual fighting, such as sailors remaining on board ships and the seamen who manned the boats bringing soldiers, equipment, and ordnance from the fleet to the battlefield.

3. Spencer C. Tucker, *The Jeffersonian Gunboat Navy* (Columbia: University of South Carolina Press, 1993), 138–42.

4. Tyrone G. Martin, *A Most Fortunate Ship: A Narrative History of Old Ironsides*, rev. ed. (Annapolis, MD: Naval Institute Press, 1997), 96–97. Preble must have had a high opinion of Dent's abilities to have left him in charge of the flagship for more than a week.

5. Christopher McKee, *A Gentlemanly and Honorable Profession: The Creation of the U.S. Naval Officer Corps, 1798–1815* (Annapolis, MD: Naval Institute Press, 1991), 246–47.

6. Capt. John Dent to Secretary Paul Hamilton, 17 Oct. and 5 Nov. 1812, in *The Naval War of 1812: A Documentary History*, ed. William S. Dudley, 4 vols. (Washington, DC: GPO, 1985–2021), 1:534–35, 584–85, hereafter cited as *Naval War*.

7. Tucker, *Jeffersonian Gun Boat Navy*, 142.

8. McKee, *Gentlemanly and Honorable Profession*, 183–85.

9. Tucker, *Jeffersonian Gunboat Navy*, 147–48.

10. Donald R. Hickey, *The War of 1812: A Forgotten Conflict*, Bicentennial Edition (Urbana: University of Illinois Press, 2012), 214: "This operation failed to divert any troops from the Gulf Coast."

11. The 1,483 refugees were about 27 percent of all those liberated from slavery by the British during the War of 1812, in all about 4,000. See also Hickey, *War of 1812*, 401n196. Alan Taylor, in *The Internal Enemy: Slavery and War in Virginia, 1772–1832* (New York: Norton, 2013), 432, argues for a higher total number of about 5,000. According to Roger Morriss, in *Cockburn and the British Navy in Transition: Admiral Sir George Cockburn, 1775–1853* (Columbia, SC: University of South Carolina Press, 1997), 117, the number 1,483 comes from a tabulation of the "registrations in the books in the ships in the squadron."

12. Mary R. Bullard, *Cumberland Island: A History* (Athens: University of Georgia Press, 2005), 119.

13. Morriss, *Cockburn and the British Navy in Transition*, 118–20.

14. John R. Elting, *Amateurs to Arms! A Military History of the War of 1812* (Chapel Hill, NC: Algonquin Books, 1991), 171–74; Hickey, *Glorious Victory*, 66–67.

15. Frank Lawrence Owsley Jr., *Struggle for the Gulf Borderlands: The Creek War and the Battle of New Orleans, 1812–1815* (Gainesville: University Presses of Florida, 1981), 98–99.

16. Owsley, *Struggle for the Gulf Borderlands*, 118–19.

17. First Lord of the Admiralty to Cochrane, 29 July 1814, folios 146–48.

18. John Shaw to Hamilton, 3 Feb. 1812, NA, RG 45, M125, CL, 1812, vol. 1, no. 28.

19. Shaw to Hamilton, 4 Aug. 1812, NA, RG 45, M125, CL, 1812, vol. 2, no. 156.

20. J. H. Laurence & Co. to Hamilton, 4 July 1812, NA, RG 45, M125, Miscellaneous Letters Received by the Secretary of the Navy (MLR), vol. 50, no. 24; Shaw to Hamilton, 27 July 1812, NA, RG 45, M125, CL, 1812, vol. 3, no. 147, including enclosure on status of ships and gunboats attached to the station; James Wilkinson to Hamilton, 22 Dec. 1812, NA, RG 45, M124, MLR, vol. 52, no. 196, criticizing Shaw for using *Louisiana* as a cruiser instead of a block ship.

21. This accounting must have been a painful ordeal for Shaw, as it took nearly a year before the department accepted and certified his accounts. In due time, Jones ordered Shaw

to assume command of the frigate *United States*, a notable assignment notwithstanding Shaw's concerns about his service in New Orleans. See McKee, *Gentlemanly and Honorable Profession*, 306–7.

22. MCdt. Daniel Patterson to MGen. Andrew Jackson, 2 Sept. 1814, NA, RG 45, Masters Commandant Letters received by the Secretary of the Navy, MCL, 1813–14, M147/5, vol. 2, no. 39 (enclosure to no. 38, Patterson to Secretary William Jones, 4 Sept. 1814).

23. Shaw to Patterson, 21 Dec. 1813, NA, RG 45, M125, CL, 1813, vol. 8, no. 94. See also *Naval War*, 2:678–81.

24. Jones to Patterson, 18 Oct. 1813, NA, RG 45, M149, 1813, SNL, 11, pp. 122–24.

25. Patterson to Jones, 25 Jan. 1814, MCL, 1814, M147/5, vol. 2, no. 25.

26. Patterson to Jones, 27 Dec. 1813, in *Naval War*, 2:681–82.

27. Jones to Patterson, 7 Mar. 1814, NA, RG 45, M149, 1814, SNL, 11, pp. 234–36.

28. Jones to Patterson, 26 Mar. 1814, NA, RG 45, M149, 1814, SNL, 8, pp. 257–58.

29. Patterson to Jones, 13 May 1814, MCL, 1814, M147/5, vol. 5, no. 127; 24 June 1814, NA, RG 45, MCL, 1814, M147/5, vol. 1, no. 151; and 8 July 1814, NA, RG 45, MCL, 1814, M147/5, vol. 2, no. 2.

30. Capt. William Percy to Cochrane, 16 Sept. 1814, PRO Adm 1/505, pp. 311–19; Wilburt S. Brown, *The Amphibious Campaign for West Florida and Louisiana, 1814–1815: A Critical Review of Strategy and Tactics at New Orleans* (Tuscaloosa: University of Alabama Press, 1969), 44–58.

31. Patterson to Jones, 4 Sept. 1814, NA, RG 45, MCL, M147/5, vol. 2, no. 38, and two enclosures.

32. Jones to Patterson, 8 July 1814, NA, RG 45, M149, 1814, SNL, 8, pp. 369–70; Patterson to Jones, 20 Aug. 1814, NA, RG 45, MCL, M147/5, vol. 2, no. 22. See also John Henley to Jones, 24 Aug. 1814, NA, RG 45, MCL, M147/5, vol. 2, no. 36. Master Commandant John Dandridge Henley (1781–1835), a nephew of George Washington, served in the First Barbary War under Commodore Edward Preble and received promotion to captain in 1817.

33. Patterson to Jones, 4 Sept. 1814, NA, RG 45, MCL, 1814, M147/5, vol. 2, nos. 64 and 65, and 14 Oct. 1814, NA, RG 45, MCL, 1814, M147/5, vol. 2, no. 67.

34. Gene A. Smith, *Thomas ap Catesby Jones: Commodore of Manifest Destiny* (Annapolis, MD: Naval Institute Press, 2000), 13–32.

35. Robert V. Remini, *Andrew Jackson and the Course of American Empire, 1767–1821* (New York: Harper & Row, 1977), 255–75.

36. Robin Reilly, *The British at the Gates: The New Orleans Campaign in the War of 1812* (New York: G. P. Putnam's Sons, 1974), 268–69.

37. A. LaCarriere Latour, *Historical Memoir of the War in West Florida and Louisiana, 1814–1815* (Philadelphia, 1816), 121–23.

38. Brown, *Amphibious Campaign*, 119–20. Major Daniel Carmick, USMC, was wounded by a Congreve rocket while commanding a battalion of volunteers and passed command of his company to Bellevue.

39. Jackson singled out Patterson's gunfire from the right bank of the river for being responsible "in great measure" for silencing the British batteries in the artillery duel of

1 January 1815. See Alfred Thayer Mahan, *Sea Power in its Relations to the War of 1812*, 2 vols. (Boston, 1905), 2:393.

40. Patterson to Jones, 13 Jan. 1815, NA, RG 45, MCL, 1815, M147/6, vol. 1, no. 11.

41. The vessels attacking Fort St. Philip included HMS *Sophie*, 26; HMS *Herald*, 20; HMS *Aetna*, 10; HMS *Meteor*, 14; and HM schooner *Pigmy*, 10. The fort was manned by US Army regulars, sailors, free men of color, and volunteers under the command of Major Walter Overton, assisted by US Navy gunboat *No. 65*, under the command of Lieutenant Thomas Cunningham, who was also in charge of the fort's water battery, two 32-pounders.

42. Tucker, *Jeffersonian Gunboat Navy*, 154–70.

43. Robert V. Remini, Jackson's biographer, praised Patterson as "one of the most important and valuable figures in the defense of New Orleans." *The Battle of New Orleans: Andrew Jackson and America's First Military Victory* (New York: Penguin, 1999), 36. See also Major Edwin N. McClellan, USMC, "The Navy at the Battle of New Orleans," *U.S. Naval Institute Proceedings* 50 (1924): 2041–59.

44. Sources are conflicted as to how many men General Lambert landed at Fort Bowyer. Owsley states 600, but Hickey maintains 5,000, a huge disparity. Elting cites 1,000 men comprising elements of the Fourth, Twenty-first, and Forty-fourth regiments of foot. This seems a reasonable number, considering the amount of ordnance that had to be moved ashore and emplaced. See Hickey, *Glorious Victory*, 115; Elting, *Amateurs to Arms!*, 319–20; and Owsley, *Struggle for the Gulf Borderlands*, 171.

45. Owsley, *Struggle for the Gulf Borderlands*, 169–85. After 1815 the fort at Prospect Bluff was called Negro Fort, defended by blacks (former British Colonial Marines) and Creek Indians who lived in the area when it was attacked and destroyed by an American force in 1816.

Chapter 13 · Sailors' Life and Work

1. Michael J. Crawford, "Avast Swabbing: The Medical Campaign to Reform Swabbing the Decks in the U.S. Navy," *Journal of Military History* 83, no. 1 (Jan. 2019): 127–56.

2. Petition of Jane Singer to Secretary of the Navy Paul Hamilton, 12 Aug. 1812, in *The Naval War of 1812: A Documentary History*, ed. William S. Dudley, 4 vols. (Washington, DC: GPO, 1985–2021), 1:261, hereafter cited as *Naval War*

3. Henry Hedley to Hamilton, 5 Oct. 1812, in *Naval War*, 1:506–7 and 507nn1, 2.

4. James Fenimore Cooper, *Ned Myers: or A Life Before the Mast*, ed. William S. Dudley, Classics of Naval Literature (Annapolis, MD: Naval Institute Press, 1989), 51–52.

5. Capt. John Cassin to Hamilton, 25 Aug. 1812, in *Naval War*, 1:222–23.

6. An Unknown Midshipman to J. Jones (114 Water St., New York), 21 Dec. 1813, in *Naval War*, 2:621–22. The midshipman's uncle, J. Jones, apparently sent the letter to Secretary of the Navy William Jones as an enclosure, with the midshipman's name clipped off. In those days, postage was paid by the recipient instead of prepaid by the sender.

7. USS *Constitution* Logbook, No. 4, 19 Aug. 1812, www.the captain's clerk.info/.

8. Tyrone G. Martin, *A Most Fortunate Ship: A Narrative History of Old Ironsides*, rev. ed. (Annapolis, MD: Naval Institute Press, 1997), 158–62.

9. Charles E. Brodine Jr., Michael J. Crawford, and Christine F. Hughes, *Interpreting Old Ironsides: An Illustrated Guide to USS* Constitution (Washington, DC: Naval Historical Center, 2007), 19–21.

10. James E. Valle, *Rocks and Shoals: Order and Discipline in the Old Navy, 1800–1861* (Annapolis, MD: Naval Institute Press, 1980), 285–96.

11. Christopher McKee, *A Gentlemanly and Honorable Profession: The Creation of the U.S. Naval Officer Corps, 1798–1815* (Annapolis, MD: Naval Institute Press, 1991), 222–23.

12. Valle, *Rocks and Shoals*, 2–3, 88–89.

13. Gaddis Smith, "Black Seamen and the Federal Courts," in *Ships, Seafaring, and Society: Essays in Maritime History*, ed. Timothy Runyan (Detroit: Wayne State University Press, 1987), 322. Smith's research agrees that the percentage of black seamen in the American merchant marine and navy was at 10–20 percent during the period 1789–1860.

14. Michael A. Palmer, *Stoddert's War: Naval Operations during the Quasi-War with France, 1798–1801* (Columbia: University of South Carolina Press, 1987), 138–39.

15. William M. Fowler Jr., *Jack Tars and Commodores: The American Navy, 1783–1815* (Boston: Houghton Mifflin, 1984), 129–30.

16. McKee, *Gentlemanly and Honorable Profession*, 219 and n.

17. Christopher McKee, *Ungentle Goodnights: Life in a Home for Elderly and Disabled Naval Sailors and Marines and the Perilous Careers That Brought Them There* (Annapolis, MD: Naval Institute Press, 2018), 104.

18. Gerard T. Altoff, *Amongst My Best Men: African-Americans and the War of 1812* (Put-in-Bay, OH: Perry Group, 1997), 13–23.

19. Cooper, *Ned Myers*, 77–92. See also Allan Taylor, "American Blacks in the War of 1812," in *The Routledge Handbook of the War of 1812*, ed. Donald R. Hickey and Connie D. Clark (New York: Routledge, 2016), 193–207.

20. Roger Knight, *Britain Against Napoleon: The Organization of Victory, 1793–1815* (London: Allen Lane of The Penguin Group, 2013), 444–47.

21. William H. White, "HM Prison Dartmoor—A Paradox in Devon, England," *Sea History*, no. 165 (Winter 2018–19): 18–21.

22. W. Jeffrey Bolster, *Black Jacks: African American Seamen in the Age of Sail* (Cambridge, MA: Harvard University Press, 1997), 102–30.

23. Ira Dye, "American Maritime Prisoners of War, 1812–1815," in Runyan, *Ships, Seafaring, and Society*, 293–320; see esp. app. 2, "A Descriptive List of Prisoner of War Journals," 315–20.

24. Donald R. Hickey, *The War of 1812: A Forgotten Conflict*, Bicentennial Edition (Urbana: University of Illinois Press, 2012), 312–13.

25. Secretary of the Navy William Jones to James Madison, 26 Oct. 1814, in *Naval War*, 3:631–36.

26. George F. Emmons, *The Navy of the United States, from the Commencement to 1853 . . . to which is added a list of Private Armed Vessels, fitted out under the American Flag, etc.* (Washington, DC: Gideon, 1853).

27. Jerome R. Garitee, *The Republic's Private Navy: The American Privateering Business as Practiced by Baltimore during the War of 1812* (Middletown, CT: Wesleyan University Press, 1977), 43, 92.

28. Brian Arthur, *How Britain Won the War of 1812: The Royal Navy's Blockades of the United States, 1812–1815* (Woodbridge, Suffolk, UK: Boydell, 2011), 210–21.

Chapter 14 · War Finance and the Blockade

1. President George Washington, *First Annual Address to Congress*, 8 Jan. 1790.

2. Donald R. Hickey, *The War of 1812: A Forgotten Conflict*, Bicentennial Edition (Urbana: University of Illinois Press, 2012), 5–6; Michael Crawford and Christine Hughes, *The Reestablishment of the Navy, 1787–1801: Historical Overview and Select Bibliography* (Washington, DC: Naval Historical Center & GPO, 1995).

3. Henry Adams, *The Life of Albert Gallatin* (Philadelphia: J. B. Lippincott, 1880), 268–69; Thomas K. McCraw, *The Founders of Finance: How Hamilton, Gallatin, and Other Immigrants Forged a New Economy* (Cambridge, MA: Belknap Press of Harvard University Press, 2012), 277–330.

4. Adams, *Life of Albert Gallatin*, 291.

5. Albert Gallatin to Thomas Jefferson, 12 Sept. 1805, in Albert Gallatin, *The Writings of Albert Gallatin*, ed. Henry Adams, 3 vols. (Philadelphia: J. B. Lippincott, 1879), 1:241–54, quoted in Adams, *Life of Albert Gallatin*, 334–35. Gallatin discusses the practical consequences of not building a larger navy and the benefits of building one from the current financial surplus.

6. By a series of orders in council the British Crown made it illegal for allied or neutral ships to trade with France and French allies. The principal order in council was that of November 1807. This was answered by Napoleon in the Milan Decree, also of 1807. Ships belonging to neutral nations, of which the United States was one, were then liable to be captured by both the British and the French navies.

7. See the section "Anglo-American Tensions: The Neutral Trade" and the ruling of Judge John Kelsall in the *Essex* case of 1805, in *The Naval War of 1812: A Documentary History*, ed. William S. Dudley, 4 vols. (Washington, DC: GPO, 1985–2021), 1:16–21, hereafter cited as *Naval War*.

8. Gallatin to Thomas Jefferson, 18 Dec. 1807, as quoted in Adams, *Life of Albert Gallatin*, 366–67.

9. Geoffrey M. Footner, *USS Constellation: From Frigate to Sloop of War* (Annapolis, MD: Naval Institute Press, 2003), 62–73.

10. Gallatin to Madison, 1 Nov. 1812, in Gallatin, *Writings of Albert Gallatin*, 1:529. See also Founders Online, National Archives, https://founders.archives.gov/documents /Madison/03-05-02-0332, originally published in *The Papers of James Madison, Presidential Series*, ed. J. C. A. Stagg et al., vol. 5, *10 July 1812–7 February 1813* (Charlottesville: University of Virginia Press, 2004).

11. Adams, *Life of Albert Gallatin*, 292–93.

12. Brian Arthur, *How Britain Won the War of 1812: The Royal Navy's Blockades of the United States, 1812–1815* (Woodbridge, Suffolk, UK: Boydell, 2011), 55–57, 230–31.

13. Hickey, *War of 1812*, 118–19, 167–68.

14. Secretary Paul Hamilton to Langdon Cheves, Chairman, Naval Committee, House of Representatives, 3 Dec. 1811, *American State Papers: Naval Affairs*, 1:247–52.

15. Adams, *Life of Albert Gallatin*, 483–86.

16. Secretary of State James Monroe to the American Commissioners, 5 Aug. 1813, quoted in Adams, *Life of Albert Gallatin*, 485–86.

17. Secretary William Jones to Madison, 21 Dec. 1813, https://founders.archives.gov /documents/Madison/03-07-02-0107, originally published in *The Papers of James Madison, Presidential Series*, ed. J. C. A. Stagg et al., vol. 7, *25 October 1813–30 June 1814* (Charlottesville: University of Virginia Press, 2012), 131.

18. Jones to Isaac Hull, 23 Apr. 1814, as quoted in Edward K. Eckert, *The Navy Department in the War of 1812* (Gainesville: University of Florida Press, 1973), 58.

19. Jones to Madison, 15 Oct. 1814, https://founders.archives.gov/documents/Madison/03 -08-02-0273, originally published in *The Papers of James Madison, Presidential Series*, ed. J. C. A. Stagg et al., vol. 8, *July 1814–1 February 1815* (Charlottesville: University of Virginia Press, 2015), 311.

20. Jones to the Honorable Joseph Anderson, Senator (D-TN), 11 Nov. 1814, *American State Papers: Naval Affairs*, 1:361.

21. Jones to Congressman Richard M. Johnson (D-KY), 3 Oct. 1814, in *Naval War*, 3:311–18.

22. Jones to Madison, 25 Apr. 1814, *Papers of James Madison, Presidential Series*, 7:437–39. In this letter, Jones wrote that he had "suffered more by the restrictive system than any person within my knowledge; yet I will never regret the zeal and felicity with which I have supported that system so long as the state of the world gave effect to its operations."

23. Jones to Madison, 11 Sept. 1814, *Papers of James Madison, Presidential Series*, 8:203–4.

24. Jones to Madison, 26 Oct. 1814, in *Naval War*, 3:631.

25. Jones to Madison, 26 Oct. 1814, in *Naval War*, 3:634.

26. Commo. Chauncey to Jones, 5 Nov. 1814, in *Naval War*, 3:637–39.

27. Jones to Chauncey, 30 Nov. 1814, in *Naval War*, 3:670–71.

28. Capt. Charles Stewart to Jones, 4 Apr. 1814, NA, RG 45, CL, 1814; Jones to Stewart, 19 Apr. 1814, RG 45, 1814, SNL; Tyrone G. Martin, *A Most Fortunate Ship: A Narrative History of Old Ironsides*, rev. ed. (Annapolis, MD: Naval Institute Press, 1997), 187–90; Claude Berube and John Rodgaard, *A Call to the Sea: Captain Charles Stewart of the USS* Constitution (Washington, DC: Potomac Books, 2005), 82–83.

29. Jones criticized the condition in which Stewart hastily left *Constellation* when he received his transfer to *Constitution*. In the aftermath of the battle of Craney Island, there had been a change of command, with first Captain Joseph Tarbell and then Captain Charles Gordon in charge of *Constellation*. Gordon reported to Jones that things were askew. According to Stewart, when he had departed *Constellation* she was in ready-for-sea condition. Apparently, equipment and cabin furniture went missing during Tarbell's tenure, and he blamed Stewart. Jones later made a quasi apology to Stewart in a letter of 28 October 1813 (in *Naval War*, 2:393). However, this could have set the tone for later accusations. Tarbell may have been ill at the time, for he died at home at Norfolk in November 1815.

30. Christopher McKee, *A Gentlemanly and Honorable Profession: The Creation of the U.S. Naval Officer Corps, 1798–1815* (Annapolis, MD: Naval Institute Press, 1991), 12–13.

31. Capt. Charles Morris to Cheves, 9 Jan. 1813, in *Naval War*, 2:20–24. Captain Morris forwarded a copy of this letter to Jones shortly after he assumed office.

32. "Re-organization and Extension of the Navy, the Establishment of a Board of Inspectors, and a Naval Academy," 15 Nov. 1814, in Jones to Senator Charles Tait (GA), Chairman, US Senate Naval Committee, 15 Nov. 1814, *American State Papers: Naval Affairs*, 1:320–25.

33. Jones to Tait, 15 Nov. 1814, 321–22.

34. Jones to Tait, 15 Nov. 1814, 322–23.

35. Jones to Tait, 15 Nov. 1814, 324.

36. Charles Tait, "Rear Admirals and Brevet Rank," 28 Nov. 1814, enclosing Jones to Tait, 15 Nov. 1814, in *American State Papers: Naval Affairs*, 1:324–25. Promotion by brevet is in effect a battlefield promotion as practiced in the US Army, but it is not a US Navy tradition.

Chapter 15 · Renewal of the US Navy

1. Samuel Eliot Morison, *The Maritime History of Massachusetts, 1783–1860* (Boston: Northeastern University Press, 1979), 93.

2. James Madison to Secretary of the Navy Benjamin W. Crowninshield, 15 Dec. 1814; Crowninshield to Madison, 26 Dec. 1814; and Crowninshield to Madison, 28 Dec. 1814, in *James Madison Papers, Presidential Series*, ed. J. C. A. Stagg et al., vol. 8, *July 1814–1 February 1815* (Charlottesville: University of Virginia Press, 2015), 436, 464; 467; 471–72.

3. See Treaty of Ghent, Yale Law School, The Avalon Project, Documents in Law, History, and Diplomacy, British-American Diplomacy, War of 1812, https://avalon.law.yale.edu/19th_century/ghent.asp.

4. Over the past year, the British had captured four US Navy schooners, two on Lake Huron and two on Lake Erie.

5. Acting Secretary Benjamin Homans to Commo. Thomas Macdonough, 27 Dec. 1815, in *The Naval War of 1812: A Documentary History*, ed. William S. Dudley, 4 vols. (Washington, DC: GPO, 1985–2021), 3:682, hereafter cited as *Naval War*.

6. MGen. Brisbane to Gov. Gen. Prevost, 22 Dec. 1814; Secretary of War Monroe to MGen. Alexander Macomb, 12 Jan. 1815; Prevost to Brisbane, 12 Jan. 1815; and Macdonough to Crowninshield, 6 Feb. 1815 in *Naval War*, 3:681, 684, 685–86. See also Thomas Malcomson, "Commodore Sir Edward W. C. R. Owen: Shaping the British Naval Establishment on the Great Lakes in the Wake of the War of 1812," *Northern Mariner / Le marin de nord* 29, no. 1 (Spring 2019); 1–24.

7. Crowninshield to Commo. Arthur Sinclair, 5 Apr. 1815, in *Naval War*, 3:702 3

8. Macdonough to Crowninshield, 12 Mar. 1815, in *Naval War*, 3:609.

9. Capt. Charles Stewart to Crowninshield, May 1815, with enclosure, "Minuets [sic] of the action between the frigate USS *Constitution* and HM Ships *Cyane* and *Levant* on 20 February 1815," NA, RG 45, M125, CL, 1815, vol. 3, no. 93; William S. Dudley, "Old Ironsides's Last Battle: USS *Constitution* versus HMS *Cyane* and HMS *Levant*," in *Fighting at Sea: Naval Battles from the Ages of Sail and Steam*, ed. Douglas M. McLean (Montreal: Robin Brass Studio, 2008), 55–85; Assheton Humphreys, *The USS Constitution's Finest Fight, 1815: The Journal of Acting Chaplain Assheton Humphreys, US Navy*, ed. Tyrone G. Martin (Mt. Pleasant, SC: Nautical and Aviation Publishing Company of America, 2000).

10. Andrew Lambert, *The Challenge: America, Britain, and the War of 1812* (London: Faber & Faber, 2012), 357–73; Capt. Stephen Decatur Jr. to Crowninshield, 2 Feb. 1815, NA, RG 45, CL, 1815, vol. 1, no. 44.

11. USS *Tom Bowline*, schooner, 14, was purchased for the US Navy in 1814. Commanded by Lieutenant Beekman Hoffman, she served as the storeship for *Hornet* and *Peacock* on their voyage to the South Atlantic after they made rendezvous at Tristan da Cunha in February 1815.

12. David F. Long, *Sailor Diplomat: A Biography of Commodore James Biddle, 1783–1848* (Annapolis, MD: Naval Institute Press, 1983), 50–59.

13. Gordon K. Harrington, "The American Challenge to the East India Company during the War of 1812," in *New Interpretations in Naval History: Selected Papers from the 10th Naval History Symposium held at the U.S. Naval Academy, 11–13 Sept. 1991*, ed. Jack Sweetman (Annapolis, MD: Naval Institute Press, 1993), 129–52.

14. The American and British commissioners at Ghent had anticipated that it would be months before all the combatants received verifiable information of the peace treaty and its ratifications. See https://avalon.documents,yale.edu/19th_century/ghent.asp.

15. In a public statement dated 2 November 1815, Warrington briefly summarized his cruise and in so doing made a statement that appeared to be an evasion of the truth. He averred that before their battle Lieutenant Boyce had known of the peace but had not told him until after the battle. Boyce maintained that he and others had informed Warrington beforehand but that the American captain had opened fire because Boyce refused to lower his colors. See *Niles Weekly Register*, 11 Nov. 1815, 188.

16. Christine F. Hughes, "Lewis Warrington and the USS *Peacock* in the Sunda Strait, Jun. 1815," in *The Early Republic and the Sea: Essays on the Naval and Maritime History of the Early United States*, ed. William S. Dudley and Michael J. Crawford (Dulles, VA: Brasseys, 2001), 115–22.

17. Hughes, "Lewis Warrington and the USS *Peacock*," 123–31.

18. Theodore Roosevelt, in *The Naval War of 1812* (New York: Random House, Modern Library, 1999), 241–42, called Warrington's attack "wanton and unprovoked." Kevin McCranie, of the US Naval War College, made a less judgmental statement: "This engagement ended the War of 1812 at sea. Considering that the conflict was precipitated by misperception, poor documentation, arrogance, and an unwillingness to compromise, the final clash served as a fitting end." Frederick C. Drake, a Canadian historian, wrote that Warrington's officers' diaries reveal that they knew of the Treaty of Ghent. It is interesting that the US Congress voted Lieutenant Boyce a life pension, indicating that Warrington might have gone one step too far in carrying out his orders. See David Heidler and Jeanne Heidler, eds., *Encyclopedia of the War of 1812* (Santa Barbara, CA: ABC-Clio, 1997), 543–44.

19. John R. Elting, *Amateurs to Arms! A Military History of the War of 1812* (Chapel Hill, NC: Algonquin Books, 1991), 325 and n.17.

20. "Reorganization of the Navy Department," 9 Jan. 1815, *American State Papers: Naval Affairs*, 1:354–59.

21. Crowninshield to Madison, 23 May 1815, https://founders.archives.gocdocuments.

22. Madison to Crowninshield, 12 June 1815, https://founders.archives.gov/.documents.

23. John H. Schroeder, *Commodore John Rodgers: Paragon of the Early American Navy* (Gainesville: University Press of Florida, 2006), 143–53.

24. "Rules, Regulations, and Instructions for the Naval Service," 7 Feb. 1815, *American State Papers: Naval Affairs*, 1:510–34.

25. A Bill for the gradual increase of the Navy of the United States, *Annals of Congress*, 16th Cong., 1st sess., 1367–72.

26. Capt. John Paul Jones to Robert Morris, 17 Oct. 1776, in *Guide to the Microfilm Edition of the Papers of John Paul Jones, 1747–1792*, ed. James C. Bradford (Alexandria, VA: Chadwyck-Healey, 1986), reel 1, no. 46.

27. William P. Leeman, *The Long Road to Annapolis: The Founding of the Naval Academy and the Emerging American Republic* (Chapel Hill: University of North Carolina Press, 2010), 70–72.

28. These points are well and amply documented in Brian Arthur, *How Britain Won the War of 1812: The Royal Navy's Blockades of the United States, 1812–1815* (Woodbridge, Suffolk, UK: Boydell, 2011).

29. Wade G. Dudley, *Splintering the Wooden Wall: The British Blockade of the United States, 1812–1815* (Annapolis, MD: Naval Institute Press, 2003), 181–82.

30. Arthur, *How the British Won the War of 1812*, 227–50 (app. B).

31. David K. Long, *Nothing Too Daring: A Biography of Commodore David Porter, 1780–1843* (Annapolis, MD: Naval Institute Press, 1970), 210.

32. Charles Beebe Stuart, *Naval and Mail Steamers of the United States* (1853; reprint, Andesite Press & Scholar Select, 2018), 13–21.

Italicized page numbers indicate figures, maps, and tables.